Voices of Exile in Contemporary Canadian Francophone Literature

After the Empire:
The Francophone World and Postcolonial France

Series Editor
Valérie Orlando, University of Maryland

Advisory Board
Robert Bernasconi, Memphis University; Alec Hargreaves, Florida State University; Chima Korieh, Rowan University; Mildred Mortimer, University of Colorado, Boulder; Obioma Nnaemeka, Indiana University; Kamal Salhi, University of Leeds; Tracy D. Sharpley-Whiting, Vanderbilt University; Nwachukwu Frank Ukadike, Tulane University

See www.lexingtonbooks.com/series for the series description and a complete list of published titles.

Recent and Forthcoming Titles

Time Signatures: Contextualizing Contemporary Francophone Autobiographical Writing from Maghreb, by Alison Rice

Breadfruit or Chestnut?: Gender Construction in the French Caribbean Novel, by Bonnie Thomas

History's Place: Nostalgia and the City in French Algerian Literature, by Seth Graebner

Collective Memory: France and the Algerian War (1954–1962), by Jo McCormack

The Other Hybrid Archipelago: Introduction to the Literatures and Cultures of the Francophone Indian Ocean, by Peter Hawkins

Rethinking Marriage in Francophone African and Caribbean Literatures, by Cécile Accilien

Two Novellas by YAE: A Moroccan in New York and Sea Drinkers, by Youssouf Amine Elalamy, translated by John Liechty

Franketienne and Rewriting: A Work in Progress, by Rachel Douglas

Charles Testut's Le Vieux Salomon: *Race, Religion, Socialism, and Free-masonry*, Sheri Lyn Abel

What Moroccan Cinema?: A Historical and Critical Study, 1956–2006, by Sandra Carter

Voices of Exile in Contemporary Canadian Francophone Literature, by F. Elizabeth Dahab

Voices of Exile in Contemporary Canadian Francophone Literature

F. Elizabeth Dahab

LEXINGTON BOOKS

A division of
ROWMAN & LITTLEFIELD PUBLISHERS, INC.
Lanham • Boulder • New York • Toronto • Plymouth, UK

Published by Lexington Books
A division of Rowman & Littlefield Publishers, Inc.
A wholly owned subsidiary of The Rowman & Littlefield Publishing Group, Inc.
4501 Forbes Boulevard, Suite 200, Lanham, Maryland 20706
http://www.lexingtonbooks.com

Estover Road, Plymouth PL6 7PY, United Kingdom

Copyright © 2009 by Lexington Books

All rights reserved. No part of this book may be reproduced in any form or by any electronic or mechanical means, including information storage and retrieval systems, without written permission from the publisher, except by a reviewer who may quote passages in a review.

British Library Cataloguing in Publication Information Available

Library of Congress Cataloging-in-Publication Data

Dahab, Elizabeth, 1952–
  Voices of exile in contemporary Canadian francophone literature / F. Elizabeth Dahab.
      p. cm.
  Includes bibliographical references and index.
  ISBN 978-0-7391-1878-8 (cloth : alk. paper) — ISBN 978-0-7391-3838-0 (electronic)
 1. French-Canadian literature—Arab authors—History and criticism. 2. French-Canadian literature—Québec (Province)—History and criticism. 3. Immigrants' writings, French-Canadian—Québec (Province)—History and criticism. 4. Exiles in literature. 5. Arabs in literature. 6. Group identity in literature. 7.
Arabs—Canada—Ethnic identity. I. Title.
  PQ3902.D35 2009
  840.9'8927071—dc22   2009011618

∞™ The paper used in this publication meets the minimum requirements of American National Standard for Information Sciences—Permanence of Paper for Printed Library Materials, ANSI/NISO Z39.48-1992.

Printed in the United States of America

Contents

Preface	vii
Acknowledgments	xv
1 Introduction: The Odyssey of Québécois/Canadian-Arabic Writers and Their Writing	1
2 Deprivation and Despair in Saad Elkhadem's *Wings of Lead*, *The Plague*, *Trilogy of the Flying Egyptian*, and *One Night in Cairo*	45
3 From Baghdad to Montréal via Paris: Naïm Kattan and His Multiple Reality	67
4 Of Suffocated Minds and Tortured Hearts: The Universe of Abla Farhoud	97
5 Of Broken Promises and Mended Lives: The War-Ravaged World of Wajdi Mouawad	135
6 "Fragments and Enigmas": Hédi Bouraoui and *La Femme d'entre les lignes*	173
Conclusion	199
Bibliography	205
Index	221
Credits	225
About the Author	229

Preface

The trajectory that brought me, *as a Comparatist*, to the study of the works of Canadian writers of Arabic origin began in the 1990s as an offshoot of my interest in literatures of French expression, especially in Québec,[1] a choice location for the study of exilic literatures. I was painfully aware of an absence of adequate tools for the study of this literature as it became increasingly clear to me that Québécois/Canadian Literature produced by writers of Arabic origin suffered from an ailment not uncommon to exilic literatures, namely, that it was weakly institutionalized and largely unknown to mainstream scholarship. No critical books or collection of papers had ever been written on those writers, no literary history had ever been undertaken, and no complete bibliography of their works had ever been published. What was available was a handful of interviews, a handful of slim anthologies, a trickle of articles and book reviews scattered here and there in non mainstream journals and magazines, written mostly by fellow Arabic scholars.

In this regard, one representative example can be pointed out: the 1988 conference held at the University of Alberta on "Literatures of Lesser Diffusion" and the proceedings of that conference (1989), which featured more than two dozen articles on the writings of various cultural minority groups, do not present anything on the topic.[2] To my knowledge, a paper I delivered at the Fourteenth Congress of the International Comparative Literature Association (ICLA)[3] (Edmonton, 1994) may have constituted the first time this topic was dealt with at a professional meeting. It was equally absent from *Other Solitudes* (1990), a collection published with the support of government agencies (notably the Department of the Secretary of State) and grouping together literary extracts and interviews from eighteen representatives of Cultural Communities.[4] Undoubtedly, this literature *as a whole* had yet to be consecrated by the Canadian government policy of support for ethnic studies, a policy institutionalized in 1971 through the official recognition of the concept of multiculturalism and epitomized by the 1988 Canadian Multiculturalism Act, which allegedly aims at the preservation and enhancement of Canada's multiethnic heritage. A monograph on Arabic-Canadian writing had not yet made an appearance amongst the books commissioned in the 1980s by the Canadian government on literatures of national minorities, including Hungarian (1987), Australian (1992), Asian (1988), Urdu (1988), and Italian (1988), to mention but a handful. Perhaps the writers themselves are to blame for that neglect, as contends one of them: "they did not seriously attempt to record, annotate, and disseminate their own artistic products and literary works, nor did they raise their voices and make themselves noticed when such studies were undertaken by others."[5]

Perhaps so, but I decided to focus my research in this neglected area and to do so from the vantage point of my own relocation from Canada to the United States via France. Before embarking on an in-depth analysis of the formal and artistic characteristics of Arabic-Canadian literature, I felt it was first necessary to unfold some of its basic aspects. Hence, a first step was the archaeological work of finding and identifying; classifying, surveying, and accounting for a growing body of literary texts, which fall under the rubric "Arabic-Canadian"; drawing a bio-bibliographical profile of the authors and addressing questions about the writers who produced these texts: Who are they? What is their social and national background? When and perhaps why did they immigrate to Canada? What did they write and in which genres; where did they publish; how much, and in which language?

With some difficulty I located and contacted the writers and their publishers; scanned libraries and bookstores for their works; ordered their books; read a great deal, and went to Canada several times to meet with the authors. Little by little a clear picture began to emerge against a hazy background. So, in August 1994, when colleagues inquired about the subject of my talk at the Fourteenth Congress of the ICLA, I told them it was about Arabic-Canadian literature, and when they invariably asked, "why, is there such a thing"? I was able to contend, with a degree of confidence, that indeed there "was such a thing": an identifiable body of writings differentiated from other bodies of work in that it manifested an internal structure closely linked to the cultural group from which it arose and that it begged acknowledgment, if not recognition. I spoke of this literature as having been born in the early seventies at the hands of First Generation Canadians of Arabic descent; having produced since then in all genres over 150 books,[6] and covering styles of writings ranging from the realist to the postmodernist. This literature was produced in French, English, and Arabic, thereby fulfilling twice over the definition given in 1975 by Deleuze and Guattari to minor literatures; namely, that a minor literature is not a literature produced in a "minor" language, but one a minority has produced in a major language.[7] I asserted that this corpus of writings bore the indelible mark of exile and sometimes genius, and could join ranks with the "other solitudes" Canada had come to acknowledge, admit, and embrace.[8]

An encouraging factor in this venture was the existence of noteworthy exceptions to the neglect I just mentioned and clear signs of an emerging interest in the topic of literature produced by Canadians of Arabic origin. A notable example in this regard was the work of the Québécois researchers Lucie Lequin, Maïr Verthuy (Concordia University, Montréal), and their team, whose research and publications focused on women-writers of Southern origins. For instance, their 1996 coedited book entitled *Multi-Culture, multi-écriture: La voix migrante au féminin en France et au Canada*, the outcome of a conference held at Concordia University (Montréal) two years earlier, was published in both Montréal and Paris and contained two studies that include women writers of Arabic origin.[9] Worth mentioning also is a large anthology (subtitled *Canadian Multicultural Literature*) that appeared in Toronto, also in 1996, with extracts from the works of Saad Elkhadem and Marwan Hassan.[10] Equally telling and symbolic of the progress that was being made is one *landmark* fraught with affiliation (in the sense in which Edward Said employed the word), namely an implicit network of cultural associations between forms and esthetic creations on the one hand and agencies and institutions on the other (1983).[11] I am referring to the fact that in 1985 the prolific Québécois-Egyptian writer Anne-Marie Alonzo was awarded the highly prestigious Québécois award *Prix Emile Nelligan* for her book of poetry, *Bleus de mine* (1985), which subsequently (and consequently) was to appear in Toronto in an English translation, under the title *Lead Blues* (1990).[12]

I wanted my work to continue this ascending trend and to fill some of the lacunas, so I drew up a bilingual agenda consisting of stepping-stones toward my ultimate goal. My research has advanced by increments, sometimes ruled by the necessity, in my view, to target in turn Francophone and Anglophone Canadian readerships, two solitudes living in the same country but each communicating solely in one language, that of one founding nation but not the other one. I delivered talks in both languages at international conferences and published likewise the results then I set up a selected bibliography of the writers' works. In Toronto, I published an annotated anthology (with a critical introduction), titled *Voices in the Desert*, featuring extracts, in English translation, from the works of nine women writers, eight of whom live in Québec.[13] I was glad this publication was considered by some as "laying foundations for a coherent canon of Arab-Canadian writing hitherto neglected in the Canadian literary landscape,"[14] and even more so when the Montréal daily, *Le Devoir*, in an email exchange with me, covered this publication in the context of a homage paid to "Exilic Writings on North-American Territory" [Des écritures de l'exil inscrites dans le territoire américain].[15]

The bulk of the present monograph consists of a detailed study of five Québécois/Canadian writers with representatively varied backgrounds, hailing from four different Arabic countries. They are of Moslem, Christian, and Jewish heritage. Four of them produced in French—they can hence be referred to as francophone[16]—and one produced in both Arabic and English. The four Franco-Canadian writers represented here come from the two largest French-speaking provinces in Canada. Hence, three of them live in Québec or share their time transnationally between Montréal and Paris; these are Abla Farhoud, Wajdi Mouawad (both originally from Lebanon), and Naïm Kattan (originally from Iraq); the *Franco-Ontarien* Hédi Bouraoui lives in Toronto (and hails from Tunisia).[17] The late Professor Saad Elkhadem, who emigrated from Cairo (Egypt) in the sixties, lived and worked in New Brunswick, then in Toronto, where he died in 2003.

To each of those five writers, I am devoting a chapter with a statement of scope, a brief biography, an overview of the author's oeuvre (with aspects of its reception) followed by an analysis of selected texts. In some cases (such as chapter 6 on Bouraoui), I focus principally on a semiotic reading of a single novel, and in other cases (such as in chapters 2 and 3 on Elkhadem and Kattan, respectively), I deal in breadth with a justifiably representative number of works. A substantial introductory chapter sheds light on the fundamental modalities of the existence of this trilingual writing produced in Canada by writers of Arabic origins. This first key chapter provides the sociohistorical context for the emergence and development of this literature, by examining factors that make of Québec a choice locus for the study of the literature of national minorities on the one hand, and by engaging the facts of the Arabic immigration to Canada, on the other. This is followed by an analysis of the quintessential characteristics of literatures of exile in general and in particular the one created by Arabic writers (mainly in French, in Québec and Ontario), thereby setting the paratextual framework within which the specificity of this particular writing is delineated. Hence, there exists in this book a continual interplay between the specific and the universal, the general and the particular, for if the introductory chapter establishes the framework, the subsequent chapters elaborate upon it and illustrate it with specific case studies.

My approach is anormative, that of the researcher as opposed to the literary critic. If it *must* be given a label, then New Criticism comes to mind, associated with an objective, empirical yet sympathetic observation of the material at hand. In my textual analyses, I look for narrative techniques, structural patterns, plots, themes, style, voice, and linguistic constructs. From repeated, close examination of the texts (literary and paraliterary), I become aware of webs of internal links, patterns of thought, and relationships within a writer's oeuvre and sometimes across writers, as well as worldviews, or *Weltanschauung*. Though I rely mainly on primary sources (the writers' works), I do refer, when deemed relevant, to secondary sources, especially so when I am studying aspects of literary reception. Likewise, even though I sometimes lean on such varied theorists as Jean Sgard, Edward Said, Pierre Nepveu, Simon Harel, or Deleuze/Guattari for their insights into literatures of exile, I partake in the view that "theories and generalizations should find their source in the texts."[18] I mainly made myself listen to the voices of the writers themselves and I recounted what I have heard. All things considered, and if I must answer succinctly the question of why I chose to study *precisely* this literature, I would reply in earnest, "Because it exists." Ontology entails epistemology, and I believe that within literary communication "all texts are only artifacts with an indeterminate communicative status until someone does something with them."[19] In the context of my subject matter, that *something* is this monograph.

I should here attempt to define some frequently occurring expressions. The term "Arab" as used in this book refers to anyone who comes from one of the twenty-one countries that make up the Arab world, namely the territory that stretches from the Arabian Gulf in the East, North to Iraq and Syria, and West across North Africa to Morocco. I will be using the terms "Arabic-Canadian" or "Canadian-Arab" interchangeably, referring to first-generation[20] Christian, Jewish, and Muslim immigrants and their offspring; who identify simply as Arabs; who have their origins directly or indirectly in the Arab states and their roots in the Arabic language and culture. The term will also apply to the second or succeeding generations.[21]

My use of the term *exile* is in line with the definition given to it by Jean Sgard (University of Grenoble) and his research team in 1986. According to Sgard, the necessary condition for being in a state of exile is "displacement, transfer to another social group, and, hence, exchange and confrontation."[22] The person who undergoes this experience and is displaced is called an *exile*. *Exilic* is an adjective I will employ to qualify the writings of such a person (or a group of people) living and working in the new environment. Even though Sgard recognizes that another necessary condition for the status of exile is forced exclusion, he admits that, *after all*, for an array of reasons, "voluntary exile" is a misleading term.[23] In fact, as will become clear in the course of my representation of the writers and their writing, I have preferred to use *exile* in the broader meaning of the term, and to think of the condition of displacement to another social group/country as both necessary and sufficient to fit under this rubric.[24] In this respect, my definition of *exile* is close to that found in *The Oxford American Dictionary*: "The state of being barred from one's native country, typically for political or punitive reasons. *A person who lives away from their native country, either from choice or compulsion.*"[25] Exile can also be metaphorical, signifying a state of mind where one may feel dislocated, displaced, and estranged in one's own country of birth. It often happens that a number of writers dwelling either in actual or figurative exile may find their true habitat or *oikos* in the very act of writing. In the words of Edward Said quoting the philosopher Theodor Adorno who lived in metaphorical exile in his native Germany (before living in actual exile in the United States for over a decade), "for a man who no longer has a homeland writing becomes a place to live."[26] This will definitely ring true for the authors studied here.

It is my hope that *Voices of Exile in Contemporary Canadian Francophone Literature* will provide a framework for the canonization of the literature of francophone Québécois writers of Arabic origin, by making it more accessible and inspiring to mainstream historical, literary, and cultural research. It is addressed to members of the literary institution and the intellectual community, to novices who want to find out about the phenomena and the writers portrayed, as well as to emerging scholars interested in pursuing research in the direction of minor literatures in Canada.

NOTES

1. Throughout this monograph, Québec will be spelled with an *accent aigu* and Québécois with two, in keeping with French orthography.

2. Except for a paper on Naïm Kattan by N. Rahimieh, "Naïm Kattan, le discours arabe and Empty Words," *Canadian Review of Comparative Literature/Revue Canadienne de Littérature Comparée* 16.3–45 (1989): 733–744.

3. International Comparative Literature Association.

4. Linda Hutcheon and Marion Richmond, eds. *Other Solitudes: Canadian Multicultural Fictions* (Toronto: Oxford University Press, 1990). Even the book by Baha Abu Laban entitled *An Olive Branch on the Family Tree: The Arabs in Canada* (1980), though containing a wealth of information, did not deal with the literature of Canadians of Arabic origins.

5. Kamal Rostom, ed. "Foreword," *Arab-Canadian Writing: Stories, Memoirs and Reminiscences* (Fredericton: York Press Ltd., 1989): no page.

6. In early 2008, the count was approximately 250 books.

7. "Une littérature mineure n'est pas celle d'une langue mineure, plutôt celle qu'une minorité fait dans une langue majeure," Gilles Deleuze and Félix Guattari, *Kafka: Pour une littérature mineure* (Paris: Minuit, 1975): 29.

8. Linda Hutcheon and Marion Richmond, eds., *Other Solitudes: Canadian Multicultural Fictions* (Toronto: Oxford University Press, 1990).

9. Lucie Lequin, "Quand le monde arabe traverse l'Atlantique," in *Multi-Culture, multi-écriture: La voix migrante au féminin en France et au Canada*, Lucie Lequin and Maïr Verthuy, ed. (Paris, Montréal: L'Harmattan, 1996): 209–219. This article deals mainly with Mona Latif Ghattas and Nadine Ltaif; Christl Verduyn, "Ecriture et migration au féminin au Québec: de mère en fille": 131–144. This article deals mainly with Nadia Ghalem and Nadine Ltaif. Also see Christl Verduyn, "Relatively political: Comparing (examples of) Québec/Canadian "ethnic"/immigrant "writings," in *Cultural Identities in Canadian Literature*, Bénédicte Maugière, ed. (New York: Peter Lang, 1998): 213–225. This article also deals with Nadine Ltaif as well as Andrée Dahan and Mona Latif-Ghattas. The author has devoted several articles to those Arabic-Canadian women writers.

10. Smaro Kamboureli, ed., *Making a Difference: Canadian Multiculture Literature* (Toronto: Oxford University Press, 1996). This anthology included the following Arabic-Canadian figures: Saad Elkhadem, "Nobody Complained": 95–98; Marwan Hassan, extract from "*The Confusion of Stones*": 330–339.

11. Edward Said, *The World, the Text and the Critic* (Cambridge, Massachusetts: Harvard University Press, 1983): 152, 157.

12. In 2004, two collections of essays appeared in the USA as a joint effort between Canadian and American scholars. These are, *Textualizing the Immigrant Experience in Contemporary Québec*, ed. Susan Ireland and Patrice J. Proulx (Westport, Connecticut: Praeger, 2004). This collection of sixteen essays contains four essays that also shed light on the work of such Arabic-Canadian writers as Abla Farhoud, Naïm Kattan, Nadine Ltaif, and Wajdi Mouawad. The second collection of seventeen essays is entitled, *Canada in the Sign of Migration and Trans-Culturalism*, ed. Klaus-Dieter Ertler and Martin Löschnigg (New York: Peter Lang, 2004). It contains a study that deals with Naïm Kattan.

13. F. Elizabeth Dahab, ed., *Voices in the Desert: An Anthology of Arabic-Canadian Women Writers* (Toronto: Guernica, 2002).

14. Julie Roorda, "Novel/Notable, *Voices in the Desert: The Anthology of Arabic-Canadian Women Writers*," *Pagicita in Toronto* 2.1 (2002): 123–124.

15. Frédérique Doyon, "Littérature-Femmes dans le Paysage; Des écritures de l'exil inscrites dans le territoire américain," *Le Devoir* (Montréal), October 21–22, 2006, www.ledevoir.com/2006/10/21/120733.html (accessed December 28, 2008).

16. The terms *francophone* and *francophonie* have been widely defined over the last two decades. For my understanding of those terms in their various shades, please see F. Elizabeth Dahab, "Visages de la francophonie; du politique, du littéraire, du sociologique," *Canadian Review of Comparative Literature/Revue Canadienne de littérature comparée* 22.3–4 (December 1995): 693–705. Also see chapter 1 (Introduction) of the present work under the subheading, "Québec as Locus for Literatures of Exile."

17. The Québec population counts over seven million individuals of whom roughly six million are French speaking (Francophone). The French-speaking community in Ontario is the largest one in Canada after Québec. It represents 5 percent of the entire population of Ontario. It is also the largest linguistic minority in Ontario. New Brunswick outdoes Ontario percentage-wise in that 33 percent of its population (the Acadians) are francophone.

18. Richard Serrano, *Against the Postcolonial: "Francophone" Writers at the Ends of French Empire* (Lanham, Maryland: Lexington Books, 2005): 8.

19. Robert de Beaugrande, "Toward the Empirical Study of Literature: A Synoptic Sketch of a New 'Society,'" *Poetics* 18 (1989): 7–27, 12.

20. The term first-generation refers either to new immigrants or their offspring. I prefer to use it in reference to new immigrants born outside Canada and to refer to their offspring as second generation. According to Rajwa G. Khouri's *Arabs in Canada-Post 9/11* (Toronto: G7 Books and Canadian Arab Federation, 2006): 75, the first expression, Canadian Arab, is favored over the second by Canadians of Arabic origin.

21. See Baha Abu Laban, "Arabs," in *Encyclopedia of Canada's Peoples*, ed. Paul Magosci (Toronto: University of Toronto Press, 1998): 203–212, 203. The Arabic speaking countries of the Middle East and North Africa (over 240 million by 1993) comprise the countries of Syria, Lebanon, Jordan, Palestine/Israel, and Iraq, known as the Fertile Crescent; the countries of the Arabian (Persian) Gulf and Peninsula: Kuwait, Bahrain, Qatar, United Arab Emirates (UAE), Oman, Saudi Arabia, and Yemen in the southwestern corner of the peninsula; in North Africa, the countries of Mauritania, Egypt, Libya, Tunisia, Algeria, Morocco, and to the south, Sudan. Somalia and Djibouti are part of the League of Arab States and Arabic is partly spoken there.

22. "Pour qu'il y ait exil, il faut qu'il yait déplacement, transfert dans un autre groupe social, et par copnséquent échange, confrontation." Jean Sgard, "Conclusions," *Exil et Littérature*, ed. Jacques Mounier (Grenoble: Ellug, 1986): 291–299, 293.

23. Jean Sgard, "Conclusions," in *Exil et Littérature*, 291–292.

24. I have also used the terms immigrant/immigration, especially when studying the Arabic presence in Canada. When discussing and classifying various types of border crossing, some critics have established a stark difference between *immigrant* and *exile*: "While both the exile and the immigrant cross the border between one social or national group and another, the exile's stance toward the new host culture is negative, the immigrant's positive" (Abdul J. JanMohamed, "Worldliness-without-World, Homelessness-as-Home: Toward a Definition of the Specular Border Intellectual," *Edward Said: A Critical Reader*, ed. Michael Sprinker (Cambridge, Massachusetts: Blackwell Publishers, 1992): 96–120, 101. Though this characterization may be applicable in a number of cases, by no means can it provide a general rule. The same critic claims that Edward Said can be considered at once an exile and an immigrant (104) or "neither quite an exile nor quite an immigrant" (109), a status perhaps applicable to the five writers portrayed here, in their border-crossing to France then Canada.

25. Emphasis mine.

26. Edward Said, "Intellectual Exile: Expatriates and Marginals," *Representations of the Intellectual: The Reith Lectures* (New York: Vintage Books, 1996): 47–64, 58.

Acknowledgments

I am grateful to California State University, Long Beach, for having granted me a semester post-tenure sabbatical leave that enabled me to bring much of this project to fruition.

I wish to recognize colleagues at large whose own scholarly endeavors or suggestions directly or indirectly influenced my very own, to mention, Steven Tötösy, François Paré, Nasrin Rahimieh, Joseph Pivato, Robert Schnucker, Lucie Lequin, Irene Sywenky, Valérie Orlando, and others.

Special thanks to my sister Nawal Kamel for her strong feedback and support, especially over the last year; to Nicolai Haydn for his input and his permission to use a photograph of his taking on the book cover.

Oliver Hoidn has meticulously and patiently read and edited the entire manuscript in June/July 2008 in Marseille/Long Beach. To him, with immense gratitude, I dedicate this book also.

1

Introduction: The Odyssey of Québécois/Canadian-Arabic Writers and Their Writing[1]

> Foreigners in Québec are afraid of becoming French, the Francophones themselves are afraid of becoming Canadian, and the Canadians are afraid of becoming American.
>
> Saad Elkhadem (*Crash Landing of the Flying Egyptian*, 29)

> *Le jugement des autres est le jugement dernier; et l'exclusion sociale la forme concrète de l'enfer et de la damnation.*
>
> [The judgment of others is the Last Judgment and social exclusion is the concrete form of hell and damnation.]
>
> Pierre Bourdieu (*Leçon sur la leçon*, 52)

Il existe au Canada, depuis une trentaine d'années seulement, des littératures minoritaires embryonnaires de langue française, très conscientes de leur origine et de leur originalité, très vivantes, très vitales, malgré l'enlisement inéluctable des communautés culturelles et ethniques dont elles émanent.

[Over the last thirty years only, there have emerged in Canada embryonic minor literatures of French expression, very conscious of their origin and originality; very lively, very vital despite the ineluctable impoverishment of the cultural and ethnic communities from which they emanate.][2]

This passage, written in 1992 by François Paré, an academic scholar and member of the *communauté Franco-Ontarienne* [Franco-Ontarian community], is taken from the critic's celebrated Ontario-published monograph suggestively titled *Les Littératures de l'exiguïté* [Literatures of Exiguïty], a work that earned its author the 1993 Governor General's Award and *Signet d'or* prize. In that monograph, Paré strongly bemoaned what he qualified as "l'arrogance de l'universel" [arrogance of the universal], inherited from Europe, which, according to him, characterized "to death" university research in Canada. He vehemently advocated the need to "reorient literary historiography, to open up its inclusionary infrastructure, and hence to account for the marginalities."[3] "Diversity is no utopia," Paré asserted in the preface to this book entirely dedicated to the cause of "small" literatures[4] (as he called literatures of national minorities in Canada), whose number make of the latter no longer a country of "two solitudes," nor even of three, but a country of a great many solitudes.[5]

The aim of this chapter is multifold. After pointing out reasons for Québec being a well-chosen locus for the study of minor literatures, I will draw a bio-bibliographical profile of the writers as a group, then I will proceed to detect tendencies in Arabic-Canadian writing (predominantly produced in Québec), and address such questions akin to those proposed by Lambert for the characterization of any given literature: What are the dominant norms; which phenomena/authors occupy a major vs. peripheral position; which language, style of writing and themes are prevalent?[6] Since this literature is still in the making, it is also relevant to mention its transmission agents, especially so when those belong to the corpus of this very literature. Because of the existence of such intermediaries, one can speak of a beginning of cohesion and of a system, defined by Lambert in 1986 as follows: "Un ensemble d'oeuvres, d'auteurs, de lecteurs . . . liés par des principes (des normes) qui les opposent aux systèmes environnnants" [a set of works, authors, readers . . . linked together by norms and principles that distinguish them from neighbouring systems].[7] In the course of this chapter, I will provide the immediate, demographic context for the study of this literature in terms of the Arabic presence in Canada and I will delineate, when dealing with the writing itself, stylistic and thematic features, some of which are shared by other Québécois writers of exile. Theoretical considerations pertaining to the choice of language by the exilic writer in Canada will be raised with regard to Ethnic-Canadian writers in general and more specifically with regard to writers of Arabic origins featured in this monograph.

Tracing some of the theoretical influences at work here, I recognize that my overall standpoint was partly influenced by Siegfried Schmidt's empirical view of literature (one that combines sociological and literary considerations) and his apt formulation of the principles underlying the development of social systems,[8] where paratextual factors pertaining to *the production and reception of literary texts* are considered relevant and worth noting. Undoubtedly, Deleuze and Guattari's *Kafka: Pour une littérature mineure* (1975), especially the chapter entitled "Qu'est-ce qu'une littérature mineure" [What Is a Minor Literature] has shed light on my subject of study.[9] And while some critics have blamed Edward Said for having exalted and overvalorized the image of the intellectual exile "caught in a historical limbo between home and the world,"[10] I find his writings on the topic inspiring, and when deemed pertinent, they may be evoked or invoked in relation to my treatment of the material at hand.[11]

QUÉBEC AS LOCUS FOR THE STUDY OF LITERATURES OF EXILE

The generic and problematic term *francophonie*, this highly debated and frequently defined construct promoted by Mitterand to strengthen ties with old colonies, refers to a full-blown political and sociological infrastructure nesting the literatures of such regions as Québec, Africa, the Caribbean, and North Africa, regions that have in common a love-hate relationship with France and perhaps a "symbiose d'énergies dormantes" [symbiosis of dormant energies] once evoked by Senghor.[12] To a certain extent, literatures of exile and literatures of national minorities produced in French (in francophone or nonfrancophone regions) belong here;[13] they tend to exhibit features similar to the literatures of postindependence nations. It has been observed that the idea of cultural dislocation inherent in the notion of hybridity and its related term *diaspora* are linked with the properties of exile (as an exterior and interior phenomenon) and can be used for approaching both ethnic identity and cultural nationalism.[14] To claim hybridity is to assert the existence of several cultures in oneself. The counterpart of hybridity in colonized countries sees the colonial encounter in terms of its disruption of domestic spaces. Thus, according to this premise, the novel of the Nigerian writer Chinua Achebe (*Things Fall Apart*), that of the Arabic-Canadian writer, Marwan Hassan (*The Confusion of Stones*) and the novel of the Québécois Jacques Godbout (*Les Têtes à Papineau*) could parallel one another within the same paradigm,[15] and could be read as "national allegories," to borrow Frederic Jameson's well-known, apt phrase.[16] Furthermore, literatures of cultural communities are often produced in more than one major language; hence, they obey the definition given by Deleuze/Guattari of minor literatures and, being twice or thrice removed from a motherland (as is the case of ethnic literatures in Québec), they offer a choice *champ d'action* for comparatists and cultural theorists alike.[17]

Convergence of Québec Minor Literatures and Québécois Traditional Literature

The choice of Québec, where over a dozen literatures of exile (or *écritures migrantes*) have emerged since the sixties,[18] is relevant in that any contrapuntal interpretation of the emergence of those literatures in this largest French-speaking community outside France has to be informed by the history of the colonization of Québec as well as an analogy between Québécois and African terms of resistance. In this sense, it is relevant to recall the handing over of Québec in 1759 to Great Britain, the subsequent invasion of Montréal by Anglo Celtic settlers and British capitals, the perceived oppression of the Québécois, and the imposition of English as the only official language in Canada until 1969.[19] The ongoing separatist impulse first manifested itself on the political front with The Quiet Revolution that began in the sixties and culminated in 1970 with the famous October Crisis, in which Pierre Eliot Trudeau, the Prime Minister of Canada at the time, declared a State of Emergency.

Literatures of exile in Québec have become visible in the eighties. They are produced by individuals of color who originated mostly from the South (including an increasing number of feminine voices) and who are "francophone, francophile, francophonisable or in the process of francophonisation."[20] In fact, those minor literatures reflect the expanded *francophonie pluraliste* stance of the nationalist immigration policy, a policy that claims to dissociate language from culture, the two main referents of French-Canadian identity, making French in Québec the rallying point for transcultural intercourse.[21] They can be said to be produced by minorities twice removed from the dominant systems, namely the French and English-Canadian literary institutions. The first degree of removal would be the political alienation in which Québec itself stands in relation to the rest of Canada (and North America): a minority within a majority. The second degree of removal for the foreign-born writer would be precisely his foreignness, his hovering at the periphery of major systems whether or not he writes in the language of the two founding nations.

Partly due to the high quotient of deterritorialization and the sense of absence inherent in literatures of exile, there exists a strong thematic link between minor literatures in Québec and some of the cultural characteristics of Québécois writing *de souche*. In fact, in his seminal work *L'Ecologie du réel: Mort et naissance de la littérature québécoise contemporaine*,[22] Pierre Nepveu showed that within traditional Québécois poetry the notions of exile/madness, alienation, and a sense of loss, as well as the feeling of an absent or incomplete country, were already quite prevalent. Those themes were partially elaborated by such poets as Octave Crémazie, who died expatriated in 1879 in Le Havre, and Emile Nelligan, exiled from his own self in a Montréal asylum where he spent forty years, dying in 1941. During the literary explosion that took place in Québec in the fifties and sixties, a period of contestation and national revival coupled with an intense quest for identity, there was a renaissance of those two writers of alienation and inner exile initiated by such Québécois figures as Nicole Brossard, Hubert Aquin, Jacques Godbout, and Gérard Bessette. In addition, theories of decolonization hailing from the Caribbean (championed by such figures as Aimé Césaire and Frantz Fanon) found fertile ground with such Québécois intellectuals as Paul Chamberland and Pierre Vallières. In 1968, the latter wrote *Nègres blancs d'Amérique* [White Negroes of America], referring to the suffering of his people at the hands of English domination, the title of which reverses Fanon's *Peau noire, masques blancs* (1952). The analogy between cultural oppression in Québec and racial oppression elsewhere was thus being made explicit, laying foundations for "other solitudes." In the words of Pierre Nepveu commenting on the state of receptivity of the *imaginaire québécois* to the "phénomène massif et incontournable"[23] [the massive and uncircumventable phenomenon] that qualifies the body of ethnic literature in Québec in the last decades of the twentieth century:

> *L'imaginaire québécois lui-même s'est largement défini, depuis les années soixante, sous le signe de l'exil (psychique, fictif), du manque, du pays absent ou inachevé et, du milieu même de cette négativité, s'est constitué en imaginaire migrant, pluriel, souvent cosmopolite.*
>
> [The Québécois *imaginaire* was largely defined, since the sixties, under the banner of exile (psychic, fictive), of a lack, of an absent or incomplete country; from the heart of this very negativity, it has re-emerged as a migrant, plural, and often cosmopolitan awareness.][24]

In this light, it is worth recalling that the Québec motto, *je me souviens* (I remember), also used on Québec issued license plates, a motto that pertains to the multiple heritage of Québec, has evolved, according to Québécois noted historian Yvan Lamonde, into an intransitive aphorism that has forgotten what it should be remembering in the first place, thus becoming strictly self-referential: reminding one to remember (that which one has forgotten).[25] This motto, then, seems to parallel the exilic text marked by the presence of an elusive absence. In the words of Nepveu: "Le texte migrant se souvient, croit se souvenir, est hanté par l'originel et l'authentique, mais doit en même temps constater, que d'une certaine manière cette hantise est sans objet" [The migrant text remembers, or believes it does. It is haunted by the authentic and the original, yet it must at the same time admit that in some way this fixation has no object].[26] Québec exilic literatures, stresses Nepveu,[27] coincide with a whole cultural movement where precisely hybridity, plurality, uprootedness, and errancy are privileged modes, not only in Québécois literature itself (witness the still popular 1842 song of *Un canadien errant*, A Wandering Canadian) but as part and parcel of postmodernism, which hence can be said to provide a point of convergence and intersection for both minor literatures in Québec and Québécois literature at large. It is that common denominator of dispossession (whose primary form is the abandonment of the native land, but which also marks the colonized Quebecer traditionally afflicted with emptiness and alienation)[28] that would become, via the medium of literature, a source for the enrichment of the French language by means of linguistic, lexical and "even syntactic" innovations.[29] In the words of a researcher expressing an idea proposed by the Italian-Canadian Fulvio Caccia on the "transcultural challenge" of present-day Québec:

> *Voici le défi transculturel. . . . La nouvelle "lingua franca" de la modernité québécoise émergera de la rencontre entre deux langues historiquement caractérisées par la faiblesse: la langue aliénée du Québec colonialisé et la langue fragile des écritures migrantes.*
>
> [Here is the transcultural challenge. The new "lingua franca" of Québécois modernity will emerge from the meeting of two languages historically characterized by weakness: the alienated language of colonized Québec and the fragile language of migrant literatures.][30]

In the final analysis, it seems that literatures of exile in particular, perhaps as a result of their vantage point of heightened creativity, and postcolonial literatures in general, may have found a solution to the problem of language in postmodernism. In this regard, one can recall Anthony Appiah's suggestive claim related to Heidegger's notion of *lichtung*, with the double meaning of light and clearing: "The post in postcolonial, like the post in postmodernism is the post of a space clearing gesture."[31] In this connection, it is worth noting a 2002 state-of-the-arts collection of essays on francophone literary studies, with an article entitled, "L'Histoire littéraire est inadmissible: le cas du Québec" [Literary History Is Inadmissible: The Case of Québec] written by a Canadian professor, Michel Biron. The conclusion consists essentially of a retake of Nepveu's thesis more than a decade earlier. After developing the idea that the Québécois context "resists the logic of any historiographic discourse," the author asserts that "the present floating epoch" feels very familiar to the literary historian who thus approaches his topic with great ease, as if "the disoriented individual of today resembled, like a brother, the individual he has always known."[32]

As mentioned above, any contrapuntal reading of Québec as a choice location for the study of literatures of exile will have to take into account the fact that the literary explosion in Québec in the fifties and sixties, characterized as it was by the self-affirmational national text, bears similarities to the anticolonial resistance of African intellectuals as well. In Québec as in Africa, the struggle was about reclaiming and revalorizing a cultural identity eroded by colonization,[33] witness the construct of *québécitude*, the North American counterpart of *négritude*, both movements valorizing stigmatized cultures.[34] Also worth mentioning in this context is a historical incidence fraught with symbolism and affiliation, one which *establishes Québec as the locus* of postcolonial struggle and resistance. It is the publication in Montréal of *Les Soleils des Indépendances*,[35] the novel of the Cameroonian writer Ahmadou Kourouma, after it had been refused in France in the late sixties because of the linguistic liberties the writer had taken in an effort to appropriate the former master's tongue.[36] Moreover, the novel won a prize called Prix de la francité, defined by the Montréal journal (*Journal D'études francaises*) that gave the prize, as francophony minus France, thus undermining the hegemony of the latter.[37] Hence, Kourouma's novel was published in the context of a picturesque parallel between French-Canadian culture and francophone African culture, witness the additional fact that in Québec too the separatist movement in the sixties had gathered momentum around the issue of the French language.[38] In any case, when used in the light of Said's notion of the worldliness of texts and the relevance of their historical, circumstantial, and affiliative reality, this particular incident of publication can be said *to provide the symbolic groove* within which will be nested literatures of exile in Québec, as well as the framework for a contrapuntal reading of the production of those literatures. Moreover, the 1985 Québécois *Prix Emile Nelligan* Prize awarded to the Egyptian-Québécois writer Anne-Marie Alonzo is another telling gesture (fraught with symbolic endorsement) recognizing a plurality in the Québécois cultural make-up, as part of a movement seeking to supplant the dated notion of the two founding nations of the "Belle Province."[39] In fact, "La pluralité des centres" [The Plurality of Centres], an expression coined by Pierre Nepveu, is the title of his conclusion to the partial death and rebirth of Québécois literature.[40]

The recognition of this cultural plurality of Québec literature on the part of scholars, critics, and the Québec government, constituted a progress if not a novelty, for before the eighties, minor literatures in Québec were largely ignored, though they had been in existence for at least two decades. The revisionist movement that took place in the eighties (partly prompted by the federal government's multiculturalism policy) within the Canadian/Québécois literary institution, claimed tangible results in the direction of dissociating "ethnicity and quebecity" [ethnicité et québécité] and advocating cultural hybridity.[41] I have already pointed out some examples in this regard. Other examples of expansion and reaching out to the Other are likewise worth mentioning in the

Québécois context: in the early 1980s, alternative literary reviews such as *La Parole Mèteque, Dérives*, and the trilingual (French-English-Italian) *Vice-Versa* (significantly subtitled *Magazine transculturel*) saw the light of day, bespeaking of the move toward the cultural heterogeneity strongly advocated by such intellectuals as the Italians Caccia and D'Alfonso as well as the Québécois *de souche*, Bertrand and Morin.[42] Furthermore, in 1991, Pierre L'Hérault drew a "cartographie de l'hétérogène" [cartography of the heterogeneous] subtitled "Dérives identitaires des années 1980" [Identity Vagrancies of the 1980s], in which he advocated breaking away from a "linear, vertical, genetic, monologic" line of thinking [pensée linéaire, verticale, génétique, monologique] in favor of a cosmopolitan and postnational reading of the Québécois text.[43] Moreover, in his essay entitled *In Italics: In Defense of Ethnicity* (1996), seeking to break-up the couple territory/national identity, Antonio D'Alfonso asserts: "It is clearly in exile that the individual will discover his true identity, and not by consuming the salts of the earth. An individual who knows how to fly lives closer to his identity, than one who crawls in the wet soil of nationhood. Here is the identity that is shared by many and everywhere across the world."[44]

In the late eighties, the University of Montréal started a vast project entitled *Montréal Imaginaire* in the framework of which a series of conferences took place (1988–1989) on the themes of transculturalism, cultural hybridity, and belonging. Similarly, in 1998, the same University of Montréal staged a colloquium entitled, "Troisièmes solitudes: écritures minoritaires canadiennes" [Third Solitudes: Canadian Minority Literatures]. Also worth mentioning that in 1992, *Lettres Québécoises*, a literary review dedicated to the promotion of Québécois literature, published an entire issue dedicated to minor literatures in Québec and entitled "De l'autre littérature québécoise" [Of the Other Québécois Literature]. That same year, *L'Institut québécois de recherche sur la culture* [The Québec Institute for Research on Culture] produced a study entitled *Montréal au pluriel. Huit communautés ethno-culturelles de la région montréalaise* [Montreal in the Plural. Eight Ethno-Cultural Communities of the Montreal region] pertaining to the socioeconomic profile of black francophone, Chinese, Italian, Portuguese, Greek, Southeast Asian and Asian communities. Two years earlier, namely, in 1990, that same institute had come up with an informative and useful tool for the study of minor literatures, consisting of a bio-bibliography of immigrant writers and works produced in Québec between 1970 and 1990.[45] Moreover, as recently as 2005, The French-Canadian critic Simon Harel produced a monograph titled *Les Passages obligés de l'écriture migrante* [The Obligatory Passages of Migrant Literature], where such writers as the Franco-Polish Régine Robin, the Iraqi-Jew Naïm Kattan, and the Haitian Emile Ollivier, are studied and celebrated.[46]

Those are all worthwhile projects. However, to what extent are Québec minor literatures de facto part of mainstream Québécois writing, and is it desirable for them to become increasingly so? Interesting dilemma to mull over! Meanwhile, it is noteworthy that the annual *Festival du monde arabe* that began in 2000 in Montréal tends to lump together Arabic writers who may sometimes feel they are being put in the same mould, under the ethnic ticket, as some cultural critics bitterly remark.[47] Furthermore, the 2000 voluminous monograph by Jacques Allard, entitled *Le Roman du Québec: Histoire, Perspectives, Lectures* [The Novel of Québec: History, Perspectives, Readings] pertains exclusively to mainstream Québécois literature, with the occasional reference to Kattan as a "néo-québécois" author.[48] Similarly, the 2004 study, *Le Roman Québécois contemporain: Les Voix sous les mots*, featuring a collection of seven essays edited by André Lamontagne, is entirely devoted to Québécois writers *de souche* (such as Jacques Ferron, Victor Beaulieu, Francine Noël, Louis Hamelin, and Jacques Poullin) with two studies on Danny Laferrière, the celebrated Haitian writer, and Régine Robin, one of the best-known immigrant writers in Québec, of European origin. Also worth mentioning in this context is the interview held with Elizabeth Dahab by the Montréal daily, *Le Devoir*, in October 2006. In view of paying homage to "Women in the [literary] landscape," as indicated by the title of the article subtitled "Des écritures de l'exil inscrites dans le territoire nord-Américain" [Of Literatures of Exile Inscribed on the North-American Soil], the journalist introduced the subject matter by referring to Alonzo and Farhoud, not only as women writers, but also as "major actors on the [Québec] cultural scene." However, in the sentence immediately following, she retracts somewhat her statement, by asserting: "L'histoire littéraire les associe toutefois à ce courant qui a pour appellation la littérature canado-arabe" [literary history associates (those writers) nevertheless, with this current called Arabo-Canadian literature].[49]

Nevertheless, all things considered, in the literary landscape of Québec an undeniable progress has been achieved in the direction of inclusion over the last three decades, as has also been recognized by other scholars in the academic world, notably by scholars in the United States.[50] Hence, in a 1996 article on the "Migratory Input into Québécois Society" [L'Apport migratoire à la société québécoise][51] of a work by Emile Ollivier, Eloïse Brière remarked that even as literary production in Québec reflects a resolutely francophone society in its language and institutions, it still manages to incorporate the exile of Others and their locus of remembrance.

It is hoped that the historiography—the emergence and ongoing development—of francophone Québécois/Canadian-Arabic literature can partially be attributed and bear witness to that laudable, intentional effort in Québec toward plurality and multiplicity—away from the "veterinarian concept of a pure race" once advocated by such right-wing nationalists as Lionel Groulx and some of his followers.[52] The fact that a large percentage of this literature is produced in French speaks of its embedment in North American *francophonie*, with its heightened likelihood of breaking new frontiers.

BIO-BIBLIOGRAPHICAL PROFILE OF QUÉBÉCOIS/CANADIAN-ARABIC WRITERS

The Canadian-Arabic Community

The Arabic community in North America numbers over three million individuals who immigrated at the turn of the twentieth century and after World War II.[53] According to official figures, approximately 216,000 immigrants from the Arab world arrived in Canada between 1882 and 1992. The first wave of immigration, also referred to as "the pioneer wave" (1882–1961) numbered approximately 15,000, and consisted mostly of Syrians, whereas "the new wave" (1962–1992), by far the larger (averaging 6,600 arrivals per year) and notably more varied, is responsible for the balance, amounting to approximately 93 percent of the total immigrant population of Canadian Arabs.[54] The sixties and seventies witnessed a marked increase in the yearly immigration figures over the earlier wave (averaging 3,500 per year as opposed to 185 per year during the pioneer wave), while the numbers continued to grow through the eighties and nineties (including large numbers of refugees and investors), with an average of 24,600 Arab immigrants for the years 1991–1992. A study conducted in 2003–2006 shows that in 2001 the settlement of Arabic immigrants by province ran as follows: Ontario (53 percent) followed by Quebec (28 percent), Alberta (5 percent), Nova Scotia (5 percent), British Columbia (4.8 percent), with the rest distributed over the other provinces.[55] As for the classification of immigrants by country of origin, the same study stipulates that for the year 2000, the percentage of total Arab immigration by country of provenance was as follows: Algeria (15.9 percent), Iraq (14.3 percent), Morocco (14.7 percent), Lebanon (10.6 percent), Egypt (9.1 percent), Somalia (8.7 percent), Jordan (8.4 percent), Syria (5.1 percent), Sudan (5.1 percent), Tunisia (2.4 percent), and the Palestinian Authority (1.5 percent).[56] However, settlement and immigration trends have waxed and waned over the decades. A noted scholar in the field claims that in the sixties and up to the nineties 40 percent of the Arab Canadians came from Lebanon, followed by Egypt (20 percent), Morocco (12 percent), and Syria (8 percent)[57] (with the remainder originating from the rest of the Arab world), and that they settled in Québec, Ontario, and Alberta, in this order.[58]

It seems that economic necessity and the desire for personal advancement were responsible for the first wave of Arab immigration to North America whereas the immediate reasons in recent decades are related to the need to escape the ravages of war: the Lebanese Civil war (1975–1990), the Algerian (1991–2002), and the Somali (1988–1995). As for religion, the first six decades of Lebanese immigration were mainly comprised of Christians, with Moslems increasing in numbers subsequently, and similarly, in the sixties, Christian Copts accounted for a large number of Egyptian immigrants while the flow of their Muslim countrymen increased in the eighties and nineties. The major wave of Egyptian immigration happened after the 1967[59] war that coincided with the tail end of Nasser's reign of terror and brutality.[60] The largest influx of Egyptian emigration began in 1973 and continued throughout the seventies, eighties, and nineties. The driving force behind it lies in the disillusionment with Anwar El Sadat's regime: His political and economic policies and the sharp social decline accompanying his policy of *infitah*, or "opening up" to foreign influences.

The Writers

There are approximately forty Arabic-Canadian writers, of whom about twenty-five have produced a major work (one or more books); the rest have a minor production (principally publications in reviews and magazines).[61] The following sample table, though *far from being exhaustive*, will give an idea of the potential of this literature. It includes only writers who published at least one book of their own writing.

Table 1.1 displays a biosociological profile fairly consistent with that of the Arabic presence in Canada and its distribution. A significant number of the writers are Egyptian and Lebanese while the others originate from the Maghreb, Iraq, and Syria. A fair number of those writers settled mostly in Québec and, to a smaller extent, in Ontario. Moreover, they are often trilingual. The languages mastered amongst them, other than Arabic, are French, English, German, Armenian, Hebrew, and Italian. They have a variety of religious backgrounds and denominations: Coptic-Orthodox, Greek-Orthodox, Catholic, Maronite, Protestant, Anglican, Muslim (both Sunni and Shi'a), and Jewish. Many have multiple ethnic origins, some very distant, others more immediate. For instance the Egyptian writer Elie Tarakdjian and the Lebanese writer Vasco Varoujean are both Armenian (they never lived in Armenia) of Syrian descent. The late Egyptian-Québécois writer Anne-Marie Alonzo had Maltese, Palestinian, and Syrian distant origins, and the late Egyptian Antoine Naaman was of Syro-Lebanese descent. Pan Bouyoucas, who

Table 1. Selected Writers and Their Writings.[1]

Name—Country of Origin—Date of Immigration—Province of Residence	Number of Publications—Genres Published Places of Publication	Literary Prizes[2] Publishing Houses/Literary Journals Founded
1-Abitbol, Bob-Oré-Morocco-?-Québec	2. Fiction (short stories and novel) Balzac (Montréal)	
2-Alonzo, Anne-Marie-Egypt-1963-Québec	21. Poetic Prose Editions Trois (Laval), L'Hexagone, Editions du Noroît (Montréal).	Prix Emile Nelligan (1985) The Order of Canada (1997) Médaille civique de la ville de Laval (1997) Co-founded Editions Trois (Laval 1985) and review, *Trois*
3-Antoun, Bernard-Lebanon-1978-Québec	25. Poetry, Non-fiction (mostly religious essays) L'Harmattan (France) Humanitas (Rosemère, Québec) Foi et vie (Montréal)	
4-Bouraoui, Hédi-Tunisia-1966-Ontario	40. Poetry, Fiction (novels), Children's books. Mémoire d'encrier, Editions du vermillon (Ottawa), Editions du Gref (Toronto), Or du temps (Tunisia).	Prix International de Poésie (Cannes 1987) Prix France-Canada (2004) Prix du nouvel Ontario (1999) Grand prix de la ville de Bergerac (France 2005) Prix du meilleur livre érudit (2005) by APFUCC[3] (Canada) Founded Centre Canada-Maghreb (York 2002)

5-Dahan, Andrée-Egypt-1968-Québec	5. Fiction (novels), Poetry Quinze, Québec-Amérique, Editions Trois (Laval, Québec)	
6-Elia, Maurice-Egypt-?-Québec	4. Fiction (novels) Humanitas, Carte Blanche	
7-Elkhadem, Saad-Egypt-1968-New Brunswick	25. Fiction (novellas, micronovels) York Press (New Brunswick)	Founded York Press Ltd. (New Brunswick 1974) Founded International Fiction Review (1975)
8-Fahmy, Jean-Egypt-1969-Québec	4. Fiction (novels), Essays L'Interligne (Ottawa)	
9-Farhoud, Abla-Lebanon-1951-Québec	7. Fiction (novels), Drama L'Hexagone, vlb éditeur (Montréal), Lansman (Belgium)	Prix Arletty de l'universalité de la langue française (1993) Prix Théâtre et liberté (France 1993) Prix France-Québec (1999) Prix du roman francophone (2006)
10-Geadah, Yolande-Egypt-1967-Québec	3. Non-fiction (essays) vlb éditeur (Montréal)	Finalist for Governor General Award (Best Essay) 1997 Prix Condorcet (Québec 2007)
11-Ghalem, Nadia-Algeria-1976-Québec	9. Poetry, Fiction (novels, short stories, children's stories). Hurtubise, vlb, Guérin literature (Montréal)	Finalist for Grand Prix Littéraire Guérin (Québec 1987) Prix Crédif (France 1995)

(continued)

Table 1. *(continued)*

Name—Country of Origin—Date of Immigration—Province of Residence	Number of Publications—Genres Published Places of Publication	Literary Prizes[2] Publishing Houses/Literary Journals Founded
12-Ghazali, Ahmed-Morocco-?-Québec/Spain	7. Drama Editions Théâtrales (France) Canada's National Arts Centre[4]	Prix SACD (Société des auteurs et compositeurs dramatiques), 2001 Prix Soni Labou Tansi (2003)
13-Hassan, Marwan (Lebanese descent) born in Ontario	6. Fiction (novels), Non-fiction (essay) Cormorant Books (Dunvegan, Ontario) Tsar publications (Toronto, Ontario)	
14-Karamé, Antoine-Egypt-1974-Québec	3. Fiction (novel) Poetry Elias Publishing (Cairo) Editions Naaman	
15-Kattan, Naïm-Iraq-1954-Québec	34. Fiction (novels, short stories), Non-fiction (essays), Drama Leméac, Editions HMH, Hurtubise, l'Hexagone (Montréal)	Prix France-Canada (1971) Prix Athanase David (Québec 2004) Prix de la francophonie (2005) Prix Hervé Deluen (France 2007)
16-Khalo, Michel-Egypt-1966-Québec	2. Fiction (novel) vlb éditeur	
17-Latif-Ghattas, Mona-Egypt-1966-Québec	13. Fiction (novels), Poetry, Music Boréal, Elias, Editions du Noroît, Leméac, Editions Trois (Laval, Québec) Elias, ESIG (Cairo)	

Author	Works	Publishers	Awards/Notes
18-Ltaif, Nadine-Lebanon-1980-Québec	7. Poetry, Poetic prose	Guernica (Toronto), Le Noroît (Montréal)	Finalist, Prix Emile Nelligan (1991)
19-Mouawad, Wajdi-Lebanon-1983-Québec	13. Drama, Fiction (one novel), Interviews	Leméac/Actes Sud-Papiers (Montréal, France/Belgium/Switzerland)	*Prix de la francophonie* (2004) *Prix Molière* (2005)
20-Mouhoub, Yamina-Algeria-1978-Québec	1. Poetry	Editions Teichtner (Laval, Québec), Les poètes du dimanche (France)	
21-Naaman, Antoine-Egypt-1966-Québec	15. Poetry, Non-fiction (essays/translations)	Editions Naaman (Sherbrooke, Quebec)	Founded: Editions Cosmos (1969) Editions Naaman (1973) Présence Francophone (1970) Ecriture Française dans le Monde (1974)
22-Nadda, Rubba, (Syrian descent) born in Montréal. Lives in Ontario	1. Fiction (short stories), 16 Films.	Sister's Vision Press (Toronto), *River's Edge Journal* (Manitoba), *White Wall Review* (Toronto)	
23-Najib, Di'un-Lebanon-1950-Québec	2. Non-fiction (Memoirs)	Archives of Coptic Church, Montréal	
24-Rostom, Kamal-Egypt-1974-Québec	30.5 Fiction (short stories/ novels	Rostom Publishing	Founded Rostom Publishing (Ottawa 1984)
5-Salloum, Habeeb-Egypt-1942-Ontario	? Essays and travel		
26-Shaker, Fouad-Lebanon-?-Québec	6. Fiction (novels, essays)		

(continued)

Table 1. (continued)

Name—Country of Origin—Date of Immigration—Province of Residence	Number of Publications—Genres Published Places of Publication	Literary Prizes[2] Publishing Houses/Literary Journals Founded
27-Tarakdjian, Elie-Egypt-1969-Québec	1. Fiction (novel) Editions pourquoi pas (Athabasca, Alberta)	
28-Varoujean, Vasco-Syria-1967-Québec	3. Fiction (novels) Editions Naaman (Sherbrooke, Québec) Tisseyre (Montréal)	
29-Wyl, Jean-Michel-Algeria-1967-Québec	4. Fiction (novels) Editions Beauchemin (Montréal)	

[1] The question marks in this table stand for the corresponding missing or unavailable information.
[2] This column lists the literary prizes earned by the authors as well as the publishing houses and literary reviews founded by them, if any.
[3] APFUCC stands for association des professeurs de français des universités et collèges canadiens.
[4] Some of Ghazali's plays were read and occasionally staged there.
[5] Only four of which were published in Canada.

was born in Lebanon and grew up there until the age of sixteen is of Greek descent and doesn't in the least consider himself Arabic.[62] The most striking features of those writers as a group are not only the diversity of their ethnic background, one that corroborates the diversity of the second wave of immigration (1962–1992), but also their relative isolation from each other,[63] the fact that they are often affiliated with a university in some capacity, and that a number of those who managed to be published held public functions.

As shown in the table above, two of the listed writers, Hassan and Nadda, are Canadian-born with Lebanese and Syrian immigrant parents. A significant proportion of Arabic-Canadian writers immigrated to Canada between 1963 and 1974 inclusively, while several did so in the fifties, late seventies, or eighties. Such is the case for Naïm Kattan who immigrated in 1954; Abla Farhoud in 1951, then again in 1973 after an interruption of eight years; Nadine Ltaif in 1980, and Wajdi Mouawad in 1983. A significant proportion are in their late fifties, a relevant fact if one wants to predict the future of this literature. Two of them (Varoujean and Naaman) died in the eighties and two prominent figures, Anne-Marie Alonzo (twenty-one books) and Saad Elkhadem (twenty-five books) died recently, in 2005 and 2003, respectively, while eight of the major surviving writers are still producing, and are the most prolific. These are Hédi Bouraoui (forty books), Naïm Kattan (thirty-four books), Mona Latif-Ghattas (thirteen books), Nadia Ghalem (seven books), Abla Farhoud (seven books), Nadine Ltaif (six books), Andrée Dahan (five books), and Marwan Hassan (six books). They write plays or documentaries for Radio-Canada or Radio-Québec; they are radio-announcers, film-script writers (Nadia Ghalem, Mona Latif Ghattas, and Rubba Nadda), film directors (Wajdi Mouawad and Rubba Nadda), stage-directors (Wajdi Mouawad), choreographers (Anne-Marie Alonzo and Mona Latif- Ghattas), or contributors to Les Grands Ballets Canadiens (Anne Marie Alonzo). They contribute to newspapers, literary magazines, and reviews such as *Le devoir*, *La Voix métèque*, *Trait-D'Union*, *La Presse*, *Liberté*, *Voix et Images*, *Humanitas*, *Trois*, *Canadian Fiction Magazine*, *The Whigstandard*, *The Georgian*, and *The Athenian*. At least five of them teach in some capacity at L'Université du Québec à Montréal (UQAM), to mention the following: Naïm Kattan (in 1991 he left the Canada Council where he had held a key position since 1967), Andrée Dahan, and Pan Bouyoucas. Hédi Bouraoui is Professor of Comparative Literature at York University and the late Egyptian Saad Elkhadem was Professor of German and Comparative Literature at the University of New Brunswick until his retirement in 1996. In Québec, they are published mostly by nonmainstream publishing houses such as Leméac, L'Hexagone, Editions des Femmes (Paris),

Editions du Noroît, Hurtubise HMH, vlb éditeur, Boréal, L'Arbre, Guérin littérature, Guernica,[64] Editions du Noroît, Editions XYZ, and La Presse. In Ontario they are published by Editions du Vermillon, Editions du Gref, and Cormorant Books. Sometimes, they are published transnationally: in France and Québec (Mouawad, Kattan), Tunisia and Québec (Bouraoui), and Egypt and Québec (Ghattas and Elkhadem). Occasionally, they have made their literary debut in Paris before being published in Québec. Such was the case for Alonzo and Kattan.

Some in the group of Canadian writers of Arabic origin are mediators who have played a significant role in the transmission and diffusion of their own products and those of other writers through the publishing houses and literary reviews they founded: Saad Elkhadem founded York Press in 1974 (where he published his entire Canadian production cast in bilingual, Arabic-English editions); the year after, he created *The International Fiction Review*. Rostom Publishing was founded in 1984 by Kamal Rostom in Ottawa; in it he published his own Arabic writings and the writings of fellow countrymen, sometimes in French or English translation; Editions Trois in Laval was cofounded by Anne-Marie Alonzo in 1985 with the Québécois Alain Laframboise, along with the bilingual literary review they created, *Trois*.[65] Noteworthy is also Hédi Bouraoui's promotion of literature of French expression in Ontario, a feat epitomized by his creation in 2002 of Centre Canada-Maghreb (York University) in Toronto, an endeavor for which he was officially recognized.

One of the major mediators of Arabic-Canadian literature between 1966 and 1986 is the late Egyptian Antoine Naaman, hailed in a Québécois newspaper as an "imposing figure": at once a Professor, Writer, Researcher, Critic, Analyst, Thinker, and Publisher.[66] He was head of the Department of French at the Université de Sherbrooke, which he joined in 1966. He founded and headed Editions Cosmos in 1969 and Editions Naaman in 1973. He created and edited two reviews: a biyearly, *Présence francophone*, in 1970, which he directed till 1974 and which he attached to the center he created in 1966 (CELEF: Centre D'Etudes des Littératures d'Expresssion Françaises) at the Université de Sherbrooke, and a quarterly, *Ecriture Française dans le Monde*, which he founded in 1969.[67] Being an ardent Francophile, he had one vast ambition at a time when France itself was not too keen to promote *francophonie* or francophone writers: that of making Sherbrooke the World Capital of literature of French expression published outside France. By 1983, Editions Naaman had produced 450 books from 40 different countries and Editions Cosmos had produced sixty. Over 10 percent of the Arabic-Québécois literature of French expression at the time was published there.

CANADIAN/QUÉBÉCOIS-ARABIC LITERATURE: EMERGENCE AND DEVELOPMENT

Looking at the selected sample bibliography of Arabic-Canadian literature, it appears that Arabic-Canadian literature emerged as an identifiable body of writing over thirty-five years ago. Naïm Kattan's essay, *Le Réel et le théâtral* (1970), (Prix France-Canada) is a first landmark. It was followed over the next few years by several works: Saad Elkhadem's Arabic novella, *Ajnihah min Rasâs* (Wings of Lead), 1971, portraying the tribulations of an Egyptian student in Vienna; Vasco Varoujean's 1972 collection of short stories, *Le Moulin du diable*, mostly depicting childhood scenes in his home village, and Kattan's first of six collections of short stories, *Dans le désert*, in 1974. The first two novels appeared in 1975. They are Kattan's *Adieu Babylone*, the first of a trilogy depicting the life of an adolescent in Baghdad, and Varoujean's *Les Raisins verts*, followed in 1977 by *Les Fruits arrachés* (Kattan), where the protagonist leaves Baghdad and discovers the West in Paris, and *Les Pâturages de la rancoeur* (Varoujean), depicting the life of a hardened and cruel landowner in a small Syrian village. These two writers, divergent as their writing may be, seem to have led the scene in the 1970s. In 1978, Elkhadem produced (in Cairo, in Arabic) *Min Rihlat Odysseus al-Misri* (From Travels of the Egyptian Odysseus), which was to appear a year later in an English translation in Fredericton, New Brunswick. The end of that decade saw the publication in Paris of *Geste* (1979), fragments of poetic prose, the first work by Anne-Marie Alonzo, whose 1985 *Bleus de mine* (Prix Emile Nelligan)—the second volume of an "Egyptian Trilogy"—is another landmark of this literature.[68]

The number of publications boomed in the 1980s and stabilized in the 1990s with Kattan, Alonzo, Bouraoui, Elkhadem, Ghalem, Ghattas, and Farhoud leading the way. Many new names materialized, scattered in various Canadian cities, creating the impression of an instant Arabic-Canadian literature. Antoine Karamé and Toufik El Hadj-Moussa were publishing in Sherbrooke; Bernard Antoun, Michel Khalo, and Nadine Ltaif in Montréal; Elie Tarakdjian in Athabasca; Marwan Hassan and Habeeb Salloum in Toronto. Books of poetry appeared: Nadia Ghalem's *L'Exil* (1980); Bernard Antoun's *Fragments arbitraires* (1989); Hédi Bouraoui's twelfth volume, *Echosmos* (1987); and a collection by Nadine Ltaif significantly titled *Entre les fleuves* (1991) [Between the Rivers]. Furthermore, Nadia Ghalem created a collection of short stories, *L'Oiseau de fer*, in 1981, followed by her novel *La Villa désir* (1988). Alonzo wrote *Droite et de profil* (1984) and *Ecoute, Sultane* (1987). Elkhadem published *The Ulysses Trilogy* (1988) and *The Plague* (1989) and Marwan Hassan produced *The Confusion of Stones: Two novellas* (1989). Mona Latif Ghattas published *Nicolas, le fils du Nil* (1985),[69] *Les Voix du jour et de la nuit* (1988), and *Le Double conte de l'exil* (1990). In 1989 Kamal

Rostom edited and published a first anthology featuring eleven writers, titled *Arab-Canadian Writing: Stories, Memoirs and Reminiscences*. This was followed in 1991 by Rostom's own collection of Arabic short stories, *Késsas Arabiya-Kanadéya: Arabic Takannad* (*Arabic-Canadian Short Stories: A Canadianized Arab*). In 1990 Alonzo produced *L'Immobile*, exploring themes of paralysis, movement, separation, absence, death, and harrowing physical pain.[70] Furthermore, Kattan published one of a number of collections of essays, *La Réconciliation* (1993).

The production continued well into the 1990s and the first decade of the new millennium. Bernard Antoun was to pursue his prolific verve in the area of spiritual (Christian) writing, with ten titles in the 1990s alone followed by an equal number at the turn of the millennium. More importantly, Wajdi Mouawad made an outstanding debut with the first part of his internationally acclaimed dramatic trilogy exploring the ravages of war: *Littoral* (1999) followed by *Incendies* (2003), and *Forêts* (2006). He published a handful of plays between each of those volumes, for a total of fifteen publications between 1999 and 2008. Farhoud discovered her talent in another genre in 1998 with a first, successful, novel, *Le Bonheur a la queue glissante*, portraying the life of an elderly female Lebanese immigrant. *Le Bonheur a la queue glissante* was preceded by half a dozen plays and succeeded by two novels: in 2001 (*Splendide solitude*), then in 2005 (*Le Fou D'Omar*). In 2006, Ghattas came up with *Ambre et lumière*, a collection of poems with accompanying CD, published simultaneously in Cairo and Montréal. Kattan and Bouaroui continued their flurry of publications, with *Bangkok Blues* (1994), Bouraoui's second novel, *Sept portes pour une brûlance* (2005), *Cap Nord* (2008), his latest novel, not to forget his acclaimed *Transpoétique: Eloge du nomadisme* (2005), his latest essay to date. *Une table de verts pâturages*, published in 2003, was Anne-Marie Alonzo's latest title before her untimely death in 2005, at the age of fifty-four.

OF LANGUAGE AND RECEPTION

Language Choice and National Affiliation

> Arabic, my native language, and English, my school language, were inextricably mixed: I have never known which was my first language, and have felt fully at home with neither, although I dream in both. Every time I speak an English sentence, I find myself echoing it in Arabic, and vice versa.[71]

The preceding passage by Edward Said describing the oppositional critic's own upbringing in a diglossic context in Cairo in the forties, can be considered as highly relevant and representative when dealing with the subject at hand, namely the choice of language as a means of literary expression by exilic writers of Arabic origin in particular and, by extension, writers of various national origins in Canada. In fact, the literary explosion in Québec in the fifties and sixties during the time of national revival and cultural liberation was paralleled in the eighties by a surge of a myriad of other literatures, sometimes written in languages other than those of the two founding nations. But how does one express exile in a language that is not one's own? What language should one choose: English, French, or a third language? A question that posed a number of existential and theoretical problems to writers and critics alike. Linguistic exile, just as physical exile, is a challenge to the immigrant writer, and more so when he/she chooses to write in a realist vein. This challenge was eloquently expressed by the Italian-Québécois writer, Antonio D'Alfonso, in the following terms: "Quand j'écris, j'ai en tête la mémoire d'une langue et j'exprime cette mémoire dans une autre langue. Un mariage des mémoires" [When I write, I think in one language and yet I express that memory in another language. A marriage of memories].[72]

How does the body of Arabic exilic literature in Canada look like? About 10–15 percent of Arabic-Canadian literature is produced in Arabic, while over 65 percent is written in French, the remainder being written in English.[73] How is that portion produced in Arabic to be classified? What bearing does the use of a third language have on the issue of the identity of the Arabic-Canadian writer, and by extension the ethnic writer? Here is a question that found resonance in other minor literatures. In fact, theoretical implications pertaining to "who is a Canadian writer" were raised as early as the 1984 Ottawa Conference on Language, Culture, and Literary Identity, becoming crucial to the debate.[74] Where do those writers who write in a nonofficial language belong? "Anyone who lives and/or writes and/or publishes in Canada must be accepted as a Canadian,"[75] will conclude a participant. However, remained unsolved was the central concern of the Ottawa conference, namely whether it would be possible for the ethnic writer and his culture to remain at once outside the mainstream and be recognized as an integral part of Canadian society. Four years later, during a 1988 Edmonton Conference on the literary life of cultural groups, questions were raised more specifically as to ways in which to classify literary texts produced in Canada in third languages. In his paper on Polish-Canadian writing, Edward Mozejko pointed out that, within Canadian cultural reality, literatures produced in third languages will function as subsystems and will belong to the primary systems of the languages from which they are derived.[76] Bisztray advocated a "multilingual Canadian literature"[77] and suggested a pentagonal model which ties third language literature to "world literature, the literature of the country of origin, the national literature of the new country, the other immigrant literatures of the new country, and literature of the same language group in other countries."[78] Ten years after the Ottawa conference, those considerations were echoed in a collection of essays, *Ethnicity and Culture in Canada: The Research Landscape* (1994) where a scholar asserts that "the idea that Canadian literature can only be written in English or French . . . has to give way to a broader, more pluralistic view of literature." [79] Exactly so, but the reality is somewhat more ambivalent, as a scholar has bitterly remarked when examining dictionaries of Canadian writers.[80] It is likewise worth noting that the bio-bibliography of immigrant novelists published as recently as 1993 by the *Institut Québécois de Recherche sur la Culture* (IQRC) lists, as one of the requirements for canonical inclusion, to have published in one of the two official languages of Canada.[81]

Canadian/Québécois-Arabic literature, in the same way as other contemporary exilic literatures, tends to fuse and mix literary genres; it is marked with the same reflexivity characteristic of postmodern literatures. The language used is often dislocated and disjointed, essentially a language that will mirror internal distance, the melancholy of the initial departure, and a sense of estrangement. In his essay *La Mémoire et la promesse* (1978), the Iraqi-Québécois writer, Naïm Kattan, when dealing with the evolution, which the concept underwent under Islam and Judaism in their relationship to the desert, defines exile precisely in terms of "the spoken word":

> *L'exil n'est plus une relation avec l'espace mais une expression de la division de l'être, du conflit entre réel et conscience, acte et théâtralité. L'exil est intériorisé. Il devient une dimension de l'être. Et d'abord l'exil de la parole.*
>
> [Exile is no longer a relationship to space but an expression of the division of the Self, of the conflict between reality and consciousness. Exile is internalized. It becomes a dimension of being. And first and foremost exile of the spoken word.][82]

Hence the relevance of the choice of language for the writer exiled not only from his origin but also from his means of expression, the spoken word, or, more literally, the written word. Broadly speaking, the problem of the choice of language for the exilic writer may well reflect the Deleuze-Guattari notion with regard to minority writers (albeit in the context of the Jews of Prague between the wars), namely the impossibility of writing in the major ambient language and the impossibility of not writing in it, an existential dilemma central to the connection between oppressed national consciousness and literary expression.[83] In the context of postcolonial literatures, a likely impossibility would be especially pronounced in former African colonies at the outset of the independence in the early sixties, for the main issue manifested itself quite sharply to militant writers and intellectuals who aimed at rebuilding anti-European nations using "that marvelous tool found in the ruins of the colonial regime,"[84] to quote Senghor. With exilic writers in Québec, however, the situation is different: French is not necessarily seen as the language of the oppressor. Quite the contrary; some of the Arabic-Québécois writers grew up in their country more versed in French as a language of thought and creative expression than in Arabic (as was the case with Alonzo, Antoun, Bouraoui, Ghalem, Dahan, Farhoud, Latif Ghattas, Ltaif, and Varoujean) as a result of the strong presence of French culture among the upper classes (in the Middle East) and its pervasive influence in the Maghreb. The choice for those authors was a natural one: "j'ai choisi le français parce que pour moi l'Occident libérateur était francophone" will say Naïm Kattan [I chose French because for me the liberating West was francophone][85] who nevertheless suffered fifteen years of silence (after he left his native Iraq) before he produced books in French. Both Kattan and Alonzo allegedly were never at ease "at home," being already *exiles* in their own country: Kattan as a young Jew growing up in Iraq and torn between the Jewish culture he alienated himself from by choosing to write in Arabic (a language he spoke with an accent), and Alonzo as a young Catholic of francophone upbringing: "me dire que j'étais refusé par tout le monde ou me dire que c'était ma chance d'appartenir à personne" [to tell myself that I was rejected by everyone or to tell myself that I was lucky not to belong to anyone] will say Kattan,[86] and Alonzo echoes him:

En Egypte je ne me suis jamais sentie égyptienne: on me faisait sentir que je ne l'étais pas. . . . Ici je n'étais pas non plus considérée comme une Québécoise ni une Canadienne

[In Egypt I never felt Egyptian: I was made to feel I was not. . . . Here too I was not considered Québécois or Canadian].[87]

au fond en vérité de pays aucun

[deep down in truth from no country].[88]

Writers who immigrated to English Canada at a fairly young age or those who are Canadian born (Marwan Hassan, Rubba Nadda) chose English as a means of literary expression. Those who left their native country at an older age, such as Emily Nasrallah or Kamal Rostom (a published writer in his native Egypt) continued to write in Arabic, sometimes becoming writers/translators.[89] Such is also the case with Saad Elkhadem who settled in Canada at the age of thirty-five. In his own words, Arabic afforded him "a direct line without pause or hesitation between [his] ideas and the images [he] uses."[90] For the Tunisian Hédi Bouraoui, the choice of French as a means of expression, even from the vantage point of his life in Toronto, was a natural one.[91]

As a rule, if an immigrant writer opts for the major ambient language as a means of assimilation into the mainstream, he will infuse it with his alienation, for his is the language of exile, a language that rewrites syntax or has the impertinence of doing so. Deleuze and Guattari will call it *reterritorialization*.[92] Other Canadian researchers have named it "the language of difference" or "ethnic writing." With the best of intentions, critics have snuggly pigeonholed minority literary voices under many such rubrics, with the natural consequence of exacerbating their marginality, albeit in so doing canonizing this marginality within the new, larger, postmodern tradition of a "plurality of centres."[93] But what is the main problem involved here? In the words of Edward Said:

> There is above all the scandal of a different language, then a different race and identity, a different history and tradition: what this results in is either the suppression of difference into complete invisibility and silence, or its transformation into acceptable, but diametrically opposed, identity.[94]

Though the above words by the late critic were written in a different context (that of an incisive analysis of Beethoven's *Fidelio*, where Florestan ends up in jail for speaking an unacceptable truth), by extrapolation they well apply to the subject at hand: the dilemma for the "ethnic" writer in Québec is one that makes him or her waver between silence and sound. The need to speak, to utter, *to express*, to make pronouncements, to reveal, to disclose, "to function as a kind of public memory," to borrow another phrase of Edward Said's, is indeed a powerful, compelling need for the artistically inclined exile who, to make matters worse, is often perfectly multilingual.[95] Unfortunately, the "language of difference" of the exilic author, I repeat, is disturbing. Moreover, some will fall into silence just because they are unable to decide upon the language of their means of expression.[96] They will thus opt not to be published at all; instead they will find an outlet for their creativity in their interpersonal relations, a fact often fraught with disappointment and *gaffes*, social blunders, for our neatly compartmentalized world does not allow for the expression of the individual *within*.

Issues and Instances of Literary Reception in Québec

The question of national literary affiliation, or *appartenance*, is one that still haunts academic discourse today; witness the debate over the literary belonging of Anglophone literature produced in Québec. I observed signs of this ongoing debate in May 2008 during the annual meeting of the Canadian Comparative Literature Association held in Vancouver, British Columbia. In a talk partially subtitled "Anglo-Québec Literature and the Figures of National Literary Identity," the speaker, a doctoral candidate at the university of Montréal,[97] expatiated on the idea that as recently as 1997, during a colloquium held at the university of Montréal on "Le Québec anglais: littérature et culture,"[98] a Québécois critic of renown (Gilles Marcotte) insisted that an Anglo-Québec literature is an oxymoron, since, by definition, true Québécois literature can only be produced in French, and that by the same token, one cannot even speak of a Franco-Québécois literature.[99] How does this strict categorization of national literary identification vis-à-vis Anglophone-Canadians living in Québec (roughly 10 percent of the population of the province) affect other Québec populations? Subsequently, that same Marcotte wrote in 1999 that it was after all easier to accept the plurality of present-day Montréal than it is to accept a still contentious French/English duality attached to the city. So is an Anglophone Quebecer English-Canadian or is he simply a Canadian Anglophone living in (mostly) francophone Québec? In a *Dictionnaire Des Ecrivains Québécois Contemporains*, the criteria of inclusion are said to be territorial, not ethnic. Hence, Acadian writers as well as anglophone writers born in Québec but having lived long enough in English Canada, are excluded. Included, however, are writers born elsewhere but having lived long enough in Québec to identify with it.[100] Alonzo, Ghalem, Kattan, Naaman, and Varoujean are thus included in this dictionary.[101]

With respect to the subject matter at hand, it seems that, ironically, *French Canadian*, if it ever did, *does not* always mean *Québécois*, witness the title of the 1994 *Anthologie Critique de la littérature Canadienne française et Québécoise* (edited by the same Gilles Marcotte) which established the distinction forthrightly. By the same *regional* logic behind the impetus guiding this distinction, Naïm Kattan was excluded as a novelist from a *Dictionnaire pratique des auteurs Québécois* (1976). One could remark that though he had lived, worked, and published in Québec for a long time, when it came to public reckoning by canon-makers, he was a North American, not a Québécois. Luckily, however, Kattan was included as Québécois thirteen years later in the above-mentioned *Dictionnaire des auteurs de langue française en Amérique du Nord* (1989)[102] by the very same researchers who had compiled the earlier dictionary, an indication of a definite progress in the direction of the *ouverture à l'autre* characteristic of the late eighties. The reception of Kattan by the Québec literary institution was well documented in 1989 by Nasrin Rahimieh (University of Alberta) who asserted that, though he produced mostly in French, Kattan fared relatively better in English Canada where he was read in translation.[103] However, the situation significantly improved in the nineties and the early years of the new millennium, witness the crowning of Kattan's career in 2004 by the most prestigious *Prix Athanase David*, a prize (accompanied by a cash value of $30,000) belonging to the elitist *Prix du Québec* series, composed of eleven prizes and officially described in the following terms:

Les Prix du Québec sont la plus haute distinction décernée chaque année par le gouvernement du Québec en reconnaissance d'une carrière remarquable dans le domaine artistique et culturel.

[The Québec prizes are the highest mark of distinction awarded every year by the Québec Government in recognition of a remarkable career in the artistic and cultural domain.] [104]

Since the foundation of this prize in 1968, Kattan can be proudly said to have been the very first migrant Québécois writer to receive a prize that has been awarded to such Québécois icons as Jacques Ferron (1977), Jacques Godbout (1985), Marie-Claire Blais (1982), Michel Tremblay (1988), Nicole Brossard (1991), and recently, Pierre Nepveu (2005) and Paul Chamberland (2007).[105]

Though she had been living in Québec since 1966, Nadia Ghalem was listed in French sources such as the *Annuaire de l'Afrique du Nord* (1981) that included a short critical bibliography of her work, as well as in the *Dictionnaire des auteurs maghrébiens de langue française* (1984). The above-mentioned Québécois bio-bibliography of immigrant writers (1993) listed her works and described her moreover as a "journaliste pigiste . . . , animatrice, recherchiste et auteure de textes documentaires et dramatiques à Radio-Canada et à Radio-Québec" [journalist . . . , animator, researcher and author of dramatic and documentary texts in Radio-Canada and Radio-Québec].[106] Of note is a very hostile review in *Le Devoir* (Montréal, 1991) about her collection of short stories *La Nuit bleue* (1991), where the critic, a Frenchman, resorted to rude language and accusations.[107] All things considered, however, Ghalem is currently well-integrated in the niche of writers *d'ailleurs* [from elsewhere] in Québec. She has been regularly invited, since the foundation in Montréal in 2000 of the annual Festival du monde Arabe [Arab world festival], to give public readings and to participate in roundtable discussions.

Elkhadem was probably (and still is, posthumously) the most isolated of the six writers studied in this monograph. As we will see in the next chapter, the great majority of reviews of his works are written by fellow Arabic scholars, and published in the author's *International Fiction Review*. Perhaps the author's reportedly intensely private demeanor shunned any attempts toward inclusiveness?[108]

Antoine Naaman's contributions were fully recognized by the three academics from Montréal and Ottawa, who compiled a *Dictionnaire des auteurs de langue française en Amérique du Nord* (1989) and who hailed him as having created an international center for the diffusion of francophone literature in Sherbrooke: "Grâce au dynamisme d'Antoine Naaman, Sherbrooke est devenu un centre international de diffusion des littératures francophones, surtout des pays en dehors de l'Europe" [Thanks to

Antoine Naaman's dynamism, Sherbrooke has become an international center for the diffusion of francophone literatures, especially countries outside Europe].[109] This recognition is relevant in light of the fact that only two other Arabic-Québécois writers were included in this dictionary, namely Anne-Marie Alonzo and Naïm Kattan.

It seems that, in terms of national literary belonging, Anne-Marie Alonzo is one of the most accepted/adopted Arabic-Canadian writers in the circle of the Québécois academic critics and writers with whom she collaborated and to whom she provided invaluable publication outlets through both the review and the publishing house she founded.[110] After making her debut as a poet in Paris, where her first two books were published (*Geste*, 1979, *Veille*, 1982: Editions des Femmes), she came to attract attention relatively fast in Québec where she lived from 1962 until her death in 2005, and where most of her voluminous production was published. For intance, in 1994, *Voix et Images*, the prestigious review published by the Université du Québec à Montréal (UQAM), totally devoted to Québécois literature, came up with an entire issue (150 pages) on Anne-Marie Alonzo. It contained eight articles by French-Canadian women scholars, an interview, and a complete bibliography of her works. Jacques Pelletier, the director of the journal, qualified her, in the introduction to the issue, as "une écrivaine majeure du Québec contemporain" [a main writer of contemporary Québec]. However, he had to add a word of caution: "Le dossier actuel . . . provoquera peut-être de la résistance chez certains quant à l'appartenance 'québécoise' de cette écrivaine migrante" [The present issue may provoke a certain resistance in some people concerned with the real Québécois belonging of this migrant writer].[111] The utterance raised some eyebrows among sympathetic, feminist Québécois critics who subsequently tried to correct the situation.[112] However, it seems that many still saw Alonzo as ethnic rather than one of them. For instance, in 1995 the feminist journal *Arcade* accorded her a lengthy *entretien* and published a bibliography of her work. The title of the issue being "Orientales . . . Orient," the interviewer (Vasseur) constantly reiterated her questions in the direction of an alleged Oriental/Egyptian substance in Alonzo's work, though the writer had mentioned a number of times that she left Egypt at the early age of twelve and spoke Arabic but a little.[113] Nevertheless, as early as the 1990s there have been some indications of an interest in Alonzo's work in Anglophone Canada and the United States. For instance, in the 1994 conference at Concordia University (Montréal) on the writing of women immigrants in France and in the United States, Walter Jakobson (Long Island, Brooklyn) talked about "Breathing Words: Exile In (other); Towards a Poetics of Anne-Marie Alonzo."[114] Moreover, William Donoghue, the translator of *Bleus de mine* (*Lead Blues*) was to remark in the preface to the English translation that "her writing burns up the lines of communication as it comes through, leaving the reader holding blackened wires and melted instruments."[115]

Upon examining the above bio-bibliographical table of writers, one cannot fail to notice a number of French/Québécois-Canadian literary prizes awarded: from Hédi Bouraoui's *Prix International de poésie* in 1987 for his collection of Poems *Echosmos*, to Anne-Marie Alonzo's Order of Canada in 1997, to Naïm Kattan's *Prix Hervé Deluen* in 2007; from Nadia Ghalem's novel, *Villa Désir*, finalist for the 1987 *Grand Prix Littéraire Guérin*, to Nadine Ltaif's *Entre les fleuves*, finalist for *Prix Emile Nelligan* in 1991, to Yolande Geadah's *Prix Condorcet* in 2007 for the promotion of secularity in Québec; and from Farhoud's *Prix France-Québec* in 1999 for her first novel *Le Bonheur a la queue glissane*, to Mouawad's *Prix de la francophonie* in 2004 and *Prix Molière* in 2005. Those are all positive instances of reception and harbingers of recognition in the Canadian literary landscape.

CHARACTERISTICS OF CANADIAN-ARABIC LITERATURE/EXILIC LITERATURES

In "Reflections on Exile," Edward Said sums up what I see as the quintessence of *that which generates* thematic clusters of binary oppositions in exilic works: "For an exile, habits of life, expression, or activity in the new environment inevitably occur against the memory of these things in another environment. Thus both the old and the new environments are vivid, actual, occuring together contrapuntally."[116] In fact, this contrapuntal consciousness described by the late Columbia professor is manifested by the recurrence, in some Arabic-Canadian texts, of such thematic dialectical pairs as enculturation/acculturation, discrimination/equality, unemployment/work, freedom/constraint, poverty/prosperity, alienation/love between parents and children, and memories of wars and times of peace. In the conclusion to a collection of essays entitled *Exil et Littérature*, Sgard has aptly described this same feature, one common to exilic literatures in general, as a double-edged sword, harbinger of both torment and creative impulse:

> *L'expérience de l'exil . . . entretient un va-et-vient entre l'ici et l'ailleurs, entre le passé et le futur, entre la nostalgie et l'espérance, entre l'exclusion et l'inclusion. . . . De là vient son malheur, mais aussi sa richesse; de là aussi son rôle dans la création littéraire.*

> [The experience of exile . . . entertains an interplay between the here and there, past and future, between nostalgia and hope, between exclusion and inclusion. . . . This is the source of its misfortune, but also of its richness; this too is the source of its role in literary creation.][117]

As will be shown in the next chapter, it is Saad Elkhadem's highly experimental *Trilogy of the Flying Egyptian* (1990–1992) which can be said to best illustrate the thematic of immigration and exile, resentment and love of one's native land, dislocation, reverse migration, disorientation, and assimilation in what the protagonist of the first volume, *The Canadian Adventures of the Flying Egyptian* (1990), ambivalently calls "the cold melting pot"[118] and "the land of courtesy and freedom."[119] Through this trilogy, Elkhadem succeeded in giving a voice to Egyptian immigrants, many of whom did not speak French and who, after the debacle of the 1967 Six Day's War between Israel and Egypt, fled en masse to Québec where they anxiously witnessed the separatist unrest culminating in the 1970 October Crisis.[120] In the first volume of the trilogy, a metafictional work that provides invaluable insights into literary creation, the writer has died in mysterious circumstances before finishing his work. The second volume, *Chronicle of the Flying Egyptian in Canada* (1991), takes the shape of an annotated biography based on recorded interviews in Canada with the protagonist's friends and acquaintances, while the third volume, *Crash Landing of the Flying Egyptian* (1992) witnesses the resurrection of the author-narrator-protagonist in nonhuman form, attempting to summarize the accumulated events of his lifetime in less than a page. The result is a hybrid novella, biographical and fictional, open-ended and unfinished, using a tone *in strife*, oppositional, disturbing, antagonistic, excessive. A tendency found in a great number of works generated by exilic writers. In the words of Edward Said: "Willfulness, exaggeration, overstatement: These are characteristic styles of being an exile, methods for compelling the world to accept your vision. . . . Composure and serenity are the last things associated with the works of exile."[121]

Whether collective, individual, spatial, sensorial or cultural, memory will play a crucial role, for the necessity to restore the past is a prevalent feature in exilic literatures, notably the one of concern to us here. In a moving passage, Edward Said characterizes "the achievements of exile" as being "permanently undermined by the loss of something left behind forever."[122] Does the exilic writer's effort consist in salvaging this loss? In fact, it is significant that "the massive referent" ["Le référent massif"], to quote Berrouët-Oriol and Fournier,[123] that marks Canadian-Arabic literature, as it does other exilic literatures, is that of the native country, the left, abandoned country, whether it is real, as when it evokes a whole youth spent there (as in the case of Saad Elkhadem, Kamal Rostom, or Naïm Kattan who went to Québec as adults), or whether it has become vague, unreal, as in the case of the Italian-Canadian Marco Micone and Anne Marie Alonzo, who all left very young. Alonzo will assert in her interviews that the Egypt she recalls in her books is "mythical"[124] and "sensual."[125] Such is also the case with Mona Latif Ghattas whose Set El Kol in *Les Voix du jour et de la nuit* (1988) is a transcendental woman endowed with multiple personalities, all representing a figure of an eternal Egypt speaking from across the ages. Writes a critic in the preface to the 1988 novel: "Il s'agit d'une Egypte de rêve, une Egypte qui transcende l'espace géographique et le temps, une Egypte que chacun de nous . . . porte en soi" [This is an idyllic Egypt, an Egypt that transcends place and time, an Egypt that each one of us has within him].[126] In a telling passage of *Le Livre des ruptures* (1988), Alonzo evokes the continuous feelings of departure and loss she associates with her native country:

> *Je suis partie*
> *Je pars et partirai encore*
> *Alexandrie n'a plus de visage*
> *Mais tant de rides qu'elle s'écroule lente délaissée.*
>
> [I left
> I am leaving and I will leave again
> Alexandria no longer has a face
> But so many wrinkles that it crumbles down, slowly abandoned.][127]

Likewise, it is in the very category of works marked by *the presence of absence* that would belong such books as Alonzo's *Ecoute, Sultane* (1987), *Mère solitude* (1983) [Mother Solitude] by the celebrated Haitian-Canadian writer Emile Ollivier, *The Other Shore* (1987) by the Italian-Québécois Antonio D'Alfonso; *Gens du silence* (1982) by the Italian-Canadian Marco Micone, without forgetting Mona Latif Ghattas's *Le Double Conte de l'exil* (1990), where the author evokes the internal exile of many a drifting character. Moreover, The French-Jewish-Polish Québécois writer, Régine Robin, in her now classic novel *La Québécoite* (1983) evokes a city of juxtaposed exiles where she looks in vain for a place to fit in.[128] *La Mémoire de l'eau* (1992) is the significant title of a novel by the eminent Chinese-Canadian writer Ying Chen. So many moments in the vast *Roman Mémoriel* (Memorial Novel), the title of a 1989 work by Régine Robin, who asserts that "tension between collective memory and cultural memory" underlines her writings since 1975.[129]

The vision of the country of origin from the vantage point of exile is not a uniform one among Québécois-Canadian writers of Arabic origins. Chafia, the protagonist of Ghalem's *Les Jardins de cristal* (1981), evokes Algeria and the trauma of war through the distorted prism of mental illness. For the author-protagonist-narrator of Elkhadem's works, childhood experiences "left all the sails of [his] life in tatters." Life in the country of origin is evoked as "dark and suffocating," "a homeland dominated by terror and corruption."[130] For Varoujean, happy recollections of his childhood in Késsab, an Armenian village in Syria, are evoked in great detail.[131]

Furthermore, in her collection of poems entitled *Entre les fleuves* (1991), Nadine Ltaif juxtaposes the Nile and the Saint Laurent rivers in a symbolic union and division. Thus, various images as well as snatches of historical moments belonging to the two countries are superposed. The author tries to find a space between the two rivers where the weight of linguistic systems is lighter and where she can feel at ease when searching for words. Likewise, the protagonist of Andrée Dahan's *Le Printemps peut attendre* (1985), who suffers from a massive loss of self-esteem as an unpopular school teacher in Québec—in her native Egypt she was a very successful one—juxtaposes contrasting scenes of school life in the two countries. Moreover, smells of spices, fruits, and honey (portrayed in the writings of Andrée Dahan, Naïm Kattan, and Hédi Bouraoui) intermingle with calls to prayers and images of desert sands superposed on Québec snow. In Ghattas's *Le Double conte de l'exil* (1990), Manitakawa, an American-Indian, and Fève, an illegal immigrant from Anatolia, meet in Montréal; despite their language barriers, they successfully exchange their mutual distant pasts and their respective alienations, in an attempt to heal their wounds through their recollections.

The notions of extraterritoriality, in-betweenness, and estrangement, notions that mark exilic literatures in general, are also found in Arabic-Canadian literature whose authors, in many cases, already belonged to ethnic minorities in their countries of origin (such as with Copts, Jews, Christians, Greeks, Armenians, Syrians, Lebanese, etc.) and who had multiple components in the make-up of their cultural background. In *Droite et de profile* (1984), Alonzo will express the feeling of hybridity and alienation she has always experienced in her native Alexandria:

> *toujours étrangère marquée là-bas comme ici*
> *de quel nom ou d'arbre.*
> *perdue cette généalogie suis française vénitienne espagnole*
> *palestienne dit ma tante syrienne pour ma mère maltaise*
> *pour la sienne si peu du nil.*
>
> [Always a foreigner, marked over there just as over here
> Of which name or which tree
> Lost this genealogy I am French Venitian Spanish
> Palestinian says my Syrian aunt for my Maltese
> Mother for her mother not too much from the Nile.][132]

For Naïm Kattan, as we will see in chapter 3, his two countries, Iraq and Canada, do not overlap. His presence in the world is one he claims to define at every step, away from "the comfort of certitudes." Speaking of his life as an intellectual who left his native Iraq to settle in Montréal several decades ago, Kattan advances the notion of "alternation in continuity," a notion akin to creation, instead of the more prevalent construct of hybridity.[133]

As for many of their counterparts across exilic and postmodern literatures, Arabic-Canadian writers seem to have challenged the very notion of *genre*. Elkhadem's works, for instance, are neither short stories, nor novellas, novels, diaries, or biographies per se, but reconstructions and deconstructions of elements of each. This is especially true of Bouraoui and also of Alonzo who, whenever possible, *purposefully* puts the word *fiction* or *contes* in the inside cover of books mostly consisting of snatches of broken and fragmented poetic prose. However, in the words of a critic commenting on Alonzo's poetry, "this seamless collage [is] unified by a narrative tension never far from the surface . . . , which functions as a ceaseless rediscovery of the themes of Self, Exile and Other."[134] Would this rediscovery, though, preclude a classification by genre? Aware that her categorization does not fit the usual acception, Anne-Marie Alonzo insists when probed:

> *Mais je suis consciente du fait que mes livres n'entrent pas dans la définition des contes et des fictions. Je préférerais ne pas avoir à les définir. Mes écrits sont à l'image de ce que je suis, à l'image de ma vie. Hybrides.*
>
> [But I am aware of the fact that my books do not fit the usual definition of narratives or tales. I would rather not have to define them. My writing is in the image of what I am, the image of my life. Hybrid.][135]

The mark of the political and the collective value of utterances Deleuze and Guattari qualified as two of three main characteristics of minor literatures can be illustrated by the following three examples:[136] In *Nicolas, le fils du Nil* (1985) Mona Latif-Ghattas deals with the question of hybrid identities. Written in exile but published in Egypt, the novel is sung from atop a minaret. The narrator tells the story of her family, her father Nicolas and her mother Jo, both "children of the Nile." Through those characters, she recalls the last Egyptian king Farouk and the first president, Nasser, with the ethnic exclusions that happened in the sixties under the latter's rule. Thus Nicolas, the protagonist whose personal and professional life and identity are deeply rooted in the soil of Egypt and whose mother belongs to an old Egyptian family, is suddenly excluded and branded a foreigner because of the Syrian nationality of his own father. The exiles that result from this ostracism mark once more the family's history of exile and the author-narrator's own immigration. Moreover, Saad Elkhadem's novels, especially *The Plague* (1989), pose the question of the political. It is a satirical novel banned in Egypt and written in Arabic, where nameless characters, which are identified by a number assigned to each, happen to meet in a visa office in Cairo as they attempt to escape from the oppression and brutality of Nasser's regime. Their conversations are restrained and marked by intense fear and suspicion of each other and of the government. The third instance illustrating the tapping of the individual into the political, considered by Deleuze and Guattari as one of the hallmarks of minor literatures, pertains to Andrée Dahan's 2005 collection of poems, *Chants de la terre morte* [Songs of the Dead Land], a book dedicated to the "dispossessed, powerless" Palestinian people, "whose despair still weaves the fabric of our days."[137] This book was, significantly, published by the Egyptian-Canadian writer Anne-Marie Alonzo in the latter's publishing house, *Editions Trois*. However, a publisher in Québec to whom Dahan had first submitted it initially refused the manuscript. The reason given by the publisher for the rejection was "a tone of propaganda and moralization" he allegedly sensed in the volume. This language prompted the author to write the publisher a rebuttal in which she pointed out (quoting a celebrated Palestinian poet) "the historical reality" that failed to achieve freedom to an entire people:

> *Ainsi l'évocation d'un pays perdu et saccagé, la révolte contre la guerre, le désir de paix, les blessures du passé sont propagande et morale? . . . Certes, ma poésie est tributaire de ma double culture moderne, la française et la québécoise, mais par les thèmes de l'engagement au pays perdu . . . j'appartiens à cette poésie arabe contemporaine qui, selon le grand poète palestinien, Mahmoud Darwish, interroge "la réalité historique dans laquelle la liberté individuelle et la libération ne se sont pas accomplies."*

> [So the evocation of a lost and ravaged country, the rebellion against war, the desire for peace, and the wounds of the past constitute for you propaganda and moralization? . . . My poetry is definitely indebted to my double modern culture, French and Québécois, but with regard to the themes of commitment to the lost country, . . . and that of exile, I belong to this contemporary Arabic poetry which, according to the great Palestinian poet Mahmoud Darwish, questions "the historical reality in which individual freedom and liberation failed to take place."][138]

Moreover, to strengthen her argument, Dahan remarks that the first poem of the collection entitled "Amers paradis" [Bitter Paradises] was recipient of a literary prize, *Brèves littéraires*. The point at issue here is the synergy at work between the poet and a whole people; the fact that Dahan, all the while recognizing her belonging to Québec/France, still conceives of her writing as a justified reflection of the tragedy of an entire nation, Palestine, with which she has distant blood ties, and in the plights of which she still partakes, albeit from the vantage point of her own artistic endeavors and her exile.

Canadian/Québécois writers of Arabic origins have in common some modalities of an "immigrant experience," assuredly. However, as with other Canadian writers, they are concerned with a great array of issues, personal, interpersonal, social, political, aesthetic, philosophical, and artistic, as will become apparent in the subsequent chapters. It is important to underscore this versatility so as not to draw a priori appraisals and conclusions. In fact, one striking feature of Arabic-Canadian writing is the diversity of the genres it harbors and the styles it embodies, from the realist strain of Kattan and Varoujean to the postmodern experimentations of Alonzo, Ghattas, Ltaif, and Ghalem. From Bouraoui's coining a great number of neologisms, a habit that becomes his hallmark, to Mouawad's uniqueness as a brilliant producer, stage-director, filmmaker, playwright, and novelist. Canadian/Québécois writing has produced great works in significant numbers. When trying to capture its quintessence, the following words by the late Anne-Marie Alonzo come to mind: "Assise noble pharaone. Scribe accroupie faisant sa marque au stylet" [sitting down noble Pharaoh. Crouched scribe making his mark with the stylus].[139]

All things considered, would it be desirable to give Arabic-Québécois/Canadian writing a permanently fixed status, one that would place it outside Canadian literature, and to assimilate it to the latter, thus naturalizing it by force? As Régine Robin has aptly remarked about ethnic literatures in Québec, once the ground is cleared, once the job of *déchiffrage* [decipherment] and ground-clearance has been achieved, it is important to pull those literatures out of ethnicity, "les sortir de l'ethnicité," studying their products for their own sake, from formal and esthetic points of view.[140]

NOTES

1. A significantly smaller version of this article was published under the title "Voices of Exile: The Trilingual Odyssey of Canadian Writers of Arabic Origins," *The Canadian Review of Comparative Literature* 28.1 (March 2001): 48–69. The facts and figures in this chapter have been updated. Also see F. Elizabeth Dahab, "Arabic-Canadian Literature: Overview and Preliminary Bibliography," *Canadian Ethnic Studies* 2 (1999): 101–111.

2. François Paré, *Les Littératures de l'exiguïté* (Hearst, Ontario: Nordir, 1992): 7. The book was reissued in a new edition in 2001 by the same publisher.

3. "Réorienter l'historiographie des littératures, ouvrir ses structures d'accueil, tenir compte ainsi des marginalités," François Paré, *Les Littératures de l'exiguïté*, 10.

4. François Paré, *Les Littératures de l'exiguïté*, 9.

5. Two solitudes is an expression referring to the descendants of the two founding nations of Canada. It originates from the celebrated 1945 novel by Hugh MacLennan; "three solitudes" is an expression referring to the group of Italian writers of the eighties. It was coined by the Italian-Canadian Filippo Salvatore in his essay, "The Italian Writers of Quebec: Language, Culture, and Politics," trans. David Homel, in *Contrasts: Comparative Essays on Italian-Canadian Writing*, ed. Joseph Pivato (Montréal: Guernica, 1991): 191–206, 199. In 1991, Linda Hutcheon

and Marion Richmond edited a book entitled *Other Solitudes: Canadian Multicultural Fictions* (Toronto: Oxford University Press, 1990).

6. José Lambert, "Plaidoyer pour un programme des études comparatistes. Littérature comparée et théorie du polysystème," *Actes du XVIème Congrès de la Société Française de Littérature Générale et Comparée, Montpellier: 1980* Montpellier: Université Paul-Valéry, 1984): 59–67, 64.

7. José Lambert, "Les relations littéraires internationales comme problème de réception," *Oeuvres et critiques* 11.2 (1986): 173–189, 176.

8. To be accepted by society, to manifest an internal structure, to fulfill a social function unique to itself, to be differentiated from other systems; see, "Looking Back—Looking Ahead," Editorial, *Poetics* 21 (1992): 1–4. Also see Siegfried Schmidt, *Foundations for the Empirical Study of Literature: The Components of a Basic Theory*, R. de Beaugrande, trans. (Hamburg: Buske, 1982). In the 1988 conference on "literatures of Lesser Diffusion" in Edmonton, Canada, it was shown repeatedly that literatures of national minorities lend themselves to systemic standpoints, which combine literary and sociological factors.

9. Gilles Deleuze and Félix Guattari, *Kafka: Pour une littérature mineure* (Paris: Minuit, 1975): 29–51.

10. See Leela Gandhi, *Postcolonial Theory: A Critical Introduction* (New York: Columbia University Press, 1998): 132.

11. The writings of Edward Said, which have proven relevant in the present context are: *The World, the Text and the Critic* (1983), *Representations of the Intellectual: The 1993 Reith Lectures* (1996), and *Reflections on Exile and Other Essays* (2000).

12. Quoted by Xavier Déniau, *La Francophonie* (Paris: Presses Universitaires de France, 1983): 25.

13. Ontario has a large number of francophone writers, witness the 2004 impressive anthology featuring the work of fifty-five writers, edited by Jacques Flamand and Hédi Bouraoui (*Ecriture Franco-Ontarienne 2003*. Ottawa: Éditions du Vermillon, 2003). Represented in this anthology (from the Arabic Canadian writers) are Hédi Bouraoui himself and Jean Fahmy. In a way, those francophone writers writing in French in a mainly Anglophone province would, to a certain extent, also fit the category of a minor literature when studied as a set.

14. Such terms as *migration, nomadism, borders, expatriation, diaspora*, and the like, have been widely defined over the last decade. Unless otherwise indicated, I am using them in their usual acceptance. For definitions of those terms, consult, for instance, Sophia McClennen, *The Dialectics of Exile* (Indiana: Purdue University Press, 2004): 14–17.

15. See Leela Gandhi, *Postcolonial Theory: A Critical Introduction* (New York: Columbia University Press, 1998): 8–12.

16. Frederic Jameson, "Third World Literature in the Era of Multinational Capital," *Social text* (Fall 1986): 65–88, 69.

17. See the definition of minor literatures in the preface of the present book.

18. "Ecritures migrantes," a widely used expression in Québec, is recognized to have been coined by Robert Berrouët-Oriol in the late eighties, in an article entitled "L'effet d'exil," *Vice versa* 17 (Décembre 1986–Janvier 1987): 20–21. Other common appellations are "littérature de minorités ethniques," de "minorités

nationales," "communautés culturelles," "moindre diffusion," "transculturelle," "minoritaire," "pluriethnique," "métissée" [literatures of ethnic minorities or of national minorities, cultural communities, lesser diffusion, pluriethnic, transcultural, minority, hybrid].

19. In 1969, French was finally added as the second official language of Canada. In 1974, it was to become the only official language of Québec.

20. "Francophones, francophiles, francophonisables ou en voie de francophonisation." See Robert Berrouët-Oriol and Robert Fournier, "L'Emergence des écritures migrantes et métisses au Québec." *Litte Réalité: Une revue d'écrits originaux: A Journal of Creative and Original Writing* 3.2 (Fall 1991): 9–35, 11.

21. The Québec 1975 bill requiring new immigrants to send their children to French schools is a reflection of the said "francophonie pluraliste."

22. Pierre Nepveu, "L'exil comme métaphore," *L'Ecologie du réel: Mort et naissance de la littérature québécoise contemporaine* (Montréal: Boréal, 1988): 43–60. Writes Pierre Nepveu: "Le poète de la 'Promenade des trois morts' [Octave Crémazie] marque le début d'une tradition, d'une tendance qui définirait l'unité fondamentale du corpus poétique québécois: étrangeté à la vie, absence au monde, aliénation intérieure" [The poet of La Promenade des trois morts [Octave Crémazie] marks the beginning of a tradition, a tendency that defined the fundamental unity of the Québécois poetic corpus: strangeness to life, absence to the world, inner alienation], 48.

23. The expression comes from Marc Angenot, in "Préface," *Romanciers immigrés: Biographies et oeuvres publiées au Québec entre 1970 et 1990*. eds. Denise Helly and Anne Vassal (Montréal: IQRC/CIADEST, 1993): xi–xii, xi.

24. Pierre Nepveu, *L'Ecologie du réel: Mort et naissance de la littérature québécoise contemporaine* (Montréal: Boréal, 1988): 200–201.

25. Yvan Lamonde, "De la difficulté d'assumer un héritage pluriel," interview by Daniel Vernet, *Le Monde*, France, Wednesday, July 2, 2008: V. This interview was about Lamonde's book entitled *Allégeances et dépendances: L'histoire d'une ambivalence identitaire* (Québec: Nota Bene, 2001). As transpired in the interview, Lamonde set the québécois identity as Q = − F + GB + USA2 − R (Québec = − France + Great Britain + USA2 − Rome).

26. Pierre Nepveu, *L'Ecologie du réel*, 200.

27. Pierre Nepveu, *L'Ecologie du réel*, 200–202.

28. Simon Harel writes: "Le Québec est malade d'une identité volée, d'un territoire usurpé. Cette vieille rengaine nous obsède" [Québec suffers from a stolen identity, a usurped territory. This old tune obsesses us]. *Braconnage identitaire, Un Québec palimpseste* (Montréal: VLB, 2006): 21.

29. Régine Robin, "A propos de la notion Kafkaïenne de 'littérature mineure': quelques questions posées à la littérature québécoise." *Paragraphes* 2 (1989): 5–14, 9.

30. Sherry Simon and David Leahy, "La Recherche au Québec portant sur l'écriture ethnique," *Ethnicity and Culture in Canada: The Research Landscape*, eds. J. W. Berry and J. A. Laponce (Toronto: University of Toronto Press, 1994): 387–409, 397.

31. Quoted in Leelah Gandhi, *Postcolonial Theory: A Critical Introduction* (New York: Columbia University Press, 1998): 54.

32. Michel Biron, "L'Histoire littéraire est inadmissible: le cas du Québec," in *Les Etudes littéraires francophones: état des lieux*, ed. Lieven D'Hulst and Jean-Marc Moura (Lille: Conseil Scientifique de l'Université Charles-de-Gaulle, 2002): 209–219.

33. Jacques Godbout wrote: "Le texte national exige des sujets, des lieux, des paysages, des ancêtres, des intentions, des champs, des fleurs, des oiseaux, des thèmes, des naissances, des amours, des alcools, des rêves MADE IN QUEBEC" [the national text demands subjects, places, sceneries, ancestors, intentions, fields, flowers, themes, births, loves, alcohol, dreams MADE IN QUEBEC], quoted by Richard Hodgson and Ralph Sarkonak, "Lire le roman québécois," *Oeuvres et critiques* 14.1 (1989): 7–17, 9.

34. To this end, writers used an array of linguistic devices including literary diglossia, or the use of *joual* in Québécois texts and local African languages in African texts; see F. Elizabeth Dahab, "Visages de la francophonie: du politique, du littéraire, du sociologique," *Postcolonial Literatures: Theories and Practice; Canadian Review of Comparative Literature/Revue Canadienne de littérature comparée* 22.3–4 (September/December 1995): 693–705. For a more recent statement on the state of the art in literary studies pertaining to *francophonie*, see the collection of a dozen essays by Lieven D'Hulst and Jean-Marc Moura, eds. *Les Etudes littéraires francophones: Etat des Lieux*, Lille: Editions du conseil scientifique de l'université Charles-de-Gaulle, 2004. This book is the outcome of a joint 2002 colloquium between universities in Belgium and in France. See in particular the introductory article by Michel Beniamino, "La Francophonie littéraire" (15–25) where *francophonie* is highly advocated as a meaningful field of studies. Richard Serrano, on this side of the Atlantic presents a recent example of an opposite stance. In his book, *Against the Postcolonial* (Lanham, Maryland: Lexington Books, 2005) he asserts that "francophone Studies is mostly a mirage and Postcolonial Studies is mostly a delusion" (1).

35. Ahmadou Kourouma, *Les Soleils des indépendances*, Montréal: Presses de l'université de Montréal, 1968. Two years later, it was published in Paris by a major publishing house, Editions du Seuil, 1970.

36. See Christopher Miller, *Theories of Africans: Francophone Literature and Anthropology in Africa* (Chicago: University of Chicago Press, 1990): 182–190.

37. André Vachon, "La Francité," *Etudes Françaises* 4.2 (1968): 117.

38. For the Québécois, whether cultural or economic, liberation began with the installation of Language laws seeking the preservation (from the invasion of English) and the promotion of the French language: for instance, in 1974, bill 22 ("loi sur la langue officielle") made French the only official language of Québec, and, in 1975, bill 101 ("charte de la langue française") entailed that new immigrants had to send their children to French schools. In 1980, bill 178 (cancelled in 1993) prevented advertisement in English.

39. A circumlocution for the province of Québec.

40. Pierre Nepveu, "Conclusion; La pluralité des centres," *L'Ecologie du réel: Mort et naissance de la littérature québécoise contemporaine* (Montréal: Boréal, 1988): 211–220.

41. See Pierre L'Hérault, "Ferron l'incertain: du même au mixte," in *L'Etranger dans tous ses états; Enjeux culturels et littéraires*, ed. Simon Harel (Montréal: XYZ, 1992): 39–52, 48.

42. In 1978, Antonio D'Alfonso founded a publishing house, Guernica, which strongly contributed to the reception of Italian literature by the Québec literary institution.

43. Pierre L'Hérault. "Pour une cartographie de l'hétérogène: Dérives identitaires des années 1980," in *Fictions de l'identitaire au Québec*, ed. Sherry Simon et al. (Montréal: XYZ, 1991): 53–114, 106.

44. Antonio D'Alfonso. *In Italics: In Defense of Ethnicity* (Toronto: Guernica, 1996): 136.

45. D. Helly and A. Vassal, eds. *Romanciers immigrés: Biographies et oeuvres publiées au Québec entre 1970 et 1990*. Montréal: IQRC/CIADEST, 1993. This book includes a handful of Canadian-Arabic francophone writers, namely Kattan, Latif-Ghattas, Alonzo, Elia, Naaman, and Dahan.

46. Simon Harel, *Les Passages obligés de l'écriture migrante*, Montréal: XYZ, 2005. In this book, an entire chapter is devoted to Kattan.

47. Such is the case with journalist Mohamed Lotfi who writes: "Beneath its image as a noble protector of the rights of "minorities," the Canadian government creates a cultural communitarianism with its multiculturalism policy; this means that even immigrants who don't want to fit into the mould are forced to. That explains the discomfort felt by Wajdi Mouawad in presenting his film *Littoral* as part of the Festival du Monde Arabe de Montréal. That also explains why his film was (wrongly) criticized for the use of Quebec actors to play Arab roles. Racism in Quebec is also fuelled by this ambiguity between diversity and cultural communitarianism." "Racism, Made in Quebec," www.citoyen.onf.ca/extraits/media/racism_quebec.pdf (accessed January 9, 2009).

48. Jacques Allard, *Le Roman du Québec: Histoire, Perspectives, Lectures* (Montréal: Québec-Amérique, 2000). Kattan is mentioned on pages 131 and 243.

49. Frédérique Doyon, "Littérature-Femmes dans le Paysage: Des écritures de l'exil inscrites dans le territoire américain," *Le Devoir* (Montréal), Octobre 21–22, 2006, www.ledevoir.com/2006/10/21/120733.html (accessed December 30, 2008).

50. See, for instance, the two companion volumes edited by Susan Ireland and Patrice Proulx, entitled respectively, *Immigrant Narratives in Contemporary France* (Westport, Connecticut: Greenwood Press, 2001) and *Textualizing the Immigrant Experience in Contemporary Québec* (Westport, Connecticut: Praeger, 2004). Both volumes, consisting of a collection of articles by international scholars, testify to the growing awareness of the tropes of immigration and exile in literary studies.

51. Eloïse Brière, "Mère Solitude d'Emile Ollivier. Apport migratoire à la société québécoise," *International Journal of Canadian Studies/Revue Internationale d'études Canadiennes* 13 (1996): 61–70, 63.

52. The expression "conception vétérinaire d'une race pure" was derisively put forth by Pierre L'Hérault in a article entitled "Ferron l'incertain: du même au mixte," in *L'Etranger dans tous ses états: Enjeux culturels et littéraires*, ed. Simon Harel (Montréal: XYZ, 1992): 39–52, 50.

53. This number is somewhat subject to debate. See Michel Suleiman, *Arabs in America: Building a New Future* (Philadelphia: Temple University Press, 1999): 2–4. According to Suleiman, the reason it is difficult to estimate with a degree of accuracy the exact number of Arab immigrants to North America is the fact that at different times American and Canadian immigration officials utilized different classification systems, and Turks, Syrians, and Armenians (in the early wave) were all lumped together under the same rubric.

54. See Baha Abu-Laban, "Arabs," in *Encyclopedia of Canada's Peoples*, Paul. R. Magosci, ed. (Toronto: University of Toronto Press, 1998): 203–212. For more recent figures, see Rajwa Khouri, *Arabs in Canada-Post 9/11*. Toronto: G7 Books and Canadian Arab Federation, 2006.

55. Rajwa Khouri, *Arabs in Canada-Post 9/11* (Toronto: G7 Books and Canadian Arab Federation, 2006): 68–70.

56. Rajwa Khouri, *Arabs in Canada-Post 9/11*, 72–74.

57. Baha Abu-Laban, "Arabs," in *Encyclopedia of Canada's Peoples*, ed. Paul R. Magosci (Toronto: University of Toronto Press, 1998): 203–212, 206.

58. Those three provinces comprised 95 percent of all Arabic immigrants. After 1971, however, Ontario became the main province of immigration, followed by Québec, Alberta, and Nova Scotia.

59. In 1967 the Canadian Arab Federation was created, in part to coordinate the various activities of Arabic organizations, and to preserve the rights of Arab-Canadians.

60. See chapter 2 on Elkhadem.

61. A change, sometimes a slight one, in the last or first name of a writer can make it difficult to identify his national origin. An added difficulty is encountered when a given writer does not identify himself or herself as Arabic.

62. According to a telephone conversation with the author in June 1994.

63. This aspect has improved with the foundation of the yearly festival du monde arabe that began in the year 2000.

64. Guernica moved to Toronto in the late 1990s.

65. The review *Trois* ceased to exist in 1999–2000.

66. Anonymous, "Antoine Naaman, un écrivain au service de la littérature." *La Tribune*, Sherbrooke, May 26, 1983, 3 (B).

67. Both publishing houses and the journals attached to them ceased to exist since 1990, four years after his death in 1986.

68. See Preface.

69. This book was simultaneously published in Cairo and in Montréal.

70. On July 5, 1966, at the age of fourteen, three years after her immigration to Québec, Alonzo became quadriplegic after a car accident.

71. Edward Said, "Between Worlds," in *Reflections on Exile and Other Essays* (Cambridge, Massachusetts: Harvard University Press, 2000): 554–568, 555.

72. Antonio D'Alfonso, *L'Autre rivage* (Montréal: VLB, 1987): 126.

73. In the early 1990s roughly a third was produced in Arabic, half in French and the rest in English.

74. On the question of language and identity, see the whole issue of *Canadian Literature*, Supplement 1 (May 1987) entitled, *A/Part*, Papers from the 1984 Ottawa Conference on Language, Culture, and Identity in Canada of Canadian Literature, ed. J. M. Bumsted, especially the paper by J. R. Colombo (90–101) and the introduction by J. M. Bumsted (7–20). Also see Henry Kreisler's article, "The Ethnic Writer in Canada," in *Identifications: Ethnicity and the Writer in Canada*, ed. J. Balan (Edmonton: Canadian Institute of Ukrainian Studies, University of Alberta, 1982): 1–13.

75. Michael Batts, quoted in "Introduction," ed. J. M. Bumsted, *A/Part*, Papers from the 1984 Ottawa Conference on Language, Culture, and Literary Identity in Canada, *Canadian Literature*, Supplement 1 (May 1987): 7–20, 18.

76. Edward Mozejko, "Ethnic or National (?): Polish Literature in Canada," *Canadian Review of Comparative Literature/ Revue Canadienne de Littérature Comparée* 16.3-4 (1989): 809–825, 824.

77. George Bisztray, "Language and Literary Institution: Hungarian-Canadian Examples," *Canadian Review of Comparative Literature/Revue Canadienne de Littérature Comparée* 16.3-4 (1989): 826–838, 834–835

78. George Bisztray, *Canadian Hungarian Literature: A Preliminary Survey*. Ottawa: Secretary of State, 1988: 6. In keeping with Henri Gobard's premises in *L'Aliénation Linguistique*, Deleuze and Guattari suggested in their 1975 book, *Kafka* . . . (43) a tetraglossic model of language: The vernacular, the vehicular (language of first deterriolization), the referential and the mythical.

79. Enoch Padolsky, "Canadian Ethnic Minority Writing in English," *Ethnicity and Culture in Canada: The Research Landscape*, eds. J. W. Berry and J. A. Laponce (Toronto: University of Toronto Press, 1994): 361–386, 380–381.

80. "Clearly if you do not write in English or French you are not a Canadian author," writes George Bisztray, "Language and Literary Institution: Hungarian-Canadian Examples," *Canadian Review of Comparative Literature/Revue Canadienne de Littérature Comparée* 16.3-4 (1989): 826–838, 834.

81. D. Helly and A. Vassal, eds., *Romanciers Immigrés: Biographies et Oeuvres Publiées au Québec entre 1970 et 1990* (Montréal: IQRC/CIADEST 1993): x.

82. Naïm Kattan, *La Mémoire et l a promesse* (Montréal: HMH, 1978): 63.

83. Gilles Deleuze and Félix Guattari, *Kafka: Pour une littérature mineure* (Paris: Editions de Minuit, 1975): 30–31.

84. Léopold Sédar Senghor, "Le Français, langue de culture," *Esprit* 1962, www.esprit.presse.fr/review/article.php (accessed January 9, 2009).

85. Jacques Allard, "Entrevue avec Naïm Kattan," *Voix et Images* 11.1 (1985): 10–32, 13.

86. Jacques Allard, "Entrevue avec Naïm Kattan," *Voix et Images* 11.1 (1985): 10–32, 24.

87. Louise Dupré, "Ecrire comme vivre: dans l'hybridité. Entretien avec Anne-Marie Alonzo," *Voix et Images* 56.2 (Winter 1994): 238–249, 247.

88. Anne-Marie Alonzo, *Bleus de mine* (Ville St-Laurent: Editions du Noroît, 1985): 33

89. Emily Nasrallah (b. 1931), the Lebanese writer, is established in Beirut and shares her time between Canada, Egypt, and Lebanon.

90. Telephone conversation with the author on June 2, 1995. As we will see in the next chapter, the originality of Elkhadem's status amongst his countrymen is the fact that virtually the totality of his Canadian production appeared in his own publishing house (York Press) cast in bilingual editions (Arabic-English). In two instances, such as *Ajnihah min Rasâs* (*Wings of Lead*, 1971) and "Rijâl" ("Men," 1967) Elkhadem himself was the translator of his own writing.

91. Though the choice of language by the ethnic writer has been considered as a key issue in the study of a "multilingual Canadian literature" (see endnote above, Bisztray 1989, 834, 835), it bears a hint of artificiality worth pointing out. I am inclined to believe that, everything else being equal, a writer is rather "chosen" by the language, which at a certain point, he feels closest to for subconscious reasons. Naturally, he can rationalize and provide reasons a posteriori, especially

if solicited in interviews and the like. Those reasons are interesting to ponder, but the onset of his choice can be a matter of inclination.

92. Gilles Deleuze and Félix Guattari, *Kafka: Pour une littérature mineure* (Paris: Editions de Minuit, 1975): 37.

93. Sherry Simon, "The Language of Difference: Minority Writers in Québec," *Canadian Literature Supplement I* (May 1987): 119–128. "La Pluralité des centres" [The Plurality of Centres] is, as previously mentioned, the subtitle of the conclusion of Pierre Nepveu's *L'Ecologie du réel*.

94. Edward Said, "From Silence to Sound and Back Again: Music, Literature and History," in *Reflections on Exile and Other Essays* (Cambridge, Massachusetts: Harvard University Press, 2000): 507–526: 521.

95. Edward Said, "On Defiance and Taking Positions," in *Reflections on Exile and Other Essays* (Cambridge, Massachusetts: Harvard University Press, 2000): 500–506, 503.

96. When speaking of Kafka as part of the Jewish minority in German-speaking Prague, Deleuze and Guattari (*Kafka*, 29–30) suggested the notion of the impossibility of writing and the impossibility of not writing in the major language, a predicament central to the connection between oppressed national consciousness and the literature that gives vent to it.

97. Richard Cassidy, "Anglo-Québec Literature and the Figures of National Literary Identity," Paper presented on May 31st at the annual meeting of the Canadian Comparative Literature Association, University of British Columbia, Vancouver, May–June 2008.

98. See www.cetuq.umontreal.ca/colloques/97-04-24.25coll.htm

99. Gilles, Marcotte. "Neil Bissoondath disait. . . ." *Quebec Studies* 26 (Fall/Winter 1998/1999): 6–11, 11. This article is the outcome of the said 1997 colloquium at the University of Montréal.

100. *Dictionnaire Des Ecrivains Québécois Contemporains*, ed. Yves Légaré (Montréal: Québec-Amérique, 1983): 7–8.

101. On pages 30, 178, 211, 289, 388, respectively.

102. *Dictionnaire des auteurs de langue française en Amérique du Nord*, Reginald Hamel et al., ed. (Montréal: Fides, 1989): 119–120.

103. Nasrin Rahimieh, "Naïm Kattan, le discours arabe and Empty Words," *Canadian Review of Comparative Literature / Revue Canadienne de Littérature Comparée* 16.3–45 (1989): 733–744. Rahimieh is presently at the University of California, Irvine.

104. See www.prixduquebec.gouv.qc.ca/prix-culturels.

105. See www.bilan.usherbrooke.ca/bilan/liste.

106. *Romanciers immigrés: Biographies et oeuvres publiées au Québec entre 1970 et 1990*. eds. Denise Helly and Anne Vassal (Montréal: IQRC/CIADEST, 1993): 31.

107. Jean Basile, "Lori Saint-Martin et Nadia Ghalem," *Le Devoir* (1991), April 13.

108. Conversation with Elkhadem's former colleague, Chris Morey, present editor of *The International Fiction Review*, in April 2008.

109. Réginald Hamel, John Hare, and Paul Wyczynski, eds., *Dictionnaire des auteurs de langue française en Amérique du Nord* (Montréal: Fides, 1989): 1020.

110. See table above.

111. Jacques Pelletier, "Avant-propos," *Voix et Images*. Special Issue on Anne-Marie Alonzo 14.2 (Winter 1994): 228–229, 228.

112. Lucie Lequin,"Quand le monde arabe traverse l'Atlantique," in *Multi-Culture, multi-écriture: La voix migrante au féminin en France et au Canada*, ed. Lucie Lequin and Maïr Verthuy (Paris, Montréal: L'Harmattan, 1996): 209–219, 211. The author asserts that this remark alone partially motivated her to organize the 1994 colloquium, whose proceedings are in the present endnote.

113. Annie Molin Vasseur, "Entretien avec Anne-Marie Alonzo." *Arcade* 34 (1995): 80–89.

114. Walter Jakobson, "Breathing Words: Exile in (other); Towards a poetics of Anne-Marie Alonzo," unpublished talk delivered at a conference on "L'écriture des femmes migrantes en France et aux Etats-Unis," Concordia University, 1994 (Montréal), 3.

115. William Donoghue, Preface, "*Lead Blues* by Anne Marie-Alonzo." Trans., W. Donoghue (Montréal: Guernica, 1990): 5–10, 5.

116. Edward Said, "Reflections on Exile," in *Reflections on Exile and Other Essays* (Cambridge, Massachusetts: Harvard University Press, 2000): 173–186, 186.

117. Jean Sgard, "Conclusions," *Exil et Littérature*, ed. Jacques Mounier (Grenoble: Ellug, 1986): 291–299, 293.

118. Saad Elkhadem, *Canadian Adventures of the Flying Egyptian* (Fredericton: York Press 1990): 33.

119. Saad Elkhadem, *Canadian Adventures of the Flying Egyptian*, 27.

120. See chapter 2 on Elkhadem.

121. Edward Said, "Reflections on Exile," in *Reflections on Exile and Other Essays* (Cambridge, Massachusetts: Harvard University Press, 2000): 173–186, 182.

122. "Exile is strangely compelling to think about but terrible to experience. It is the unhealable rift forced between a human being and a native place, between the self and its true home; its essential sadness can never be surmounted, And while it is true that literature and history contain heroic, romantic, glorious, even triumphant episodes in an exile's life, these are no more than efforts meant to overcome the crippling sorrow of estrangement. The achievements of exile are permanently undermined by the loss of something left behind forever," Edward Said, *Reflections on Exile*, 173.

123. Robert Berrouët-Oriol and Robert Fournier, "L'Emergence des écritures migrantes et métisses au Québec." *Litte Réalité: Une revue d'écrits originaux: A Journal of Creative and Original Writing* 3.2 (Fall 1991): 9–35, 17.

124. Louise Dupré, "Ecrire comme vivre: dans l'hybridité. Entretien avec Anne-Marie Alonzo," *Voix et Images* 56.2 (Winter 1994): 238–249, 248.

125. Annie Molin Vasseur, "Entretien avec Anne-Marie Alonzo." *Arcade* 34 (1995): 80–89, 84.

126. Jacques Hassoun, Préface, "*Les Voix du jour et de la nuit* par Mona Latif-Ghattas" (Montréal: Boréal, 1988): 7–9, 9.

127. Anne-Marie Alonzo, *Le Livre des ruptures* (Montréal: Editions de l'Hexagone, 1988): 104.

128. Régine Robin, *La Québécoite* (Montréal: Québec/Amérique, 1983): 186.

129. Quoted by Pierre L'Hérault, in "Pour une cartographie de l'hétérogène: Dérives identitaires des années 1980," in *Fictions de l'identitaire au Québec*, eds. Sherry Simon et al. (Montréal: XYZ, 1991): 53–114, 65.

130. *Crash Landing of the Flying Egyptian*, trans. Saad El Gabalawy, Bilingual edition, English-Arabic (Fredericton, New Brunswick: York Press, 1992): 12.

131. Vasco Varoujean, *Le Moulin du diable* (Ottawa: Le Cercle du Livre de France, 1972).

132. Anne-Marie Alonzo, *Droite et de profil* (Montréal: Lèvres urbaines 7, 1984): 5.

133. Naïm Kattan, *Le Réel et le théâtral* (Montréal: Editions HMH, 1970; Paris: Editions Denoël, 1971): 188.

134. Walter Jakobson, "Breathing Words: Exile in (Other): Towards a Poetics of Anne-Marie Alonzo," unpublished talk delivered at a conference on "L'écriture des femmes migrantes en France et aux Etats-Unis," Concordia University, 1994 (Montréal), 3.

135. Louise Dupré, "Ecrire comme vivre: dans l'hybridité. Entretien avec Anne-Marie Alonzo." *Voix et Images* 56.2 (Winter 1994): 238–249, 241.

136. The third characteristic is the deterritorialization of language. See Gilles Deleuze and Félix Guattari, *Kafka: Pour une littérature mineure* (Paris: Minuit, 1975): 29–33.

137. Andrée Dahan, *Chants de la terre morte* (Laval: Editions Trois, 2005): dedication page, no number.

138. Email from the author to myself on March 19, 2006.

139. Anne-Marie Alonzo, *L'Immobile* (Montréal: Editions de L'Hexagone, 1990): 19.

140. Régine Robin, "Sortir de l'ethnicité," *Métamorphose d'une utopie*, eds. Jean-Michel Lacroix and Fulvio Caccia (Paris/Montréal: Presses de la Sorbonne/Nouvelle-Tryptique, 1992): 25–43.

2

Deprivation and Despair in Saad Elkhadem's *Wings of Lead, The Plague, Trilogy of the Flying Egyptian*, and *One Night in Cairo*[1]

> He traveled abroad to quench his thirst for freedom, knowledge, and love, but his heavy wings could lift him no higher than a few feet before he fell down, shattering his dreams.
>
> Saad Elkhadem (*Wings of Lead*, Epigraph)

> This was an insane period in the history of Egypt, an era that must be compared to the days of Hitler, Stalin, Caligula, and Nero, as well as other rulers who raised themselves to the status of gods, reducing other human beings to the state of bugs, worms, and bats.
>
> Saad Elkhadem (*Crash Landing of the Flying Egyptian*, 13)

> Where will you publish, brother? . . . publishing houses are up to their ears these days printing and distributing the President's speeches, his so-called "Covenant," and the manifesto of his Socialist Union . . . leave it on God, brother!
>
> Saad Elkhadem (*The Plague*, 30)

SAAD ELKHADEM AND HIS LEGACY

Saad Elkhadem (1932–2003) was born in Cairo, Egypt, where he grew up and received his Bachelor of Arts degree. He earned his doctorate in Graz, Austria, and then worked for the government in both Egypt and Switzerland for a short while, before teaching at the university of North Dakota. In 1968, he was hired as Associate Professor in the Department of German at the University of New Brunswick (Canada) where he taught

German and Comparative Literature. He spent the rest of his career there, becoming Professor Emeritus in 1995 and relocating to Toronto where he lived until his death in 2003. During his distinguished academic career, Saad Elkhadem chaired the interdisciplinary Comparative Literature Program, and was Chair of the Department of German and Russian for nearly seventeen years. Elkhadem is hailed in an obituary published by *The International Fiction Review* as "a creative writer, an editor, a translator, and a publisher who left a mark as founder of York Press."[2]

In three decades, Elkhadem produced more than twenty-five books, of which sixteen are fiction—some of them are banned in Egypt—and the rest are reference books. The latter include such titles as *The York Dictionary of English-French-German-Spanish Literary Terms and Their Origin* (1976), *History of the Egyptian Novel: Its Rise and Early Beginnings* (1985), *The Concise Dictionary of Greek, Roman, Norse and Egyptian Mythology* (1991), *Life Is Like a Cucumber: Colloquial Egyptian Proverbs, Coarse Sayings, and Popular Expressions* (1993), and *Brief Definitions of All Essential Literary Terms* (2000).

This prolific Egyptian-Canadian novelist, playwright, publisher, editor, and academic also translated works from German and Arabic into English, including, in some instances, some of his own writing from Arabic, such as *Ajnihah min Rasâs* (Wings of Lead) (1971/1994) and *Rijâl wa Khanâzîr* (Men and Pigs) (1967/1977)[3], much in the tradition of Brecht and Beckett who were themselves writers/translators of their own writing. In the words of a critic commenting on this aspect of Elkhadem's literary achievements: "Elkhadem's systematic publication of bilingual editions of his works from the 1980s was instrumental in opening up part of the literary scene in Egypt and a different realm of thought and experience to the Western mind."[4]

Moreover, and as mentioned in the introduction to this study, Saad Elkhadem was among those Egyptian-Canadian mediators (such as Alonzo and Naaman) who played a significant role in the transmission and diffusion of their own and other writers' products through the literary reviews and the publishing houses they founded. In 1975, Elkhadem created the eminent *International Fiction Review* and the year before a publishing company, York Press. As General Editor, he set up a series entitled "Authoritative Studies in World Literature" that became very successful. He published internationally recognized intellectuals such as Roger Moore, Alain Robbe-Grillet, M. P. Gillespie, Victor Terras, Anthony Boxhill, Edward Wasiolek, and many others, a valuable endeavor in its own right. Nevertheless, asserts the writer of the aforementioned obituary, Saad is probably best known for his creative work.[5]

Elkhadem's literary production, a major contribution in the area of Canadian writing of Middle Eastern origins, not only spans three decades, from 1971 to shortly before his death in 2003, but is also credited with providing one of the first landmarks of Arabic-Canadian literature, an identifiable, trilingual body of works born in the seventies at the hands of First Generation Canadians of Arabic descent. Thus, in 1971, his *Ajnihah min Rasâs* (Wings of Lead), written in Arabic in Canada, appeared in Cairo (an English translation by the author followed in 1994). In 1978, Elkhadem produced (in Cairo, in Arabic) *Min Rihlat Odysseus al-Misri* (From Travels of the Egyptian Odysseus), which was to be published a year later in an English translation in New Brunswick. A few years later, *Thulathiyat Ûlis* (The Ulysses Trilogy) (1988) and *Al-Tâ'ûn* (The Plague) (1989) appeared, followed in 1990–1992 by the experimental *Thulathiyat al-Misri al-Tâir* (Trilogy of the Flying Egyptian).

It seems that the originality of Elkhadem's status, amidst his fellow writers of Arabic origins, is not only the fact that he continued to write in Arabic after settling in Canada (at the relatively mature age of thirty-six) but also that virtually the totality of his Canadian production was published by York Press, translated by the Egyptian critic, Saad El Gabalawy (Professor Emeritus of English at the University of Calgary) and cast in bilingual editions (Arabic and English): two languages, two countries, multiple awareness, and an array of shifting perspectives partaking in the larger postmodern vision shared by a number of transnational writers.

The majority of the reviews of Elkhadem's oeuvre, over four dozens reviews, are written by fellow Arabic scholars, and published in *International Fiction Review*. Only a fifth, approximately, of the total references on him are written by English Canadians or Americans, also published in *World Literature Today* or in *Canadian Book Review Annual*. Most of these tributes tend to stress the intercultural aspect of his work rather than the wealth of technical devices and artistic craft inherent in it. Ironically, a very perceptive appraisal of *The Plague* (1989) was written by Paradela, a Spanish scholar from the Universidad Autónoma de Madrid who rightly pointed out the marginality of Elkhadem's status in Egypt as a result of Western influences in his narrative techniques. Nevertheless, by far the best, most thorough, and truly analytical appraisal of the writer's work comes from his translator and critic Saad El-Gabalawy who contributed a lengthy critical introduction to each of the volumes he translated. El-Gabalawy rightly considers Elkhadem to be "an artist of great power, versatility and craftsmanship."[6] The translations themselves are excellent renditions, at once close to the original and dynamic, preserving some of the characteristic patterns of Arabic narrative discourse without detracting from the quality of the English prose.

The aim of this chapter is multifold: its main purpose is to examine four of Saad Elkhadem's major works, namely *Wings of Lead* (1971/1994), *The Plague* (1989), *Trilogy of the Flying Egyptian* (1990–1992), and *One Night in*

Cairo (2001). My focus will be the underlying narrative techniques and the transnational themes at play in these complex experimental novels that seem to bear the mark of the political and the collective value of utterances. Elkhadem's relatively recent death in 2003 engenders yet another goal, that of drawing a profile of the writer's contribution to Arabic-Canadian literature, his reception in Canada, and the linguistic choices he was faced with as a minority writer.

WINGS OF LEAD (1971–1994)

> Egyptians come to Europe carrying two sacks on their shoulders. One bulges with psychological complexes and emotional sores, and the other is inflated with naive hopes and crazy dreams. . . . Thrilled with their new freedom, they run in every direction. A train that has jumped off its rails. . . . [7]

This is how the antihero of *Wings of Lead* sums up the collective experience of expatriation, one which sheds light on the title of this experimental work that beautifully portrays the flight to Europe of a young man, his struggles, downfall, disintegration, and final crash when he is deported to Egypt at the very end of the novella. The very last sentence, "my new life begins tomorrow," is a poignant reminder of the tenacity of human vice—in Europe he got acquainted with, and then became addicted to, alcohol—, the fragility of willpower, and the clinging force of the illusion of possible redemption. That sentence occurs several times throughout the novella, especially so whenever the protagonist encounters a major setback.

The nameless protagonist-narrator unfolds his woes in diary form, a dramatic monologue consisting of alternating fragments of unequal length. We learn that he succeeded, after a number of difficulties, to travel to Vienna to study medicine, with next to no financial resources—his low-middle-class father sends him the paltry monthly sum of twenty Egyptian pounds, roughly the equivalent of forty dollars in the sixties—and with no prior knowledge of German, "a barbarous language in which the exception is the rule, and the exemption is the norm."[8] He believes he can learn German "in a month or two."[9] He studies it arduously for three months then fails the compulsory language entrance examination. This first failure—"I came to Europe to satisfy my hunger for knowledge, for freedom, and for love. I tripped on the first obstacle on the road to knowledge"[10]—marks the beginning of the protagonist's descending curve, his subsequent failures in his studies three years later, his alcohol addiction, and his disastrous amorous ventures. I fail to agree with the claim that the protagonist's immaturity, his "cultural shock," and "abuse of freedom"[11] are the sole factors that led to his ruin, for I think the novel can also be interpreted from a stance whereby the socioeconomic background would provide a reliable prognosis for success. The protagonist of this novel was bound to fail in his venture. It is also from that standpoint that I would tend to read the portrayal of the wasted life of Egyptian students in Europe—"they talk about nothing but dance halls and girls and discuss nothing but trivial matters and obscene affairs"[12]—in glimpses scattered throughout the novel. Much like the Egyptians in Canada whom we encounter in the trilogy (see below), the students in Vienna are portrayed as "the travelers who never arrive, the eternal outsiders who never belong, the aliens who are constantly isolated from the center."[13]

The "emotional sores" in the opening quotation of the present section are related to the protagonist's flashbacks into his past, one full of "all kinds of hunger. Hunger for freedom. Hunger for knowledge. Hunger for love"[14]; his parents' "tyranny and rigidity," his mother's utter submissiveness, and his father's preference for his older brother, "the first-born. The breast of the chicken. The heart of the watermelon."[15] In a relatively small number of pages, the past, the present, and the future of this problematic antihero interweave to provide a full picture of a life marked by doom.

> I spent six weeks turning the pages of my life. I didn't find one thing that I would like to keep. I didn't come across a single ray of light that might illuminate my way. I made more than one decision. I designed more than one plan. I don't know what to do with myself. Or what myself would do to me.[16]

Such statements provide a complete, albeit condensed, picture of the mental state of the protagonist, and though they abound throughout the novel, the reader never gets an impression of rambling and redundancy. On the contrary, there is a lack of effusion in the protagonist's discourse, one which, though punctuated with despair, retains nevertheless a manner of restraint and discretion. As Saad El Gabalawy remarked,[17] with a careful selection of narrative details, Saad Elkhadem makes use of a great economy of style in those long and short highly poetic fragments that give the reader insights into the protagonist's life.

THE PLAGUE (1989)

> *The Plague* depicts potently the dark force of dictatorship, with its tempestuous fury, which leaves people vulnerable and defenseless against the insidious power of evil. This is a haunting novella with unusual complexity.[18]

The above statement by the author's translator, Saad E-Gabalawy, is an accurate depiction of the spirit of this work. In fact, Saad Elkhadem's *The*

Plague, reminiscent in its structure of Boccaccio's *The Decameron*, in which ten characters are fleeing plague-ridden Florence, is a satirical novel (banned in Egypt) that demonstrates with stark frankness the ethos of the years between 1952 and 1970 under the presidency of General Gamal Abd El-Nasser. *The Plague* features ten nameless middle-class characters, seven men and three women (instead of the seven women and three men of Boccaccio's work). Those characters are an engineer, a teacher of French, a young girl, a businessman, a journalist, a television actress, a student, a translator, an older housewife, and a commander of a military prison. They happen to meet in a visa office in Cairo as they are waiting for their exit visa in order to escape from the oppression and brutality of Nasser's tyrannical regime. In an attempt to while away the time and to alleviate the boredom of waiting, each character in turn introduces him/herself to all the others, telling something of their near future plans. The title, *The Plague*, evokes the confinement in which they find themselves:

> I don't know why these bastards prevent people from leaving and hold them as if they had the plague and must be kept in quarantine. . . . The whole country is in quarantine. . . . the whole nation is under house arrest. Oh, if I could just set foot abroad, I would never come back again.[19]

The above statement is part of an internal monologue of character number nine. In fact, the characters in *The Plague* are identified numerically from one to ten, a number that is also the title of each of the corresponding ten chapters that constitute the novella. There are no fewer than four sets of points of view in this complex experimental work:

1. An omniscient voice (an eleventh invisible character that has the function of a chorus), indicated by parentheses marked with an asterisk, that speaks of the past and future of each character.[20]
2. Each of the nine characters who pursue their internal monologue while one of them is speaking aloud.
3. The voice of the person introducing him or herself to the others.
4. The inner discourse of the speaker, again in parentheses, but with no number attached this time.

Since there are ten characters, the outward dramatic monologue they proffer in turn is constantly interrupted by a sequence of numerical parenthetical inserts belonging to the inward utterances of their fellow visa-seekers. Those consist partly of ruminations about the conditions of life in Egypt, and reactions to the speakers' monologues. There are more than twelve abrupt shifts in points of view in any given section of the narrative, which constitutes a tight flow with no paragraph breaks. The following extract taken from chapter 2 (the one devoted to the teacher) illustrates this scheme:

> Is it my turn? (*the speaker was a thirty-two-year-old man, elegant and bald, with a bushy mustache that endowed him with an air of gravity and dignity which belied his diminutive size and soft voice). I am Magdi Na'im, a teacher of French (5—which means he's a blue boned son of a bitch; . . . the rest of his name might be John or George or Christian, . . . they are all sons of bitches posturing as modish Westerners) (9—He seems to be a Christian; resembles the handsome young man who married princess Fathiya and the King kicked them out of the country).[21]

The narrative harbors not only multiple points of view but *also* multiple registers of language, a multiplicity that brings together form and content, one that further enriches *The Plague* with several dimensions (social, political, and psychological), endowing it with the collective value of utterances and the mark of the political, characteristics pointed out by Deleuze and Guattari with regard to minor literatures. The novel becomes, through the wealth of its linguistic constituent, "an important social document, which reveals manners, morals, customs, habits, and ways of life in contemporary Egypt."[22] The omniscient voice that functions as an all-knowing chorus revealing to the reader the future that awaits each character uses classical Arabic, in a matter-of-fact, objective, arid tone, devoid of any judgments, in stark contrast with the speeches of the three other points of view, a fact that adds a level of irony to the entire narrative. Furthermore, there are also the spoken words and the internal monologues of the characters, in stark contrast to one another. The language the characters speak in public is standard Arabic, polite and correct, well edited, restrained, polished, free of insults and popular idioms, and full of patriotic and civic commitment to the reigning regime. Unlike *The Decameron* where the spoken word is a vehicle for escapism and entertainment, here it is an instrument of restraint and self-control. The language used in the internal soliloquies, on the other hand, is full of profanities, proverbs, idioms, humor, irony, and popular jokes. It betrays the suspicion they all have of their countrymen as well as their intense, seemingly paranoid fear lest an intelligence agent be hidden amongst them, ready to retract their visa at the last moment, or even after they have boarded the plane: "I think, and I do not say what I think, therefore I am,"[23] seems to be their mode of discourse and communication, if one can qualify as *communication* an assemblage of juxtaposed monologues, whether internal or external, and a total absence of dialogue.

Given that predicament, the biggest fear of the ten characters is, understandably, to utter something that would prevent them from leaving Egypt. Thus, the University Professor cautions himself before speaking: "Don't say anything about your doctorate or mention it at all, lest they should cancel the visa at the last moment . . . they have blocked the departure of those with Ph.D.'s because the state needs them to erect its new renaissance."[24] The businessman will reflect in the same vein:

> It's only one hour at the most and the window will be opened, then each will get his visa and go his way; even after giving you the visa, they may retract their word for whatever reason . . . a presidential decree for general mobilization . . . they can cancel the visa even when you are about to board the plane . . . or force you to leave it . . . or order it back from the sky . . . they'll never lack means to do it.[25]

This very fear constitutes the leitmotif of the novel, with the visa office taking the role of an "objective correlative"—this theme was slightly dealt with in the earlier novella, *Wings of Lead*—that triggers associations of suppression and suspicion, as the translator rightly pointed out.[26] Moreover, it leads the characters to claim aloud that they will go back to Egypt as soon as they have achieved the purpose of their trip, even though they all know this to be untrue and that none of them ever intends to return. Thus speaks the scholar, his inward thoughts (in parenthetical inserts) belying his hypocritical public stance: "I will publish the results of my research immediately after my return to Cairo (I'd be a real son of a bitch if I ever come back again of my own volition)."[27]

The young woman, similarly speaks and thinks simultaneously:

> and I shall return to Egypt before the opening of the great Alexandria festival in order to take part in organizing it (there is my face, spit on it, one by one, if I ever set foot in Egypt as long as you are in power, you dirty pimps! . . . enough is enough! . . . God never tasks a soul beyond its limits!).[28]

The truth of the matter is that all those characters have been wounded, directly or indirectly, by a sociopolitical system marked by brutality and autocracy. However, not a word pertaining to their woes is ever revealed to their companions. We have a glimpse of those woes *only* through their internal monologues and the mysterious, omniscient voice that informs the reader of their past and future: the gifted scholar whose fellowship obtained from an American university was diverted by his deputy minister in favor of the latter's nephew; the Coptic teacher of French who faced religious persecution; the government employee, victim of the fanatic religious clerk, his boss, who used religion as a pretext for controlling and intimidating others; the young woman forced to marry an "old, impotent, crippled rhinoceros, with dirty fingernails and a paunch sagging in front of him,"[29] and the student pushed into exile by his older brother to protect the latter's newly acquired, heightened social status. The list is long, and Nasser seems to be the ultimate culprit. The older housewife thinks to herself, while pitying character number three, the young girl:

Oh, poor child, she's no older than nineteen or twenty; . . . why are you too, my girl, compelled to leave your homeland?! . . . may God deprive you, Nasser, of all His blessings and make you wander aimlessly all your life, just as you did to us and all our children.[30]

Wealthy as it may be from the standpoint of modernist experimentation, *The Plague* is first and foremost an indictment of Egypt under Nasser, from the death of the last king (Farouk) to the 1952 coup d'état that overruled the monarchy and established the republic, to the rise of Sadat in the seventies.

As one critic rightly stated, and as mentioned above, *The Plague* is "One of the most ironic and scathing critiques of Nasser's regime to be found in the pages of a literary creation."[31] The last character (number ten),[32] the commander of the military prison, Hasan Safwat, now out of favor with his superiors, evokes people he tortured, crippled, and killed, and how one of them sat trembling with a pool of urine, blood, and excrements underneath him. Ironically, embittered by his demotion, this ex-commander thinks of himself as a victim: "for whom did I torture the traitors and crush the enemies of the Revolution? . . . for my mother? . . . wasn't it for you, sons of whores,"[33] he exclaims in an internal invective addressed to his enemies, his ex-bosses. Similarly, referring to the Québec 101 law (issued in 1975) that mandates the use of French by all immigrants, character number two, the teacher about to leave to Montréal, thinks to himself: "They [the Québécois] should just ask Nasser and he'll send them some intelligence officers who would keep beating, terrifying, and torturing the people until they are forced to stop uttering a single word except in French."[34]

All things considered, in this novel, Elkhadem dares taking up the two most divisive issues in Egypt and perhaps in much of the world, namely politics and religion, for it is not just an Egyptian ethos that transpires through *The Plague*. The wealth of fragmentary perceptions contained in it, as well as the intensity of these perceptions shot from a multitude of angles and expressed in a compelling language contribute to make this novel "[a work] of both regional and universal significance."[35]

TRILOGY OF THE FLYING EGYPTIAN (CANADIAN ADVENTURES OF THE FLYING EGYPTIAN, 1990; CHRONICLE OF THE FLYING EGYPTIAN IN CANADA, 1991; CRASH LANDING OF THE FLYING EGYPTIAN, 1992)

Canadian Adventures of the Flying Egyptian

Saad Elkhadem's highly experimental *Trilogy of the Flying Egyptia*n (1990–1992) illustrates the themes of exile and immigration nested in a host of ambivalent feelings toward both the new and the old country. The entire trilogy seems to make use of a multiplicity of languages, in that the narrator is constantly debating about whether to use classical or colloquial Arabic when dealing with any given topic, an aspect that, most unfortunately, does not come through in the English translation, hence the invaluable bilingual editions (Arabic/English) in which the trilogy, as with most of Elkhadem's works, is cast. In the words of a reviewer commenting on that aspect of Elkhadem's writing: "In a sense, this is a true polyglot work, a product of what Elkhadem himself calls 'the complex art of the mosaic.'"[36]

Through a variety of self-reflexive devices, the trilogy writes a story that portrays at once the dual experience of immigration and artistic creation. It reflects the ontological link between spatial displacement and linguistic estrangement, and it is marked with the collective value of utterances characteristic of minor literatures. In fact, Elkhadem expressed the predicament of Egyptians, many of whom did not speak French, who went en masse to Québec where they anxiously witnessed the separatist unrest culminating to the 1970 October Crisis. Trudeau's declaration of the War Measures Act in order to counter the Québec Liberation Front's acts of terrorism reawakens painful memories and the trauma experienced under Nasser's military regime by hundreds of other Egyptian immigrants. Writes the protagonist narrator of *Canadian Adventures of the Flying Egyptian*:

> We arrived in 67, leaving Egypt humiliated and beaten and in ruins, and came to rich, lovely, joyful Canada . . . and right away, brother, in the same year political disturbances started, followed by assassination, sabotage, suspension of the rule of law and mass arrest, without a hint or warning.[37]

In the first volume of the trilogy, a metafictional work in the form of a soliloquy, one that provides invaluable insights into literary creation, the writer/character struggles to design a story that embodies the themes of exile and immigration. Kafka's opening sentence of *Metamorphosis* ("As Gregor Samsa awoke one morning from uneasy dreams he found himself transformed in his bed into a gigantic insect") is transposed and played upon a number of times, with variations:

> As Hasan Gum'a awoke one morning from uneasy dreams he found himself transformed in bed into an emaciated, frightened dog.[38]

Or:

> Hasan awoke one morning from uneasy dreams to find himself transformed in bed into a confused, lost, frightened, and sickly dog.[39]

The state of mind of the protagonist, we learn, is caused by the military defeat of 1967, which delayed the exit visa the he had applied for. This theme of being trapped in the country with little or no hope of escape, as we have seen above, is highly reminiscent of the thematic fabric of *The Plague*. The reader further becomes aware that the writer-narrator of *Canadian Adventures* has returned to Egypt and has died there in mysterious circumstances before finishing his manuscript about his immigration to Canada—he had successfully left Egypt after great difficulties— where he landed during the centennial celebration of 1967. This celebration is juxtaposed with reflections on the demoralizing effects of the devastating military defeat suffered by the Egyptian army at the hands of Israel during the 1967 Six Day's War, which, in the eyes of many Egyptians, constitutes the betrayal of the Egyptian people by Gamal Abd El Nasser—"from humiliation, fear, and despair to freedom, joy and security"[40]—and the deceitful, misleading role played by the Egyptian media in this context, claiming victory for the Egyptian army and defeat for the Israelis. This juxtaposition, charged with irony as it is, creates a contrapuntal mood, that of a simultaneous transnational awareness of disparate events, with disparate affects, in a manner much reminiscent of Edward Said's pronouncement in "Intellectual Exile: Expatriates and Marginals" about the vividness of both the new and the old environments in the awareness of the expatriate: "Because the exile sees things in terms of what has been left behind and what is actual here and now, there is a double perspective that never sees things in isolation. Every scene or situation in the new country draws on its counterpart in the old country."[41]

The manuscript is punctuated with a variety of comments in parenthetical inserts from an editor who is preparing it for publication in Cairo and who takes issue with many of the bitterly critical remarks that the original writer-narrator has made concerning his homeland in the wake of the 1967 debacle, the era of "the rabid dogs," as the writer calls it. The editor fulfills the function of the unreliable narrator with the information he provides for the sake of "clarification" and "documentation" and through which four elements transpire:

1. His fear of Egypt's government and his paying lip service to it
2. His ludicrous ignorance about Canada—"Calgary is a city in the state of Albertina"[42]
3. The pedantic clutter of editorial commentary as well as the tedium of documentation
4. Ultimately, Elkhadem's own metafictional endeavors, namely his interest in the interchangeability of documentary and fictional devices characteristic of modernist experimentations.

Canadian Adventures is written now in the second person, now in the first person point of view (with abrupt shifts), both pointing to the same protagonist, Hasan. In the words of Saad El-Gabalawy: "As an accomplished artist, Elkhadem attempts to comprehend the reality of the moment by means of shifting particles which accentuate a lack of stability and permanence."[43]

Chronicle of the Flying Egyptian in Canada

The second volume of the trilogy, *Chronicle of the Flying Egyptian in Canada* (1991) takes the shape of an annotated biography based on transcribed interviews a new Egyptian editor conducts in Canada with the protagonist's friends and acquaintances who convey at random their subjective perceptions and memories of him. Some of them claim that he may have faked his death and moved to a distant land after all. These commentaries often express the biases of the interviewees and their own fears. The testimonials seem to belong to unreliable narrators who admit to not having known the writer and yet seek, at the same time, to give accurate pronouncements on him: "you want me, sir, to discuss the stages of his life one by one but my relationship with the deceased lasted for a very brief period of time. . . . I could hardly know much about him, all just observations. . . ."[44]

Instead of the parenthetical inserts characteristic of the first volume, here the editor uses extensive footnotes where quotations from previous works by Elkhadem reappear, sometimes as short as one sentence, an intertextuality that may be puzzling and disconcerting (and intended to be such) to readers unacquainted with those works, but one that enriches the author's legacy and gives readers who recognize these recurring passages a sense of satisfaction when they actively participate in this web of cross-references.

It is truly as if the author wanted to educate the reader and to prevent him from becoming complacent. "Writing, in the true sense of the word is . . . a great ethical responsibility shared by the reader, the publisher, and the writer,"[45] the narrator/protagonist remarks. In the same vein, he adds, "the true artist . . . is like mercury, never stops in one place, never melts, and never freezes."[46] This is a theme we encounter again in the last volume of the trilogy, a theme accompanied by a poignant complaint pertaining to the reception of his works and his fate as a writer: "But it seems to me, now that I am close to the end of this long journey, that what I wrote and published was nothing but a mute dialogue which required no response, a suppressed cry which left no echo."[47] Is this a reminder of the fact that Elkhadem's modernist innovations never found favor among literary critics in Egypt?

Crash Landing of the Flying Egyptian

The third volume of the trilogy, *Crash Landing of the Flying Egyptian* (1992), witnesses the resurrection of the author/narrator/protagonist in an indefinite form, perhaps a butterfly, hovering on the margin of oblivion and attempting to summarize the accumulated events of a lifetime in fewer than two hundred words, an economy of form, a search for *compactness* and density full of irony and deep philosophical implications pertaining to the void of one's existence. This novella is haunted by nightmarish memories of the protagonist/narrator's childhood in his not-so-beloved native land, Egypt, whom he calls "the land of nonexistent opportunities."[48]

In fact, for the author/protagonist/narrator of Elkhadem's works, childhood experiences "left all the sails of [his] life in tatters."[49] Life in the native country is evoked as "dark and suffocating." Mostly in this volume, but throughout the entire trilogy, we encounter references to Nasser's reign of brutality, "an insane period in the history of Egypt. An era that must be compared to the days of Hitler, Stalin, Caligula, and Nero."[50] The author seems to refer to years marked with regular "disappearances" of whomsoever uttered (or was accused of such) a word that could be [mis]taken to be critical of the 1952 "revolution," a revolution thought by a number of historians to be a coup d'état rather than a revolution per se. In this context emerges a poignant personal allusion to Hamada, the protagonist's brother, who was taken by secret police in the middle of the night, "shivering from the effects of rheumatic fever," never to return.[51] The sentence, "I have created in you a spirit of pride and dignity,"[52] a sentence that Nasser pronounced during one of his public speeches, ironically appears in the middle of the description of Hamada's ruthless arrest. In fact, this sentence comes back in other works as well, juxtaposed with descriptions of the plight of the Egyptian people, a vast portion of whom—and this may remain a mystery of mass psychology!—adored Nasser. Referring to the Cairo Fire and the events that led to the 1952 overthrow of the last king (Farouk), the narrator/protagonist relates:

> The mobs smashed the store windows, office panes, and shop doors, especially those owned by foreigners and Jews. That was the Egyptian Night of Shattered Glass, which paved the way for the rule of iron, fire, and blood. Then came the foremost teacher [Nasser], the greatest thinker, the beloved of millions, who broke the backbone of the Egyptian nation to teach it the meaning of real pride, and rubbed the noses of the whole population in the mud to instill in them the basics of true dignity.[53]

The protagonist's colossal anger toward his past and his native land equally engulfs the figure of the father as "absolute evil, unadulterated malice, and distilled venom."[54] "From a household full of insults and screams to a homeland dominated by terror and corruption"; "from a piece of shit to the sewer, rejoice my heart,"[55] he adds sardonically, after having, in a typical instance of narrative self-reflexivity, decided that "coarse and obscene colloquial Arabic is the only language capable of describing your father."⁵⁶ It seems that his was "a house which resounded with slaps . . . and abuses,"⁵⁷ where the father was "the raging rhinoceros," "the monstrous beast," "the insane dinosaur."⁵⁸ There are numerous vivid instances of the latter's cruelty and violence—they are reminiscent of Strindberg's portrayal of his father's cruelty—least of which, for example, when he ripped his daughter's clothes and shaved her hair with a razor when he caught her singing and dancing in front of the mirror.⁵⁹ As a pervasive shadow looming over the entirety of the trilogy, the protagonist's miserable childhood is a burden and a permanent "sore." The following quotation taken from *Crash Landing* sums it up:

> A man's family is a macrocosm of himself and a microcosm of his country. Wherever you went, you found yourself chained to what you had experienced in the early days of your life; and however far you moved, you were always tied to what you had endured during your boyhood and youth.⁶⁰

In this last volume of the trilogy, the protagonist further ruminates on the reasons for his immigration to Canada: an abusive father, the war, and a cruel homeland are not the only reasons (and those are reasons that are not usually dealt with in Egyptian fiction!). There is also mention of sexual and religious oppression, poverty, and inflation. After recounting the ordeal he went through to find a country to immigrate to, he evokes in strong terms what it was like for him and his countrymen to be in Montréal in the midst of the separatist unrest, with the mounting linguistic tensions of the seventies when French became the only official language of Québec: "And they hated us in Montréal. We can't speak it. We don't want to speak it" will say the protagonist of *Canadian Adventures*.⁶¹ The writer/narrator of *Crash Landing* further recalls the various fears and dangers that loomed on the horizon, especially for Anglophone immigrants of various ethnic backgrounds, a number of whom ended up relocating, mostly to Western Canada (especially Ontario) and to the United States. The impetus behind their relocation was their fear of assimilation and acculturation, due to the 1975 Québec law that required immigrants to send their children to French schools. Those immigrants feared that "Québec could separate overnight and [they] find [themselves] sitting between two chairs, without any right to either."⁶² In the words of a Greek acquaintance encountered by the protagonist of *Crash Landing*: "Foreigners in Québec are afraid of becoming French, the Francophones themselves are afraid of becoming Canadian, and the Canadians are afraid of becoming American."⁶³

In the conclusion of a brief book review of the first volume of the *Trilogy of the Flying Egyptian*, Roger Allen, the eminent critic, exclaims: "Perhaps *Canadian Adventures of the Flying Egyptian* . . . is destined to remain in a state of limbo between the two languages of Arabic and English in which the volume itself is couched."[64] This commentary can also be applied to the state of unrest and the feeling of estrangement the protagonist of Elkhadem's Egyptian trilogy experiences. Is this an attempt by the author to reestablish balance? It is probably true that the exile's writing, as one critic rightly put it, "aims to win back the land" and that "its longed-for destination is that one place where it can never be."[65] If this is so, we here hold the key to deciphering the feeling of being in-between that haunts the complex protagonist of the *Trilogy of the Flying Egyptian*.

ONE NIGHT IN CAIRO (2001)

One Night in Cairo: An Egyptian Micronovel with Footnotes, written barely two years before the author's death, features a nameless narrator/writer/protagonist who feels bound, trapped as he is "by a peculiar country that [he] cannot desert, by an incompatible marriage that [he] cannot dissolve, and by an ancient religion for which [he] cannot find an acceptable alternative."[66] Here we recognize the familiar paradoxical voice that is the hallmark of Elkhadem's narrators: somber, self-reflexive, honest, analytic, self-critical, sarcastic, crude, and sometimes humorous. The narrative first-person pronoun *I*, much like that of the protagonist of *Wings of Lead*, reveals to the reader that this protagonist has also studied in Europe. However, although the 1989 novel ends with the deportation of the protagonist/narrator from Vienna to Cairo, the present 2001 work features one night in Cairo in contemporary Egypt of the early eighties—hence the title of the novella—in the life of the protagonist who is now a mature Cairo resident with a family.

One Night in Cairo is in a way a retake of some of the themes encountered in Elkhadem's earlier work dealt with in this chapter. In this novel the narrator/artist is once more struggling with the idea of a topic and a working plot for a new novel. He is on deadline and he is supposed to submit an installment to the journal he writes for. Throughout the narrative, which is interspersed with several long footnotes (a few pages each) that constitute stories nested within the larger frame of a story itself multidimensional, we are presented with the topics our narrator/writer dallies with. In the words of a critic: "he is at once the 'artist-hero' and the artist as his own subject."[67] Even though the narrator is again an antihero who is suffocating in the not-so-loved city of his birth, he presents the facts in an objective tone far removed from any hint of judgment. Writes a critic:

> Saad Elkhadem writes as a realist and does not yield to the pious moralizing, gushing sentimentality, and melodrama that often afflict writers depicting a "tormented heart" or a "soul on fire." The fictional form Elkhadem constructs

in *One Night in Cairo* attracts and focuses the reader's imagination on the narrator and his plight. He has succeeded in presenting us with a work that delightfully and sensitively describes the creative process at work and the problems the novelist faces.[68]

The subject matters the narrator/writer considers include but are not limited to stories of Egyptian students abroad: "I may write a collection of short stories that revolve around those lost souls. What they went through in Europe will be the common denominator."[69] Thus the reader is told of Husni, the young peasant who went with his young wife to London where he became a famous gambler while his wife, whom he eventually divorced, ended up marrying a Pakistani student and then disappeared. There is also Shawqi who quit his job at the ministry of education and went abroad to do his Ph.D., marrying a pregnant English girl with whom he immigrates to Brazil to flee the opprobrium of his peers.

Throughout this rambling narrative with shifting points of view, from the first to the second to the third and back, there emerges, like a recurring leitmotiv, a piercing note, one that tells of Karen, the girl the antihero met abroad in his student days and who committed suicide when she discovered that he was leaving her (he would have been accused of murder had it not been for the testimonial of a friend). The entire European experience is set against that sacred memory of the one aborted love of his, the truest in his life. Thus, he qualifies his European sojourn in the following terms:

> Bleak days full of fraud, trickery, and deceit. Although I yearn for them from time to time. Not really! Karen is the only one who forces me to live in the past, and to remember days I am intently trying to erase from my memory.[70]

This recurring Karen motif is reminiscent of Beckett's dramatic monologue, *Krapp's Last Tape*. I am referring to the boat scene between Bianca and Krapp, who, much like our protagonist of *One Night in Cairo* with Karen, has forsaken his only true chance at love to pursue instead empty dreams and to become a lonely embittered old man. Like Beckett, Elkhadem uses his art to evoke the time-cursed pathos of human existence. Throughout the novel, the shadow of death is looming as the narrator complains of chest pains that may kill him before he has time to write his story about Karen, "a story of passion and betrayal, of devotion and deceit."[71] In fact, the novel ends with our protagonist in a drunken stupor in a Cairo bar, postponing the moment of returning home to his nagging wife. He fantasizes about his own death and he imagines his funeral attended by a dead Karen who laughs at jokes his father is making.

The footnotes that give the novel its subtitle are themselves long, self-contained narratives in their own right, each outlining a possible plot, and each based on a true story from the protagonist's childhood and youth. They all have in common a documentary realist style; they describe a specific incident, and, without any nostalgia, they bear witness to times bygone. As such, they shed light on the making of a novel insofar as they suggest that a writer's themes and subject matters will best be drawn from a pool of past biographical experience. Thus we have the story of "Sayyid Al-Tumatiki," the Cairo young man who, out of dire need and desperation, takes a self-created job underneath the disk of a merry-go-round, moving it up and down, emulating an "automatic" mechanism (hence his moniker *Tumatiki*, a colloquial Arabic deformation of the word *automatic*) until he is crushed to death one day when the disk collapses on him; "Dr. Simon," the story of the Paris drunk and trickster who would go from bar to bar, freeloading on drinks at the expense of lonely, suffering souls whom he would console by telling tall tales full of miseries from his own life; "Torpedo," the story of the cowardly Cairo merchant with the scary eyebrows, huge stature, and heavy mustache, who loses his power of speech one day during a raid, presumably during World War II, shaking and crying with fear, and refusing to leave the safety of the shelter to rescue his son trapped in the family store in front of which an unexploded torpedo had just fallen (hence his nickname "torpedo" thereafter); "Stupid," the story of a simpleton who would not be called "stupid" and who physically assaults whoever called him so, causing the poor fellow to go to jail four consecutive times, and "Accident," the story of an accident witnessed by the protagonist when he was eleven years old (around 1952) and featuring a man who sees his young son hit by a car and killed and who, with great dignity and compassion, refuses to express anger at the driver who ran his son over, pleading instead with the angry crowd to stop assaulting the driver, kindly bidding the latter to wait for the police in the safety of his car:

> The man we took for a physician or a male nurse looked at Amm Hysayn, then gave him his back and took off his coat. We all expected a bloody fight, but the man knelt beside the child, folded his jacket, put it under the boy's head, then stood up and asked the people standing around: "did anyone call the police?"
> But Amm Hysayn ... was the first to talk: "I said, what business is it of yours? Did anyone call for your help, mister respected physician? Or have you appointed yourself custodian of this neighborhood?"
> Without looking at Amm Hysayn's face, the man said in a very soft and calm voice: "I am the father of this poor child. May God have mercy on his soul."[72]

In the end, none of those footnotes make it in to the main text, a point worth mulling over in light of the fact that the narrator/artist/protagonist punctuates his entire narrative with reflections on the novel as a genre and the literary devices he finds useful. Wherein lies the failure of the writer to secure satisfactory topics? Perhaps the ultimate suggestion here is that the only valid remaining topics to broach must be fragments and snatches lifted more or less faithfully from slices of a writer's life, whether or not he or she is the main actor in those "slices." The following transparent remarks will delineate the essence of the metafictional nature of *One Night in Cairo*:

> From its inception, the novel has always relied on love and adventures, This is what I learned at the university. And this is what I have never done in my stories till now.[73]
>
> The novel is the literary genre closest to the masses. That is why it should remain simple and exciting. Literature for popular consumption.[74]
>
> I will narrate a genuine experience, and deal with something I know extremely well. And to add to that a style which reflects all kinds of experimentation. Successive, superimposed images, thoughts that flow with the stream of consciousness, impressions that rush like a torrential current.[75]
>
> Would I ever be able to write an imperishable work? Literary immortality is a commercial idiom that benefits no one but publishers.[76]

In light of Elkhadem's preoccupation with form and literary techniques, the above comments, set against the reoccurring self-reflexive themes of the antihero/writer of the *Trilogy of the Flying Egyptian* studied above, provide continuity in the type of characters featured in Elkhadem's works, characters who, when dealing with their native country (to borrow the words of the antihero of *One Night in Cairo*) attempt "to defeat the feeling of isolation," which overwhelms them "in a country that had become alien to [them]."[77]

ON SAAD ELKHADEM'S EXPERIMENTAL LEGACY

The vision of the native land from the vantage point of exile, the recurring themes in patterns of binary oppositions, the linguistic experimentations in the form of fragments, mute dialogues and abrupt time-shifts, the use of situational irony, and sudden changes in points of view, those are features of Elkhadem's writings shared by a number of contemporary exilic writers. In fact, as with many of the writings of his counterparts, Elkhadem's works are neither short stories, nor novellas, novels, diaries, or biographies per se.

They lie somewhere between novels and novellas in length and they are hybrid reconstructions and deconstructions of elements of each.[78] As his translator has eloquently put it in the introduction to *The Ulysses Trilogy*: "It seems that emotional and geographical distance from his homeland has liberated Elkhadem as a writer-in-exile, giving him a special vantage point from which to observe his past and reshape it into fiction."[79]

To conclude, the overall effect of Elkhadem's works is that of self-reflexive hybrids of biography and fiction, open-ended and unfinished. His metafictional writings are endowed with an unsettling, estranging, and oppositional tone. Furthermore, the writer's use of situational irony, crude language, and internal monologues, accompanied with sudden shifts in points of view and linguistic registers, is quite dazzling. This is what his translator, Saad El-Gabalawy, was referring to when he asserted: "With his strong emphasis on flux and process [Saad Elkhadem] can aptly be described as a 'shape shifter' who designs a wonderfully complex pattern: a tale within a tale within a tale."[80] Perhaps it is worth pointing out that the notions of extraterritoriality and estrangement shown in Elkhadem's work analyzed above are further exacerbated by the fact that some of the characters portrayed belong to ethnic minorities in their country of origin. Before their displacement to their new adoptive country, they had already experienced a sort of mental exile in their own native land: "We are, if you will pardon the phrase, foreigners in any godforsaken place! foreigners here, foreigners there, foreigners everywhere!" will painfully remark an Egyptian-Canadian of Greek descent in the *Chronicle of the Flying Egyptian*.[81]

However, as with a number of writers in the diaspora, it seems that the space carved by writing is space that can be inhabited, one's true home, even if it is a space punctuated with continuous motion. This assertion certainly applies to Saad Elkhadem himself as well as to the writer-protagonist portrayed in *Chronicle of the Flying Egyptian in Canada*, who, upon commenting on his own mission as an experimental, avant-garde author, vehemently asserts: "the true artist . . . lives in absolute freedom, constant motion, and perpetual experimentation."[82] That statement could well be said to sum up the legacy of Saad Elkhadem as an exilic writer in Canada.

NOTES

1. A shorter version of this chapter was published in *Canadian Ethnic Studies* (38.2 (2006): 72–85) under the title, "Poetics of Exile and Dislocation in Saad Elkhadem's *Wings of Lead* (1971), *The Plague* (1989), and *Trilogy of the Flying Egyptian* (1990–1992)."

2. Anonymous, "In Memoriam: Saad E. A. Elkhadem: 1932–2003," *The International Fiction Review* (January 2004), no page. Since Elkhadem's retirement in 1995–1996, Chris Lorey, Professor of Culture and Language at the University of New Brunswick, has been editor of *The International Fiction Review*.

3. Appeared in Arabic in the collection of short stories entitled *Rijâl wa Khanâzîr* (Men and Pigs), Cairo: Matba'it al-Dâr al-Misriyyah, 1967. Translated into English in 1977. Likewise, *Ajnihah min Rasâs* first appeared in Arabic in 1971 and then in English in 1994.

4. A. F. Cassis, "Saad Elkhadem: One Night in Cairo" (book review), *The International Fiction Review* 29 (January 2002): 97–98, 98.

5. Anonymous, "In Memoriam: Saad E. A. Elkhadem: 1932–2003," *The International Fiction Review* (January 2004), no page.

6. Saad El-Gabalawy, "Introduction," *Canadian Adventures of the Flying Egyptian* (Fredericton: York Press, 1990): 3–8, 8.

7. Saad Elkhadem, *Wings of Lead: A Modern Egyptian Novella* (Fredericton: York Press, 1994), 14.

8. Elkhadem, *Wings of Lead*, 16.

9. Elkhadem, *Wings of Lead*, 3.

10. Elkhadem, *Wings of Lead*, 9.

11. Saad El-Gabalawy, "Introduction," *Modern Egyptian Short Stories* (Fredericton: York Press, 1977): 5–11, 10.

12. Elkhadem, *Wings of Lead*, 4.

13. Saad Elkhadem, *Crash Landing of the Flying Egyptian* (Fredericton: York Press, 1992), 6.

14. Elkhadem, *Wings of Lead*, 3.

15. Elkhadem, *Wings of Lead*, 1.

16. Elkhadem, *Wings of Lead*, 19.

17. Saad El-Gabalawy, "Introduction," *Modern Egyptian Short Stories* (Fredericton: York Press, 1977): 5–11, 10.

18. Saad El-Gabalawy, "Introduction," *The Plague* (Fredericton: York Press, 1989): 3–6: 6.

19. Saad Elkhadem, *The Plague* (Fredericton: York Press, 1989), 31–32.

20. In the words of El-Gabalawy on the chorus: "The prophetic voice of the chorus amplifies the time of the novella into wide-ranging geographical and emotional voyages, transporting the reader to such remote places as Montreal, Philadelphia, Hollywood, Detroit, London, Paris, Hamburg, Mecca, and Indonesia. Whereas some of the characters will realize their dreams in the most unpredictable of ways, others will be lifted up only to be dashed down," Saad El-Gabalawy, "Introduction," *The Plague* (Fredericton, New Brunswick: York Press Ltd., 1989): 3–6, 5.

21. Elkhadem, *The Plague*, 11.

22. Saad El-Gabalawy, "Introduction," *The Plague* (Fredericton: York Press, 1989): 3–6, 5.

23. Nieves Paradela, "Arabic Literature in Exile: *The Plague* by Saad Elkhadem," *The International Fiction Review* 22 (1995): 47–53, 50.

24. Elkhadem, *The Plague*, 29.

25. Elkhadem, *The Plague*, 18.

26. Saad El-Gabalawy, "Introduction," *The Plague* (Fredericton: York Press, 1989): 3–6, 3.
27. Elkhadem, *The Plague*, 29.
28. Elkhadem, *The Plague*, 25.
29. Elkhadem, *The Plague*, 25.
30. Elkhadem, *The Plague*, 15.
31. Nieves Paradela, "Arabic Literature in Exile: *The Plague* by Saad Elkhadem," *The International Fiction Review* 22 (1995): 47–53, 50.
32. Saad El-Gabalawy writes: "It is most appropriate that the novella should end with the portrait of . . . the commander of the military prison. . . . Pathologically sadistic and venomous, he epitomizes the evil of the Revolution, lashing out in fury at its enemies, real or imagined," *The Plague*, Introduction, 6.
33. Elkhadem, *The Plague*, 34.
34. Elkhadem, *The Plague*, 3.
35. Janeen Werner-King, "Review of *The Plague* by Saad Elkhadem," *The International Fiction Review* 16.2 (1989): 154–156, 155.
36. Joshua S. Mostow, "Complex Art of the Mosaic: Saad Elkhadem, *Canadian Adventures of the Flying Egyptian*," *Canadian Literature* 132 (1992): 174–176, 175. The expression "the complex art of the mosaic" occurs in Elkhadem's *Canadian Adventures of the Flying Egyptian*, 18.
37. Elkhadem, *Canadian Adventures of the Flying Egyptian*, 35.
38. Elkhadem, *Canadian Adventures of the Flying Egyptian*, 9.
39. Elkhadem, *Canadian Adventures of the Flying Egyptian*, 22.
40. Elkhadem, *Canadian Adventures of the Flying Egyptian*, 24.
41. Edward Said, "Intellectual Exile: Expatriates and Marginals," *Representations of the Intellectual: The Reith Lectures* (New York: Vintage Books, 1996): 47–64, 60.
42. Elkhadem, *Canadian Adventures of the Flying Egyptian*, 24.
43. Elkhadem, *Canadian Adventures of the Flying Egyptian*, 3.
44. Saad Elkhadem, *Chronicle of the Flying Egyptian in Canada* (Fredericton: York Press, 1991): 9.
45. Elkhadem, *Chronicle of the Flying Egyptian in Canada*, 26.
46. Elkhadem, *Chronicle of the Flying Egyptian in Canada*, 26.
47. Saad Elkhadem, *Crash Landing of the Flying Egyptian* (Fredericton: York Press, 1992): 27.
48. Elkhadem, *Chronicle of the Flying Egyptian in Canada*, 16.
49. Elkhadem, *Chronicle of the Flying Egyptian in Canada*, 112.
50. Elkhadem, *Chronicle of the Flying Egyptian in Canada*, 13.
51. Elkhadem, *Canadian Adventures of the Flying Egyptian*, 14.
52. Elkhadem, *Canadian Adventures of the Flying Egyptian*, 14.
53. Elkhadem, *Crash Landing of the Flying Egyptian*, 14.
54. Elkhadem, *Crash Landing of the Flying Egyptian*, 9. The use of Arabic is reflected upon by the narrator also in a more positive context, as in the following statement when he is speaking to himself: "Look, Brother, if you want to write realistic and unaffected literature, actually expressing what people think, feel, and say, then you must use the same idiom adopted by the majority of the people, even if the style is weak, or improper, or ungrammatical" (*Crash Landing*, 18).
55. Elkhadem, *Crash Landing of the Flying Egyptian*, 12.

56. Elkhadem, *Crash Landing of the Flying Egyptian*, 8.
57. Elkhadem, *Crash Landing of the Flying Egyptian*, 5.
58. Elkhadem, *Crash Landing of the Flying Egyptian*, 7.
59. Elkhadem, *Crash Landing of the Flying Egyptian*, 7.
60. Elkhadem, *Crash Landing of the Flying Egyptian*, 12.
61. Elkhadem, *Canadian Adventures of the Flying Egyptian*, 35.
62. Elkhadem, *Crash Landing of the Flying Egyptian*, 15.
63. Elkhadem, *Crash Landing of the Flying Egyptian*, 29.
64. Roger Allen, "Review of *Canadian Adventures of the Flying Egyptian*, by Saad Elkhadem," *World Literature Today* 65.2 (Spring 1991): 356–357, 357.
65. Amy Kaminsky, *Reading the Body Politic: Feminist Criticism and Latin American Women Writers* (Minneapolis: University of Minnesota Press, 1993): 58.
66. Saad Elkhadem, *One Night in Cairo* (Fredericton: York Press, 2001): 11
67. A. F. Cassis, "*One Night in Cairo* by Saad Elkhadem," Book Review, *The International Fiction Review* 29 (2002): 97–98, 97.
68. A. F. Cassis, "*One Night in Cairo* by Saad Elkhadem," Book Review, *The International Fiction Review* 29 (2002): 97–98, 98.
69. Elkhadem, *One Night in Cairo*, 10.
70. Elkhadem, *One Night in Cairo*, 14.
71. Elkhadem, *One Night in Cairo*, 37.
72. Elkhadem, *One Night in Cairo*, 21.
73. Elkhadem, *One Night in Cairo*, 8.
74. Elkhadem, *One Night in Cairo*, 8.
75. Elkhadem, *One Night in Cairo*, 3.
76. Elkhadem, *One Night in Cairo*, 23.
77. Elkhadem, *One Night in Cairo*, 11.
78. "There is an ironic intent behind this compacting of experience," Smaro Kamboureli, *Making a Difference: Canadian Multicultural Literature* (Toronto: Oxford University Press, 1996): 95.
79. Saad El-Gabalawy, "Introduction," *The Ulysses Trilogy* (Fredericton: York Press, 1988): 1–9, 2.
80. Saad El-Gabalawy, "Introduction," *Canadian Adventures of the Flying Egyptian* (Fredericton: York Press, 1990): 3–8, 3.
81. Elkhadem, *Chronicle of the Flying Egyptian in Canada*, 16.
82. Elkhadem, *Chronicle of the Flying Egyptian in Canada*, 26.

3

+

From Baghdad to Montréal via Paris: Naïm Kattan and His Multiple Reality[1]

Je n'accepte pas la fixité des lieux sûrs et le confort des certitudes
[I do not accept the fixity of safe places or the comfort of certitudes].

Naïm Kattan (*Le Réel et le théâtral*, 188, 142)

Nomade, toute la terre m'appartient
[Nomad, the whole earth belongs to me].

Naïm Kattan (*La Mémoire et la promesse*, 15)

La proximité de Naïm Kattan fait en sorte que son oevre est souvent décrite comme l'un des témoignages les plus représentatifs de l'écriture migrante au Québec
[The proxinity of Naïm Kattan is such that his oeuvre is often described as one of the most representative testimonials of migrant writing in Québec].

Jacques Allard (*Les Passsages obligés de l'écriture migrante*, 128)

KATTAN AND HIS OEUVRE

Naïm Kattan (1928–) grew up in Baghdad, where he was born to a middle class Jewish household. In 1947, he went to Paris on a scholarship, to study literature, and a few years later, in 1954, he moved to Canada where he still lives and where he became active in publishing and editing, founding the first Montréal Jewish newsletter in French, and contributing literary criticism in such newspapers as *La Quinzaine Littéraire*, *Critique*, and especially the daily *Le Devoir* (from 1962 to the present). He held a key position in the Canada Council for twenty-four years (1967–1991), promoting the development of a Canadian literature and being dubbed "la fée des bourses à Ottawa [the grant fairy of Ottawa]."[2] Over the last thirty-six years, he has produced a total of thirty-four novels, essays (reflective rather than formal), and collections of short stories, a vast body of works for which he was awarded the *Prix Athanase David* (2004) considered one of the highest honors belonging to the very prestigious *Prix du Québec* series. Kattan is the first Arabic-Canadian writer to receive this honor granted to such famous Québécois figures as Anne Hébert (1978), Jacques Godbout (1985), Michel Tremblay (1988), Nicole Brossard (1991), and recently, the celebrated Québécois critic, Pierre Nepveu (2005). Naïm Kattan is also the recipient of such Honors as the Order of Canada (1983) and the French Legion of Honor (2002). Furthermore, in 2005, he received the annual prize of *francophonie* from the Centre International d'Etudes francophones (CIEF). In 1990, he was made Knight of the National Order of Québec. He is Associate Professor at the Department of Literary Studies (*Département d'études littéraires*) at the University of Québec in Montréal (UQAM), and he was awarded three honorary doctorates, in Canada (Concordia University, Montréal, 2006), Serbia (University of Novi Sad University, Vojvodina, 2004), and in the United States (Middlebury College, Vermont, 2003) where, on this occasion, a week-long conference was held on the writer's work. Moreover, in 2007, Kattan was the first writer to receive the newly founded *Grand prix Hervé Deluen Grand Prize* awarded by the French Academy "to reward every year an individual or an institution efficiently contributing to the defense and the promotion of French as an international language."[3]

Naïm Kattan's very first book, an essay entitled *Le Réel et le théâtral*, was published in Montréal in 1970, then in Paris the following year, and soon after in 1972, in Toronto, in an English translation. This work has the double merit of having been awarded the prestigious *Prix France-Canada* (1971), and providing the first landmark of Arabic-Canadian literature as a distinct body of writing. It was soon to be followed in the seventies by the first two volumes of his transcontinental trilogy, namely *Adieu, Babylone* in 1975 and two years later, *Les Fruits arrachés* (with the third volume, *La Fiancée promise*, appearing in 1983); four collections of short stories, *Dans le désert* (1974), *La Traversée* (1976), *Le Rivage* (1979), and *Le Sable de l'île* (1979), and an essay, *La Mémoire et la promesse* (1978), making of Kattan one of the most prolific writers of Arabic origins in Québec at the time. Kattan's output steadily continued in all three genres (essay, short-story, novel) throughout the eighties and nineties, with titles such as *La Réconciliation* (1993) and *La Célébration* (1997), and up to the twenty-first century, with his latest novel, *Le Gardien de mon frère*, appearing in Montréal in 2003 and in France shortly after (2005). Both this novel and its predecessor, *L'Anniversaire* (2000), which was hailed in 2007 as one of the finest novels in *francophonie*,[4] partake in a new structural form, unique in Kattan's work, as will be shown below. Kattan's one but latest collection of short stories, *Je regarde les femmes*, was published in 2005 in Montréal. It was followed in 2006 by another collection entitled *Châteaux en Espagne*. Kattan's style is typically very transparent, simple, with little imagery, and in general, it obeys what Barthes has called the zero degree of writing, *le degré zéro de l'écriture*,[5] i.e., the neutral, blank style that came to be associated with the writings of Camus. It is a style that betrays and conveys a sense of absence as will be discussed in this chapter.

In 1977, a Canadian book reviewer described Kattan's first novel, *Adieu, Babylone*, as "a portrait of the Artist as a Young Iraqi Jew Trying to be French,"[6] while the year before another critic titled his review, "Why an Arabic-speaking, Baghdad Born Jew Is a Perfect Guide to the Modern Canadian Experience."[7] Notwithstanding the potentially ironic tone inherent in such characterizations, those do convey, nevertheless, a portrayal of Kattan with regard to the multiplicity of his cultural, linguistic, and ethnic make-up, a multiplicity that affixes its indelible stamp on the vast body of works he has produced from 1971 to the present.

In an article partially entitled "Iraquébec" on Naïm Kattan, Michael Greenstein has aptly advanced that "in order to accommodate boundaries, borders, and the homelessness of Diaspora," it would be useful to borrow the notion of "trans-mimesis" or "the representation of more than one reality in transcultural societies" when studying Québécois migrant literature in general and Kattan's world of fiction in particular.[8] Moreover, a recent study on "the obligatory passages of migrant literatures" (*Les Passages obligés de l'écriture migrante*) by a Québécois critic qualified Kattan's abundant literary production as one of the most representative of "migrant literature" in contemporary Québec.[9] Moreover, Kattan's lifelong production was celebrated in 2002 in a collection of essays and interviews edited by an influential Québécois critic (Jacques Allard) under the title *L'Ecrivain du passage* (The Writer of the Crossing) and, as recently as 2005 appeared another token of recognition, namely a substantial volume of interviews recounting Naïm Kattan's intellectual trajectory conducted by Sophie Jama, entitled *Les Temps du nomade: Itinéraire d'un écrivain* [The Times of the Nomad: Itinerary of a Writer].

In light of the aforementioned comments, the aim of the present chapter is as follows: The first part consists of a study of Kattan's transcontinental trilogy, highlighting its leitmotifs, narrative style, and especially the sociohistorical conditions it reflects, with *Adieu, Babylone*, undoubtedly the richest of the trilogy, receiving particular attention. I will then study two of Kattan's latest novels, namely, *L'Anniversaire* (2000) and *Le Gardien de mon frère* (2003) followed by two collections of short stories, an earlier one, *La Reprise* (1985), then a recent title, *Je regarde les femmes* (2005), none of which have been translated to date. Having done so, this chapter will move on to tie the themes of exile and expatriation as reflected in Naïm Kattan's fiction, notably in the trilogy, to the writer's own professed views pertaining to the passage of his multiple being across various nations, as transpired in interviews he gave, as well as in his very first essay, *Le Réel et le théâtral* (recipient of Prix France-Canada in 1971), itself a landmark in Arabic-Canadian literature.[10]

TRILOGY: *ADIEU, BABYLONE* (1975), *LES FRUITS ARRACHÉS* (1977), *LA FIANCÉE PROMISE* (1983)

It is noteworthy that, of the handful of translated works of Kattan's voluminous production, two belong *precisely* to this semiautobiographical, par excellence transcultural, transnational trilogy. *Adieu, Babylone*, first published in French in 1975, appeared in 1976[11] in an English translation, which went out of print soon after, whereas its French counterpart remained available. In 2005, a new English edition saw the light of day in the Canadian West, this time with an added subtitle, *Coming of Age in Jewish Baghdad* (translated by Sheila Fischman) and in November 2007, a small publisher in Boston reissued the book, with a new preface by the author.[12] The second volume of the trilogy, *Les Fruits arrachés*, was translated in 1979 under the title *Paris Interlude*,[13] while the third volume, *La Fiancée promise* (The Promised Bride), has yet to be translated into English.

The trilogy as a whole mirrors perfectly well the author's personal trajectory: The first volume is an account of a twelve-year-old boy growing up in Baghdad between 1940 and 1947 as part of the Jewish community that constituted roughly 30 percent of the total population (approximately 700,000 in 1947). The second volume of the trilogy sees the protagonist-narrator, Meir—he is never named in the first volume—in Paris, studying at the Sorbonne and undergoing his sentimental education, while the third volume is about Meir's 1954 immigration to Canada, where he settles and works in Ottawa and in Montréal.

Since *Adieu, Babylone* is not only the first volume of the trilogy but also the author's very first novel written after fifteen years of silence, it constitutes a landmark that inscribes the beginnings, intentions, method, and the life-long project of Kattan-the-novelist. An eminent Québécois critic has qualified it as "one of the most beautiful autobiographical works of contemporary Québécois literature,"[14] while a 2005 Montréal reviewer, alluding to current events, has written, "If anything, the book is more important now than it was then."[15] Moreover, a Canadian critic, echoing the new subtitle added to the 2005 edition (*Coming of Age in Jewish Baghdad*), asserts in *Quill and Quire*, that in this novel "Baghdad is realized as a whole world, not the simplistic, military theater it has become."[16]

ADIEU, BABYLONE (1975): *FAREWELL, BABYLON* (2005)

Throughout this first in line of the trilogy, a novel where narration abounds and where dialogues are relatively scarce, a fact the author himself recognizes,[17] the reader encounters an array of scenes that make up the fabric of the narrator's adolescence: scenes of domestic life and friendships, discussions on art and the future of the nation, menial bureaucratic jobs, school excursions to Babylon, swimming in the Tigris, night picnics of grilled fish on an island, "fleeting, isolated pleasures that did not make up for our painful need for woman."[18] In fact, a major theme in this first volume of the trilogy speaks of the torturous pangs of desire and the dictates of a conservative society where women are either veiled or altogether invisible. There are descriptions of the protagonist's first sexual experiences in the brothels of the red light district of Baghdad where dwelled the antithetical, bold woman: "Nous passions de la femme voilée à la femme nue, sans transition" [we went from the veiled woman to the naked woman without transition],[19] says the narrator.

The reader also witnesses the protagonist's pride in his Judeo-Islamic heritage, his conviction of his predestination as a writer, and his literary debut. There are statements revealing his ardent love of Arabic literature and language, which he mastered better than most of his Moslem peers, a love that did not abate even after he was about to go to France: "My passion for our own literature, rather than being weakened at the prospect of leaving, was rekindled."[20] There are pages disclosing his strong *francophilie* and his discovery of French literature through his French teachers at the Alliance Israélite school; his enthusiasm for Péguy, Rolland, Aragon, and Gide—with Gide's epiphanic injunction, "Pars! Quitte ta famille. Va ailleurs. Sois libre. Ta vie t'appartient" [Travel. Leave your family. Go elsewhere. Be free. Your life belongs to you].[21]—and his strong desire to go to France—"My chosen country, which would satisfy all my desires, quench my insatiable thirst"[22]—where everything good seemed to be happening: "We lived in the unformed, in the pain of gestation and the delight promised by life," the narrator asserts about himself and his close friends.[23]

Why not *Farewell, Baghdad* instead of *Farewell, Babylon* as a title for the first volume of the trilogy? When asked about this in a 1985 interview by Allard, Kattan is very clear: "Ce n'était pas *Adieu, Bagdad* parce que Bagdad continue, l'Irak continue. Mais Babylone ... est terminé" [It was not

Farewell, Baghdad because Baghdad continues, Irak continues. But Babylon has ended].[24]

The novel also tells the story of the end of a Jewish community in Baghdad, a community that began some 2,500 years ago when Nebuchadnezzar brought Jewish prisoners from Jerusalem. When given the choice of return a few generations later, their descendants opted instead to stay in Babylon. They came to be known as the Babylonian Jews, contributing to world Judaism by writing the Talmud and enduring the test of time all the way up to postwar Iraq, a country in which they had been active and well-integrated citizens living alongside other ethnic and religious communities, such as Kurds, Armenians, Assyrians, Chaldeans, as well as Shia and Sunni Moslems.

The opening scene of *Farewell, Babylon* takes place during the Second World War, in a Baghdad café, where the protagonist and his Jewish friend Nessim are discussing the future of Iraqi literature with a group of mostly Moslem friends:

> *Dans notre groupe, nous n'étions ni Juifs, ni Musulmans. Nous étions Irakiens, soucieux de l'avenir de notre pays, par conséquent de notre avenir à chacun de nous. Sauf que les Musulmans se sentaient plus Irakiens que les autres.*[25]

> [In our group we were neither Jew nor Muslim. We were Iraqis, concerned about the future of our country and consequently the future of each one of us. Except that the Muslims felt more Iraqi than the others.][26]

Everybody spoke Arabic but with varying accents and vocabulary. Nessim made a statement that night by insisting on using the Jewish dialect (full of Hebraic and Persian words), commonly a source of mirth and mockery in the ambient Moslem community. The narrator challenged his friend's audacity by speaking literary (Koranic) Arabic (used in books, in formal occasions, and in news reports). The Moslem friends who spoke the Iraqi-Arabic dialect ended up paying attention to Nessim and even emulating his language, with not a trace of derision, and the narrator triumphantly comments:

> *A la fin de la soirée, la partie était gagnée. Pour la première fois, des Musulmans nous écoutaient avec respect. . . . Nous sommes là dans notre lumineuse et fragile différence. Et ce n'était ni signe d'humiliation ni symbole de ridicule.*[27]

> [By the end of the evening, we had won the game. For the first time the Muslims were listening to us with respect. . . . We stood there in our luminous and fragile difference. And it was neither a sign of humiliation nor a symbol of ridicule.][28]

The "luminous and fragile difference" speaks of the internal exile the narrator and his Jewish friends were born to and under the mark of which the whole book unfolds. Schooled mainly in Hebrew and Arabic at the Alliance Israélite Universelle School in Baghdad (tied to France), the adolescent protagonist, unlike his Jewish peers who went to the Shamach school (tied to Britain), later on opted for a Muslim high school, insisting on using Arabic as the language of study and literary expression, one he had a passion for and in which he excelled, but one he had to speak differently in order to be accepted, an endeavor he did not always achieve. In the words of Rahimieh, "For the protagonist as for the young Kattan, the most conventional form of speech becomes a mark of internal exile,"[29] a fact further emphasized, as the critic points out, by mastering *Suki*, Arabic written with the Hebrew alphabet, a transposition in which the protagonist excelled. That skill was applied in the job the latter held when still under age, a job that consisted of deciphering *Suki* documents for Muslim officials granting commercial permits to Jewish merchants. Thus *Suki* becomes the emptied-shell-language and the symbol of absence par excellence.

Despite occasional interethnic conflicts, unlike Western Jews (inhabitants of *shtetels*) Baghdad Jews had always been well integrated and constituted "the backbone and sinews of the Iraqi state."[30] In a country where illiteracy rates were very high, the Jewish community was literate, versed in foreign languages, especially English (best taught in Jewish schools), and was respected by Moslems who, considering Jews "people of the book,"[31] never tried to convert them. When the British marched on Baghdad in 1917 to break down the Ottoman stronghold, Jews were called upon as interpreters, and with the subsequent establishment of the Iraqi state, they held jobs in public (railways, post office, etc.) as well as private sectors, though they were not permitted to become army officers or diplomats.

The narrator describes how, throughout Baghdad, there were districts reserved to the various ethnic groups. People usually respected the "invisible boundaries" that "isolated each group within its neighborhood."[32] In a vivid passage of *Farewell, Babyon,* we are told how, having sprained his elbow as a young boy of eight, and after the Rabbi had nursed it and prayed over it in vain, the narrator's parents decided to take their child to a well-known Moslem healer, owner of a coffee shop. After having taken "every precaution to disguise [his] Jewish origin"[33] when dressing him for the occasion, father and son—the latter was very nervous—were getting ready "to cross the frontiers of [their] own country."[34] They walked through the Moslem neighborhoods uneventfully:

> Quelle ne fut ma surprise en faisant mon entrée dans ces ruelles étrangères, d'apercevoir des portes semblables aux nôtres, des fenêtres identiques à celles de nos maisons.[35]

[How surprised I was when I entered these foreign alleys to see doors that looked like ours, windows that were identical to those of our own houses.][36]

The kindly *Haj* who exercised his art pro bono, fixed the damaged elbow; father and son went their way unnoticed, much to the increased astonishment of the young child: "so we were not so different from the others after all," the narrator exclaims.[37]

Harmony failed to last, however. There had been a rising anti-Jewish sentiment in the thirties fueled by the pro-Nazi propaganda of Radio Berlin, which reached Baghdad through Bari, Italy. This sentiment culminated in early May of 1941 in an unfortunate incident, the *Farhoud*, when "thirteen centuries of shared life and neighborliness"[38] with Muslims "crumbled like a structure of mud and sand,"[39] leaving the Jews of Baghdad traumatized thereafter. At the time, a pro-Nazi nationalist government headed by Rachid Ali El Gaylani had taken over the country. That Iraqi government was allied with the Germans against the British who still held Iraq under mandate (Iraq had gained its independence in 1922). The struggle lasted over a month with the British army finally prevailing against Rachid Ali and his pro-Nazi insurgents; the ousted young king who had taken refuge in Iran was on his way back home to form a new government. Between the departure of one government and the return of another, however, there was a gap of two or three days during which the country was on its own. During this lapse of time, Bedouins marched on the city, armed with picks and daggers, to attack, kill, and steal. Their target was only Jews and the Jewish districts of town. The young protagonist describes in vivid terms his anguish and his fear of death—"I had barely glimpsed the richness of life and now it was going to be snatched away from me, forever"[40]—as the noise of shotguns was getting closer to his house throughout the night, suddenly stopping at dawn. His family made a narrow escape. The Iraqi army was back in town, repelling the attackers and protecting the Jewish population. We are also told how, during the *Farhoud*, Moslem neighbors defended, hid, and protected their Jewish countrymen against the attacks, often at great risk to themselves.

Even though order was restored and many belongings recovered, fear had indelibly left its mark on hearts and minds, and Jewish families started applying for passports, thinking of leaving the country. The situation steadily escalated in the following years and was to culminate in a crisis. Jews were often detained under charges of communism and/or Zionism. Import permits became very difficult for them to obtain, so was being allowed to leave the country. Hundreds were fleeing illegally to Teheran, then to Israel. Some remained in Iran. Crumbled were dreams of life in postwar Iraq and crumbled were the hopes for a world where, in the words of the young narrator: "Juifs, Musulmans, et Chrétiens vivront dans une éternelle euphorie, découvrant les joies d'une entente sans tache et d'une harmonie retrouvée"[41] [Jews, Moslems, Christians would live in an eternal euphoria, discovering the joys of a spotless rapport and of a new found harmony].[42]

In 1947, the narrator of *Farewell, Babylon* received a long-awaited scholarship to study at the Sorbonne, weeks before exit visas for Jews became hard to obtain. The last scene of the novel is a farewell scene, with his family (whom he would not meet again till 1952, in Israel) at a bus station, heading to Beirut by bus, then to Marseille by boat, never to return to Babylon:

> *Ces visages qui me regardent, qui s'éloignent, que je regarde à travers la fenêtre de l'autobus, ce sera l'irak. Tout ce qui me restera. Pourvu que je puisse en emporter à jamais, en moi le dernier reflet. Il le fallait. Ainsi mon enfance sera preservée, je ferai mon entrée dans le monde nouveau sans m'amputer d'une part privilégiée, sans disperser en pure perte ce monceau de rêves et de souvenirs.*[43]

[These faces looking at me, moving away from me, which I saw through the window of the bus—they were Iraq. All that remained of it for me. And I hoped I would be able to take away forever, within myself, its last reflection. It had to be so. In that way my childhood would be preserved. I would enter the new world without cutting off a privileged part of it, dispersing my dreams and memories.][44]

LES FRUITS ARRACHÉS (1977): *PARIS INTERLUDE* (1979)

The opening scene of *Paris Interlude* is a telephone conversation where the priest who shared the protagonist's cabin on the trip to France announces to him the creation of the state of Israel by the United Nations. The news does not cause the narrator any joy, for that meant the imminent compulsory departure of his family. In contradistinction to the first volume of the trilogy, this second one has a large number of dialogues and very few narrative descriptions, a fact recognized by Kattan himself. He explains that feature by pointing out that when he wrote this Parisian interlude, it was not Paris he wanted to describe, for that can be found in many books, but his first social encounters in the Western world, hence the importance of the dialogical exchange in the structure of this novel.[45]

Throughout this second volume of the trilogy, we witness Meir, the now-named protagonist of *Farewell, Babylon*, in his daily Parisian life, frequenting French literary circles, including Gide, Breton, and the surrealists; having a string of girlfriends from various European countries through whom he undergoes his apprenticeship as a newcomer to the idealized West; writing for Arabic-Iraqi newspapers under a French pseudonym, and going to Germany to purge the memory of the genocide in an attempt *to understand*, something he rightly refuses to achieve.

The main interest of this transitional volume that has not fared as well as its predecessor lies in the various comments and reflections found in it on the situation of postwar Iraqi Jews. Those Jews are indeed "the uprooted fruits," or *les fruits arrachés* the French title strongly evokes and the English one fails to transmit. The reader is informed that the news from home is bad. Meir's best friend Nessim has escaped from Iraq via Iran to Israel. His brother was arrested, and upon release from prison, he too went to Israel where he shared the fate of Sephardic Jews, looked down upon by the Ashkenazi Jews. The latter referred to their less fortunate counterparts, somewhat derisively, as "Babylonian Jews," as witnessed in the following letter addressed to Meir by his friend:

> En Irak, on ne voulait pas de nous. Nous étions juifs. Ici, on nous reproche d'être irakiens, arabes. Partout, on nous rejette. Personne ne veut de nous. Il ne nous reste que le fonds de l'océan. Même l'Hébreu . . . il faut le prononcer comme les Juifs de Pologne. Ils méprisent nos traditions, notre nourriture. Ils veulent nous civiliser, nous placer sur la voie du progrès.[46]

> [In Iraq we were not wanted. We were Jews. Here, we are blamed for being Iraqis. We are rejected everywhere. Nobody wants us. The bottom of the ocean is our last refuge. Even Hebrew we have to pronounce like the Jews of Poland. They despise our traditions, our food. They want to civilize us and to put us on the road to progress.][47]

As for Meir himself, he realizes that he cannot remain in Paris and that he has no future there. The Promised Land, once more, fails to prove to be the last landing place. He consequently decides to leave for the United States. His friend Nessim has sent him a ticket and some money from Iran. The last scene of the novel, as in *Farewell, Babylon*, is a departure scene. This time, however, no family or friends are bidding Meir farewell. He is alone at the harbor and no one, except Anne, his last Parisian girlfriend, knew about his sailing from Rotterdam to New York. Meir arrives there on a hot summer evening in 1949, with a stateless identity card, the renewal of his Iraqi passport having been denied.

This second volume of the trilogy, nested between life in Iraq in the thirties and forties and life in Canada in the fifties and thereafter, will function as a bridge and the axis upon which will be played the protagonist-narrator's transcontinental trip, toward the construction of a new national, literary, and personal identity.

LA FIANCÉE PROMISE (1983) [THE PROMISED BRIDE]

The third volume of the trilogy, La Fiancée promise, opens on a scene where Meir is on a train from Halifax to Montréal in the winter of 1954, with the total sum of a hundred dollars to begin his new life.⁴⁸ His obnoxious compartment companion is a Jew from Poland who promises to find him a fiancée, a relative of his in Toronto, hence the title of the book, The Promised Bride.⁴⁹ As plotless as Paris Interlude, this last volume of the trilogy portrays the protagonist's efforts to secure proper lodging and to find his place in the new society. More importantly, the narrative illustrates Meir's difficulties in finding employment. From interview to interview he wades, facing numerous disappointments, for his is a most unusual profile. He does not fit into any of the ambient ethnic and cultural moulds, and he finds himself, once more, out of place, an oddity-of-sorts, even within the local Iraqi community. For a time, he works for an Iraqi businessman (who does not sympathize with his intellectual and literary ambitions), selling wholesale, imported cloth. To add to Meir's alienation, Montréal Jews at the time were Anglophone Ashkenazi who spoke Yiddish, while he was a Sephardic Jew, Francophone, and he spoke Hebrew. His background, which he is called upon to explain and to justify time and again, disconcerts and intrigues prospective employers, including officers at the Jewish Employment Office, some of whom insist he should belong to a Christian parish since he spoke French!⁵⁰

In a first move toward the construction of an ethnic-religious identity, like Kattan himself, Meir ends up founding the first Jewish newsletter in French, Le Bulletin du cercle Juif, a successful endeavor and a door opener. As in his Paris Interlude, he has a number of amorous relationships that ease his initiation to the new country, with the last woman, Claudia, herself an immigrant, becoming the "fiancée promise," The Promised Bride. Like a musical leitmotiv, a major theme resurfaces in this last volume of the trilogy where, as in the previous volume, dialogues abound: The theme of the multiple identities to renegotiate and to repackage, in order to succeed and to assimilate in yet another new context. Thus at the end of Paris Interlude, before leaving Europe for America, when he was about to immigrate and to become uprooted once more, Meir exclaims: "J'avais déjà une double peau. Elle sera triple, infranchissable carapace"⁵¹ [I already had a double skin. It will soon become triple, impervious shell].⁵²

Meir's existential multiplicity is unfortunately accompanied by the perpetual need to justify his difference (the plight of every literate immigrant in search of a career) and to explain his trajectory, and by the continual necessity to account for his multiple personae, in order to avoid being looked upon with suspicion and mistrust. This is what he writes after a brief encounter with a priest, the brother of a girlfriend, who questions him about his background:

> *Encore des explications. Il fallait toujours que je me justifie. Pourquoi le Canada? Pourquoi pas la France? Pourquoi pas l'Irak? je tramai une biographie comme un vieux disque, j'étais un marchand ambulant et j'offrais à la criée mon passé.*
>
> [More explanations. I always had to justify myself. Why Canada? Why not France? Why not Iraq? I constructed and played my biography like an old record; I was like a street vendor crying out his past on the market place.]⁵³

In a touching passage at the closing of the novel, Meir will announce to Claudia his intention to seek another job altogether, one where his ethnic and religious affiliations would not be involved: "Je suis malheureux de faire de mes origines et de mes convictions une profession, une carrière"⁵⁴ [I am tired of making of my origins and my convictions a profession and a career]. Significant reflection on the part of the perpetual wanderer! The closing of this last volume of the trilogy epitomizes the figure of the promised bride—Claudia—and sets it as the symbol for the new, last landing place both Meir and Kattan found in Canada, where they were able to negotiate an identity that positively absorbs migrancy and nomadism.

L'ANNIVERSAIRE (2000) [THE BIRTHDAY]

Written two and a half decades after *Adieu Babylone*, *L'Anniversaire* (The Birthday) constitutes a perfect counterpoint to Kattan's first novel, and closes a cycle of identity quests culminating in the final grand statement where the protagonist declares his affiliation with "every man who refuses to die, to disappear without leaving a name."⁵⁵

As Allard has pertinently pointed out,⁵⁶ this novel tells the reader in an explicit manner that which minor writing does not commonly narrate, namely, how integration in Québec society can sometimes be accomplished. *L'Anniversaire* functions as an actualized counterpart to the abstract notion of cultural assimilation. With its bipolar structure and the themes it portrays (the truth behind human rapport, the meaning of success and failure, the interpenetration of the personal and the professional, the trials of assimilation, and the arduous road to reconciliation), this novel offers invaluable insights into the trajectory of the exilic intellectual in search of that which is forever lost to him: a homeland and a former, initial self. A Québécois critic has spoken of *L'Anniversaire* in the following laudatory terms:

> L'Anniversaire *se donne ainsi comme l'un des grands romans médidatifs que l'on voit paraître au Québec depuis un demi-siècle. C'est l'un des plus riches de la littérature contemporaine.*
>
> [L'*Anniveraire* comes forth as one of the main reflective novels published in Québec for the last fifty years. It is one of the richest novels of contemporary literature.][57]

The novel combines the epistolary and the diaristic forms. It consists of eleven pairs of entries written by René Shems, a history professor in Québec, on the aftermath of his seventieth birthday celebration hosted by his Québécois peers: Thus, there are eleven letters coupled with eleven diary entries or internal monologues. The letters are elaborate thank-you notes that purport to describe in eloquent terms the more or less significant role each of the addressees has played in Shems's life. The first of those letters is addressed to the colleague organizer, Maurice, and the other ten, in this order: To his estranged daughter (Deborah), to Adrien, his enemy-colleague; Diane, his first love; Jacques, a distant millionaire cousin who lost his fortune; Marianne, his ex-wife of twenty years; Nadine, his great (estranged) love and ex-graduate assistant; Dominique, a colleague writing an essay on him; Agnès, a young student-admirer; Jean-Marc, the publisher preparing a collected edition of his works, and finally, Renaud, his one and only true friend. The diary entry (written in italics) that follows each letter acts as an explicit subtext not intended for public consumption. It reflects on the true nature of Shems's feelings toward his correspondent, disclosing his innermost thoughts pertaining to each relationship, whether bygone or current. Those reflections act as "counterletters," to quote a term used by Kattan himself, or as darker doubles revealing to the reader that which is otherwise concealed behind the seemingly sincere and courteous tone of the social missives.[58]

As with the structure of Saad Elkahdem's *The Plague*, the reader gets the impression of a forked tongue mode of expression, one that reveals the existential duality inherent in every gesture one poses, every human rapport one has, and everything one appears to be or to do. To Jacques, Shems writes, for instance, "tu es certes mon cousin, le seul avec lequel j'ai un véritable rapport" [You are certainly my cousin, the only person I have a close rapport with],[59] yet his counterletter belies this statement: "*Je n'ai jamais compris la vraie nature de ma relation avec Jacques. Je le décris comme cousin et c'est une exagération*"[60] [*I have never understood the true nature of my relationship to Jacques. I describe him as cousin but it's an exaggeration*]. Likewise, "Mon cher Adrien" turns out to be the rival colleague, the "*young wolf*" of his early professional days[61] who would strive to debunk Shems's work, often successfully, for nobody would dare to disbelieve "*the genuine Canadian*" who tells the story of his worthy ancestors in favor of a mere Shems, a *"stranger,"* a *"parasite nobody had invited"* to study the history of the French Canadians.[62]

The first letter reveals the protagonist's childhood and origins: Jewish by birth, an only cherished child, he was born in Aleppo (Syria) where he spent the first years of his childhood; he later moved to Sao Paulo with his parents (his father, a Syrian Jew and his mother, of Turkish descent). A few years later, having failed in Brazil, the family moved to Brooklyn where it finally fared well. After studying at Brandeis and Yale, Shems decides to get a doctorate in history at Rochester and to do research, not on the Ottoman Empire, the subject of his master's thesis, nor the Bible or the USA, as either parent had hoped, but on the history of French Canada, precisely because he had no ties to that country.

Cut from his native city Aleppo by virtue of his religion, and deprived of the ties developed in Sao Paulo, his is the bitter cup of the thrice immigrant-exile, resentful of his parents for having "deprived him of his past"[63] and striving to conquer a future and a city to call his own, an endeavor he does accomplish in Montréal. In the monologue following the letter to his ex-lover Nadine, he exclaims:

> *N'avais-je pas été seul depuis ma naissance! Mes parents m'avaient interdit l'accès à la ville, que ce soit Alep ou Sao Paulo, j'avais dû me résoudre à inventer la mienne, Montréal.*

> [Was I not alone since birth? My parents had forbidden me access to the city, whether Aleppo or Sao Paulo, I had to resort to inventing my own, Montréal.][64]

Furthermore, he later reflects in his private commentary on the letter to his publisher: *"Montréal fut pour moi l'Alep qui ne fut pas, qui n'a pas eu lieu"* [Montréal was for me the Aleppo that has not been, that has not happened].[65]

Shems is the image of the perfectly assimilated, successful immigrant who finds a country to adopt and one that adopts him, but is he really at home there? He admits never having felt at ease "in this country whose history [he] chose as a daily, vital occupation,"[66] a choice taken perhaps as an escape route (*échappatoire*), one meant to conceal his profound *malaise*, uneasiness. This is what he writes in the counterletter to his ex-wife, Marianne:

> *Je m'identifiais à la recherche, non pas à l'histoire, mais à l'existence que je lui consacrais. J'étais devenu l'histoire du Canada et mon adhésion au pays était viscérale, une nécessité de subsistance. Il était facile de confondre ce processus avec celui d'une parfaite intégration, d'un amour inconditionnel du pays d'adoption.*

> [I identified with my research, not with history as such, but with the type of life I devoted to it. I had become the history of Canada and my connection to the country was visceral, a necessity of survival. It was easy to mix up that

process with that of a perfect integration and an unconditional love of the country of adoption.][67]

Shems's birthday celebration is heavily attended. But is he really loved? His letters to his daughter, his ex-wife, his female admirer, and his ex-love exude disappointment, a sense of betrayal, lack of communication and utter failure. "Et on appelle cela une vie réussie"[68] [and you call this is a successful life], he bitterly writes to his daughter Debbie whom he failed to recognize during the reception—he had not seen her for eight years—and to whom he confesses having channeled toward her all his love at the expense of her mother (his ex-wife), a fact that did not prevent him from losing the love of both mother and daughter alike: *"Je suis un être mutilé. Rien n'est plus horrible que de perdre un enfant qui est encore en vie"*[69] [I am a mutilated being; nothing is more horrible than losing a child who is still alive], he adds in the commentary following that letter.

His career is that of the eminent scholar-historian, esteemed and recognized by all on the most prestigious of all fronts, the intellectual one. Is he really successful and integrated in this regard, though? As a scholar, he considers himself merely an artisan, and yet he will secretly admit that all he was looking for in the study of French-Canadian history is his own history, that of his robbed past, heavy with losses. In a moving passage on the quest for immortality that drives dispossessed peoples who have nothing but a legend left to save, he confesses that the tale he has told all his life in his research was his very own: *"Je parle de ma vie. Je me raconte"*[70] [I speak of myself, I narrate myself].

Throughout the novel, we witness not only a duality of genres (the letters and the diary entries), but also a duality of discourse (the private versus the public), and a duality of modes of existence (the insider and the outsider/the Jew who is both Québécois and immigrant). *Palimpsest* is the word used by Greenstein to rightly qualify "the form of the text reflecting Shems's split consciousness and immigrant status."[71]

This sense of estrangement, of loss and alienation, coupled with the painful feeling of an absent or incomplete country, act as catalysts: having been robbed once and for all of the cities of his birth to which Jews were no longer allowed access, and that of his childhood from which he was uprooted, Alep and Sao Paulo respectively, Shems finally grafts his own history onto the history of the French-Canadians in their adamant attempts to survive as a distinct society, in opposition to the English-Canadian majority. For Shems, history has transcended and supplanted geography, and he has become one with his subject of study. The story he tells is now his very own. It is in this sense that he "had become the history of Canada" [J'étais devenu l'histoire du Canada] as is shown in the extract above from the monological reflection on the letter to his ex-wife.[72]

The coincidence of *the personal and the collective*, typical of migrant writing in Québec, as mentioned in the introduction to this work, is explicitly enmeshed in the fabric of this novel, making of its author a spokesman for his own community, and by extension for others as well. In the words of Greenstein: "Kattan's equation of immigrant and Québécois history runs throughout the novel to such an extent that the mystery of survival for Jews and French-Canadians becomes interchangeable."[73]

Against the fixity of national monologic identity that equates ethnicity with territory and identity with native land, perhaps *L'Anniversaire* can be said to be a novel of the eternal rebirth of the wanderer, the perpetual Exile. Like the phoenix who is reborn from its ashes, Shems, a name that means "sun" in Arabic, is reborn (*renaît*) in his adopted Québec. Kattan intentionally chose the homonym René as first name to Shems, to convey this idea of cyclical and luminous renewal,[74] an idea, as mentioned above, that reflects Kattan's notion of exile versus immigration: "Pour tout immigrant, changer de lieu, ce n'est pas s'exiler, c'est renaître" [For every immigrant, to change residence does not mean to go into exile, it is to be born anew],[75] a view that will become clear with the discussion of Kattan's 1971 essay, *Le Réel et le théâtral*.

LE GARDIEN DE MON FRÈRE (2003) [MY BROTHER'S KEEPER]

The binary structure of *L'Anniversaire* (the juxtaposition of letters and italicized reflections on the letters) is corroborated in Kattan's subsequent novel, the latest written to date, *Le Gardien de mon frère* (My Brother's Keeper), which also obeys a binary composition, albeit of a slightly different nature. The novel consists of a series of thirteen diary entries, each forming a chapter featuring, alternatingly, the voice of two brothers whose names provide the titles of the respective chapter entries.

The title of the book is obviously of biblical inspiration. It evokes Cain's statement when, in his rebellion and his jealousy of Abel, he exclaims rhetorically: "Am I my brother's keeper," and, indeed *Le Gardien de mon frère* is a tale of sibling rivalry transcended and conquered at the very end, at the father's deathbed.

Seven of the letters are from Gabriel whose entries begin and end this chronicle, which features reflections on the brother's mutual rivalry in relation to parental love and attention, careers, girlfriends, and, as the first entry tells us, a fight over inheritance. From the standpoints of each of the two siblings who respond to each other through the reader, we learn that "[their] parents did everything in their power to separate [them], to distance [them] from each other;"[76] that Gabriel was his mother's favorite and Raphaël his father's, and that each of the two brothers incarnated a side of their parents' character that was never fully developed: the father loved music but was a failed businessman; the mother loved social action and was only a cold, frustrated housewife. The brothers themselves are of divergent dispositions: Gabriel is practical, strong, assertive, and loud; Raphaël contemplative, soft, timid, and weak. Gabriel is a gifted businessman and womanizer, and Raphaël is an ardent musician and composer.

Throughout the novel, the leitmotiv is apparent: "you are my brother,"[77] "We are brothers,"[78] "Take care of your brother."[79] These are statements that come back with slight variations on the theme, and the very first sentence of the novel, "A brother remains a brother," points in this direction.[80] Interestingly enough, the title of the book, *My Brother's Keeper*, is itself an elliptic affirmation of Cain's rhetorical question. Raphaël does prove to be his brother's keeper at the end, and Kattan himself stated in a 2005 interview that despite the brothers' fights and disagreements, "there is the affirmation, according to which, despite the difficulties and the contradictions, there is a path one can follow."[81] Does this affirmation reflect the notion of the totality and unity of Being Kattan asserts to have acquired from his Judeo-Islamic heritage?[82]

In reference to Kattan's *L'Anniversaire*, Jacques Allard has pointed out, shortly after its publication in the year 2000, that the theme of exchange is best accommodated in that novel through the epistolary form. This mode, also displayed in *Le Gardien de mon frère*, celebrates this time too, albeit in relation to a different rapport—the indissoluble tie of fraternity rather than social interaction—the theme of exchange, intercommunication, a theme the Québécois critic rightly considers a cornerstone in the work of Kattan.[83] But is this theme always portrayed in a successful light when it comes to family relations? A study of some of Kattan's collections of short stories is enlightening in this regard.

LA REPRISE (1985) [THE REBOUND]
JE REGARDE LES FEMMES (2005) [I LOOK AT WOMEN]

About Kattan's first four collections of short stories (1974–1979), Michael Greenstein was writing in 1984: "The stories encompass a variety of cultural situations—Arabic, Jewish, European, North and South American—each characterized by a sense of absence—whether spatial, temporal, or existential."[84] This is still roughly the case with the two collections produced decades later (1985 and 2005), *La Reprise* and *Je regarde les femmes*. In fact, Kattan's world of short stories is one of wasted lives, where couples, mostly living in Montréal, are often breaking-up; children are moving out and living in distant countries, having little contact with their estranged parents; lonely widows endure the misery of their solitude, and old couples face their past and recapitulate their empty, loveless, and pathetic lives. Kattan points out, in an interview, that readers have mentioned to him his pessimism and the fact that "there isn't a single love story that ends well, nothing works, and everything is bad."[85] To this the author replies that the world around him compels him to write the way he does, but that after all, the title *La Reprise* (The Rebound) has a positive note to it, since it suggests the triumph of "life, fragile and weak, but persistent and real."[86]

In "La Reprise," the story that gives its title to the entire collection, an old widow, Julie, who worked as a secretary for twenty years, is given a retirement party. She tells her coworkers during the speech she is asked to make: "Désormais je vais me consacrer entièrement à mes plantes, à mes perruches et à mes poissons"[87] [I will from now on devote myself to my plants, my birds, and my fish]. She looks forward to her new status, but her life, which had been dictated so far by her work schedule, falls apart when she finds herself in charge of her own time. Her pets die, wither, or escape. When one of her two children (Marie and Thérèse) phones her at the end of the story and questions her about her ailing voice, she replies: "Je trouve mon appartement un peu exigu. Peut-être faudrait-il que je déménage"[88] [I find the apartment a bit small. Maybe I should move out]. The ending thus marks a glimmer of hope toward a new beginning, or is this yet another illusion?

In a similar vein, "La Conquête" (The Conquest) features Habiba, a Montréal widow and Jewish immigrant from Baghdad. Her daughter, Linda, is married in Israel. Her recently deceased husband, Mourad, was in the real estate business. At his death, Habiba takes over the business and prospers. She discovers herself, her body, her skills, and her freedom: "à peine se souvenait-elle de son veuvage sinon pour soupirer d'aise"[89] [barely did she have any time to remember her widowhood and then, what a feeling of relief]. She begins going out, traveling, does a cosmetic surgery that leaves her looking less old than before. At the end of the story, however, she suddenly realizes that her time is over, and she resigns herself to visiting her grandchildren in Israel. A kindred character is found in "Les Mémoires" (The Memoirs), a story that features a protagonist, Esther, whose daughter Caroline lives in Greece and whose husband, Jacob, an important public figure, just died, leaving her to face a long-awaited freedom: "Et maintenant elle était libre. Libre et seule" [And now she was free, free and alone].[90] But again hers is an empty, aimless freedom. In "Se retrouver" (To find oneself), for instance, Sarah, an older woman, faces old age and sadness. She has two adult children, Bruno and Tina, living far away, and to whom she had sacrificed all notions of pleasure and self-fulfillment for the sake of their education and well-being.

When finally she and her husband begin going on leisure trips, she fails to enjoy the travels—"elle passait d'une diarrhée à une constipation et n'arrivait pas à dormir" [she would go from diarrhea to constipation and could not sleep]—and she exclaims to her ailing husband in a moment of epiphany: "Nous avons trop attendu, Raphaël. Il est trop tard" [we have waited too long, Raphaël. It is too late].[91]

It seems that when they have no one to blame and when there are no longer any hindrances to their freedom, usually an unloved spouse or a meaningless job, the protagonists still cannot find happiness. Perhaps nobody is to blame but the emptiness of life itself, seems to suggest the author.

With titles such as "Deux amis dans le métro," "Une femme riche," "L'enterrement," "La Mort du voisin," "Derniers jeux de patience," "Tous des obsédés" [A Rich Woman, The Burial, The Neighbor's death, Last Games of Patience, All Obsessed], *Je regarde les femmes* (2005) (I Look at Women) harbors largely the same themes of departure, broken love affairs, and divorce, as did *La Reprise* twenty years earlier, with an emphasis on the vagaries of old age, chance meetings between ex-lovers or friends after a great number of years, sudden deaths and deaths from old age, funerals, encounters accompanied with lies and hypocrisy. The volume is divided into three sections (with roughly the same number of stories in each) titled, respectively, "Je regarde les femmes," "Théâtre des veuves," and "Il n'y a pas d'âge" (I Look at Women, Theatre of Widows, There Is No Age). The stories themselves—Montréal is the usual setting—are often peopled with characters who have failed their lives, not having lived up to their emotional or intellectual potential.

"Le Trio" features an elderly man, Aurèle, a widower who finds himself under the harsh authority of Irène, his married middle-aged, domineering only daughter. In a reversal of roles, whenever he introduces his potential girlfriends to her, she unfailingly applies severe judgments on them. "Jamais il ne l'avait entendue faire l'éloge d'une femme de moins de soixante-dix ans"[92] [He had never heard her praise a woman under seventy years of age]. At the end of the story, there is a psychological break-up between daughter and father. The latter decides to shun his daughter, and he declares his love to Diane, his latest encounter, despite his daughter's usual animosity. "David etait mon ami" is a story of two friends from the "native country" (we are not told which), a businessman and an engineer. The relationship had always been one of measuring up to the other as a validation of one's success—"Je n'étais que le témoin de ses victoires, j'en étais la mesure"[93] [I had been merely the witness of his victories, and the measure of them]. When David dies, his friend does not go to his funeral and hence feels liberated from the "last witness" of his childhood.[94]

Sometimes the protagonists are losers who extract some personal glory from the city they live in. In "Deux amis dans le métro" [Two Friends in the Subway] for instance, Xavier, a cook stationed in Austin, Texas, goes to Montréal to meet his childhood friend (a supermarket employee), Sebastien—they had grown up together as *pieds noirs* in Tunisia—after twenty years of separation. The two friends with their miserable jobs and their failed marriages and offspring try to impress each other; they resort to lies and half-truths in an effort to conceal their respective failures. When Sebastien takes his friend around Montréal, he is very proud of his city: "elle lui appartenait. Il en faisait l'éloge comme pour substituer sa renommée à son propre échec"[95] [It belonged to him. He praised it as if to substitute his own failure with the fame of the city].

As we have seen, Montréal is the setting for much of Kattan's fiction and the site of his characters' familiar world. Shems, the protagonist of *L'Anniversaire*, speaks of Montréal as his beloved city, one he invented and loves,[96] and where "the familiarity of the streets, stores, even the faces, spares [him] any effort of discovery or recognition."[97] Likewise, Gabriel, the protagonist of *Le Gardien de mon frère*, is comforted upon his return to Montréal "where everything seemed familiar,"[98] and Daniel, the protagonist of "Une ville à vendre" [A City for Sale], endows Montréal with everything meaningful in his life: "For him, the streets of Montréal overflowed with life."[99] In a chapter entitled "Le Roman de la métropole" published in the 2000 voluminous study entitled *Le Roman du Québec*, Jacques Allard mentions Naïm Kattan as part of a wave of writers who continue to partake in the modernity of the Québécois urban novel where the protagonist emerges as an anticlerical counterpart to a formerly rural society. In this context, along with names such as Yves Beauchemin, "the novelist par excellence of Montréal,"[100] Allard refers to Kattan as one of the neo-Québécois writers who "give Montréal a new humanity."[101] In the words of Kattan himself speaking of his exposure to this city upon his arrival in 1954:

> *Quand je suis arrivé à Montréal, je me suis dit que cette ville ressemblait beaucoup à Bagdad parce qu'il y avait des quartiers. A Bagdad il y avait le quartier des Juifs, le quartier des Musulmans, des Arméniens, des Chrétiens, etc., et quand je suis arrivé à Montréal j'ai constaté qu'il y avait un quartier canadien-français, un quartier canadien-anglais, un quartier juif, un quartier italien, un quartier grec.*[102]

[When I arrived in Montréal, I told myself that this city resembles a lot Baghdad because there were districts. In Baghdad there were the Jewish, Moslem, Armenian, Christian neighborhoods, and when I arrived in Montréal, I noticed that there were French-Canadian, English-Canadian, Jewish, Italian, and Greek neighborhoods.]

Montréal is thus for Kattan the physical and mental dwelling, the habitat, the *oikos*, to borrow Harel's apt word,[103] similar to, yet so dissimilar from his native town, Baghdad, where cultures can peacefully cohabitate in their plurality. French for Kattan-the-writer becomes the necessary yet chosen vehicle for this cohabitation, much like Arabic had once been, before his definitive departure from Babylon for the West in 1947. As Greenstein writes in his study entitled "Iraquébec: Naïm Kattan's Trans-Mimetic Disapora": "Kattan sees Montreal as an American city that is at once francophone, European, and international, and the centripetal and centrifugal forces acting upon Kattan's imagination thus lead to his adoption of a trans-mimetic mode of writing."[104] That mode of writing is, in my view, closely linked to Kattan's resolution of the problem of identity for the transcultural writer, as will be further demonstrated below.

FROM FICTION TO ESSAY AND BACK TO KATTAN-THE-TRAVELER

A 1977 reviewer of *Farewell, Babylon* uses terms such as "a world of shadows," "disembodied," and "unreal" in reference to this first volume of the trilogy.[105] The critic (Spettigue) attributes that impression partly to the Canadian readers' unfamiliarity with a world "two or three times removed from [them]."[106] Moreover, in an incisive 1989 study by Nasrin Rahimieh, where the latter refers to Spettigue's comments, she asserts that the disembodiment effect produced by Kattan's novel has to do with Kattan's replicating in Canada (by choosing to write in French) the same linguistic alienation and conflict he had experienced and knew so well growing up in Baghdad (where he chose to write in Arabic), a situation that would further corroborate, she asserts, Kattan's desire to live on the margins. "He is a man who has forever lost his orientation,"[107] Rahimieh concludes, and she supports her assertion notably with some statements made by Kattan himself, including the epigraph to this study taken from *The Real and the Theatrical*: "je n'accepte pas la fixité des lieux sûrs et le confort des certitudes."[108]

Regardless of the fact that the above-mentioned comments may be partly due to the deterritorialization effect pointed out by Deleuze and Guattari with regard to literatures written by minority writers in a major language, absence is itself a motif that, though latent, permeates the first volume of the trilogy. It also leaves its mark in *Les Fruits arrachés* where Meir becomes stateless by virtue of the creation of the state of Israel in 1948 and the ensuing exodus of Iraqi Jews: "comment expliquer que je n'appartiens plus à mon pays" [How to explain that I no longer belong to my country],[109] he writes when reminded that his French scholarship was about to expire. Likewise, in *La Fiancée promise*, about an attractive girl (Rose) who courts him and whom, because she is Iraqi, he considers sexually off-limits, he asserts, evoking a day when he was unable to respond to her advances: "Elle était là, toute l'Amérique, et son visage n'était qu'absence" [She was right here, America in its entirety, and her face was mere absence].[110]

Even though those insights are relevant, we should also turn to Kattan himself for guidance in this reading. In the preface to the 2005 English edition of *Farewell, Babylon*, Kattan writes the following from the vantage point of retrospection, exactly three decades later: "*Farewell, Babylon* is not a work of nostalgia, nor is it one of resentment."[111] Juxtaposed with an interview conducted by Jacques Allard some two decades earlier, this authorial statement is enlightening, as Kattan himself explains that if his novels are autobiographical in nature, this is due to the fact that he strives to defy loss of memory (*l'oubli*, which he equates to absence and death) by salvaging memory, thus challenging death.[112] The author adds in this interview that what he fears most is absence: "J'ai beaucoup vécu dans l'absence" [I have lived a lot in absence],[113] and he asserts having attempted to transmit to the readers of his first novel that which he carried within himself. Quoting Chateaubriand, he adds: "Chacun de nous transporte en lui sa patrie" [We each carry in us our native land].[114] The absence noted by the critics above may be ultimately the place left by the underlying "référent massif,"[115] the "massive referent," that of the lost homeland—should we recall Pierre Nepveu's well-documented studies on exilic literatures[116]—and in the case of Kattan-the-writer, the thrice-lost homeland: 2,500 years ago, in 1947 and again in 1954. Conquering that void, hence, will be the mark of *Farewell, Babylon,* this novel written in the absence of the native country, Iraq, and in the presence of the new homeland, Canada. The endeavor will reflect the collective value of utterances Deleuze and Guattari pointed out as being another feature exhibited in minor literatures.[117]

In a most enlightening 2002 interview entitled *"D'où je viens, où je vais"* [where I come from, where I am going], Kattan links his personal trajectory to that of his ancestors, the Jews of Babylon who wrote the Talmud. Babylon was crucial because it was in Babylon that, in the words of the author, *"we got freed from a feeling of exile while remaining ourselves."*[118] He goes on to assert that this achievement, namely, "how to remain oneself" across the ages and to assert one's presence all the while "totally participating in another culture" and being part of it, stayed with him all his life, *even in Canada.*[119]

Here we come to a fundamental worldview of Kattan's, one that dictates his premises as an essayist and a fiction writer as well: He refuses the condition of exile altogether on the basis that "the Exile who lives in the current country while thinking of another country"[120] is neither here nor there, neither in the initial vanished country nor in the new one. And despite the fact that Kattan did lose entitlement to an Iraqi passport in 1948 and could not go back home, in order to avoid living in the "unreal" country of the exilic individual, he chose instead to call his departure to Canada *immigration* or "chosen exile," possibly an oxymoron.[121] In his own words: "J'ai été plus ou moins renvoyé, on m'a enlevé mon passeport, mais finalement, cet exil-là j'en ai fait un choix" [I was more or less kicked out; my passport was taken away from me, but in the final analysis, I have chosen that exile].[122] Why? Because, according to Kattan, in the exile's relationship to the new land, there exists a profound refusal of the crossing, *"un refus du passage,"*[123] and here Kattan will link once more the biblical text, not only with his own personal history, but also with that of his community: He reminds us of how Abraham became an *ivrit* (a passerby in Hebrew) when he obeyed God's injunction to move on and to leave his native Chaldea, fifty kilometers from Baghdad (Kattan's native town), to go to another chosen land which he made his own by choosing it, by accepting to cross over to it. Kattan reiterates this idea in a magnificent passage of *La Mémoire et la promesse*, an essay where he explicitly links the biblical exile to the genealogy of his own family:

> Je suis parti de Bagdad, emportant le rêve d'un lieu fixe, héritier de vingt-cinq siècles d'histoire en un point donné. Nous étions entourés de nomades, les empires s'étaient édifiés puis effondrés, et nous, les fils de prisonniers de Nabuchodonosor étions toujours là et pourtant nous étions nous aussi des nomades, nous avons appris qu'il n'y a de lieu que de passage et que Dieu habite tous les lieux.
>
> [I left Baghdad and took with me the dream of a fixed place, heir of twenty-five centuries at a given point. We were surrounded by nomads, empires had risen and crumbled, and we, the sons of prisoners of Nebuchadnezzar were still there and yet we too were nomads. We have learned that all places are passageways and that God inhabits all places.][124]

We have learned that all places are passageways and that God inhabits all places. Is this to be taken as an exaltation of the nomadic state? It occurs in a chapter of *La Mémoire et la promesse* entitled "Les nomades et les errants" [Nomads and Wanderers] from which one of the epigraphs to the present study is borrowed.[125] In that chapter, Kattan makes the distinction between wanderers and nomads. The latter are at home in all places they cross because when they travel from oasis to oasis, they meet members of their tribe and they feel at home. "All of earth belongs to them."[126] Their world is rich, richer than the world of Europeans who live under the illusion that they will *appropriate* and make theirs an ancestral property after three or four generations of inhabiting it with a fence around. "Les Nomades sont des pèlerins qui parcourent le désert, psalmodiant . . . la parole donnée et qui est leur seule demeure"[127] [Nomads are pilgrims who go through the desert chanting the given word that is their only home]. Is that not the case also for the intellectual-writer, Kattan himself or Shems, his counterpart in *L'Anniversaire*, both having made of words their ultimate dwelling? Both having inscribed their presence on their new country by their writing, much in the same fashion as the Jews of Babylon did in Iraq when they wrote the Talmud?

The refusal of the mental stance of exile is also entertained in Kattan's essay, *Le Réel et le théâtral*, mentioned above. Since this is the writer's very first work, one that precedes his large production of works consisting of roughly fourteen essays, ten novels, and ten collections of short stories, it is worthwhile pointing out one of its most fundamental concepts, for, as Douek has noted,[128] in this essay is found the "foundation of [Kattan's] thoughts," and those tend to spill over onto his fiction as well. Hasn't Greenstein rightly asserted that "Kattan's cross-fertilization of genres forms an integral part of his migratory experience"?[129]

In *Le Réel et le théâtral*, Kattan puts forth the idea that three types of rapports dictate the march of civilizations: Man to Man, Man to God and Man to Nature. The latter rapport forms the essence of one's concept of reality, exhibited in language itself. In Semitic languages there is an immediate coincidence between word and object, just as there is between man and nature, whereas in Hellenic civilization, the relationship between man and nature (and Man and God) is mediated through what he calls the theatrical, by which he signifies the carnivalesque, the figurative, or the illusionary. In Arabic, a language whose genius is in the noun, not in the adjective, he asserts, an object lives because it is named;[130] a thing is not *qualified*, it is *said*. In contradistinction, Western thought is so heavily mediated that it cannot grasp the power of evocation Semitic languages enjoy, and Kattan concludes: "L'homme occidental est, par conséquent, un homme divisé, partagé" [Western man is consequently a divided, split man].[131]

In the very context of the notion of the totality of being—he also claims it comes to him from Judaism,[132] and he elsewhere calls it desire[133]—Kattan ascertains his refusal to live in-between two worlds, two cultures or two worldviews. His answer to the existential dilemma of multiplicity, sometimes the predicament of the migrant, and certainly his own, is *creation*, which he likens to "alternation within continuity."[134] Thus, he writes at the conclusion of *Reality and Theater*:

> Mes deux univers ne se superposent pas. Ils se continuent, se prolongent dans le mouvement de la vie. J'ai opté pour une langue que j'invente à chaque moment. J'ai choisi un lieu que je dote de ma présence en y inscrivant mon invention.[135]

[My two universes are not superimposed, they complement each other, prolong one another in the movement that is life. . . . I have opted for a language I invent at every moment. I chose a place I endow with my presence by inscribing my invention upon it.][136]

To learn how to "endow" a place with one's presence, thereby creating it anew—transforming it into a home and a refuge—means possibly to become a passerby who has *effected his crossing*, or translated into Canadian official parlance, to become a *landed immigrant*. This constitutes a notion present in some of Kattan's fiction as well, such as *L'Anniversaire* (as demonstrated above), where Shems, the protagonist immigrant-exile, just like Kattan himself, adopts his new country, French-Canada, so intimately and so well that he grafts his own history, and by extension, that of his Jewish community, upon the history of Québec. Perhaps herein lies the quintessence of Kattan's writing:

Le grand mérite de l'oeuvre de Naïm Kattan est d'insister sur la plasticité de l'expérience culturelle. L'oeuvre de cet auteur n'oppose pas l'intégration à l'assimilation. Elle ne met pas en relief de façon rigide l'enracinement et la liberté de déplacement.

[The great merit of Kattan's oeuvre is to insist on the plasticity of cultural experience. This writer's oeuvre does not oppose integration and assimilation. It does not contrast, in a rigid way, integration with freedom of movement.][137]

The above statement by the eminent critic Simon Harel sums up the achievements of Naïm Kattan and his transmimetic writing, for having been born, having lived, and having created his oeuvre under the sign of the multiple, Naïm Kattan evokes that very "plasticity of cultural experience" of which he is a proud specimen.

NOTES

1. A distinctly smaller version of this article, entitled "Naïm Kattan's Transcontinental Trilogy: Under the Sign of the Multiple" is forthcoming in *Canadian Ethnic Studies*.
2. Nasrin Rahimieh, "Naïm Kattan, *le discours arabe*, and Empty Words," *Canadian Review of Comparative Literature/Revue Canadienne de Littérature Comparée* 16.3-4 (1989): 737-744, 737.
3. "Pour récompenser tous les ans une personne ou une institution qui contribuent efficacement à la défense et à la promotion du français comme langue internationale," Pierre Nora, "Discours sur les prix littéraires" (29 novembre 2007), www.academie-francaise.fr/immortels/discours_SPA/nora_2007.html

4. Pierre Nora, "Discours sur les prix littéraires," www.academie-francaise.fr/immortels/discours_SPA/nora_2007.html (accessed 29 November 2007).

5. Roland Barthes, *Le Degré zéro de l'écriture*. Paris: Editions du Seuil, 1953 and 1972.

6. D. O. Spettigue, "Farewell, Babylon," *Queen's Quarterly* 84.3 (1977): 510–511, 510.

7. I. M. Owen, "Bridge of Tongues: Why an Arabic-speaking, Baghdad-Born Jew Is a Perfect Guide to the Modern Canadian Experience," *Books in Canada* 12.5 (1976): 5–6, 5.

8. Michael Greenstein, "Iraquébec: Naïm Kattan's Trans-Mimetic Diaspora," in *Textualizing the Immigrant Experience in Contemporary Québec*, ed. Susan Ireland and Patrice J. Proulx (Westport, Connecticut: Praeger, 2004): 117–126, 117–118.

9. Simon Harel, *Les Passages obligés de l'écriture migrante* (Montréal: XYZ éditeur, 2005): 128.

10. See F. Elizabeth Dahab, "Voices of Exile: The Literary Odyssey of Canadian Writers of Arabic Origins." *Canadian Review of Comparative Literature/Revue canadienne de littérature comparée* 28.1 (March 2001): 48–69.

11. The first French edition was published by La Presse (Montréal, 1975) and the second one by Leméac (Montréal, 1986). Quotations in French are from the 1986 edition.

12. David Godine. Kattan has been invited since to a number of university campuses to speak about this book. The publication of *Adieu, Babylone* in an Italian translation is forthcoming.

13. By the same translator as the first volume, Sheila Fischman.

14. Sylvain Simard, "Lettre à qui refuse le tragique," in *L'écrivain du passage, D'où je viens, où je vais, Saluts. hommages et lectures*, ed., Jacques Allard (Montréal: Hurtubise HMH, 2002): 84.

15. Mary Soderstrom, "Farewell, Babylon: Coming of Age in Jewish Baghdad," *Montreal Review of Books* 9.1 (2005), www.aelaq.org/mrb/article.php?issue=15452&cat=4 (accessed February 13, 2006).

16. Andrew Kett, "Farewell, Babylon: Coming of Age in Jewish Baghdad," *Quill and Quire* (May 2005): 33–34, 34.

17. Jacques Allard,"Entrevue avec Naïm Kattan," *Voix et Images* 11.1 (1985): 10–32, 20.

18. Naïm Kattan, *Farewell, Babylon: Coming of Age in Jewish Baghdad*, translated from the French by Sheila Fischman (Vancouver: Raincoast Books, 2005): 139. Unless otherwise indicated, all English quotations of *Farewell, Babylon* are from the 2005 English edition. Throughout this chapter, whenever a text has not been translated into English, I give the French original followed by my own English translation.

19. Naïm Kattan, *Adieu, Babylone* (Montréal: Leméac, 1986): 169. This is my translation as the sentence is absent in the English edition.

20. Kattan, *Farewell, Babylon*, 176.

21. Kattan, *L'Ecrivain de passage*, 26.

22. Kattan, *Farewell, Babylon*, 124.

23. Kattan, *Farewell, Babylon*, 176.

24. Jacques Allard, "Entrevue avec Naïm Kattan," *Voix et Images* 11.1 (1985): 10–32, 16.

25. Kattan, *Adieu, Babylone*, 12–13.
26. Kattan, *Farewell, Babylon*, 15.
27. Kattan, *Adieu, Babylone*, 13.
28. Kattan, *Farewell, Babylon*, 15.
29. Nasrin Rahimieh, "Naïm Kattan, *le discours arabe*, and Empty Words," *Canadian Review of Comparative Literature/Revue Canadienne de Littérature Comparée*, 16.3–4 (1989): 737–744, 741.
30. Kattan, *Farewell, Babylon*, 54.
31. Moslems consider Christians and Jews as "People of the Book" because of the Bible and the Gospels.
32. Kattan, *Farewell, Babylon*, 53.
33. Kattan, *Farewell, Babylon*, 49.
34. Kattan, *Farewell, Babylon*, 49.
35. Kattan, *Adieu, Babylone*, 49–50.
36. Kattan, *Farewell, Babylon*, 49–50.
37. Kattan, *Farewell, Babylon*, 50.
38. Kattan, *Farewell, Babylon*, 20.
39. Kattan, *Farewell, Babylon*, 20.
40. Kattan, *Farewell, Babylon*, 26.
41. Kattan, *Adieu, Babylone*, 182.
42. Kattan, *Farewell, Babylon*, 170.
43. *Adieu, Babylone*, 237.
44. Kattan, *Farewell, Babylon*, 217.
45. Jacques Allard, "Entrevue avec Naïm Kattan," *Voix et Images* 11.1 (1985): 10–32, 20–21
46. Naïm Kattan, *Les Fruits arrachés* (Montréal: Hurtubise HMH, 1977): 212.
47. My own translation.
48. A discrepancy of five years from the year of departure at the end of *Paris Interlude*.
49. Kattan explains in an interview that the image of the promised bride symbolizes the promise Canada held in store for the immigrant. See Jacques Allard, "Entrevue avec Naïm Kattan," *Voix et Images* 11.1 (1985): 10–32, 27.
50. Naïm Kattan, *La Fiancée promise* (Montréal: Hurtubise HMH, 1983): 18–19.
51. Naïm Kattan, *La Fiancée promise*, 229.
52. Translations of passages from *Paris Interlude* are mine.
53. Kattan, *La Fiancée promise*, 165.
54. Kattan, *La Fiancée promise*, 228
55. Naïm Kattan, *L'Anniversaire* (Montréal: Québec-Amérique, 2000): 143.
56. Jacques Allard, "L'Anniversaire ou l'hommage raconté," in *L'Ecrivain de passage. D'où je viens, où je vais. Saluts. hommages et lectures* (Montréal: Hurtubise HMH, 2002): 151–155, 151.
57. Jacques Allard, "L'Anniversaire ou l'hommage raconté," in *L'Ecrivain de passage. D'où je viens, où je vais. Saluts. hommages et lectures* (Montréal: Hurtubise HMH, 2002): 151–155, 155.
58. Sophie Jama, ed., *Les Temps du nomade: Itinéarire d'un écrivain* (Montréal: Liber, 2005): 166.
59. Kattan, *L'Anniversaire*, 60.

60. Kattan, L'Anniversaire, 67.
61. Kattan, L'Anniversaire, 46.
62. Kattan, L'Anniversaire, 48.
63. Kattan, L'Anniversaire, 19.
64. Kattan, L'Anniversaire, 111.
65. Kattan, L'Anniversaire, 155–156.
66. Kattan, L'Anniversaire, 58.
67. Kattan, L'Anniversaire, 92.
68. Kattan, L'Anniversaire, 28.
69. Kattan, L'Anniversaire, 36.
70. Kattan, L'Anniversaire, 143.
71. Michael Greenstein, "Iraquébec: Naïm Kattan's Trans-Mimetic Diaspora," in *Textualizing the Immigrant Experience in Contemporary Québec*, eds., Susan Ireland and Patrice Proulx (Westport, Connecticut: Praeger, 2004): 117–126, 122.
72. Kattan, L'Anniversaire, 92.
73. Michael Greenstein, "Iraquébec: Naïm Kattan's Trans-Mimetic Diaspora," in *Textualizing the Immigrant Experience in Contemporary Québec*, eds., Susan Ireland and Patrice Proulx (Westport, Connecticut: Praeger, 2004): 117–126.
74. Telephone conversation with the author on March 30, 2006.
75. Naïm Kattan, *L'Ecrivain du passage. D'où je viens, où je vais. Saluts. hommages et lectures*, ed. Jacques Allard, (Montréal: Hurtubise HMH 2002): 40.
76. Naïm Kattan, *Le Gardien de mon frère* (Montréal: Hurtubise HMH, 2003): 68.
77. Kattan, *Le Gardien de mon frère*, 68.
78. Kattan, *Le Gardien de mon frère*, 36.
79. Kattan, *Le Gardien de mon frère*, 31.
80. Kattan, *Le Gardien de mon frère*, 9.
81. Sophie Jama, ed. *Les Temps du nomade. Itinéarire d'un écrivain* (Montréal: Liber, 2005): 152. "Il y a donc l'affirmation selon laquelle, malgré les difficultés, les contradictions, etc., il y a un chemin qu'on peut suivre."
82. Naïm Kattan, *La Mémoire et la promesse* (Montréal: Hurtubise HMH, 1978): 37.
83. Jacques Allard, *Le Roman du Québec: Histoire, Perspectives, Lectures* (Montréal: Québec-Amérique, 2000): 19.
84. Michael Greenstein, "The Desert, the River and the Island: Naïm Kattan's Short Stories." *Canadian Literature* 103 (1984): 42–48, 42.
85. Jacques Allard, "Entrevue avec Naïm Kattan," *Voix et Images* 11.1 (1985): 10–32, 30–31.
86. Jacques Allard, "Entrevue avec Naïm Kattan," *Voix et Images* 11.1 (1985): 10–32, 31.
87. Kattan, *La Reprise* (Montréal: L'Arbre HMH, 1985): 61.
88. Kattan, *La Reprise*, 67.
89. Kattan, *La Reprise*, 115.
90. Kattan, *La Reprise*, 5.
91. Kattan, *La Reprise*, 14.
92. Kattan, *Je regarde les femmes* (Montréal: Hurtubise HMH, 2005): 195.
93. Kattan, *Je regarde les femmes*, 61.
94. Kattan, *Je regarde les femmes*, 64.
95. Kattan, *Je regarde les femmes*, 143.

96. Kattan, *L'Anniversaire*, 111.
97. Kattan, *L'Anniversaire*, 131.
98. Kattan, *Le Gardien de mon frère*, 33.
99. Kattan, *Je regarde les femmes*, 268.
100. Jacques Allard, *Le Roman du Québec: Histoire, Perspectives, Lectures* (Montréál: Québec-Amérique, 2000): 131.
101. Jacques Allard, *Le Roman du Québec: Histoire, Perspectives, Lectures* (Montréál: Québec-Amérique, 2000): 131.
102. Naïm Kattan, *L'Ecrivain du passage*, 44.
103. Simon Harel, *Les Passages obligés de l'écriture migrante* (Montréal: XYZ éditeur, 2005): 125.
104. Michael Greenstein, "Iraquébec: Naïm Kattan's Trans-Mimetic Diaspora," in *Textualizing the Immigrant Experience in Contemporary Québec*, ed. Susan Ireland and Patrice J. Proulx (Westport, Connecticut: Prager, 2004): 117–126, 119.
105. D. O. Spettigue, "Farewell, Babylon," *Queen's Quarterly* 84.3 (1977): 510–511, 510.
106. D. O. Spettigue, "Farewell, Babylon," *Queen's Quarterly* 84.3 (1977): 510–511, 511.
107. Nasrin Rahimieh, "Naïm Kattan, *le discours arabe*, and Empty Words," *Canadian Review of Comparative Literature/Revue Canadienne de Littérature Comparée*, 16.3–4 (1989): 737–744, 743.
108. Nasrin Rahimieh, "Naïm Kattan, *le discours arabe*, and Empty Words," 743.
109. Naïm Kattan, *les Fruits arrachés* (Montréal: Hurtubise HMH, 1977): 61.
110. Naïm Kattan, *La Fiancée promise* (Montréal: Hurtubise HMH, 1983): 175.
111. Kattan, *Farewell, Babylon*, 8.
112. Jacques Allard, "Entrevue avec Naïm Kattan." *Voix et Images* 11.1 (1985): 10–32, 27.
113. Jacques Allard, "Entrevue avec Naïm Kattan." *Voix et Images* 11.1 (1985): 10–32, 27.
114. Jacques Allard, "Entrevue avec Naïm Kattan." *Voix et Images* 11.1 (1985): 10–32, 14.
115. Robert Berrouët-Oriol and Robert Fournier, "L'Emergence des écritures migrantes et métisses au Québec." *Litte Réalité: Une revue d'écrits originaux: A Journal of Creative and Original Writing* 3.2 (Fall 1991): 9–35, 17.
116. Pierre Nepveu, *L'Ecologie du réel: Mort et naissance de la littérature québécoise contemporaine*. Montréal: Boréal, 1988.
117. Gilles Deleuze and Félix Guattari, *Kafka: Pour une littérature mineure* (Paris: Les Editions de Minuit, 1975).
118. Kattan, *L'Ecrivain du passage*, 22. Emphasis mine.
119. Kattan, *L'Ecrivain du passage*, 22
120. Kattan, *L'Ecrivain du passage*, 41.
121. Kattan, *L'Ecrivain du passage*, 41.
122. Kattan, *L'Ecrivain du passage*, 41.
123. Kattan, *L'Ecrivain du passage*, 41.
124. Kattan, *La Mémoire et la promesse* (Montréal: Hurtubise HMH, 1978): 14.
125. "Nomade, toute la terre m'appartient" [Nomad, the whole earth belongs to me], Naïm Kattan, *La Mémoire et la promesse*, 15.

126. Kattan, *La Mémoire et la promesse*, 15.

127. Kattan, *La Mémoire et la promesse*, 15.

128. Simone Douek, "Naïm Kattan: *D'où je viens, où je vais*," in *L'Ecrivain du passage. D'où je viens, où je vais. Saluts. hommages et lectures*, ed. Jacques Allard (Montréal: Hurtubise HMH, 2002): 11–76, 66.

129. Michael Greenstein, "Iraquébec: Naïm Kattan's Trans-Mimetic Diaspora," in *Textualizing the Immigrant Experience in Contemporary Québec*, eds. Susan Ireland and Patrice Proulx (Westport, Connecticut: Praeger, 2004): 117–126, 118.

130. Naïm Kattan, *Le Réel et le théâtral*, 16.

131. Naïm Kattan, *Le Réel et le théâtral*, 17. Translation mine.

132. Sophie Jama, ed., *Les Temps du nomade: Itinéarire d'un écrivain* (Montréal: Liber, 2005): 219.

133. Naïm Kattan, *Le Désir et le pouvoir* (Montréal: HMH, 1983).

134. Naïm Kattan, *Reality and Theater*, translated by Alan Brown (Toronto: Anansi, 1972): 142.

135. Naïm Kattan, *Le Réel et le théâtral* (Montréal: Editions HMH, 1970): 188.

136. Naïm Kattan, *Reality and Theater*, translated by Alan Brown (Toronto: Anansi, 1972): 142.

137. Simon Harel, *Les Passages obligés de l'écriture migrante* (Montréal: XYZ éditeur, 2005): 128.

4

Of Suffocated Minds and Tortured Hearts: The Universe of Abla Farhoud

Pourquoi pourquoi pourquoi je dirai pourquoi jusqu'à la fin des temps jusqu'au jour où ma langue sèchera dans ma bouche je dirai pourquoi pourquoi pourquoi jusqu'à ce que mon gosier éclate et personne ne me répond et personne ne me répondra.

[Why why why I will say why to the end of time to the day my tongue dries in my mouth I will say why why why until my throat explodes and nobody answers me and nobody will answer me.]

Abla Farhoud (Jeux de patience, 41 and Splendide solitude, 49)

Quoiqu'il fasse l'étranger attire les regards. Plus il essaie de se fondre dans la foule, plus il se sent remarqué, comme une femme enceinte qui voudrait cacher son ventre.

[Whatever he does, a foreigner attracts attention. The more he tries to melt into the crowd the more he feels noticed, like a pregnant woman who wishes to hide her belly.]

Abla Farhoud (Le Bonheur a la queue glissante, 131)

FARHOUD AND HER OEUVRE

Abla Farhoud was born in 1945, in Ain-Hirsché, a village in South-East Lebanon. When she was six years old, she immigrated with her parents to Montréal, in a francophone neighborhood. In 1965, the family returned to Lebanon where the twenty-year-old Abla reluctantly spent four unhappy years, after which she went to Paris where she studied theater for another four years. In 1973, she moved back definitively to Montréal and joined the Université du Québec à Montréal (UQAM) earning a master's in Theater in 1985. Having worked in Montréal as a professional actress from the age of eighteen to the age of twenty, performing on stage and television for *Radio Canada*, Abla Farhoud continued acting in Lebanon and France for a while, then she eventually left the stage and has devoted herself entirely to her writing since 1990, contending she would rather be heard as a writer than seen as an actress.[1] That seems to have been the impetus behind her twofold career and her continuing interest in drama.

The idea of universe, as suggested by the title of this chapter, is quite compelling when dealing with Abla Farhoud as a rising Québécois-Lebanese novelist and playwright who chose French as a means of literary expression. At the outset, one is struck by the relatively recent emergence of her literary production: Three innovative novels published in the relatively short span of seven years (*Le Bonheur a la queue glissante*, 1998, *Splendide solitude*, 2001, *Le Fou d'Omar*, 2005) preceded by five equally innovative plays (several of which became finalists of such prizes as *Radio France Internationale*) published over a decade (1988–1999), of which *Les Filles du 5-10-15 cents*, recipient of the prestigious French prize, *Prix Arletty* (1994). This play was initially written in the mid-eighties and performed in 1986 at the *Théâtre de Quat' Sous* in Montréal. A reviewer of the popular daily newspaper, *Quotidien de Paris*, who saw it performed in Limoges (France) in 1992, at the *Festival des francophonies*, asserts that it was "the most human and the most current" play of the entire festival.[2] Likewise, Farhoud's sixth play, *Les Rues de l'alligator* (published in Montréal in 2003) was first performed in 1998 in Lille (France), at *Théâtre la Licorne*.

It is noteworthy that, even though she has published six titles, Farhoud has in point of fact written several collections of short stories and more than thirteen plays, many of which were staged in Canada, Belgium, France, Lebanon, the United States, and even Africa. The first of the series, *Jeux de patience*, written in 1982, was performed the following year in Montréal, during the festival of Montréal's *Théâtre Expérimental des Femmes* and again at *La Licorne* in 1995. Moreover, one of Farhoud's unpublished plays, *La Possession du prince* [The Prince's Possession] was staged in France in 1993 at the *Festival International des francophonies* where it received the *Prix Théâtre et Liberté* award.

Interestingly enough, even though *Les Filles du 5-10-15cents* (published in Belgium in 1993), *Quand j'étais grande* (published in France in 1994), and *Jeux de patience* (published in Montréal in 1997) were initially written and performed in French, their very first appearance in print was not in French but in English editions, translated from the French by Jill MacDougall. They had first been published by the New York–based company, Ubu Reportory Theater, under the titles, respectively, of *The Girls from the Five and Ten* (1988), *When I Was Grown Up* (1989), and *Games of Patience* (1994). Moreover, of Farhoud's three published novels, only the first one, *Le Bonheur a la queue glissante* (1998), recipient of *Prix France-Québec* in 1999, was translated into English (by the same translator) under the title Dounia-a-World. It is still pending publication, whereas an Italian translation of it came out in 2002, titled *La felicità scivola tra le dita* by the translator Elletra Zorzi. Ironically, as some Québécois critics have duly recognized,[3] *Le Bonheur a la queue glissante*, the first novel of the first Arabic-born Québécois playwright to have dramatized the collective experience of immigration, has attracted more critical attention than her plays, even though the plays had preceded it, had been staged overseas, and had already won several prizes by the time *Le Bonheur a la queue glissante* was published. Farhoud's latest novel, *Le Fou d'Omar* (2005), rightly hailed by some as "a jem of a book," one written with "a superb hand,"[4] was laureate of the *Prix du Roman Francophone* in 2006, shortly after it saw the day. It promises to catapult Farhoud to the foreground of the literary ranks of Québécois writers of *other* origins. Already two years before the publication of *Le Fou d'Omar*, Lucie Lequin, a Québécois critic, was asserting that Abla Farhoud as a "Québécois-writer of Lebanese origin . . . occupies an increasingly larger place in Québécois literature."[5]

Abla Farhoud is admittedly the first Arabic-Canadian writer to have dramatized the communal experience of exile, and more specifically the horrors of the civil war in Lebanon (1975–1990), in plays destined for the stage, plays indelibly marked with the collective value of utterances qualified by Deleuze and Guattari, as previously mentioned, as one of the main characteristics of minor literatures. To capture a major contribution of the author, and as Louise Forsyth has aptly pointed out, Farhoud is "one of the first Québec writers to represent the experience of immigrant girls and women,"[6] as will be shown in this chapter.

Amidst other Arabic-Québécois/Canadian writers, Farhoud stands unique in that she uses no fewer than five registers of language in her writings: Québécois slang (*joual*), standard French, colloquial French, English, colloquial Lebanese-Arabic and classical Arabic. In fact, she is to be credited for having been the first of those writers to have infused her works with transliterated Arabic phrases when representing characters of Lebanese origin speaking with each other or involved in a dramatic or internal monologue. Farhoud often glosses the Arabic utterances by having the character repeat herself in French; otherwise, a footnote gives the readers the meaning of the Arabic expression. Sometimes, the Arabic word occurs in context and is not translated. By so doing, Farhoud can be said to partake in linguistic strategies to "other" the French language, strategies in use by postcolonial African writers of French expression who are involved in a quest for national identity. Like them, Farhoud makes use of a great deal of syntactic calques, i.e., literal transcriptions of proverbs and idiomatic expressions, especially so in her first novel, the very title of which, *Le Bonheur a la queue glissante*, consists of an exact translation of an Arabic proverb literally meaning "happiness has a slippery tail," a title displayed in (literary) Arabic script in the inside cover of the novel, immediately under the French transcription of it, an original and apt editorial gesture worthy of emulation.

Death and the preoccupation with death, whether through war or the process of aging, seems to be the one overruling leitmotif of Farhoud's entire literary production, as Lequin has pointed out,[7] and as the writer herself acknowledges in an interview conducted in 1997 with the Montréal daily, *La Presse*:

> *S'il n'y avait pas la mort, je n'écrirais pas. Tout mon travail vise à comprendre cette chose insaisissable. Comprendre toutes les morts, pas juste les morts physiques, mais aussi les petites morts faites de maladie, d'amis disparus, de pays perdus et de perte de contact avec la réalité. Je n'accepte pas la mort, aucune mort. Pour moi, c'est la question fondamentale.*
>
> [If death did not exist, I would not write. All my work aims at understanding this unfathomable thing. To understand all deaths, not only physical deaths, but also small deaths made of illnesses, disappeared friends, lost countries, and loss of touch with reality. I do not accept death, any death. To me this is the fundamental issue.][8]

In light of the characteristics outlined above, the present chapter purports to study a cross-section of three of Farhoud's major plays spanning a decade, from 1986 to 1998, as well as her three novels published thereafter (1998–2005), followed by a concluding statement on the thematic crossover in the writer's oeuvre.

LES FILLES DU 5-10-15 CENTS (1986/1993)[9]
[THE GIRLS FROM THE FIVE AND TEN]

Les Filles du 5-10-15 cents is divided into nine sections (the word "scene" is not used). It dramatizes the life of two French-speaking adolescent girls, nineteen-year-old Amira and her sixteen-year-old sister Kaokab, both having emigrated from Lebanon to Montréal when still quite young. Despite their high academic performance, the two girls were pulled out of school by their father, while their eighteen-year-old brother Mounir is allowed to pursue his education and to rest during the holidays. Amira and Kaokab are solely made to work long, tedious, and stifling hours, with no vacation time, six days a week, in their father's 5-10-15 cents utility store located in the Montréal suburb of Saint-Vincent-de-Paul. The setting is cast in the early sixties, in "a climate of boredom, of routine,"[10] in the bitter cold of a Québecois winter. The store, a bleak "trappe à rats" [rat trap], as Kaokab calls it,[11] is piled up with a hodgepodge of merchandise and boxes to be sorted. It gradually closes in on the sisters, literally and increasingly so as they toil away, trying to make sense of their implacable plight. The energetic Kaokab, whose anguish is palpable, is the one deeply aware of her dead-end lot. She tries to push her more complacent older sister to rebel, and will eventually succeed in doing so, using such objectifying ploys as pretending to be an interviewer questioning Amira about her life and her family. Referring to their life, Kaokab will say: "C'est comme une roue qui tourne . . . qui tourne à vide! [It is like a wheel that turns . . . that turns on empty],[12] as she is acutely aware of her dreary prospects for the future: an arranged marriage, like other female relatives, perhaps with a boorish, older, ill-looking husband—with "a banana nose," she will say—and continuing lack of education.[13]

Her childhood memories aiding, Kaokab has idealized Lebanon as the sunny paradise of her tender childhood, when she was "running barefoot on the red earth"[14] instead of wasting her life in the store. The transliterated Arabic sentence, "Ma'ad Fiyé, Ma'ad Fiyé" [I can't take it any longer, I can't take it any longer][15] is cried by her toward the end of the play, a play that marvelously portrays the mounting physical and psychological *suffocation* and consequent breakdown of two young girls, up to the final tragedy that ensues from their decision to burn the family store in order to set themselves free. It can be said that at the end the sisters have lost the game of patience, the cards taken away by Amira early in the play,[16] in what can be seen as a symbolic gesture of renouncing patience as a traditional value of Arabic culture, one that fosters endurance and can sometimes serve as a tool for oppression. The grieving Mariam in *Jeux de patience*, as we will see below, is also one who refuses "games of patience." She rejects the expression "Noshkour Allah," "thanks be to God," a highly popular, overused expression in the Arab world, one that stands for resignation, submission, and equanimity in the face of any adversity "God" chooses to send one, including man-made calamities.[17]

Les Filles du 5-10-15 cents also indicts the injustice made to young girls in favor of young boys in some uneducated Middle-Eastern families, and the obsession with financial success that skews the outlook of some immigrants on their children's future. Furthermore, it portrays the linguistic alienation children of immigrants are often faced with: Unable to properly communicate with their monolingual parents in Arabic, the sisters are equally unable to communicate in French with their Anglophone Lebanese acquaintances (the only ones they are allowed to frequent), who, unlike Amira and Kaokab, were schooled in English. On the other hand, they do not feel part of the Québécois community their father carefully shuns out of bigotry.

Throughout the play, the energetic Kaokab speaks to a tape recorder (a staging device reminiscent of Krapp in Beckett's *Krapp's Last Tape*) in which she tries to tell her parents her complaints in a frustrated, interrupted, incomplete medley of Arabic and French. The very first sentence of the play, in fact, is addressed (in French and Arabic) to her parents. The utterance, "Ya bayé, ya immé.... Je veux vous dire... je veux vous dire.... Ya bayé, ya immé.... Je veux vous dire" [Dad and Mom, I want to tell you, I want to tell you ... Dad and Mom, I want to tell you. . .].[18] reoccurs a number of times, with variations. Kaokab cannot find the right words to tell her parents, either in French or Arabic, since her knowledge of the latter is limited to "everyday words, words to drink and eat."[19] When her sister asks her what she intends to do with the "niaiseries" [stupidities][20] she is taping, Kaokab answers that she hopes one day, when she is old, to be able to make sense of things, "to understand why."[21] In a moment of epiphany, at the end of the play, Kaokab suddenly knows what to say to her parents. Her final outburst, when she drops the microphone and wildly runs through the store screaming, is a *trilingual diglossic protest* against the *living death* the author herself refers to in the aforementioned citation, and a savage refusal to submit to such death. In her own words:

> Je vous hais, je vous déteste, je vous déteste de m'avoir fait tant souffrir. Je veux vous dire que Kaokab est indestructible, indestructible. Vous ne l'empêcherez pas de vivre. ... Je veux vous dire que je ne mourrai pas malheureuse. Je veux vous dire que malgré vous, je suis vivante, vivante! Enough is enough. Bi Kaffé, bi kaffé, bi kaffé. On ne se laissera pas enterrer vivante. Jamais. Jamais!
>
> [I hate you, I detest you, I detest you for having made me suffer so much. I want to tell you that Kaokab is indestructible, *indestructible*. You will not prevent her from living.... I want to tell you that I will not die unhappy. I want to tell you that in spite of you, I am alive, *alive!*[22] Enough is enough. Bi Kaffé, bi kaffé, bi kaffé. We will not let ourselves be buried alive. Never. Never!][23]

The tape recorder, symbol of Kaokab's living testimonial, with its mixture of French and Lebanese Arabic dialect, is the last object heard on stage after she rushes inside the store to rescue it from the fire she set to the store. Farhoud's 1997 play toys with the construct of patience built in the very title of it.

JEUX DE PATIENCE (1992/1997) [GAMES OF PATIENCE]

J'offre cette pièce à toutes celles et à tous ceux qui ont perdu leur enfant, leur pays, leurs rêves, le goût de la vie.

J'offre ces mots aux oublié-e-s et à tous ceux et celles qui essaient d'oublier.
A ceux qui affrontent chaque jour, chaque instant, le silence de la mort.

[I offer this play to all those who have lost their child, their country, their dreams, their taste for life.
I offer those words to the forgotten ones and to all those who are trying to forget.
To those who face every day, every moment, the silence of death.][24]

The above passage is Farhoud's dedication of *Jeux de patience*, a self-reflexive play, slightly reminiscent of Pirandello's meta theatre. It is divided into five sections indicated with a roman numeral in the original French edition only. In this play, death is approached with a straightforward, direct, and intentional gaze. There are three characters, once more, only female ones: Two Lebanese women, this time in their forties: Mariam or the Mother, who just arrived in Montréal from war-torn Lebanon to live with her cousin, a successful Québécois writer by the dual name of Monique/Kaokab, who is given to playing Solitaire when her writing is in gestation. Monique/Kaokab, emigrated from Lebanon thirty years before, at the age of six, in the early fifties, and has practically forgotten her Arabic except for some obsolete expressions that amuse her cousin. The third character, Samira (a character-actor who is actually the incarnation of living memory) is the sixteen-year-old dead daughter of Mariam who occupies the entire theater (on and offstage). Samira died two months earlier on the streets of Beirut. It is not clear at the outset whether her death was voluntary or accidental. The crux of the action, though, which consists of an attempt to mourn, to grieve, and to remember, is played between the two cousins who resort to Arabic more frequently than Amira and Kaokab did in *Les Filles du 5-10-15 cents*. Monique/Kaokab, perhaps the spokeswoman of the author herself, *must* understand, remember, and write the tragedy of her niece and her native country, in order to remain alive.[25]

In the opening of the play, Kaokab, who is occupying a large stage space on the right, is seen throwing away the game of patience she had been playing and running frantically, breathless, crying:

La patience a des limites. Grouille, Kaokab! Décolle! Bouge! "On peut tout essayer. Devant la mort, tous les risques sont faibles." Ecris Kaokab!

[Patience has its limits. Move, Kaokab! Get going! Budge! "Try as much as you will. With death all risks are weak." Write, Kaokab!][26]

The point of fact is that since her cousin's arrival, Monique/Kaokab has suffered from an acute writer's block, partially caused by Mariam's constant challenging of her desktop suffering in the safety of her well-to-do Montréal home, away from the bombs and the destruction. Mariam, who is seen in a small light spot upstage, is the loud voice of her cousin's and her own survival guilt, guilt to have escaped the dangers of war while others, the omnipresent Samira, for instance, are constantly subject to it. On the back of the stage, which is supposed to represent Kaokab's house, there is a map of the world with drawers at the hot war zones, from which sporadically emerge body parts, including those of Samira. At the end of the play, limbs rain down the stage near the two characters. No specific country is mentioned, for the author's aim is clear. As the opening quotation of this section indicates, Farhoud's intention is an indictment of global violence even if the historical event that forms the backdrop of the play is specifically the Lebanese civil war, which has dispersed thousands of people. "Leaves in the wind. Orphans. Everyone gone where he could,"[27] will say Mariam when her cousin asks her news of her siblings. Farhoud's endeavor is part of "the witnessing project," to borrow an apt expression of the critic Malpede describing newer trends in twenty-first-century theater. She refers to "the witnessing imagination" as a construct developed with a psychiatrist she worked with.[28] Monique/Kaokab seeks to "write the invisible"[29] and expresses her urgency to bear witness and to write about the war. Throughout the play, she repeats the same line, with variations: "Je ne veux pas mourir avant d'avoir écrit. Je ne veux pas mourir avant d'avoir compris" [I do not want to die before writing. I do not want to die before understanding].[30]

At the end of the play, the writer does achieve a manner of reconciliation, if not of understanding, when she starts recording her niece's story and when it becomes clear to her, in the process, that the young girl who "loved life too much,"[31] like Antigone before her, refused to compromise, to live a *living death*, and to die "piece by piece, eaten away by fate." Monique/Kaokab realizes that Mariam's daughter wanted "to make a choice, just once in her life."[32] By means of a mise-en-abyme technique, we learn from Samira-the-character and Monique/Kaokab-the-author who narrates in a poetic monologue the plight of Samira-the-daughter, that, in fact, the latter had chosen to die, purposefully exposing herself to the "death machinery,"[33] as an act of protest over the killing of her best girlfriend, Amal. When the outraged Mariam, the Mother, who would insist that "they killed her,"[34] gradually comes to consider that conjecture as a possibility, she seems somewhat appeased, and finally connects with her writer-cousin who scolds her for her refusal to accept the facts and her equal refusal to mourn Samira's death.[35] Mariam finally agrees to let go of the folded rug she was clutching and rocking throughout the play.

A critic has remarked that the dialogue between the cousins "condemns the Arab tendency to glorify suffering and blame others for their misery."[36] I do not agree with that comment, for one cannot fail to note the bias inherent in such a pronouncement on an alleged "Arab tendency." I would rather advance the following simple interpretation of the mother in Mariam: that a mother's awareness of her daughter's choice to die may be more devastating to her than the idea of an involuntary death, hence Mariam's initial resistance to the idea that her daughter's death was an act of suicide rather than an act of murder carried on by Israelis.

The last line of *Jeux de patience* is a popular Arabic proverb: "El Sabr méftèh el faraj,"[37] which translates to "patience is the key to freedom." Uttered by the playful, teasing Samira who had refused resignation and patience much as her counterpart Kaokab in *Les Filles du 5-10-15 cents* had done, those words add a semblance of ironic relief to the otherwise ominous atmosphere of the play. The feeling of loss and dispossession pervasive in this play is taken to a new dimension in Farhoud's rather ludic and more lighthearted 2003 play.

LES RUES DE L'ALLIGATOR (1998/2003) [ALLIGATOR STREETS]

Les Rues de l'alligator (2003) is an absurdist play from which transpires the universal themes of loneliness, integrity, filial and parental love, sibling relationships, nomadism, poetry, the love of words, and of course, death. In the words of Pierre L'Hérault who prefaced the play and whose very first sentence asserts: "S'il ya une constante dans l'écriture d'Abla Farhoud, ce serait sans doute celle de la disparition, de la perte, de l'amputation" [if there is a constant in the writing of Abla Farhoud it would undoubtedly be that of disappearance, loss, and amputation].[38]

In an epigraph to the play, the word "Alligator (or crocodile)" is defined, in an entry quoted by the author from the *Dictionary of Symbols*, as an epigraph to the play, as the god connected to the "primordial forces of death and rebirth."[39] It is therefore safe to contend that it is under the auspices of such a symbol of life renewal that the play unfolds.

The setting is in "nowadays"[40] Montréal or anywhere "where there are four seasons,"[41] at "the angle of a main street and a quieter one with side streets,"[42] along which life unfolds its course. The play is divided into nine *tableaux* (with the five seasons, beginning with winter and ending with winter) with eighteen characters, nine women and nine men, and some nameless passers-by, as befits streetscapes. The main figures are Sonia Bélanger, a sixty-two-year-old street-crosser, perhaps the same character as the protagonist encountered in *Maudite machine* (1999) who recounts her failed life and the tyranny of social mores in the Québec of her youth; Sophie-Catherine, a fourteen-year-old girl holding a rag doll named Coralie; Blanche Villalobos, a street poet and performer; and Tancrède, a tramp in love with Sonia. Apart from a Mrs. Findley with no part, those are the only characters with a name. All the others are designated by their function or the activity they are engaged in, such as La Femme à la Mallette [the woman with a briefcase], L'Homme Effacé [the effaced man], or Monsieur Cigarette. They all seem to be looking for something or other, one for his lost dog, the other for his lost wife, one for a cigarette, yet another for his lost son, always repeating the same sentences with variations, and in the process, disclosing more details about the object of their quest, a device mimicking the repetition of days and the reenactment of the street as a continual passageway.

The character of Sonia provides the little action there exists in the play, with a revival of the theme of the dead child left behind (Samira in *Jeux de patience*) and the theme of living death we have encountered in our study of *Les Filles du 5-10-15 cents* (the young Kaokab). The illiterate Sonia befriends and tames the reluctant Sophie-Catherine, and there is some hint that the latter is the reincarnation of Sonia's beloved grandmother. Sonia is seduced by the beauty of "the music coming out" of the girl's mouth when the latter is heard reading out loud to her doll,[43] and she convinces the child to teach her how to read, something they begin to do, with tales of times bygone. One of those tales is precisely that of a little girl named Gertrude who was locked and left behind by her parents in a room where she died alone. Through the dialogue, we learn that Coralie (the doll) is the name of Sophie-Catherine's sister. She died seven years before. At the funeral, Sophie had thrown her own doll (bearing her own name, Sophie-Catherine) in the tomb and took her sister's doll instead, Coralie. Sophie-Catherine thus lives with the burden of the identity exchange with a dead sibling whose effigy she always carries on her: "Le jour où ma soeur est morte, je suis morte moi aussi" [The day my sister died, I died too].[44] Furthermore, she believes her parents don't love her but love solely her dead sister through her: "Ils m'aimeraient si j'étais morte" [they would love me if I were dead],[45] she will say. When Sophie-Catherine does not show up for the reading lesson, we learn that she wants to kill herself because her mother has cut up her rag doll Coralie and flushed her down the toilet. She has escaped somewhere. Sonia tries to find her and eventually succeeds. Her love saves the child's life, and the play ends on a note of hope: "J'ai pas encore trouvé ce que je cherche . . . mais . . . j'ai toute la vie devant moi" [I have not found . . . what I am seeking . . . but . . . I have my whole life ahead] says the child.[46] The last image of the play is snow falling and Sonia, cold, "helping people to cross,"[47] she who helped Sophie-Catherine at a difficult crossing of her disturbed adolescence.

Sonia stands out as the figure of the quintessential metaphorical exile Edward Said qualified as marked with a state of "restlessness, movement, constantly being unsettled and unsettling others" and a "dislike of the trappings of accommodation."[48] She is Québécois *de souche* (despite having a Ukranian grandmother), yet she is marginal, poor, childlike, and rather ignorant of the ways of the world.⁴⁹ She enjoys simple things, despises wealth, power, and the unkindness of the establishment. She is an object of mockery for the frustrated executive who lost her job, La Femme à la Mallette, who accuses Sonia of being an eyesore in their clean city, and shouts at her to "go back home."⁵⁰ That Sonia stands for the heart of *Alligator* is hinted at by the fact that she is the one who reads aloud the literal dictionary definition of the alligator, whose mythical definition, as noted above, is used as an epigraph to the whole play: "caractérisé par de fortes mâchoires et un revêtement cuirassé" [characterized by strong jaws and a leather-like hide].⁵¹ She defends the reptile when La Femme à la Mallette calls her "scaled alligator."⁵²

Les Rues de l'alligator stages a community based on the exchange of words, its own and others', a fact that constitutes the main structural theme around which the play revolves. What Sonia seeks above all are words and the beauty of words, worrying about ways to access them. Whoever asks her a question must first give her "a line."⁵³ When, throughout the play, Tancrède declares his love to her, for instance, she constantly asks him to "give" her a sentence, usually a poetic utterance, in exchange for which she shows him kindness. Additionally, the poet Blanche Villalobos, whose domain is the spoken word, declaims poetry taken from Pablo Neruda, Anne Hébert, Gatien Lapointe, and others, and her character constitutes a center of intertextuality to which gravitate and in which participate other characters. Sometimes Sonia's recitation gets enmeshed with some of the other characters' dialogue in what makes for a highly poetic effect. It is not surprising thus that the first tableau of the play opens and closes with a poem Blanche recites, beginning and ending with the importance of the spoken word, *la parole*, a theme we have encountered with the two plays analyzed above:

> *Il me reste la parole.*
> *Qui a des yeux m'entende*
> ...
> *Tous les mots, toutes les chansons portent le poids du silence.*
> *Il me reste la parole*
> *pour ne pas mourir enterrée par le bruit.*
>
> [I still have words to say
> Whoever has eyes can listen to me
> ...
> All the words, all the songs carry the weight of silence.
> I still have words to say
> in order not to die buried by the noise.]⁵⁴

But as with Monique/Kaokab, the protagonist of *Jeux de patience*, the poet Blanche Villalobos, on a symbolic level this time, communicates a sense of urgency that does not necessarily provide an index for success: The need to express oneself may be accompanied by failure, or by a sort of existential impossibility, perhaps due to the nature of language itself. In this regard, it is not surprising that Blanche quotes the Chilean poet Pablo Neruda: "Entre les lèvres et la voix quelque chose s'en va mourant" [between the lips and the voice something dies out][55] when Sophie-Catherine asks her how much she loves Tancrède.

It is interesting to note that *Les Rues de l'alligator* was read as a play several years before its publication, the same year that saw the publication of Abla Farhoud's very first, acclaimed novel, *Le Bonheur a la queue glissante*.

LE BONHEUR A LA QUEUE GLISSANTE (1998) [HAPPINESS HAS A SLIPPERY TAIL]

In an interview about *Le Bonheur a la queue glissante*, Abla Farhoud pointed out that the initial chosen title of that first novel was going to be *Le Livre de ma mère* [My Mother's Book] in reference to the author's own mother, a woman "who does not write and speaks little,"[56] a motivational factor for Farhoud's endeavor: "Si je veux prendre la parole, c'est parce que ma mère ne l'a pas fait" [If I want to speak, it is because my mother has not done it].[57] The genesis of Farhoud's novel, one that nevertheless belongs to the realm of fiction despite the transposition of some of the mother's account, is mirrored in the *mise en abyme* framework of the novel itself.

Dounia, the protagonist-narrator of *Le Bonheur a la queue glissante*, is a seventy-five-year-old illiterate Lebanese immigrant woman who has lived in Montréal some forty years. She narrates her life to her daughter Myriam, a prolific writer who realizes that though she has written fifteen books so far, not a single one reflects her mother. Myriam proceeds to fill this gap in what becomes a project of self-revelation. Daughter and mother, twice a week, meet for the whole day. In the words of Dounia: "Avec du café ou du vin, des questions ou de la patience, Myriam m'aidait à dérouler ma vie" [with coffee or wine, questions or patience, Myriam helped me unravel my life].[58] The protagonist's daughter will write her mother's memoirs, in a similar way the writer Monique/Kaokab in *Jeux de patience* writes Samira's story for her cousin Mariam (Samira's mother) who could not do it herself. The quality of *orality* of the transmitted testimonial will be retained and will color the style of this vibrant narrative, a fact that betrays the novelist's indebtedness to the stage, where she is used to dealing with characters in the flesh, as she herself acknowledges.[59] In the words of Naïm Kattan commenting on the tone of this narrative:

Abla farhoud [qui] réussit à emprunter le langage de cette femme qui ne parle que l'arabe, nous donne l'impression de transcrire un récit oral truffé de proverbes, de dictons . . . jetant ainsi un regard neuf et frais sur le Canada, le Québec dont [la vieille dame] cherche, à sa manière, à comprendre les moeurs et la politique.

[Abla Farhoud . . . succeeds in conveying the language of this woman who speaks only Arabic, and gives us the impression of transcribing an oral tale enriched with proverbs and sayings . . . thus casting a fresh and novel gaze on Canada, on Québec whose customs and politics [the old woman] tries, in her own way, to understand.][60]

Because Dounia is illiterate, the spoken word is the only means at her disposal to bequeath the account of her life to her daughter who records it for her in a long dramatic monologue with shifting points of view, sometimes the third person singular, and most of the time the first person singular. In both cases it is Dounia speaking, perhaps momentarily trying to distance herself from her own account when using the third person point of view. As one would expect from a monologue characterized by introspection, little by little Dounia relates her life, not in a linear fashion but in leaps, beginning a theme, pursuing it for a moment, leaving it as she flashbacks to an incident in her youth, beginning a new theme or sub-theme, pursuing it, then picking up an adjoining topic that sheds new light on the previous one. Throughout the narrative there are references to Dounia having lost her voice; questionings as to what could have possibly happened to the chatty little girl Dounia once was, and to her words being transformed in adulthood "into grains of wheat, rice, vine and cabbage leaves" instead.[61] She asserts she sometimes wishes to be able "to speak with words"[62] instead of "branches of parsley . . . , bell peppers and zucchini."[63]

Amongst the themes harbored in the monologue are childhood memories, immigration and reverse migration, with the difficulties entailed each time when beginning anew or readjusting, and added difficulties as well. As we slowly learn, Dounia's universe is dominated by a husband (Salim) to whom she "conceded her tongue"[64] once and for all, and who is portrayed as stubborn and unloving, as well as her relationship with six children and five grandchildren. Other themes include the Québec separatist movement, the choice of French schooling for her children as a gesture of gratitude to the Québécois,[65] and the civil war in Lebanon, one that "dispersed thousands of families across the world."[66] The leitmotivs of the narrative are impending death, the slow decrepitude of her body—"I tame death," she will say[67]—and, only later in the narrative, the mental illness of her oldest child, Abdallah, the guilt and shame she felt pertaining to pivotal moments of her existence, and an acute need to make sense of it all. In her own words:

> *mieux comprendre avant de mourir. Juste pour le plaisir de comprendre. Pour savoir pourquoi j'ai souffert, pourquoi j'ai parfois envie de quitter ce monde.*
>
> [to better understand before dying. Just for the pleasure of understanding. To know why I suffered, why I sometimes feel like leaving this world.][68]

The whole narrative is punctuated with profound quasi-philosophical reflections on human nature, interspersed with parables and proverbs, including, as befits the title of the novel, on "the slippery," elusive nature of happiness. No fewer than sixty-five proverbs, pertaining notably to pain, solitude, and old age, enrich the narrative, a fact that accounts for the lexicon put at the end of the novel of some of those proverbs in French and Arabic scripts. To mention but a handful: [Only your nails will scratch your skin and relieve you];[69] "Si jeunesse revenait un jour, je lui raconterais ce que vieillesse a fait de moi . . . " [If youth came back to me some day I would tell her what old age has made of me];[70] "Celui qui souffre s'accroche aux cordes du vent" [He who suffers will hang on even to the ropes of the wind];[71] "Une main vide est une main sale" [An empty hand is a dirty hand];[72] and "Je ne suis pas une pastèque qui, en plus de nourrir et d'étancher la soif, sert de repas à l'âne" [Am I a watermelon whose meat and juice quench thirst and whose peel serves as food to donkeys?].[73]

We learn in the course of the monologue that Dounia, daughter of a respected village priest, lost her mother as a young child. Dounia's siblings, except for the youngest brother Mounir, all immigrated to Argentina later on, when she was still young. She marries at eighteen, leaves her village Chaghour to the nearby village of her husband, Bir-Barra (incidentally the same village where Mariam in *Jeux de patience* comes from), where she experiences "deprivation and nostalgia,"[74] and where she spends twelve years, perceived and feeling as "a stranger." After immigration to Canada in the fifties with three young children, the family lives in Montréal for fifteen years, goes back to Lebanon (with six children) for ten years in the midsixties and returns again to Montréal at the onset of the Lebanese civil war in the midseventies. Before the first immigration to Canada, Salim, the husband, who has lost his father young, goes alone to Montréal for two years to pave the way for the family, during which time he lives with his mother, a disastrous experience. He is thirty years old and a total stranger to his mother—the latter never got over her daughter's death—who had immigrated to Canada when Salim was very little, leaving him behind with extended family, as was not unusual at the time in the Middle East.

Dounia refers to her feeling of utter suffocation when she first arrived in Canada, finding the climate "at once cold and suffocating,"[75] and living with her mother-in-law "who hated [her] as if [she] had killed her children.[76] Dounia mentions the financial difficulties and the fact that Salim, the great storyteller, the magician of words accustomed to telling his stories to all and sundry on the village square,[77] had no audience in Canada. Not even his children, because of the language barrier. Says Dounia, "stories remained imprisoned in his throat and choked him."[78] She sums up their first years of immigration in the following words:

> Les premières années passées ici, nous étouffions tous les deux, lui regardant par en dehors en frappant, en cassant tout ce qu'il touchait, et moi, j'éclatais par en dedans ne sachant où déverser mes peines.
>
> [The first years spent here, we both suffocated, he looking outward and hitting, breaking everything he touched, and me, imploding, knowing not where to pour my pain.][79]

She adds that both she and her husband, "two orphans in need of affection and gentleness,"[80] could have died asphyxiated had it not been for the children,[81] and that she managed to breathe just enough so she would not die.[82]

Most of all, Dounia has begun seeing her life in a different light since Myriam has started questioning her.[83] In the face of despair, what she is really attempting to achieve, as a noted psychologist (Erik Erickson) would say, is *ego integrity*, or a sense of acceptance of one's life and one's meaningful relationships in life. She attempts to "redeem" herself and "to throw bridges between past and present," as a critic has rightly pointed out.[84] One senses throughout Dounia's narrative a terrible secret she holds back, one she will not disclose but fiercely keeps locked in. She refers to an "insidious ailment that invaded [her] head and [her] heart,"[85] and she alludes once in a while to "having been crushed by destiny without ever getting up again,"[86] and to a mysterious ailment of her son Abdallah's, a sort of "rapacious bird that eats the inside of his head," leaving him "dispossessed" and "disoriented."[87]

Toward the last third of the narrative, and herein transpire the difficulties her daughter has in extracting information from her, Dounia has a falling out with her daughter Myriam who indirectly attempts to probe the difficult issue of her brother Abdallah. Dounia evades Myriam's questioning about "the event in her life that marked her most," and instead, answers with the first proverb that comes to mind, one she knows her daughter particularly detests: "whoever is born is trapped, whoever dies is liberated."[88] When Myriam insists on getting a genuine answer, the mother blows up and repeats the same proverb, contending that whether her daughter wants it or not, that proverb defines her life. It cannot be brushed aside and treated as if it had not influenced Myriam's life as well.[89]

The mother-daughter narrative session is interrupted, but Myriam's interrogation has opened the floodgates, and Dounia is overwhelmed by her once well-guarded grief. Connected, grafted onto the Abdallah motif, is an array of negative feelings she cannot communicate to Myriam without betraying her engrained values of discretion and propriety: "how to say the truth I have hidden for so long":[90] Shame, guilt, suppression, anger, hatred, and loss of voice, as if the secret of Abdallah's tragedy—she calls him the sacrificial lamb of the family, the one on whom the knife fell[91]—and illness were a microcosm of her own existence, and in fact, she does connect the two when she says that both herself and Abdallah have been broken somewhere in the trajectory of their lives:[92] she, when she married at eighteen; he when he became ill at eighteen[93] and went to the hospital forever burdened with the stigma of madness.[94] She begs her daughter not to write about Abdallah because no book can witness what she and her son have endured together. "Vingt livres ne suffiraient pas" [twenty books would not suffice],[95] and nobody could understand anyway except the husband who witnessed it all. In the words of Dounia explaining her loss of voice:

Le résultat de ma vie est là devant moi. . . . J'ai attendu longtemps pour élever la voix. Trop longtemps. Je ne savais plus comment faire et ma voix ne faisait peur qu'`a moi-même. C'était trop tard. . . . Ma peine, je l'ai poussée à l'intérieur de la jarre comme je le fais avec les courgettes. . . . Quand mon fils tombe en enfer, c'est plus fort que moi, . . . je tombe avec lui, j'éclate en mille morceaux et ma peine devient déraisonnable.

[The outcome of my life is here in front of me. . . . I waited a long time to raise my voice. Way too long. I no longer knew how it was done and my voice scared only myself. It was too late. My grief I have shoved inside the jar as I did with zucchini. . . . When my son falls into hell, I cannot help it, . . . I fall with him, I explode into a thousand pieces and my pain becomes excruciating.][96]

Toward the end of her monologue, Dounia makes reference to an ashtray "the size of three plates" that flew from the hands of "the one I cannot call my husband because I detest him so"[97] and hit Abdallah on the forehead. One is made to understand that the ashtray incident caused Abdallah brain damage. On this occasion Dounia blames herself virulently for having failed to protect her children from their father, for not having stood up to her husband whose violence she endured all her life. She now knows that her loss of voice began with her marriage.[98] She recalls especially one particular incident, when she was still in Lebanon, six months pregnant with her third child, and Salim, for no reason, hit her hard in the face in front of her own father who did nothing to intervene, but insulted her instead. This memory still outrages her "after fifty years," and she discloses her hidden despise and hatred for both father and husband alike—"I should have killed him"[99]—but especially her own lack of self-respect: "Je suis lâche. Je ne suis qu'une peureuse et une lâche, une femme sans dignité, sans colonne vertébrale" [I am a coward. I am only a chicken and a coward, a woman without dignity or spine],[100] she cries as she further realizes that "once you have resigned one time, it's over, you will resign for the rest of your life."[101]

In the context of submission and resignation to her husband's abusiveness, Dounia recalls with bitterness some proverbs inculcated with mother's milk, proverbs that have taken the place of her voice as nutshells of ready-made formulas passed on from generation to generation by men and women alike, for the submission of women to men: "Leave your pain in your heart and suffer in silence; disclosed suffering is but dishonor and scandal." All the women were "imbibed with those proverbs and murmured them silently."[102] This is how she was able to stifle the pain.[103] Dounia's voicelessness and patience (as pointed out by a critic)[104] are thus reinforced by the proverbs repeated as mantras and functioning as built-in devices for self-silencing, as when Dounia admits earlier in the monologue that replying with proverbs (when asked difficult questions) is easier than "having to look for truth, to say it and to live it."[105] Thus, when Myriam asks her if she is afraid her children may abandon her in her old age, she replies, "Allah is with the weak to astonish the strong,"[106] as she could not admit to such a lack of confidence in life and in her children.

The opening sentence of the novel has already expressed the thought of solitude and abandonment in a disguised form:

J'ai dit à mes enfants: "le jour où je ne pourrai plus me suffire à moi-même, mettez-moi dans un hospice pour vieillards." Ils ont répondu: "Mais non, mais non, tu es notre mère, nous nous occuperons de toi."

[I told my children, "the day I can no longer take care of myself, put me in a retirement home." They answered: "No, no. You are our mother. We will take care of you."][107]

In the closing chapter of the narrative Dounia is indeed alone, invalid, in what seems to be a nursing home. Her husband Salim is dead. An unspecified number of years have elapsed. The following is perfectly foreshadowed by the very first sentence of the novel. Dounia speaks thus:

Elle est assise sur une chaise parfois, la plupart du temps dans son lit, la femme épave que je suis devenue. Elle regarde dehors, la femme sans jambes. Ses yeux ne voient presque plus, la femme muette. Elle parle à la vitre devant elle, la femme qui s'est toujours tue. Dehors il n'y a personne, à côté d'elle il n'y a personne.

Pour l'aider à manger quelqu'un vient. . . . Ses enfants viennent parfois la voir comme s'ils lui faisaient une faveur, la femme qui les a tant aimés.

[She is sitting on a chair sometimes, most of the time in her bed, the wreck I have become. She looks outside, the woman without legs. Her eyes are almost blind, the silent woman. She talks to the windowpane in front of her, the woman who always kept quiet. Outside there is nobody, besides her there is nobody.

To help her eat somebody comes. . . . Her children come to see her sometimes as if they were doing her a favor, the woman who has loved them so much.][108]

At the very end of the narrative, Dounia has a dream of her husband where he is very kind to her and tells her that because of her he had had a good life and that his heart had always been for her and with her. He also tells her that perhaps their son Abdallah was sent by destiny to make them understand something. "You must forgive, Dounia, you must,"[109] he adds. Here, once more, as we have seen with both *Les Filles du 5-10-15 cents* and *Jeux de patience*, a note of hope transpires at the end of this otherwise somber narrative where, much like the characters staged in the plays studied above, Dounia hated resignation and submission, even if she gave in to them. All things considered, Dounia beheld someone who could listen to her, albeit belatedly. Perhaps the reader has to wait until Farhoud's next novel in order to experience the ultimate portrayal of solitude, as the title itself, *Splendide solitude*, indicates.

SPLENDIDE SOLITUDE (2001) [SPLENDID SOLITUDE]

Elle marche. Elle veut comprendre. L'âme. Point d'interrogation. L'âme. Point d'exclamation. L'âme. Points de suspension.

[She is walking. She wants to understand. The soul. Question mark. The soul. Exclamation mark. The soul. Ellipses.][110]

Splendide solitude, the second of Farhoud's novels and the least acclaimed of the three, consists of a diary-monologue of an upper middle-class Québécois woman in her early fifties, who faces her total aloneness. Her husband left her many years before; so did, one after the other, her three children (two boys and a girl), the youngest of whom recently. Only her aging body remains, "a country at war" she says[111]—this is the first entry of the monologue—as she faces the various discomforts associated with menopause. Unaccustomed to this utter loneliness, which is one of the leitmotifs of the novel, she strives to battle, to confront, and to tame her splendid solitude. To this end, she shuns the outside world to a maximum, a feat she can easily accomplish, as she is financially independent and does not need to work. Much like her Lebanese counterpart, Dounia, in *Le Bonheur a la queue glissante*, all she wants is to understand:

> Comprendre où est parti l'amour. L'amour que j'ai donné, l'amour que j'ai cru recevoir.
>
> [To understand where the love went. The love I gave, the love I thought I had received.][112]

For an indeterminate amount of time, she will reflect on her life as she conducts a painful introspection full of questioning. Reflections on the meaning of life, love, death, and family happiness, permeate this moving account of a seemingly failed life.

In her attempt to achieve understanding (an impulse she shares with many a character in Farhoud's *oeuvre*), to figure out "how to inhabit time,"[113] and to continue living, this nameless protagonist-narrator, orphaned at the age of twenty-one when she loses both parents, revisits her past as the story of her marriage unfolds: she is the one to have discovered her husband, a talented composer, when he was young, poor, and still unknown. She relives what his music meant to her and the place it occupied in her life. Recalling her very first encounter with him at a concert where he was playing, she says: "Lui et la musique sont indissociables. Ce jour-là j'ai entendu le secret de son âme en même temps que j'ai vu son corps" [He and music are inextricably linked. That day I heard the secret of his soul at the same time as I set eyes on his body].[114] Having married him and provided him with the financial means to launch a successful musical career, she became the facilitator of his talents, and subsequently, of those of her three children, all able musicians. Herself a musician (like her mother before her), she failed to pursue her own interest, devoting herself instead to what she understood to be her mission.[115] Nevertheless, with every new departure of each member of her family, she refused to let go of the piano,[116] the only remaining relic of her past happiness. In point of fact, hers is an intense, passionate love of *live* music in the process of becoming,[117] which is the second leitmotiv of this sad monologue. She explains: "C'est le miracle que j'aime. Le miracle de la création . . . qui se fait *live*, en vie, vivant, embryon de vie" [It is the miracle I love. The miracle of creation . . . that is being made *live*, living, alive, living embryo].[118] Sometimes, musical terminology itself will be used to express pain as, for instance, on the very first page of the diary when the tone for the entire upcoming narrative is being established:

> On m'a tranchée quatre fois, concerto en quatre mouvements avec thème récurrent: le père de mes enfants, puis l'aîné en âge de partir, puis le cadet, et puis la benjamine qui n'arrivait plus à respirer.

[I was cut four times, concerto in four movements with recurring theme: the father of my children, then the eldest, the middle one and the youngest who could no longer breathe.][119]

Like Sonia Bélanger, the metaphorical exile of *Les Rues de l'alligator*, this nameless narrator-protagonist, also a nonethnic Québécois, is nevertheless made stateless by her husband's abandonment. *S'expatrier* [to expatriate himself] is the term her husband used to announce his moving out of her life and their house. *Stateless* is the one she uses to describe her status after his departure, her exile from what was her native country, the music of her husband, the man she loved.[120]

In the last chapter of the monologue, the narrator seems to have journeyed at length since the beginning of her voluntary confinement, as she undergoes an epiphany where she redefines the meaning of solitude: it is not so much missing loved ones, but missing the vanished *Self*. In this light, she sees solitude as "a lost belonging, an earthly disconnection, a loss of meaning, a dislocation of ties."[121] She confesses to having been a mere spectator instead of an actor and to having lived through the talents of others in avoidance of the fulfillment of her own potential. While music allowed her body, her mind, and her soul to be in touch with the essence of life itself, absence of musical creation meant being in touch with death itself.[122] Herein lies the crux of her existential plight. At the close of the diary, she is suddenly enabled to mourn her parents' death of three decades earlier. She invites her nine girlfriends to a travel-log reading of an alleged (nonexistent) trip she claims to have taken to *Le Grand Nord*. She repaints her house, throws away all the dried flowers in a symbolic gesture of renewal, and refurbishes the newly tuned piano. The last sentence of the novel, "Tout le monde est parti, mais le piano est encore là" [Everybody is gone but the piano is still here],[123] suggests that she is on a new track, recovering her autonomy and becoming her own person.[124] Is this, then, the ultimate solitude the title of the novel suggests?

In a 2001 book review published in a Québécois daily, titled "*Splendide solitude*: Un titre trompeur" [Splendide Solitude: A Misleading title], the reviewer, Jean Vigneault, in an effort to contest the title of Farhoud's novel and to warn the prospective readers, qualifies the solitude found in it, not as "splendid," but as "oppressante, écrasante" [oppressive, crushing].[125] Even though I agree that the narrator's frame of mind is bleak, I believe the adjective *splendide* here should not be taken as the dictionary definition of *resplendent, gorgeous, glorious, sublime,* or *superb*. Rather, it should be understood in the sense of an uninhabited space, vast, immense, and formidable in size. This view is suggested by such statements as "Le chemin de moi à moi est si long et si ardu" [the path from me to myself is so long and so arduous],[126] statements that speak of the space of an internal journey, one undertaken "without make-up, with nothing. To experience the nothing, the alone."[127] The frequent shifts in points of view, from the third person singular to the first person and back, also suggest a voyage inward, through a land where both detachment and involvement are required stances. In the words of the Québécois critic, Lucie Lequin, commenting on the narrator's revival:

> Pour la première fois, elle partage avec ses amies sa parole écrite; elle leur lit des pages de son "récit de voyage," voyage vers soi. . . . Tout au long du roman, les jeux entre le je et le elle sont significatifs de ce regard autonome.
>
> [For the first time, she shares with her friends her written word. She reads them pages of her "travel log," travel towards the self. . . . All along the novel, the play between the *I* and the *she* are relevant to this autonomous gaze.][128]

It is worth pointing out the heavy use of intertextuality present in *Splendide solitude*, a fact reminiscent of *Les Rues de l'alligator* mentioned above. Unlike the latter, however, where the texts quoted belong mostly to French-Canadian writers as we have seen, here, it is rather a collection of mostly nineteenth and twentieth-century French writers who are heard in little snatches of poetry and prose alike: Pascal, Marceline-Desbordes Valmore, Baudelaire, Rimbaud, Beckett, Gide, Camus, and Proust. The latter is evoked in a lengthy passage where the narrator-protagonist gives a reader's response to the French writer's oeuvre: "L'auteur a transcendé sa souffrance en la transposant en oeuvre d'art" [The author has transcended his pain by transposing it in a work of art],[129] she comments, in the context of the manner in which Proust helped her connect her own suffering to that of humanity at large. The intertextuality embedded in this monologue adds a second dimension to the background and speaks of the interconnection of humans (great and less great) across time, the theme of Proust's last sentence of *Combray*, which she records (109).[130]

LE FOU D'OMAR (2005) [OMAR'S MADMAN]

When speaking of the genesis of her third novel, Abla Farhoud asserts that instead of the current theme elaborated by the renowned French Canadian psychoanalyst Guy Corneau,[131] of the absent father figure resulting in an utterly failed son, she wanted to come up with an all too present father and arrive at the same result, namely the failed, deprived son, an inspiration that led her to imagine a man waking up some morning totally alone, after having lived all his life with his father whom he finds dead in bed.[132]

Le Fou d'Omar, Farhoud's latest fictional endeavor (recipient of *Prix du roman francophone*), as the author herself admits, is more complex than her earlier novels *Le Bonheur a la queue glissante* and *Splendide solitude*. In fact, instead of the one long dramatic monologue of the two previous novels, *Le Fou d'Omar* is composed of six dramatic monologues titled *livres* [books], each one of which headed by an epigraph consisting of a literary quotation borrowed from Stefan Zweig, Cervantès, Omar Khayyam, Sony Labou Tansi, and Emily Dickinson, a device never used before by the author, and one she attributes to her concept of literature as something that needs to circulate.[133]

The six dramatic monologues that make up *Le Fou d'Omar* consist of personal diaries written by four characters: Radwan Abou Lkhouloud (Books 2 and 6), his brother Rawi (Book 3), their father Omar (Book 5), and the family's Montréal neighbor (Books 1 and 4), Lucien Laflamme, a philanthropic fellow in his late fifties, originally from Chicoutimi (Québec), who has read the Koran. The novel opens with Lucien Laflamme commenting on his Moslem Lebanese neighbors' lives, which fascinates him and intrigues him at the same time—"there is something wrong" with the family, he remarks[134]—for, after fifteen years, he has yet to know them, a situation due to a "frustrating" and excessive privacy on their part. He has come to notice, especially after the mother's death, an extraordinarily strong bond between father and son. Laflamme also recounts a mysterious incident when the mother was still alive, one day when he saw the son, Radwan, whom he describes as otherwise gentle and delicate,[135] suddenly going on a rampage in the garden where he tore everything up, then ran onto the streets while his parents were desperately calling out for him in vain. This is the first foreshadowing the reader has of the manic-depressive disorder which Radwan, the adored son of Omar, suffers from. The theme of madness, peripherally at work through the character of Abdallah in Farhoud's first novel, is also encountered in *Quand le vautour danse* [When the Vulture Dances], Farhoud's 1997 play where the *vulture*, madness, hits the brother of the protagonist, Suzanne, and leads the latter to suicide. However, it is not until *Le Fou d'Omar* that Farhoud explores this theme in a full-fledged proportion.

Written from the first person point of view, in a French infused with English sentences—especially when uttering profanities—as well as highly colloquial Québécois expressions, with the occasional Arabic (transliterated) idioms, *Le Fou d'Omar*, "Omar's Madman," is a hauntingly vibrant and compelling multiple account of the agonies of mental illness and its impact on the members of an entire family, in particular two brothers and their father, whose diaries vividly record their parallel woes. Fraternal, filial, parental love, sibling rivalry, death wishes, failure, and the immense burden of responsibility are some of the subthemes that permeate this "little gem of a book," to borrow a French-Canadian critic's qualification.[136] Particular attention will be paid in this chapter to the two brothers' accounts.

Radwan's Book

Book 2, the longest one, is Radwan's first monologue. It unfolds basic facts about his life and those of his family. Radwan is around thirty-seven years of age and suffered the first onset of his mental illness at the age of fourteen. He is the fourth of six offspring (the third one was stillborn), and the first long-awaited male adored by his father at the expense of his siblings. There are four remaining adult children in the family—he tells us that he "drank all the water of their wells":[137] His older sisters Salma and Nabila and his younger brother Rawi, alias Pierre-Luc Duranceau, a highly prosperous Québécois writer who changed his name and hid his Arabic origin from the public. His second younger brother, Hafez, broke up with the family long ago and disappeared altogether, and Soraya, a younger sister whom Radwan adored, perished at fourteen in a fire. Radwan's siblings—he is convinced they detest him, and that he is the blight, "the chewing-gum they cannot unglue from their soles"[138]—all live away from Montréal, in Canada and Europe. At the death of the mother, we learn, Radwan suddenly finds himself alone with his father, though "pieces of [his siblings'] skin remained attached" to his own.[139] Radwan expresses resentment mostly toward his brother Rawi, notably for having changed his name and disowned him and his father. A year younger, Rawi nevertheless seems to have played the role of Radwan's protector during childhood and to have functioned as Radwan's alter ego and a successful one at that: "Je voulais être écrivain, c'est mon frère qui l'a été" [I wanted to be a writer, it's my brother who has become one],[140] he will bitterly exclaim, a sentiment echoed in Rawi's monologue, as will be shown below.

In the opening scene of his monologue, when he finds his father dead in his sleep, Radwan is surrounded by his five salvaged dogs which, in his utter helplessness, he will gradually come to call his "beloved children."[141] The very first, fragmented sentence of Radwan's first book (Book 2) is in English. It summarizes at once his disjointed personality and broken life: "Father. My father. My father is. My father is dead."[142] This is repeated throughout, with variations, almost always in English, a fact that can perhaps be explained by the need to register the reality of the father's death with the attention and distance afforded by a non-native language: "My father is dead and I'm not,"[143] "My father is dead and I'm alive. Almost alive,"[144] "My father is dead and I can't walk anymore. I won't kill myself. I won't";[145] "My father is dead. Dead. Dead. And I'm dying."[146] Examining these utterances, one notes an increasing sense of breakdown conveyed by the mere repetition of "My father is dead" juxtaposed with gradually more compelling signs of incapacitation (difficulty to walk, suicidal thoughts, paralysis). What transpires here is

Radwan's inability to make a move to bury his father, though he repeatedly points out that Islam requires washing the body and burial within twenty-four hours. The mounting urgency of burial, accompanied with the incapacity to act—after a great deal of agonizing, he calls his brother Pierre Luc Duranceau, the writer, then he hangs up the receiver when his brother answers—is perhaps an offshoot of the illness itself. It permeates this account of intense fear, of a paralyzed will and a suffocated soul. Thus, as Radwan continues to watch his father's "smooth face," he is glued to his deathbed and can't get up:

> *Je n'arrive pas à enlever mes yeux, sortir, fermer la porte. . . . Des mots. des mots. Il faut des gestes [I am unable to remove my eyes, to go out, to close the door. . . . Words. Words. I need acts].*[147]

At the end of the sixth book, his second monologue, he implores the help of his dogs:

> *Prendre mon père dans mon bras. Le mener à. Aidez-moi. Aidez-moi. Bamako, Ego, Bacha, Abel, Solo. Aidez-moi. Il me reste vous.*
>
> [To take my father in my arms. To bring him to. Help me. Help me. Bamako, Ego, Bacha, Abel, Solo. Help me. I still have you.][148]

Intense, excruciating fear, one that marks his entire life, seems in this moment of crisis, to have further contributed to the above-mentioned paralysis. Radwan describes himself as "a crazy scared child"[149] and invokes his father's help, begging him to extract that lump of fear from his stomach,[150] so that he may accomplish his burial duty. Though Radwan's first monologue ends with his having given up on burying his father, in the second monologue, at the end, he will finally make it as far as the garden where he drags the body and shovels snow on it, to the alarm and utter disbelief of his neighbor Lucien Laflamme who happens to be sitting on his balcony. His brother Rawi will come to the rescue and take over from the neighbor who meanwhile has extended a helping, compassionate hand.

Despite his illness, Radwan cannot pass for an unreliable narrator, for his is a keenly lucid awareness of himself and his place in his family and in society at large, one echoed and corroborated by both his father's and his brother's subsequent monologues. This lucidity is also apparent in his social criticism. It does not curtail, however, the existence of a large number of incomplete sentences, a fact that reflects perhaps a state of mind characterized by discontinuity and a sense of incompleteness. To give but two examples: "J'aurais pu en apprendre plusieurs si" [I could have learned several if],[151] he says, in reference to foreign languages, or "Je suis dans la possibilité de. La torture. J'aime mieux la torture. Mettre le feu" [I could consider. Torture. I prefer torture. To set fire]¹⁵² in reference to his panic over his father's impending burial and the course of action to follow.

In his monologues, Radwan expatiates on the nature of mental illness and recounts his first episode when he was fourteen. His torment is expressed in concise but moving passages that inform the reader and enlighten him about the added social stigma attached to mental illness. The horror, we learn, is one associated with the continuous *va-et-vient* "between the internal and the external, between the external and the internal,"¹⁵³ from hospital to home with "a head heavy with shame,"¹⁵⁴ back to the hospital, escorted by two policemen, like a common criminal. Radwan will come to question his very humanity. Openly so when he asks outright, several times, whether a "madman is still a man"¹⁵⁵ or when he asserts at the end that he is "a madman, not a man,"¹⁵⁶ or in a more subtle linguistic switch at the end of his second and last monologue when he invokes the help of his "beloved sons" (his five dogs), calling them "bons chiens" [good dogs], followed by the singular form *bon chien* [*good dog*], which he repeats, obviously referring to himself.¹⁵⁷ A sharp sense of failure will hence mar the awareness of this antihero:

> "I am a coward. I'm a loser. I'm a frog."¹⁵⁸ "Tous mes efforts n'ont jamais servi à rien. Je suis né fils. Et je mourai fils. Possédé et dépossédé" [All my efforts were always in vain. I was born son. And I will die son. Possessed and dispossessed].¹⁵⁹

Those statements, constituting variations on the theme of *the eternal son* and on that of being orphaned (a theme encountered in all three of Farhoud's novels), "son of no one, father of nobody,"¹⁶⁰ abound and speak of a filial symbiotic link: "My father and I were living in a blender. Un broyeur de vie. Il a broyé ma vie, j'ai broyé la sienne" [a life crusher. He crushed my life. I crushed his],¹⁶¹ and he goes as far as reproaching his oversolicitous dead father: "I didn't deserve your love. Why did you love me so? Why? Why?"¹⁶²

Rawi's Book

The third book is told by Rawi, alias Pierre-Luc Duranceau, a writer like Monique/Kaoakab in *Jeux de patience* and like her preoccupied with questions related to a writer's integrity. Rawi's diary is mostly devoted to Radwan's illness and to a lesser degree, to a codependent rapport he has with his brother: "Mon frère est fou et c'est moi qui suis aliéné, . . . qui suis devenu son esclave" [My brother is crazy and I am the alienated one . . . who has become his slave].¹⁶³ In his monologue, Rawi discloses his love-hate relationship with Radwan, one compounded by the lack of fatherly love he had to endure as a child. His account begins and ends with his brother Radwan whose aborted phone call makes him intuit the father's death, especially so since he is at a point of his novel where his protagonist is about to lose her father. He speaks, among other things, of an all too familiar sensation of heart palpitations and acid in his stomach he would always feel when he worried about Radwan.[164] In a moving passage, Rawi-Duranceau describes the day his brother returned home after the first hospitalization, and how seeing him in bed, broken down, swollen, foaming at the mouth, dispossessed of himself, and murmuring the words: "To die . . . I . . . want . . . to die . . . ," he, Rawi, was invaded by the desire to die.[165] The two brothers were born, we are told, "head to head"[166] (Rawi being a year younger), according to an Arabic expression referring to two chronologically immediate siblings, an expression Rawi translates as "cat and dog." We learn that even as an adult, despite having moved thousands of miles away and having changed his name in hopes of escaping the suffocating emotional stronghold of his sibling, Rawi still feels vulnerable. He asserts that every time Radwan "crumbles," he himself feels like vanishing,[167] hence the need for self-protection. Referring to his brother's ascendancy over him, in an expressive statement corroborating Radwan's own admittance as transpired above, Rawi writes: "ses tentacules sont si poreux qu'ils suceraient toute l'eau de mon corps si je me laissais aller" [his tentacles are so porous that they would suck all the water out of my body if I were not careful].[168]

In an interesting twist of sibling rivalry, Rawi considers his life to be the carbon copy of his brother's; his brother, in turn, functions as an alter ego. Corroborating his brother's statement on the issue, Rawi contends that by becoming a writer he fulfilled Radwan's failed dream of becoming one himself: "Ma vie s'échafaude en réaction à celle de mon frère. Si le destin ne l'avait pas foudroyé, j'aurais eu une toute autre vie"[169] [My life is scaffolded in reaction to that of my brother's. If destiny had not struck him, I would have had an altogether different existence].[170] He admits that if, socially speaking, he, Rawi, is the light, then, on a different dimension, his brother Radwan is himself the light and he, Rawi, darkness.[171] A telling comment in light of what the reader can perceive of Radwan's astuteness.

Rawi's monologue is a compelling record of the family life of six people "agglutinated in misery,"[172] a family who, in times of crisis, becomes "a talking mill," endlessly repeating the same words,[173] invaded as one tribal entity, with no longer any sense of individuality, by one thought, one concern, and one mission championed by the father: to save at all costs Radwan,[174] whose "misfortune" was the misfortune of the entire family and who, at the onset of the illness, stopped being referred to by name, but by the personal and possessive pronouns, *he* or *him* instead. Having lost his name, Radwan suddenly "occupied the entire space."[175] In times of remission, when the family barely had time to recover, the "hurricane" would strike again, most unexpectedly, each time more violently, a theme handled by the father as well. In the words of Rawi-Duranceau:

> Quand nous n'étions pas en train de parler de lui, nous étions en train de courir les papiers des médecins, de téléphoner à la police ou de le chercher à travers la ville. Et nous revenions tout raconter: Comment il avait refusé de nous accompagner, comment il était habillé, ce qu'il avait fait et dit. . . . C'était sans fin. Comme si nos propres vies n'avaient plus aucune importance.
>
> [When we were not talking about him, we were busy running around to physicians, phoning the police, or looking for him across town. And we came back to tell everything: how he had refused to follow us, how he was dressed, what he had said and done. . . . It was endless. As if our own lives no longer mattered at all.][176]

The title of the novel, *Le Fou d'Omar*, occurs for the first time in Rawi's monologue, namely in the third book. It refers to a tragedy in which the writer Pierre Luc Duranceau—his name at birth, Rawi, means storyteller in Arabic—imagines the role of each and everyone in his family: Radwan, *le fou*, is his father's madman. As such he holds the main role. *Omar*, the father "who only loved one child. The only one. The unique" is his adjuvant.[177] The mother is the coryphée, and Rawi and his siblings, the choir.[178] It is of relevance that the novel would bear the name Omar, the name of the father whose own contribution, a mere fifteen pages of the total One-hundred-sixty-nine pages, is obviously minimal. Perhaps it could be contended that the theme of the father's excessive love for one son to the relative exclusion of the other offspring, is the overarching theme to which everything else, especially the conflicted relationships between siblings, becomes subservient and can be considered as mere subthemes.

Omar's Book

"Je suis mort étouffé. Etouffé par trop d'amour, trop d'espoir déçu" [I have died choked. Choked by too much love, too much betrayed hope].[179] Such is the first sentence of Omar's monologue (Book 5), a portrayal of the agony of an intensely devoted father over his ailing son, expressed in terms more painfully vivid than the previous monologues. Omar's is a sweeping statement where he renounces God and where he discloses his awareness of the negligence with which he treated his other children (who had to carry their sick brother's burden), his failure as a father, and his stifling adoration of his favorite son Radwan, whose devastation devastated in turn his own being:[180] "Tous les jours, qu'il soit à la maison ou à l'hôpital ou perdu quelque part dans la ville, je vivais l'échec. L'échec de ma vie" [Everyday, whether he was at home, at the hospital, or lost somewhere on the streets, I was living failure. The failure of my life].[181] Furthermore, referring to his torment over his mentally ill son, Omar asserts: "avec le temps je suis devenu une pensée unique à circuit fermé" [with time I had become one single thought in a closed circuit].[182] The death of his wife Hoda, whom he tenderly loved—*Hoda la magnifique*, he calls her—exacerbated his concern over his son's mental illness.

Perhaps the following statement, one that intimates the inherent unpredictability of psychotic episodes as well as the impossibility of escape from them, will sum up this father's outlook on the biggest trial of his life:

J'ai connu guerre et folie, et à un soufle de la mort, je choisirais la guerre, si je pouvais encore choisir, sans l'ombre d'un doute, sans aucune hesitation.

[I have known both war and mental illness. On the brink of death, if I were to choose again, I would choose war, without the shadow of a doubt, without any hesitation.][183]

In the above enlightening passage, psychotic episodes are likened to the Lebanese civil war (1975–1990): For fifteen years, every time it subsided, like Radwan's illness, it would suddenly flare up one more time and resume the devastation, relentlessly so. However, unlike war raids during which an intense sense of solidarity flourishes between people facing a common danger, binding them together, with psychotic attacks, on the other hand, a family is in total solitude, burdened with shame, isolated from the entire community, neighbors and strangers alike, by "that mass of shadow that one can neither disclose nor name."[184] The family, moreover, is alienated from the dispossessed member himself whose psychotic attacks are an adversary with an ever-changing face. In the words of Omar:

Chaque fois que la folie frappe, c'est la première fois. Comme chaque membre de ma famille, j'ai été catapulté, en vingt ans, dans quarante pays inconnus, où rien ne ressemblait à rien . . . , où aucun geste n'avait de rapport avec l'autre.

[Every time madness strikes, it is like the first time. As for every member of my family, in twenty years, I was catapulted to forty different unknown countries, where nothing resembled anything . . . , where not a single gesture had any connection with any other gesture.][185]

Perhaps the state of mind of this unfortunate Omar, the figure of the eternal father, is singularly akin to that of Dounia, the protagonist-narrator of *Le Bonheur.* . . . Dounia too, as a devoted mother, was tortured over the fate of her mentally ill son Abdallah. Moreover, she, much like her male counterpart in the 2005 novel, had sinned from excessive hope or trust in life's clemency. She had endured her plight in hopes it would be alleviated, only to find out that hope had betrayed her: The *trop d'espoir déçu* [too much disappointed hope] expressed by Omar was also the predicament of Dounia, the protagonist of *Le Bonheur a la queue glissante*, who likewise realized that "to be touched through the suffering of one of your children is the biggest of all sufferings."[186]

OF THEMATIC CROSSOVERS IN THE UNIVERSE OF ABLA FARHOUD

Immanently a playwright, both in the genesis of her career, as described above, and in the making of her works, Abla Farhoud, a latecomer to the world of novel-writing, has admittedly written her novels the way she conveived of plays,[187] hence the dramatic monologues (at times with different voices) that her novels consist of, providing an instance of crossover, albeit of a structural nature, between fiction and drama in her oeuvre. The cross-fertilization of genres, and especially themes, constitutes a hallmark of Farhoud's writing. Hers is a world where loneliness, fear, acute mental pain, alienation, and shame haunt some of the characters, often orphaned protagonists; where the need to bear witness, to mourn, to grieve, to understand and to forget, or to understand in order to forget, is prevalent; where the urge and the necessity to write, to narrate oneself or someone close to oneself, provide the only hope for salvation.

Farhoud's universe—incidentally, Dounia, the protagonist's name in the first novel, which means *world* in Arabic, while Kaokab, which means *star*, is the first name of the main female character in two of the plays studied in this chapter[188]—is one where mental illness (the ultimate state of exile) and the agonies of the mentally ill are painted with vivid colors and a subtle hand. When it comes to leitmotifs in Farhoud's oeuvre, within and across genres, one can think first and foremost of the theme of the lost child loved by a parent to the detriment of the other children, and the tyranny exercised by the dead and the mentally ill on the survivors of that loved one *lost* either through death or mental illness. Such is the case with Sophie-Catherine in *Les Rues de l'alligator*, who mourned her sister's loss and her parents' preference of her dead sister. Such is also the case with Mariam in *Jeux de patience* who could not accept the death of her daughter Samira whose physical presence on the stage stood for that refusal; of Kaokab and Myriam in *Les Filles du 5-10-15 cents* who suffered from their parents' stark preference of their brother Mounir; of Salim, Dounia's husband, who was left behind in Lebanon as a child and was disliked by his mother who loved her dead daughter, his sister, instead; of the protagonist in *Splendide solitude* who had yet to mourn the loss of her own parents when still a young girl; of Suzanne in *Quand le vautour danse* who was destroyed by her brother's madness, and last, of Rawi in *Le Fou d'Omar* who felt controlled by his brother's mental illness and his father's exclusive concern for that one brother. The list is long.

Seeking other thematic and structural similarities or unique instances in Farhoud's oeuvre, one should also note that the mark of the political, in the shape of themes pertaining to the Lebanese civil war and the related issue of the Palestinian situation, often only implicit in her drama and fiction, as I have pointed out throughout this chapter, become suddenly much more explicit in her latest novel, *Le Fou d'Omar*, and more specifically so in Radwan's diaries where we initially learn about the family's reasons for immigration and where, in a very lyrical passage, he merges the figure of his younger sister Soraya who died accidentally in a fire at the age of fourteen, with that of a fourteen-year-old female Palestinian suicide bomber he happened to have read about. Additionally, referring to the massacre conducted by Israel in Southern Lebanon on two Palestinian refugee camps, in which 1,700 people were killed,[189] Radwan writes, addressing the Israeli Sharon:

> S'il n'y avait que toi de charognard, on n'en serait pas là. 1982. Sabra et Chatilla, ce n'était pas assez. Ça ne t'a pas suffi. Du sang. Encore du sang. Et le peuple israelien t'a élu. Je hais le genre humain.
>
> [If you were the only butcher, we would not be here. 1982. Sabra and Chatilla, that was not enough. Blood. More blood. And the Israeli people have elected you. I hate the human species.][190]

Radwan launches a three-page indictment of the violence made to the Palestinians with the help of "God of the universe, Bush . . . son of Bush the Great";[191] of the silence the rest of the world keeps in this regard, and of the fact that the victims of the Holocaust became in turn executioners. In this context, 9/11 is seen as part of a murderous chain that will never stop. It is deemed as an event blown out of proportion—"as if there had never been any violence before"[192]—in order to further the injustices committed by G. W. Bush. The latter, Radwan contends, received "all the blessings" after 9/11. His own terrorism (that of "the stronger") is not called by the same name as the terrorism of "the weaker" (presumably the Palestinians) when the latter, in turn, seeks to gain a semblance of power. "Deux poids deux mesures" [two weights two measures] is the expression used by Radwan[193] to point out the stark double standard involved and the political correctness of the terminology used by the media when covering the Middle East, in favor of Israel and the United States. One is led to wonder what compelled Farhoud who, in her previous work never openly refers to precise sides of political conflicts, to suddenly come forth with openly engaged statements in her latest novel? Is the fact that those statements are written by a mentally ill protagonist relevant insomuch as he can be made to express thoughts the author would not otherwise come up with?

In relation to the backgrounds of the protagonists of Farhoud's oeuvre within and across the two genres she practices (fiction and drama), one can conclude that *Splendide solitude* (2001) is to the other two novels, *Le Bonheur a la queue glissante* (1998) and *Le Fou d'Omar* (2005), what *Les Rues de l'alligator* (2003) is to the plays *Jeux de patience* (1993) and *Les Filles du 5-10-15 cents* (1993). The 2001 novel, like the 2003 play and unlike the other works mentioned, does not represent immigrant characters, but rather old-stock Québécois ones (for instance, Sonia Bélanger in *Les Rues de l'alligator* and the nameless woman-narrator of *Splendide solitude*) confronted with some of the same issues and dilemmas as their immigrant counterparts: vast solitude, fear of aging, and a record of suppression and failed aspirations. In that regard, Farhoud can well be said to have managed to *transcend* the specific attributes associated with ethnic experience by portraying characters whose plights have universal resonance, a worthwhile achievement great writers have sometimes shared. In what light does Abla Farhoud consider the aspect of her writing pertaining to the "ethnic experience"?

In a 1994 *table ronde* [roundtable discussion] with other minority Québécois writers, when confronted with the issue of the minority writer in Québec, Farhoud asserts repeatedly that her being a *migrant* writer is peripheral to her work, and somewhat accidental. She contends that immigration is not a major theme in her work, but merely a background landscape[194] and that her own experience of immigration can stand as a metaphor for human life, an assertion that lends credence to my claim pertaining to the universality of some of Farhoud's themes. Writes the author in this vein:

> *Mon écriture est migrante dans la mesure où je suis toujours à la recherche de l'ailleurs. Enfant, j'ai expérimenté la déchirure, l'arrachement, comme tout être humain a dû quitter un jour le sein de sa mère. C'est dans ce sens que mon expérience d'immigrante est une métaphore du trajet humain.*
>
> [My writing is migrant to the extent that I am always in search of the elsewhere. As a child, I have experienced loss and displacement, as every human being who has had to leave one day his mother's womb. It is in that sense that my immigrant experience is a metaphor for the human trajectory.][195]

That "metaphor for the human trajectory," at once poetic, eloquent, vivid, lyrical, and vibrant, describes Farhoud's entire oeuvre, inscribing it in a vast project of transmission of memory, text, and beauty, both personal and collective.

The notion of universe, as the title of the chapter suggests, imposes itself when studying Abla Farhoud, not only because of the author's literary creation and the time span in which it was conceived, written, stage-read, produced, performed, and published; but first and foremost because of the recurrence of themes harbored at various degrees throughout this body of works, within and across genres, as the first epigraph to this chapter, a citation occurring at once in a novel and in a play, strongly suggests. Abla Farhoud has etched a universe stamped with the mark of the political, and where exiles are not only those characters who chose to leave in the fifties for economic reasons, or who have been compelled by the civil war (1975–1990) to leave their native Lebanon for Québec, but also some Québécois *de souche* who have been abandoned or orphaned by their loved ones, and in the process made into exiles, albeit metaphorically so. All things considered, the writing of Abla Farhoud, perhaps like the author herself, may be qualified as *preoccupied* [*soucieuse*], as a critic has remarked and as this chapter has unfolded.[196]

NOTES

1. Gilbert David, "Ecrire pour surmonter son impuissance," *Le Devoir*, Montréal, 27 February 1991, Théâtre, C3.

2. Gilles Costas, "Le Français tel qu'ils le jouent," *Le Quotidien de Paris*, Friday, 2 October 1992, Page B2, "Festival des francophonies".

3. Lucie Lequin, "Abla Farhoud et la fragilité du bonheur," *Rocky Mountain Modern Language Association (RMMLA)* 58.1 (Spring 2004), rmmla.wsu.edu/ereview/58.1/articles/lequin.asp (accessed July 5, 2006), 1.

4. Karine Projean, "*Le Fou D'Omar*," *Choq FM*, August 3, 2005, web.choq.fm/article.php?id=1546 (accessed August 3, 2006).

5. Lucie Lequin, "Abla Farhoud et la fragilité du bonheur" [Abla Farhoud and the Fragility of Happiness], *RMMLA* 58.1 (Spring 2004), rmmla.wsu.edu/ereview/58.1/articles/lequin.asp (accessed July 5, 2006): 1–9, 1.

6. Louise Forsyth, "Resistance to Exile by Girls and Women: Two Plays by Abla Farhoud," *Modern Drama* 48.4 (Winter 2005): 800–818, 817.

7. Lequin asserts: "L'écriture d'Abla Farhoud, Romanesque ou dramatique, tend toujours vers la compréhension du sens de la vie, et implicitement du sens de la mort, que celle-ci soit physique ou qu'elle soit émotive ou spirituelle" [the writing of Abla Farhoud, whether fiction or drama, always tends to comprehend the meaning of life, and implicitly, the meaning of death, be it physical, emotional, or spiritual], in "Abla Farhoud et la fragilité du bonheur," *RMMLA* 58.1 (Spring 2004), rmmla.wsu.edu/ereview/58.1/articles/lequin.asp (July 5, 2006): 1–9, 9.

8. Unless otherwise indicated, all the translated quotes from Farhoud's works are mine. Interview conducted by Raymond Bernatchez, "Abla Farhoud: 'S'il n'yavait pas la mort, je n'écrirais pas'" [If Death Did Not Exist I Would Not Write] *La Presse Montreal*, Théâtre, 13 September, 1997, no page.

9. The first date refers to when the play was first performed on stage, and the second to the publication date
10. Abla Farhoud, *Les Filles du 5-10-15 cents* (Carnières, Belgium: Lansman, 1993), 7.
11. Farhoud, *Les Filles du 5-10-15 cents*, 53.
12. Farhoud, *Les Filles du 5-10-15 cents*, 49.
13. Farhoud, *Les Filles du 5-10-15 cents*, 24.
14. Farhoud, *Les Filles du 5-10-15 cents*, 62.
15. Farhoud, *Les Filles du 5-10-15 cents*, 48.
16. Farhoud, *Les Filles du 5-10-15 cents*, 33.
17. Abla Farhoud, *Jeux de patience* (Montréal: VLB Éditeur, 1997), 28–29.
18. Farhoud, *Les Filles du 5-10-15 cents*, 16.
19. Farhoud, *Les Filles du 5-10-15 cents*, 10.
20. Farhoud, *Les Filles du 5-10-15 cents*, 39.
21. Farhoud, *Les Filles du 5-10-15 cents*, 39.
22. Bolded words in the original.
23. Farhoud, *Les Filles du 5-10-15 cents*, 54. The bolded words are by Farhoud.
24. Abla Farhoud, *Jeux de patience* (Montréal: VLB Éditeur, 1997), 11.
25. Farhoud, *Jeux de patience*, 43.
26. Farhoud, *Jeux de patience*, 14.
27. Farhoud, *Jeux de patience*, 31.
28. Karen Malpede, "Theatre at 2000: A Witnessing Project." *The Year 2000: Essays on the End*, eds. Charles Strozier and Michael Flynn (New York and London: New York University Press, 1997), 299–308. The psychiatrist in question is Stevan Weine.
29. Farhoud, *Jeux de patience*, 55.
30. Farhoud, *Jeux de patience*, 51.
31. Farhoud, *Jeux de patience*, 68.
32. Farhoud, *Jeux de patience*, 68.
33. Farhoud, *Jeux de patience*, 72.
34. Farhoud, *Jeux de patience*, 72.
35. Farhoud, *Jeux de patience*, 53.
36. Jane Moss, "Immigrant Theater: Traumatic Departures and Unsettling Arrivals," in *Textualizing the Immigrant Experience in Contemporary Québec*, ed. Susan Ireland and Patrice P. Proulx (Wesport, Connecticut: Praeger, 2004): 65–81, 69.
37. Farhoud, *Jeux de patience*, 77.
38. Pierre l'Hérault, Préface, *Les Rues de l'alligator* par Abla Farhoud (Montréal: VLB Éditeur, 2003): 7–10, 7.
39. *Jeux de patience*, 12.
40. Abla Farhoud, *Les Rues de l'alligator* (Montréal:VLB Éditeur, 2003), 14.
41. Farhoud, *Les Rues de l'alligator*, 14.
42. Farhoud, *Les Rues de l'alligator*, 14.
43. Farhoud, *Les Rues de l'alligator*, 30.
44. Farhoud, *Les Rues de l'alligator*, 56.
45. Farhoud, *Les Rues de l'alligator*, 56.
46. Farhoud, *Les Rues de l'alligator*, 85.
47. Farhoud, *Les Rues de l'alligator*, 87.

48. Edward Said, "Intellectual Exile: Expatriates and Marginals," in *Representations of the Intellectual* (New York: Vintage Books, 1996): 47–65, 53.
49. Farhoud, *Les Rues de l'alligator*, 42.
50. Farhoud, *Les Rues de l'alligator*, 21.
51. Farhoud, *Les Rues de l'alligator*, 43.
52. Farhoud, *Les Rues de l'alligator*, 66.
53. Farhoud, *Les Rues de l'alligator*, 40.
54. Farhoud, *Les Rues de l'alligator*, 15, 21.
55. Farhoud, *Les Rues de l'alligator*, 32.
56. Marie-André Chouinard, "La Voix de Dounia," *Le Devoir*, Montréal, Saturday and Sunday, March 28, 1998, D1–D2.
57. Marie-André Chouinard, "La Voix de Dounia," *Le Devoir*, Montréal, Saturday and Sunday, March 28/29, 1998, D1–D2.
58. Abla Farhoud, *Le Bonheur a la queue glissante* (Montréal: L'Hexagone, 1998), 124.
59. Marie-André Chouinard, "La Voix de Dounia," *Le Devoir*, Montréal, Saturday and Sunday, March 28, 1998, D2.
60. Naïm Kattan, "Les Écrivians immigrants et les autres," *International Journal of Canadian Studies/Revue internationale d'études canadiennes* 18 (Fall 1998): 185–191, 190.
61. Farhoud, *Le Bonheur a la queue glissante*, 16.
62. Farhoud, *Le Bonheur a la queue glissante*, 15.
63. Farhoud, *Le Bonheur a la queue glissante*, 14.
64. Farhoud, *Le Bonheur a la queue glissante*, 16.
65. Farhoud, *Le Bonheur a la queue glissante*, 51–52.
66. Farhoud, *Le Bonheur a la queue glissante*, 121.
67. Farhoud, *Le Bonheur a la queue glissante*, 65.
68. Farhoud, *Le Bonheur a la queue glissante*, 94.
69. Farhoud, *Le Bonheur a la queue glissante*, 35. "Seuls tes ongles gratteront ta peau en te soulageant."
70. Farhoud, *Le Bonheur a la queue glissante*, 11.
71. Farhoud, *Le Bonheur a la queue glissante*, 33.
72. Farhoud, *Le Bonheur a la queue glissante*, 23.
73. Farhoud, *Le Bonheur a la queue glissante*, 125.
74. Farhoud, *Le Bonheur a la queue glissante*, 45.
75. Farhoud, *Le Bonheur a la queue glissante*, 31.
76. Farhoud, *Le Bonheur a la queue glissante*, 31.
77. Farhoud, *Le Bonheur a la queue glissante*, 42.
78. Farhoud, *Le Bonheur a la queue glissante*, 43.
79. Farhoud, *Le Bonheur a la queue glissante*, 43.
80. Farhoud, *Le Bonheur a la queue glissante*, 41.
81. Farhoud, *Le Bonheur a la queue glissante*, 43.
82. Farhoud, *Le Bonheur a la queue glissante*, 34.
83. Farhoud, *Le Bonheur a la queue glissante*, 138.
84. Samira Farhoud, "Déchirement ou délivrance: écriture autobioraphique dans *Les Saisons de passage* d'Andrée Chédid, *Le Bonheur a la queue glissante* d'Abla farhoud et *La Prisonnière* de Malika Oufkir et Michèle Fitoussi," *Présence Francophone* 58 (2002): 138–151, 142.

85. Farhoud, *Le Bonheur a la queue glissante*, 82.
86. Farhoud, *Le Bonheur a la queue glissante*, 30.
87. Farhoud, *Le Bonheur a la queue glissante*, 10.
88. Farhoud, *Le Bonheur a la queue glissante*, 125.
89. Farhoud, *Le Bonheur a la queue glissante*, 126.
90. Farhoud, *Le Bonheur a la queue glissante*, 153.
91. Farhoud, *Le Bonheur a la queue glissante*, 142.
92. Farhoud, *Le Bonheur a la queue glissante*, 143.
93. Farhoud, *Le Bonheur a la queue glissante*, 145.
94. Farhoud, *Le Bonheur a la queue glissante*, 142.
95. Farhoud, *Le Bonheur a la queue glissante*, 145.
96. Farhoud, *Le Bonheur a la queue glissante*, 139–140.
97. Farhoud, *Le Bonheur a la queue glissante*, 151.
98. Farhoud, *Le Bonheur a la queue glissante*, 139.
99. Farhoud, *Le Bonheur a la queue glissante*, 152.
100. Farhoud, *Le Bonheur a la queue glissante*, 151.
101. Farhoud, *Le Bonheur a la queue glissante*, 151–152.
102. Farhoud, *Le Bonheur a la queue glissante*, 150.
103. Farhoud, *Le Bonheur a la queue glissante*, 63.
104. Patrice J. Proulx, "Migration and Memory in Marie-Céline Agnant's *La dot de Sara* and Abla Farhoud's *Le Bonheur a la queue glissante*," in *Textualizing the Immigrant Experience in Contemporary Québec*, ed. Susan Ireland and Patrice P. Proulx (Westport, Connecticut: Praeger, 2004): 127–136, 132.
105. Farhoud, *Le Bonheur a la queue glissante*, 30.
106. Farhoud, *Le Bonheur a la queue glissante*, 35.
107. Farhoud, *Le Bonheur a la queue glissante*, 9.
108. Farhoud, *Le Bonheur a la queue glissante*, 163.
109. Farhoud, *Le Bonheur a la queue glissante*, 166.
110. Abla Farhoud, *Splendide solitude* (Montréal: L'Hexagone, 2001), 131.
111. Farhoud, *Splendide solitude*, 99.
112. Farhoud, *Splendide solitude*, 11.
113. Farhoud, *Splendide solitude*, 95.
114. Farhoud, *Splendide solitude*, 60.
115. Farhoud, *Splendide solitude*, 189.
116. Farhoud, *Splendide solitude*, 10.
117. Farhoud, *Splendide solitude*, 38.
118. Farhoud, *Splendide solitude*, 39.
119. Farhoud, *Splendide solitude*, 7.
120. Farhoud, *Splendide solitude*, 35.
121. Farhoud, *Splendide solitude*, 195.
122. Farhoud, *Splendide solitude*, 195.
123. Farhoud, *Splendide solitude*, 196.
124. Farhoud, *Splendide solitude*, 189.
125. Jean Vigneault, "Splendide Solitude," *Le Courrier*, 12 December 2001, www.lecourrier.qc.ca/archives/2001/2001_12_12/707L15X.html (accessed February 9, 2006).
126. Farhoud, *Splendide solitude*, 146.
127. Farhoud, *Splendide solitude*, 10.

128. Lucie Lequin, "Abla Farhoud et la fragilité du bonheur," *Rocky Mountain Modern Language Association (RMMLA)* 58.1 (Spring 2004), rmmla.wsu.edu/ereview/58.1/articles/lequin.asp (July 5, 2006), 7 of 9 (accessed August 3, 2006).

129. Farhoud, *Splendide solitude*, 110.

130. Farhoud, *Splendide solitude*, 109.

131. Guy Corneau is a celebrated Canadian psychoanalyst whose book, *Père manquant, fils manqué* (*Absent Fathers, Lost Sons: The Search for Masculine Identity*, New York: Random House, 1991) is alluded to by Farhoud in reference to her protagonist Radwan, during her interview with Simard. In Radwan's case, the father figure is not absent; it is, on the contrary, omnipresent; yet, the outcome is equally amiss.

132. Mathieu Simard, "Abla Farhoud: Le Fou d'Omar ou être à l'origine de sa propre vie," *Le Libraire* 28 (May–June 2005): 1–16, 6.

133. Mathieu Simard, "Abla Farhoud: Le Fou d'Omar ou être à l'origine de sa propre vie," *Le Libraire* 28 (May–June 2005): 1–16, 6.

134. Abla Farhoud, *Le Fou d'Omar* (Montréal: VLB Éditeur, 2005), 14.

135. Farhoud, *Le Fou d'Omar*, 17.

136. Karine Projean, "*Le Fou D'Omar*," *Choq FM*, August 3, 2005, web.choq.fm/article.php?id=1546 (accessed August 3, 2006).

137. Farhoud, *Le Fou d'Omar*, 29.

138. Farhoud, *Le Fou d'Omar*, 23.

139. Farhoud, *Le Fou d'Omar*, 37.

140. Farhoud, *Le Fou d'Omar*, 33.

141. Farhoud, *Le Fou d'Omar*, 175.

142. Farhoud, *Le Fou d'Omar*, 21.

143. Farhoud, *Le Fou d'Omar*, 30.

144. Farhoud, *Le Fou d'Omar*, 33.

145. Farhoud, *Le Fou d'Omar*, 47.

146. Farhoud, *Le Fou d'Omar*, 62.

147. Farhoud, *Le Fou d'Omar*, 68.

148. Farhoud, *Le Fou d'Omar*, 175.

149. Farhoud, *Le Fou d'Omar*, 78.

150. Farhoud, *Le Fou d'Omar*, 75.

151. Farhoud, *Le Fou d'Omar*, 74.

152. Farhoud, *Le Fou d'Omar*, 171.

153. Farhoud, *Le Fou d'Omar*, 75.

154. Farhoud, *Le Fou d'Omar*, 75.

155. Farhoud, *Le Fou d'Omar*, 64.

156. Farhoud, *Le Fou d'Omar*, 172.

157. Farhoud, *Le Fou d'Omar*, 175.

158. Farhoud, *Le Fou d'Omar*, 63. In English in the text.

159. Farhoud, *Le Fou d'Omar*, 67.

160. Farhoud, *Le Fou d'Omar*, 55.

161. Farhoud, *Le Fou d'Omar*, 56.

162. Farhoud, *Le Fou d'Omar*, 57. In English in the original text.

163. Farhoud, *Le Fou d'Omar*, 122.

164. Farhoud, *Le Fou d'Omar*, 93.

165. Farhoud, *Le Fou d'Omar*, 118.
166. Farhoud, *Le Fou d'Omar*, 94.
167. Farhoud, *Le Fou d'Omar*, 86.
168. Farhoud, *Le Fou d'Omar*, 104.
169. Farhoud, *Le Fou d'Omar*, 122
170. Farhoud, *Le Fou d'Omar*, 122.
171. Farhoud, *Le Fou d'Omar*, 123.
172. Farhoud, *Le Fou d'Omar*, 88.
173. Farhoud, *Le Fou d'Omar*, 89.
174. Farhoud, *Le Fou d'Omar*, 89.
175. Farhoud, *Le Fou d'Omar*, 120.
176. Farhoud, *Le Fou d'Omar*, 90.
177. Farhoud, *Le Fou d'Omar*, 98.
178. Farhoud, *Le Fou d'Omar*, 97.
179. Farhoud, *Le Fou d'Omar*, 151.
180. Farhoud, *Le Fou d'Omar*, 67.
181. Farhoud, *Le Fou d'Omar*, 164.
182. Farhoud, *Le Fou d'Omar*, 161.
183. Farhoud, *Le Fou d'Omar*, 158.
184. Farhoud, *Le Fou d'Omar*, 159.
185. Farhoud, *Le Fou d'Omar*, 159.
186. Farhoud, *Le Bonheur a la queue glissante*, 145.
187. Mathieu Simard, "Abla Farhoud: *Le Fou d'Omar* ou être à l'origine de sa propre vie," *Le Libraire* 28 (May–June 2005): 1–16, 6.
188. *Les Filles du 5-10-15 cents* and *Jeux de patience*.
189. Presumably Sabra and Shatilla.
190. Farhoud, *Le Fou d'Omar*, 60.
191. Farhoud, *Le Fou d'Omar*, 60.
192. Farhoud, *Le Fou d'Omar*, 62.
193. Farhoud, *Le Fou d'Omar*, 62.
194. Michel Vaïs and Philip Wickham, "Le Brassage des cultures: Table ronde" (interviews), *Jeu* 72 (no issue number) (1994): 8–38, 36.
195. Michel Vaïs and Philip Wickham, "Le Brassage des cultures: Table ronde" (interviews), *Jeu* 72 (no issue number) (1994): 8–38, 29.
196. Lucie Lequin, "Abla Farhoud et la fragilité du bonheur," *RMMLA* 58.1 (Spring 2004), rmmla.wsu.edu/ereview/58.1/articles/lequin.asp (accessed July 5, 2006): 1–9, 9.

5

Of Broken Promises and Mended Lives: The War-Ravaged World of Wajdi Mouawad

Il faut casser le fil.

[We have to break the thread.]¹

Wajdi Mouawad (Incendies)

*L'enfance est un couteau planté dans la gorge.*²

[Childhood is a knife stuck in the throat.]³

Wajdi Mouawad (Incendies)

Lorsqu'on me demande si je suis québécois, français ou libanais, je réponds que je suis juif et tchèque.

[When I am asked whether I am Québécois, French or Lebanese, I reply that I am Jewish and Czech.]

Wajdi Mouawad (Architecture d'un marcheur, 69)

MOUAWAD (1968–) AND HIS OEUVRE

Wajdi Mouawad stands unique among his fellow Arabic-Québécois/ Canadian writers in that he has achieved international fame at the relatively young age of thirty-two. He created and stage directed a dozen unpublished plays, and the entirety of his production spans barely over a decade.⁴ In this relatively short time (from 1996 to the present), he wrote, stage-directed, and published, all in French, twelve plays, with his latest to date, *Le Soleil ni la mort ne peuvent se regarder en face* (2008) being staged at the Théâtre National de Bordeaux (May/June 2008);[5] he also wrote a single novel, *Visage retouvé* (2002), made into a children's play retitled *Un Obus dans le Coeur* (2007). Mouawad's very first published play, *Alphonse* (1996),[6] and the latest, *Assoiffés* (2007), are both youth drama.

Wajdi Mouawad's career as a very successful playwright is intimately intertwined with his career as a highly talented stage director, a duality that seems to be the hallmark of his entire oeuvre, and perhaps one of the secrets of his success. A critic hailed him as "the greatest Québécois playwright"[7] and the French daily *Le Monde* dubbed him "one of the most innovative writers of francophone theatre."[8] Regarding his 2006 production of *Forêts* at the Malakoff Théâtre in Paris, the same critic writes:

> *Sa puissance narrative et poétique . . . laisse les spectateurs de* Forêts *. . . bouleversés, en larmes, ovationnant longuement le spectacle.*
>
> [His narrative and poetic power leaves the audience of *Forêts* . . . moved, in tears, applauding the show for a long time.][9]

Time and again, the emotional impact of Mouawad's plays on his audiences will be pointed out as being the special "Mouawad touch."[10] In the words of a reviewer:

> French theatre audiences generally applaud more courteously than passionately, never clapping at intermissions, seldom granting standing ovations. But at the end of the *Forêts* performance I attended in Grenoble, the crowd jumped to its feet, to show its appreciation.[11]

Wajdi Mouawad was born in Lebanon to a Christian family, in Deir El Qamar (in Arabic, meaning monastery of the moon), a village of stone houses with red-tiled roofs, located in the Chouf district in South-Central Lebanon and known as the birthplace of a number of well-known artists and writers. In 1976, a year after the onset of the Lebanese civil war, a war that lasted fifteen years and claimed over 200,000 victims, the young Wajdi moved with his family (his parents and two siblings) to Paris, with the intention of returning back home three months later. However, because of the continuing turmoil in Lebanon, in 1983 (when Mouawad was fourteen) the family left once more, this time to Montréal where it settled for good. Wajdi graduated in 1991 with an acting diploma from the prestigious Montréal-based *Ecole Nationale de Théâtre du Canada*. From 1990 to 1999, he directed with Isabelle Leblanc a theatre the two cofounded, *Le Théâtre Ô parleur*, where he started staging his own plays as well as a variety of other plays, from Shakespeare's *MacBeth*, to Pirandello's *Six Characters in Search of an Author*, to Irvine Welsh's *Trainspotting*. From 2000 to 2004, Mouawad held the position of Artistic Director of The *Théâtre de*

Quat'sous in Montréal, and in 2005 he founded two parallel companies that echo each other transatlantically, one in Québec and the other in France, respectively named *Abé carré cé carré* and *Le carré de l'hypoténuse*. In 2006, Mouawad moved to Ottawa to become director of *Théâtre français du centre national des arts*, and in 2007, he was named artistic director of the French theatre section at The National Arts Centre for 2008-2009. His career entails an enormous amount of travel, and to the question of whether he resides in Paris, Montréal, or Toulouse, his evasive answer is that he lives "wherever work takes him."[12]

Mouawad's very first published book, *Alphonse* (1993/1996),[13] which appeared in an English translation in 2002, was finalist for the *Prix du Gouverneur Général* [Governor General Award]. It stages the flight from home of a fourteen-year-old who goes walking alongside a country road, meeting wonderful imaginary characters who are for him very real. *Pacamambo* (2000), Mouawad's third title, is also a youth drama about Julie, a little girl with a dog, who hides for a long time near the decomposing body of her grandmother while thinking of Pacamambo, a place full of lights. It was preceded and followed by *Les Mains d'Edwige au moment de la naissance* (1995/1999), a tale of burial and deceit, and *Rêves* (1999/2002), a quintessentially metafictional play bearing the mark of Pirandello. Follows *Willy Protagores enfermé dans les toilettes* (1993/2004), first produced when Mouawad was still a student—ten years elapsed between its creation and appearance in book form. It tells of a young boy who stages a family rebellion and refuses to get out of the bathroom as long as the unwanted house guests are not gone. This play won the *Masque* award and was voted best Montréal-based production by the *Association Québécoise des critiques de Théâtre*. Throughout its production, Mouawad filled all at once his quadruple role of writer, actor, stage-director, and producer.

As for *Littoral* (1999), the first of a tetralogy in the making, it was first staged at the author's *Théâtre des quat'sous* in 1997, then in 1998 in Limoges, at the fifteenth international festival of *francophonies* in the Limousin, and the following year at the celebrated *Festival d'Avignon*. The play nearly single-handedly catapulted Mouawad to the foreground of the Montréal-French scene. In 2000, he received the most prestigious Canadian award, The Governor General Award in Literature for theatre (for *Littoral*) and in 2004, he was awarded the *Prix de la francophonie* bestowed by the international *Société des auteurs et compositeurs dramatiques* (SACD) for his oeuvre. Speaking of *Littoral* and the fact that it was produced all over the world, over 175 times, in Lebanon, France, and North America, Mouawad recognizes the impetus it gave to his career: "*Littoral* m'a mis au monde artistiquement, m'a fait naître aux yeux du milieu théâtral québécois" [*Littoral* gave birth to me artistically, handed me a place in the Theatrical Québécois milieu].[14]

The Governor General Award was not the only award bestowed on Mouawad. In 2002, he became *Chevalier de l'Ordre national des arts et des lettres,* a membership awarded to him by the French Ministry of Culture for his entire oeuvre. Furthermore, three years later, in 2005, Mouawad was awarded the Molière Prize for the best francophone playwright of the year, making him the first Québécois playwright to have ever been offered this prestigious French award. Mouawad declined it, however, stating that his love of theatre prevented him from competing with other fellow playwrights. On that occasion, he shamed the many theatre directors who do not do so much as write letters of acknowledgment to the playwrights whose plays thus become "lost texts" that often remain unread.[15] Because of this incident, he was dubbed "l'enfant terrible de la scène québécoise" [the terrible child of the Québec stage].[16]

The present chapter purports to study the first three volumes of Mouawad's tetralogy-in-the-making (*Littoral,* 1997/1999, *Incendies,* 2003, *Forêts,* 2006) followed by a concluding statement on Mouawad's own outlook on his status as an *exilic* writer as well as his outlook and methods as stage-director and playwright. My decision behind choosing to study this trilogy was dictated by the representative thematic motifs found across the three plays, namely the preoccupation with the ravages of war on individuals and collectivities alike (the mark of the political), the grafting of individual quests onto national histories (the collective value of utterances), and the search for redemption through love and solidarity. Those plays also bear semblance with Greek tragedies from which they seem inspired; in fact, Mouawad often grafts long quotes from the Classics into his plays. As in Farhoud's works, the characters, often orphans, also need to bear witness. They seek reconciliation with the past by trying to recover their dignity, and to provide a public record by breaking the silence. Although Farhoud and Mouawmad both portray war horrors, Mouawad differs in that his plays exude a strong sense of humor expressed in the vernacular. Profanities of all sorts crop up in long strings of typical québécois slang, producing a highly comic effect; characters masturbate and curse while others speak of lofty dreams of peace and fraternity in most poetic terms. A highly scatological language is often juxtaposed with one infused with a puissant "souffle littéraire,"[17] or literary breath, as Mouawad himself calls it. To juxtapose the mythical with the real and the vulgar with the poetic is a conscious, professed aim of this innovative playwright.[18] In fact, he views the stage as a place of "stark consolation," *lieu de consolation impitoyable,*[19] as well as a place where a *prise de parole* [speaking up][20] is inscribed and registered in a fashion that places Mouawad's dramaturgy in the newly founded tradition of the *théâtre engagé* of contemporary Québec.[21]

LITTORAL (1999), *INCENDIES* (2003), *FORÊTS* (2006)

It is hardly surprising that of the five plays of Mouawad's translated into English and published by the Toronto-based Playwrights Canada Press, two belong to his somewhat autobiographical, par excellence transcultural, transnational trilogy (soon to become a tetralogy, since the projected fourth volume, *Ciels*, was announced by the author for 2009). *Littoral* and *Incendies* appeared in English in Toronto, under the titles, respectively, *Tideline* (2002) and *Scorched* (2005).[22] Together with *Forêts* (2006), whose publication in English is forthcoming, they form a cluster related to the question of provenance and exile and, in the very words of Mouawad, "the question of promise: renounced, betrayed, kept then forgotten, then kept again, forsaken, rejected, disclaimed, mocked, then regretted."[23] The last volume of the tetralogy, *Ciels*, is supposed to close the cycle opened by *Littoral* with a premise that, asserts the playwright, will reverse that of the three plays preceding it.[24]

In my opinion, even though *Littoral* is the most celebrated of the three plays, *Incendies*, the middle volume (It received the *Prix de la critique* of *L'Association québécoise des critiques de théâtre* in 2004), incidentally the one with the most credible plot and the least surrealistic dramaturgy (notwithstanding the fact that the dead reappear to narrate and play out their stories), is also the most powerful of the trilogy. In the words of an eminent Québécois critic, *Incendies* is "the most beautiful and the strongest play of Mouawad's" as well as the "most remarkable Québécois production of the season."[25] Consequently, it is the play to which I will devote particular attention.

Far from constituting a trilogy in the traditional acceptance of the term, since they do not trace the same narrative line and since they present different characters, settings, and situations, those three plays nevertheless have in common that all three portray, with increasing intensity, the issue of the unknown forces that mysteriously shape our identities. It is noteworthy that the title of each volume consists of a sole plural common concrete noun, except for the first one, which is singular (littoral). The starting point for all three plays is present-day Montréal. In *Incendies* the setting switches to Lebanon, and in *Forêts*, to France, as far back as 1870. Despite the correct assumption of critics[26] that *Littoral* is set in Lebanon, there is actually nothing definitive in the play indicative of that or of any other country in particular. No place, no village, no country is ever named, and there is not a single Arabic proper name amidst the characters staged. One can consequently assume that the action in *Littoral* takes place anywhere where war has occurred and where there is a coastline. The nameless country is perhaps a sure way to reach various international audiences who can identify with the dramaturgy, an assumption substantiated by the fact that *Littoral* has been translated in several European countries, as well as Mexico.

LITTORAL (1997/1999) [TIDELINE (2002)]

Littoral is composed of fifty-two scenes or tableaux and six divisions, or acts, titled, sequentially, "Here, Yesterday, Over There, The Other, Road, and Tideline." Those titles follow the thread of the narrative, suggesting that past and present will sometimes be simultaneously staged, the dead sharing the stage with the living. Wilfrid, who lives in Montréal (the *Here*), receives a phone call announcing the death of his father while he is reaching sexual climax with a partner. His parents' troubled past (the *Yesterday*) and the mystery of his birth are suddenly revealed to him through his discovery of unsent letters his father had written him over the years. We learn that the mother's family had objected to his parents' marriage and that his mother died giving birth to him in the old country. Wilfrid is raised by his maternal aunts who, by rejecting the father and blaming him for the mother's death, drive him into exile. Some comic scenes of family dynamics are staged between the aunts and Wilfrid over the question of the father's burial. At first Wilfrid hesitates, but then he is entrusted with a mission by his alter ego (the kind, ethical, imaginary Arthurean knight Guiromelan) to bury his father in his native land. Wilfrid reluctantly embarks on the journey, leaving all his commitments behind. He is accompanied by his irritating father's talking cadaver as well as a film crew that continuously records his movements in what constitute humorous, ironic touches that alleviate the weightiness of the overarching theme. *Over There*, in the nameless father's country, Wilfrid finds a place decimated by war, with no more plots left for burial. He first encounters Ulrich, an old sage who quotes the opening of the *Iliad* and the passage where Priam beseeches Achilles to remit him the body of his slain son Hector, an endorsement that gives Wilfrid's quest a mythical dimension. In his father's homeland, he continues to encounter the *Other*, first hostile villagers who tell him to go away, and eventually, one by one, what comes to form a collection of sympathetic young orphan-survivors (Simone, Amé, Massi, Sabbé, Joséphine) who help him fulfill his mission by traveling with him on the *Road* they finally discover, one that leads them all the way to the *Tideline*. The father is buried in the water from which he addresses the group of young folks, ending the play on a note of universal hope, resilience, and rejuvenation:

> *Tout juste après les amours et les peines*
> *Les joies et les pleurs,*
> *Les pertes et les cris,*
> *Il y a le littoral et la grande mer,*
> *Qui emporte tout*
> *Et qui m'emporte d'ailleurs,*
> *Qui m'emporte, qui m'emporte, qui m'emporte*[27]

[Right after loves and sorrows
Joys and tears,
Losses and laments
There is the tideline and the great sea,
The great sea
That carries everything away
And that's now taking me,
That's taking me, taking me, taking me].[28]

The last line, "that's taking me, taking me, taking me" is repeated six times as the father's voice presumably grows fainter as he sinks into the sea. The collective mission is thus accomplished. What is exactly that mission?

As a critic, Jane Moss, has rightly remarked, if "the ethical burden placed on those who survive historical trauma is to mourn the dead and bear witness, . . . this is exactly what *Littoral* does."[29] Wilfrid and his friends form a cohesive group bound together by a sacred, communal sense of bereavement, as they have each been through a war-related trauma; after having lost all her family, Simone (who is somewhat reminiscent of Nawal in *Incendies* and of Sonia, the crossing guard in Farhoud's *Rues de l'alligator*), the unique survivor of her entire village, continues, despite opposition, to play the violin from place to place to celebrate life and to commemorate the war victims. Her task is to tell people the stories of what has happened[30] as she longs to liberate herself and to enjoy life: "Aujourd'hui, la guerre est terminée et je suis encore en prison"[31] [Now the war is over and I'm still in prison][32] she cries to the villagers who admonish her for her carefree demeanor. She is the one who, along the way, collects other orphans who end up following her; we learn that Massi has never known his father, Amé unwittingly killed his own father, and Sabbé was plagued with laughing fits after being forced to watch the dismemberment of his father, and to hold the decapitated head in his hands, not to forget Joséphine, the Antigone-like figure whose vocation, in Mouawad's words, "is to bear the memory of the vanquished."[33] She carries a heavy load of books where she scrupulously records the names of all the war victims, and when she runs out of pencils she commits to memory the names, repeating them unceasingly to avoid memory loss. She will find no rest until the father has received proper burial, and when the group reaches the tideline where the body is collectively washed, Joséphine uses the weight of the memorial books to anchor it onto the seabed when he is thrown into the sea.

In a noteworthy article by Pierre L'Hérault, subtitled "l'hospitalité comme instance dramatique" [Hospitality as dramatic instance],[34] the eminent Québécois critic remarks that, in the final analysis, Wilfrid's quest in *Littoral* involves *words* rather than *territories*. Joséphine literally discloses the identity of members of the group by giving them back their names,[35] and if the plot stages deterritorialization (here taken literally as the destruction of a country, the absence of burial ground, and the consequent burial in water) enhanced by the burial ritual that is enacted, it ultimately deals with the dual theme of encounter (*rencontre*) and hospitality, or lack thereof, on the ground.

Furthermore, the communal sense of bereavement, the quintessential leitmotif of the play, ties in with the figure of the father himself, a figure that acquires the added symbolic status of a collective father. In the introduction to the play, speaking of the genesis of *Littoral*, Mouawad himself states that he had in mind the figure of the father, whether the absent father, as in Dostoyevski's the *Idiot*, or the father to be avenged, as in *Hamlet*, or the father who is unwittingly killed by the son, as in *Oedipus*,[36] respectively, represented by the characters of Massi, Sabbé, and Amé. The universality of the image of the father, against the backdrop of the leitmotif of the play, is explicitly signified by Sabbé's injunction to the reluctant Amé, weary of helping in the arduous task of finding a burial ground for Wilfrid's father:

> *Ouvre les yeux. Reconnais en lui le père disparu, le père assassiné, le père ensanglanté. Reconnais en lui père de toutes nos douleurs.*[37]
>
> [Open your eyes and recognize in him the father who disappeared, the father who was murdered, the father covered in blood. Recognize in him the father of all our pain.][38]

Just as they are reaching the sea, Simone declares that the story they will be telling henceforth to everybody, will be that of a man who wants to bury his father and who seeks a burial ground to this purpose. The circle is closed and the play ends in a metatextual, self-reflexive fashion that ties the dénouement to the starting point, the initial situation of Wilfrid himself at the opening scene. Wilfrid summarizes that initial situation when he is asked by Massi to tell his story and, in yet another touch of humor juxtaposed with the sacred nature of the leitmotif (a juxtaposition Mouawad cultivates and enjoys), Wilfrid irreverently recalls the sexual climax connected to the telephone ring, bearer of the death news:

> *C'est un type qui a couché avec son père parce qu'il faisait l'amour avec une fille au même moment où son père mourait. Puis là le type va éjaculer d'une sonnerie de téléphone. Ça le surprend! Il répond. On lui dit qu'on vient de retrouver son père mort assis sur un banc.*[39]
>
> [It is a guy who slept with his father because he was making love with a girl at the same time that his father was dying. Here the guy will ejaculate a telephone ring. He is surprised! He answers. He is told that his father was just found dead on a bench.][40]

Guiromelan, the imaginary companion of Wilfrid's dreams, and one of the humorous ploys at use by the playwright, retires at the closing of the play and bids farewell to Wilfrid. It is time for the latter to become his own person, in what opens the door for a coming-of-age or hero's journey reading of *Littoral*.

INCENDIES (2003) [*SCORCHED* (2005)]

The second volume of Mouawad's projected tetralogy, *Incendies*, was first produced in France in the Spring of 2003, and then, later that year, in Montréal, during the *Festival de Théâtre des Amériques*.

Speaking of the genesis of this play, Mouawad writes: "*Incendies* serait la seconde partie de quelque chose dont *Littoral* est la première [*Incendies* would be the second part of something of which *Littoral* is the first part].[41] The *Association Québécoise des critiques de l'art* in the press release announcing the prize award for this second volume asserts: "Cette âpre remontée vers les origines, soutenue par un travail d'ensemble d'une grande cohésion, nous a bouleversés" [This harsh travel to the origins, set in a very cohesive framework, has deeply moved us].[42] In fact, Mouawad himself states in the introduction to the play that *Incendies* picks up once more the reflection "on the question of origin."[43] In 2003 Mouawad thought of *Incendies* as the best of his productions to date; to quote from a performance review of his stage-direction of that play:

> *Transposé sur la scène, le texte de Wajdi Mouawad demeure percutant, pertinent, et d'une beauté foudroyante.*
>
> [Transposed on the stage, Wajdi Mouawad's text remains pertinent, striking, and of overwhelming beauty.][44]

Of the three volumes of the projected tetralogy, *Incendies* is the one which most clearly refers to incidents pertaining to the Lebanese civil war. "Frère contre frère, soeur contre soeur. Civils en colère"[45] [brother against brother, sister against sister. Angry civilians][46] will lament one of the characters. Although, as in *Littoral*, the word Lebanon is never pronounced, most of the names of characters and towns encountered in *Incendies* are clearly Arabic names. Two of the main characters (Nawal and Sawda) repeat together the Arabic alphabet[47] and recite Arabic poetry[48] and, as we will see below, some of the incidents referred to in the narrative are altered versions of documented incidents that occurred during the Lebanese civil war. But is war a leitmotif in *Incendies*? Is incest an overarching theme in this play, even though it is enmeshed in the drama? What are the leitmotifs that transpire in this second volume?

Incendies is composed of thirty-nine tableaux or scenes and four divisions or acts titled, sequentially, "Nawal's fire, Childhood on Fire, Jannaane's Fire, and Sarwane's Fire." As we can see, those titles are composed of a proper noun and a common noun (forming a possessive case) as opposed to those of *Littoral*, which consist of single common nouns (see above). An attentive reader will rightly suspect at the outset that the heart of the drama in this second play will be not so much action-oriented (a ritualized burden to carry) but rather person-oriented, related to self-image, quest for truth, and ego integrity. As with *Littoral*, the divisions in *Incendies* will follow the thread of that quest, albeit roughly so this time, given the nature of the action, largely focusing on the crisis, or *fire*, lived in turn by each of the three main characters (Nawal, Jeanne/Jannaane, and Simon/Sarwane) who have been or will be *scorched*, as the judiciously chosen title for the English translation suggests.

Nawal Marwan, a sixty-five-year-old Montréal woman of Lebanese origin, has just died. The play opens on the reading of her will by a kindly notary and friend, Hermile Lebel. Other than the customary bequest of property, the will contains some unusual items (a blue vest with the number 72 inscribed on it for her daughter and a red copybook for her son) and unusual, elaborate burial instructions. She wished to be buried in the ground face down "against the world," naked, with no casket, no name, no tombal stone, and no epitaph. She entrusts her twin children, twenty-two-year-old Jeanne/Jannaane and Simon/Sarwane—they had lived so far under the impression that their father had died a hero in Lebanon and that they had no other siblings—with a letter each, asking them to go to her native land to find their father and brother and to deliver the letters to each of them. Then and only then, when the letters are remitted to their father and brother respectively, the will explains, can silence be broken and can her tomb be marked with her name. The very "cohesion" mentioned above by the Québec association that granted the prize to *Incendies* is partly the outcome of the careful crafting of the structure: the will that opens the play, the letters that close it, and the narrative that unfolds in between. Those letters and the accompanying will constitute the key around which the various tenets of the narrative will gravitate. As Nawal herself says in her will:

> *Pas d'épitaphe pour ceux qui ne gardent pas leurs promesses*
> *Et une promesse ne fut pas tenue.*
> *Pas d'épitaphe pour ceux qui gardent le silence.*
> *Et le silence fut gardé.*
> . . .
> *Lorsque ces enveloppes auront été remises à leur destinataire*
> *Une lettre vous sera donnée*
> *Le silence sera brisé*

> *Et une pierre pourra alors être posée sur ma tombe*
> *Et mon nom sur la pierre gravé au soleil.*⁴⁹
>
> [No epitaph for those who don't keep their promises
> And one promise was not kept.
> No epitaph for those who keep the silence.
> And silence was kept.
> . . .
> Once these envelopes have been delivered to their recipients
> You will be given a letter
> The silence will be broken
> And then a stone can be placed on my grave
> And my name engraved on the stone in the sun.]⁵⁰

The reader/audience is made aware that the quintessence of the play will thus revolve around the following contradictory, intertwined leitmotifs:

1. The necessity to break the silence/the necessity to have kept the silence in the first place.
2. The sacred nature of promises.

Is there more than one silence in the drama? We learn as early as the second scene that Nawal, not very loquacious to begin with, suddenly stopped speaking altogether five years before her death. As the tableaux or scenes flash into her past and as dead characters come on stage to reenact episodes from their lives (Nawal's Fire and Childhood's Fire, scenes 1 to 20), we learn that Nawal was pregnant at the age of fifteen. She promised her lover Wahab—he was forcibly taken away from the camp and she never saw him again—that she would love their unborn baby for two, *always and no matter what happens*. A few months later, she gave birth to a boy to whom she also *promised repeatedly*, "quoiqu'il arrive je t'aimerai toujours"⁵¹ [I'll always love you, no matter what].⁵² Her mother forced her to give up the baby who was taken to an orphanage in Kfar Rayat by the midwife Elhame. Shortly after, Nawal's grandmother Nazira, on her deathbed, beseeched Nawal to refuse, and to "break the thread"⁵³ ("Il faut casser le fil"),⁵⁴ the vicious circle of misery that causes violence and hatred from mother to daughter, from generation to generation. She advises her to leave the village and to "learn to read, to speak, to write, to count, to think,"⁵⁵ and then to come back and engrave her name on her tomb, as the *first literate person* in the entire village. Those two promises, namely to love her son unconditionally *and* always, and to "break the thread"⁵⁶ ("casser le fil")⁵⁷ of hatred and misery—by educating herself—became Nawal's guiding path until her death. She fulfilled the promise to Nazira, engraving her grandmother's name in Arabic on her tombstone, then she left in search of her son. The vicissitudes of life would not allow her to keep the promise made to the latter, however, as the play takes a fateful turn reminiscent of the life of Oedipus.

Jeanne's quest will result in breaking the silence mentioned in the will. From scenes 21 to 30 (Jannaane's fire), Jeanne (a mathematics instructor), haunted by her mother's silence and by the *blindness* in which she has lived so far, takes up the challenge to find her origin. She feels she is loosing it: "Le gouffre dans lequel je vais tomber, celui où je glisse déjà, c'est celui de son silence"[58] [the hole I'm about to tumble into, the hole I'm already slipping into, is that of her silence][59] she tells her reluctant brother Simon, a boxer who first refuses to join in the quest and who, in his anger at his mother whom he detests for her coldness and lack of affection, comes up with a long and unexpected (given the context) string of profanities and insults in perfect Québécois slang after the notary has finished reading the mother's will.[60]

Jeanne, now in Lebanon, is led to a string of people, the prison guide Mansour, the former prison janitor Fahim, and the peasant Malak, who will each in turn provide a missing piece of the puzzle. Jeanne finds out that the younger Nawal failed to find her son; that the latter had been adopted from the orphanage by a childless couple who renamed him Nihad Harmanni. At the age of forty (in 1978), Nawal, having joined the resistance movement, was imprisoned in the Kfar Rayat prison, after killing the head of the militia, Chad. The ruthless prison director, Abou Tarek, used to torture and rape her. As a result, she gave birth to twins who, instead of being thrown down the river as was customary with rape children born in prison, were entrusted to a peasant (Malak) who named them Jannaane and Sarwane and took care of them. A couple of years later, Malak returned the children to Nawal (who was then forty-five) after her release from prison cell number 72, the cell that became famous thereafter as the cell of "the woman who sings" [la femme qui chante][61] because she used to sing when her prison mates were being tortured, in a gesture reminiscent of Simone, the violin player in *Littoral*.

Jeanne's twin brother later joins the quest ("Sarwane's Fire," scenes 31–39), accompanied by the debonair Hermile Lebel whose demeanor and language alleviate the otherwise somber atmosphere of the text—in a manner reminiscent of Lucien Laflamme, the kindly québécois neighbor in Farhoud's *Le Fou d'OMar*. As the rest of the drama unfolds, it becomes clear from the account given by Shamseddine, head of the resistance during the war, who had known Nihad Harmanni and given him a job for a while, that Abou Tarek and Nihad Harmanni were one and the same person. He too had been looking for his mother, then suddenly gave up, changed his name to Abou Tarek, and became a ruthless sniper. He was eventually hired by the enemy as the prison director at Kfar Rayat. Jeanne and Simon finally find their brother/father Nihad/Abou Tarek and give him the two letters addressed to him by their mother and entrusted to them by the notary Lebel. The latter gives the twins the letter addressed to them now that their mission is accomplished. The play ends with the reading of those three posthumous letters: "Letter to the father" (Abou Tarek/Nihad), "Letter to the son" (Nihad/Abou Tarek), and "Letter to the twins" (Jeanne/Jannaane, Simon/Sarwane), and finally, a cassette recording by the mother to all three children.[62] Thus Nawal's final action in life is at the heart of the legacy handed down to her by her grandmother.

The legacy left by the grandmother, we learn through the unfolding of the action, came into effect at crucial moments of Nawal's life. The formulation of the promise made to Nazira occurs no fewer than four times, with variations throughout the play. Thus, the forty-year-old Nawal invokes that very promise to her friend Sawda in an effort to dissuade the latter from getting back at the enemy who had decimated her refugee camp, and hence to avoid new carnage and the vicious circle of revenge:[63]

Mais j'ai fait une promesse, une promesse à une vieille femme d'apprendre à lire, à écrire et à parler, pour sortir de la misère, sortir de la haine. Et je vais m'y tenir, à cette promesse, coûte que coûte. Ne haïr personne, jamais, la tête dans les étoiles, toujours.[64]

[I made a promise. . . . I promised an old woman I would learn to read, to write and to speak, so I could escape poverty and hatred. And this promise is going to guide me. No matter what. Never hate anyone, never, my head in the stars, always.][65]

Nawal will also invoke that promise in her testimonial against Abou Tarek during trials held in Montréal against war criminals, which she assiduously attended. Addressing him directly (in the red notebook bequeathed to her son Simon) she will claim a sense of dignity as the last remaining vestige of hope, condemning the circle of violence that pit against each other people belonging to the same land, the same language, and the same history, a circle engulfing victims and executioners alike, ultimately rendering each camp responsible for the other. She concludes:

Vous parler comme je vous parle témoigne de ma promesse tenue envers une femme qui un jour me fit comprendre l'importance de s'arracher à la misère.[66]

[Speaking to you as I do today bears witness to a promise I kept for a woman who once made me understand the importance of rising above misery.][67]

From the above quotes one can surmise that a pattern unfolds and crystallizes as it becomes clear that a personal promise made some day to a grandmother grafts itself onto a collective situation (a civil war), *just as a personal quest upheld*[68] leads to acquaintance with historical moments of an entire country.

Incendies supplants the standard association of kinship and blood ties, elevating the notion of personal origin to new heights, that of spiritual struggles undertaken and promises fulfilled. Thus, at the end of the "Letter to the twins," Nawal repeats that which she already put down in her will. Now that Jeanne and Simon have broken the silence and opened the letter (given to them by the notary after finding the brother and father), they can go back, engrave her name on a stone, and place it on her tomb.[69] Isn't that the very request made by Nawal's grandmother Nazira fifty years earlier?[70] The same expression, "to break the thread" of hatred, misery, and violence by learning to think and to read, an expression used by the grandmother Nazira on her deathbed, is utilized by Nawal in her "letter to the twins," albeit posthumously, along with variations of the aphorism, "L'enfance est un couteau planté dans la gorge"[71] [childhood is a knife they've stuck in my throat].[72] That aphorism, hardly metaphorical in the context, is repeated throughout the play.[73] It occurs for the first time in the mouth of fifteen-year-old Nawal and her lover Wahab when they are about to be forcibly separated by their respective parents. The scene in question (scene 7), in fact, has that aphorism as a title, suggesting the unfortunate and universal reality of harsh errors and violent punishments that parents subject their children to. This view is reinforced by the preceding scene (entitled "carnage" [bloodshed]), which stages the young pregnant Nawal and her mother Jihane, with the latter forcing her daughter to agree to give up the baby or else to leave the house. Whereas in Nawal's case "breaking the thread" and removing the knife entailed the basic endeavors of learning how to read, write, and speak, for Nawal's literate children it means to study the history of their mother's life and to absorb the harsh truths associated with their own origin. Writes Nawal in her "Letter to the twins":

> *A présent, il faut reconstruire l'histoire.*
> *L'histoire est en miettes.*
> *Doucement consoler chaque morceau*
> *Doucement guérir chaque souvenir*
> *Doucement*
> *Bercer chaque image.*[74]
>
> [Now, history must be reconstructed.
> History is in ruins.
> Gently
> Console every shred
> Gently
> Cure every moment
> Gently
> Rock every image.][75]

In a magnificent and revealing passage in that same letter, Nawal asks Jeanne and Simon to look for the beginning of their own story, *not at their birth*, for that "begins in horror"; not at the birth of their father/brother, though that is immersed "in a beautiful love story," but to look for it on the "day when a young girl went back to her native village to engrave her grandmother's name Nazira on her gravestone."[76] The fulfillment of the promise made by Nawal to her grandmother thus becomes the one willful, conscious act, powerful enough to mark the beginning of a new era, an act far more significant than the whims of fate or tyranny (that plunge knives in children's throats), and one that inscribes Nawal's history, and especially that of her offspring, onto a new page, superior to the legacy bestowed by genetics or blood ties.

Perhaps one of the underlying themes of *Incendies* ensues from the twists of fortune the narrative unfolds. If love can engender horror, as Nawal's love for Wahab engenders the executioner Abou Tarek, horror can in turn engender love and beauty. Such is the gist of the peasant Malak's comment to the reluctant Nawal, returning her twins after her release from prison:

> Les fruits de la femme qui chante sont nés du viol et de l'horreur, ils sauront renverser la cadence des cris perdus des enfants jetés dans la rivière.[77]

> [The offspring of the woman who sings were born of rape and horror, but they will restore the lost cries of the children thrown into the river.][78]

A premonitory statement echoed by Nawal herself some two decades later in a passage of her trial testimonial in which she addresses Abou Tarek directly, asserting that the children born of rape and horror (Jeanne and Simon) "are beautiful, intelligent, sensitive . . . , already seeking to give a meaning to their lives, their existence. . . . "[79] Why then, did she refuse to speak to them for years?

The muteness Nawal chose to keep is also consistent with her world outlook. That sudden muteness, as we learn as early as scene 2, began five years before her death, a time that corresponds to the end of the Abou Tarek trial. During the trial, she suddenly discovered Abou Tarek's true identity when he produced a clown's nose Nawal identified as the object her midwife had put in the baby boy's diaper before taking him to the orphanage. Thus, her hated ex-torturer was the very son she had looked for in vain for over two decades and Jeanne and Simon's father/brother. Notwithstanding the shock and the utter horror that must have accompanied that discovery, the latter also *meant* that *she had broken the solemn promise*—repeated no fewer than eight times throughout the play—she had made to the baby son (and to her lover Wahab, his father) some forty years earlier, to "always" love him, "no matter what" (see above). In the "letter to the son," posthumously delivered by Simon to his brother/father, a letter full of affection and pardon toward her ex-torturer whom she is now addressing as a beloved offspring and to whom she tells her efforts to find him, Nawal explained her vow of silence: "Pour préserver l'amour, aveuglément, j'ai choisi de me taire" [to preserve love, blindly, I chose to keep quiet].[80] To speak would mean to *disperse* the remaining legacy of love she desperately wanted to salvage. In this sense, silence, one upheld in a double bind provoked by a promise made then unwittingly broken, is taken literally, as the total absence of speech, as opposed to the omission of certain topics of conversation from one's utterances.

In the final analysis, the strongest theme of *Incendies* is perhaps the bond of affection that ties people together. The sentence, "maintenant que nous sommes ensemble ça va mieux" [now that we are together things are better][81] is the most frequently occurring sentence in the play. It was uttered the first time by Wahab and taken up thereafter by Nawal herself, with variations: "Il n'y a rien de plus beau que d'être ensemble"[82] [there is nothing more beautiful than being together].[83] In fact, the one time Nawal breaks her silence shortly before her death, it is to pronounce that sentence that comes back one last time at the very end of the play, in the "letter to the son"[84] and in "the last cassette," the last of a series of cassettes on which Nawal's Canadian nurse recorded her silence in hopes that she would break it.

I began the discussion of *Incendies* by mentioning the Lebanese civil war. It is worth devoting some attention to the backdrop against which the drama of *Incendies* is set, one that constitutes a fifth *incendie*, or fire (partly responsible for the title of the play) on which the four other personal fires (Nawal's Fire, Childhood on Fire, Jannaane's Fire, and Sarwane's Fire), each of which corresponds to one of the four divisions or acts, are superimposed.

War is evoked at the outset by the very cover illustration of the book: a small square and inside it a red wolf eating from a bowl resting on the lap of a figure in black, probably a woman. This is far from being a fortuitous illustration. "La terre est blessée par un loup rouge qui la dévore" [The earth is being devoured by a red wolf][85] exclaims Sawda, referring directly to the war, in scene 13 when she encounters Nawal for the first time and convinces the latter to take her along and teach her how to read, in the same way youngsters attach themselves to Simone and follow her in *Littoral*. Similarly, Sawda, much like Simone, complains about adults trying to ignore the war; she becomes inseparable from Nawal in what constitutes another instance of extraordinary feminine friendship encountered in *Forêts* as well. Furthermore, *les loups rouges* [The red wolves], an image that is also central to *Visage retrouvé*, constitutes the title of scene 30 of *Incendies*: Simon is about to join Jeanne in her quest, and his "fire" is about to begin (scenes 31–39).

The dead Nawal reemerges and asks him the reason for his tears and tells him she needs his "fists to break the silence." He replies that he is afraid that a red wolf with blood in its mouth will devour him, and he wonders whether red wolves really exist. Nawal answers that he should find out for himself by discovering the true identity of his brother *now that he knows that of his father*: "Tu sauras alors si les loups rouges existent ou s'ils n'existent pas" [86] [find him and you will find out whether there's such a thing as red wolves],[87] she concludes. Perhaps Simon discovers the answer at the end, but for our purpose here an *explicit connection* is established between war, blood, red wolves, fear, fists, finding out, and *breaking the silence*, a lexical field suggesting semantically that forcefully breaking the silence and unveiling the truth, a way of bearing witness on more than one level, *personal and collective*, may free one of one's fears and provide the courage to confront those fears, real and imagined; the courage to look horror in the face and to *start* a new thread thereafter.

The burning bus incident, yet another fire (albeit a literal one) is encountered twice in *Incendies*, in scenes 24 and 25.[88] It is told in very vivid terms by Nawal to Sawda. The former had made a narrow escape as she was on that very bus. Armed men suddenly showed up, pouring gasoline on the bus before gunning down the passengers who were instantly set ablaze along with the vehicle. A woman who tried to escape from the window with her baby was shot down and remained on the window sill.[89] The notary Hermile Lebel also refers to that incident, recounting it to Jeanne and Simon when he mentions Nawal's phobia of the Montréal bus transportation system.[90] That same event, with slight variations, constitutes a central image in *Visage retrouvé*[91] (2002), Mouawad's only novel. The bus incident is equally mentioned in *Architecture d'un Marcheur*[92] (2005) by the playwright himself as an event he witnessed from his parents' balcony in Beirut, when he was seven years of age.

It is noteworthy to specify that the aforementioned bus attack is a well-documented event known to have occurred on April 13, 1975, when a Maronite Christian Militia group opened fire on a busload of Palestinian workers to avenge an attack that had happened shortly before on a Maronite church in a suburb of South Beirut. This event triggered an escalating, infernal cycle of violence that lasted in Lebanon for fifteen years (from 1975 to 1990). In *Incendies* the bus is filled not with workers but with Palestinian refugees and the incident is set in 1978, three years later than its historical counterpart.[93] Apart from that discrepancy, however, the core of that sorry incident is transposed into the play accurately enough to be identified by whomsoever is at all familiar with that somber page of Lebanese history.[94]

Also worthy of note is the hardly veiled reference in *Incendies* to the infamous 1982 Sabra and Shatilla massacre. In September of that year,

Maronite Christian Militias went on a rampage upon the killing of their popular leader Bachir Gemayel. With the aid of Israeli forces, they invaded two Palestinian refugee camps located in South Beirut, killing an estimated 2,000 people.

Quite faithfully transposed into the play, the tragedy is set in 1978, four years earlier than its historical occurrence. It is after this very massacre—it lasted three days—that Nawal is seen planning the killing of the militia leader responsible for the invasion, an act that leads her to the Kfar Rayat prison, as mentioned above. The guide showing the prison (transformed into a museum in 2000) to Jeanne refers to the Sabra and Shatilla camps by their fictional names, Kfar Riad and Kfar Matra. No religious or ethnic affiliation is ever given, however. The Lebanese Maronites are referred to as "the militia," and Israel is referred to, obliquely, as "the foreign army. The one from the South. Who helped the Militia."[95] Nevertheless, it is hardly difficult to make a direct connection between the events portrayed in the play and the 1982 genocide committed in the Sabra and Shatilla refugee camps. In the words of Sawda, inhabitant of those camps, recounting the massacre to her friend Nawal in terms reminiscent of what occurred during the historical genocide:

> *Ils sont entrés dans les camps comme des fous furieux. Les premiers cris ont réveillé les autres et rapidement on a entendu la fureur des miliciens! Ils ont commencé à lancer les enfants contre les murs, puis ils ont tué les hommes qu'ils ont pu trouver. Les garçons égorgés, les jeune-filles brûlées. Tout brûlait autour, Nawal, tout brûlait, tout cramait! Il y avait des vagues de sang qui coulaient des ruelles.*[96]
>
> [They stormed into the camps like madmen. The first screams woke the others and soon everyone heard the fury of the militiamen! They began by throwing children against the walls, then they killed every man they could find. They slit the boys' throats and burned the girls alive. Everything was on fire, Nawal, everything was on fire, everything went up in flames! Blood was flowing through the streets.][97]

Referring to that same massacre, Sawda tells of a devastating incident, a mere instance amidst scores of similarly horrendous acts of war she herself witnessed from a safe hiding place: an elderly woman was forced to choose between her three sons aligned against a wall, and about to be executed. The man pulled the mother by the hair and hurriedly shouted to her to choose which one to save, or else all would be shot. Out of her mind, and pressed to speak, she haphazardly named one of her three sons. When the other two were shot dead at her feet, she ran around the camp, crazed and out of her mind, yelling "that she had killed her sons.

Dragging her heavy body, she kept screaming that she was her sons' assassin."[98]

The above description takes place not so much for its own sake, but in the context of a conversation where Nawal, with some difficulty, manages to dissuade Sawda from perpetrating the cycle of revenge. Nawal convinces her friend not to retaliate against an entire collectivity. She opts instead, as already mentioned, to take matters in her own hands, and to target *only* the top person responsible for the bloodshed.

Finally, it is also worth mentioning, in the context of the historical background of *Incendies*, that the Kfar Rayat prison where Nawal spent five years most likely stands for the actual Khiam prison in Southern Lebanon—Mouawad was aware and outraged of its existence[99]—where Lebanese hired by Israelis tortured other Lebanese. Like its semifictional counterpart, the Khiam prison closed down in 2000, after Israeli forces withdrew from Southern Lebanon, becoming a museum thereafter. The executioners who had worked in it later found refuge either in Israel or in Canada. Hence the character of Abou Tarek (the director of the Kfar Rayat prison) ending up in Montréal, where he is supposedly tried, a detail that may be puzzling at first, but one which is otherwise consistent with that historical footnote.

Nevertheless, and despite the presence of war, in the final analysis, *Incendies* is not a play *about* war per se. The latter is the background of the action, and undoubtedly there is a stark denunciation of the evils of it, but it does not constitute the central motif of the play, just as it does not constitute the central motif of *Littoral*. It could easily have been replaced by another calamity where the inner beasts of man are let loose under the guise of legitimate action and reform. Rather, *Incendies* is about life, about promises; about resilience, solidarity, human suffering and the possibility of new, luminous beginnings emerging from foul and evil endings. Mostly, *Incendies* is about the intersection of the collective and the personal, a theme taken up and intensified in *Forêts*, the third volume of Mouawad's tetralogy in progress.

FORÊTS (2006)

Created in France (Chambéry), *Forêts*, the third play of Mouawad's tetralogy, is a Franco-Québécois production of the aforementioned Franco-Québécois companies, *Abé carré cé carré* and *Le carré de l'hypoténuse*, a production on which eighteen French theatre companies collaborated. After first touring France in March 2006, it was performed in Montréal in February 2007. A critic of the Montréal daily *Le Devoir* qualified it as "one of [Mouawad's] most ambitious and most coherent performances."[100]

Writes the playwright in an introduction to *Forêts* entitled "La Contradiction qui fait tout exister" [Contradiction That Makes Everything Be]:

> *Avec Forêts s'achève pour moi . . . une manière de raconter et de déplier une histoire, s'achève aussi cette conviction de la necessité des origines et de l'héritage.*
>
> [*Forêts* ends for me . . . a way of telling something, of unfolding a story; it also ends the conviction of the necessity of origin and heritage.][101]

Furthermore, in that same introduction, Mouawad announces his scheme regarding the last volume of the tetralogy (the forthcoming *Ciels*, 2009): he plans to bring forth a new theme that will "magnificently contradict everything that came before it in the manner of a final organ note."[102]

The title *Forests* (a plural common noun, like *Incendies*) has a double meaning, literal and figurative. The former refers to the Ardennes forest in France, and the latter alludes to the complexity of the action portrayed and, especially, that of the characters involved. It also refers to memory, "a forest where all the trees have been felled," as one of the characters will exclaim, struggling in vain to remember his past.[103] That multiple figurative meaning, the more prevalent of the two, is suggested at the outset by the cover illustration of the book, a small square featuring the head of a man: the top of it is cut off and a panther-like black figure (probably a representation for the inner bestiality of man) is walking on the remaining (horizontal) part.

Of the three volumes of the tetralogy published so far, *Forêts* contains the smallest number of scenes (24) and yet the largest number of acts (vii), with titles referring to body parts belonging to the seven generations of women featured achronologically in consecutive sections or acts: from "Le Cerveau d'Aimée" (I), "Le sang de Léonie" (II), and "La mâchoire de Luce" (III), to "Le ventre d'Odette" (IV), "La peau d'Hélène" (V), "Le sexe de Ludivine" (VI), and finally, "Le coeur de Loup" (VII) [Aimée's Brain (I), Léonie's Blood (II), Luce's Jaw (III), Odette's Belly (IV), Helen's Skin (V), Ludivine's Sex (VI), Loup's Heart (VII)].[104] The title of the last division alone is figurative, while the others are literal and loosely related to the action that goes back and forth, with numerous time shifts, from 1871 France at the end of the 1870–1871 Franco-Prussian War, through the two World Wars, up to present-day Montréal where the first scenes are set.

The intersection of the personal and the collective, as well as promises made, forsaken, and redeemed, themes already prevalent in the play's predecessors, find their culmination in this third volume. As will be demonstrated below, there is a strong intimation throughout *Forêts*, one that resonates in the two preceding plays as well, especially in *Incendies*, that as long as promises remain unfulfilled, one becomes and remains prisoner of one's existence; that vows that are violated continue to haunt the descendants of the perjurers, destroying their lives as much as they do the lives of the forsaken loved ones. One critic called *Forêts* "an ode to friendship, a hymn to the triumph of companionship over kinship,"[105] and Darge rightly asserts about the playwright:

> *ses identités multiples et successives ont produit une interrogation sans équivalent dans le théâtre francophone d'aujourd'hui sur les imbrications entre les histoires individuelles et la grande histoire.*
>
> [his multiple and successive identities have produced an unprecedented debate in today's Francophone theatre regarding the imbrications between individual history and History with a capital H.][106]

The plot of *Forêts*, without the numerous time shifts it unfolds, runs as follows: in 1989, a pregnant Montréal woman, Aimée, is found to have a strange extraneous bone in her brain around which a cancerous tumor has formed, making it inoperable. She has to choose between abortion and chemotherapy on the one hand or a continued pregnancy, no chemotherapy, and a considerably reduced life span, on the other. She opts for the latter and has a baby girl, Loup. Aimée dies around 2002. The bone is extracted by a paleontologist, Douglas Dupontel, who studies it for four years. His own father, also a paleontologist who had worked in Nazi cemeteries to "pull from the void those who were thrown in it"[107] discovered in 1946, in Dachau, the badly shattered skull of a young woman, most likely killed with a hammer. Having spent years reconstructing the skull, he lost his mind over it, obsessing over the last missing part, the upper jaw. On his deathbed, he entrusted his son Douglas to find it. The son promised to pursue his father's mission and was entreated by the dying father to rely "only on coincidences."[108] In 2005, Douglas finds out that the bone extracted from Aimée's skull after her death is indeed the missing cranium bone his father looked for in vain. He convinces Aimée's daughter Loup to go with him to Europe in search of her mother's origin. He entreats Loup "to elucidate the enigma that shackles" her existence and his own,[109] and to decipher the message hidden behind the reappearance of part of that young woman in one of her presumed descendants. "Le fil du passé nous lie et nous relie" [The thread of the past binds us and connects us],[110] he asserts to a skeptical Loup. Similarly, Luce, Loup's grandmother (like Nawal's grandmother Nazira in *Incendies*) enjoins her granddaughter to "break the thread of [their] shattered childhoods" [briser le fil de nos enfances concassées] by seeking the missing piece of the puzzle.[111]

In Europe, Douglas and Loup follow the trail of a French couple, all the way back to 1871, with the lineage it begets, punctuated with two cases of incest, a suicide, a fratricide/parricide, and a matricide. In 1874, Albert Keller and his wife Odette left Strasbourg and settled in the forest of the Ardennes where they created a zoo, living in a utopian Arcadian dream amidst wild animals, in total isolation from the outside world. The female lineage is thus begun with Odette who gives birth to twins, Albert's half-siblings—she had an affair with Albert's father, Alexandre, shortly before marriage—the twins Edgar and Helen, and then Edmond, later known as *Edmond le Girafon* because of his marked affinities with giraffes. Around 1892, Helen in turn begets a string of children, notably by Albert, her half-brother/stepfather, and later by her twin brother Edgar who rapes her and kills Albert before throwing himself to his death in the cage of the American bears.

When Helen wants to escape from the Ardennes shortly after the murder and suicide of Albert and Edgar respectively, her kindly brother Edmond decides to go to the city by himself in order to pave the way, and to come back later to get his sister and her children. Much as he repeats his promise, "Je ne t'abandonnerai jamais" [I will never abandon you],[112] he never does make it back, becoming thereafter alienated and obsessed with that forsaken vow. After Edmond's departure, Helen begets twins (the fruit of incest and rape), Léonie and a monster who, years later, ends up keeping his mother prisoner in a deep trench. In 1917, Léonie, now seventeen years old, falls in love with Lucien Blondel, a deserting soldier who is carried half-dead by the nearby river to this remote part of the Ardennes. Léonie nurses Lucien back to life and begets with him a girl, Ludivine. Lucien is killed trying to save Helen from her monster-son and Ludivine is given away by her mother Léonie to an orphanage in the nearby city of Nancy. Before doing so, Léonie tattoos the failed promise made by her uncle to her own mother—"Je ne t'abandonnerai jamais"[113]—on the back of Ludivine, and puts in the baby's clothes a letter asking whomsoever to remit the child to Edmond le Girafon.

When, during the Second World War, Ludivine, an adult in search of her own origin, finally manages to locate the whereabouts of her reluctant uncle Edmond in a lunatic asylum, the latter agrees to disclose the family's past only at the sight of the inscription on Ludivine's back, the forsaken promise he made to his sister Helen a quarter of a century earlier, a sight that jolts him back to reality and to the past he suddenly recalls and which he accepts to recount to his entreating niece. Ludivine, however, does not have the opportunity to advance further in the search for her roots: she is part of a resistance network (*La Cigogne*) responsible for the rescue of British, Canadian, and American soldiers whose planes have crashed in occupied territory. "Ludivine la divine" [Ludivine the divine], as she is sometimes called,[114] stoically decides to switch her identity with that of her pregnant friend and coresistance mate, Sarah Cohen, in an effort to save two lives. She ends up gladly sacrificing her own life in what makes for another instance of heroic feminine friendship already encountered in *Incendies* between Nawal and Sawda (see above). Shortly later, in 1944, Ludivine, under the name of Sarah, is in fact taken away and killed in the concentration camp of Dachau, her skull shattered by means of a hammer. Her friend Sarah's newborn baby-girl, Luce, is entrusted to a French-Canadian aviator, Armand Godbout, who delivers the baby to his own parents in Québec before getting killed in Normandy shortly after. As instructed by his French rescuers, he tells his parents before his departure that some day the mother will come back to recover her child. However, Sarah never comes back, having lost all trace of her daughter's whereabouts. Luce spends her childhood and youth waiting in vain for her mother's return. In early adulthood she becomes alcoholic, helpless, and increasingly self destructive as she gradually understands that her wait is fruitless. Because of her condition, she is eventually forced to give up her daughter Aimée to adoptive parents, and she ends her days in an asylum, "looking at the pieces of [her] shattered life."[115]

It becomes clear toward the end of *Forêts* that the extraneous bone found in the brain of Aimée (Luce's daughter and Sarah's granddaughter) belongs not to Sarah herself, Luce's biological mother, but to Sarah's friend, Ludivine, who switched her name with Sarah's and then posthumously engendered "a fragment of herself" in Sarah's descendant.[116] This mysterious occurrence effectively constitutes a patent message that great self-sacrifices beget an inheritance at least as strong as that bestowed by genetics, and that friendship "saves us from blood ties,"[117] themes highly reminiscent of *Incendies*. The reappearance of that part of Ludivine's cranium in Sarah's granddaughter Aimée is foreshadowed in an anachronistic scene (22) set in 1944, where the young Ludivine is seen urgently beseeching her reluctant friend to accept her sacrifice before the Gestapo arrives to take Sarah Cohen. Ludivine assures the reluctant Sarah:

Sarah, un jour quelque chose viendra témoigner de ce que toi et moi nous aurons fait l'une pour l'autre et aura le visage de notre jeunesse sacrifiée.[118]

[Sarah, one day something will bear witness to what you and I will have done for each other and people will recognize our sacrificed youth.][119]

When Loup (Aimée's daughter and Luce's granddaughter), who has no blood ties whatsoever to Ludivine, understands the message transmitted thereof by the reappearance a generation later, of that "something" (Ludivine's jaw bone in Loup's mother's cranium) that bears witness to a great act of altruism, an act that bequeaths her own existence, she suddenly achieves a sense of continuity hitherto missing from her disconnected life,[120] henceforth conceived as a bridge between past and future. In Loup's words in the last scene where she addresses the seven preceding generations of women (Odette, Hélène, Léonie, Ludivine, Sarah, Luce, Aimée) that make up the backbone of the plot:

> *Moi qui croyais être liée par mon sang au sang de mes ancêtres*
> *Je découvre que je suis liée par mes promesses*
> *Aux promesses que vous vous êtes faites.*
>
> [I used to believe I was bound by blood to my ancestors' blood
> I have discovered that I am bound by my promises
> To the promises you made to each other.][121]

In fact, the very last line of the play, "I will never abandon you," is repeated three times by Loup addressing her future female offspring[122] in exactly the same terms used a century earlier by Edmond le Girafon as he was taking leave of his sister Helen. As for Douglas Dupontel, the representation of the voice of conscience and the guardian angel—he is reminiscent of the ethical knight in *Littoral* who helps Wilfrid find a burial ground for his father in the latter's homeland, or the kindly notary Lebel in *Incendies*, who aids Jeanne and Simon in their search for their brother/father in their mother's native country, also Lebanon—by the end of the play he has also fulfilled the promise made at his father's deathbed, namely, to find the identity and the personal history of the owner of the missing cranium bone. Moreover, by linking his own quest to the quest undertaken by Loup, Douglas, the middle-aged childless paleontologist, finds in the young Loup the daughter he has never had, promising in turn never to abandon her, as he bids her farewell.[123]

From the analysis above, it becomes clear that *Forêts* pays tribute to great friendships and to the human linkage they engender, with an ironic wink in the direction of the cyclical recurrence of personal failings—will Loup hold her promise or will she, like some of the women before her, abandon her child? This twist is typical of the subtle humor characteristic of Mouawad's style.

Furthermore, we find in both this play and the earlier parts of the tetralogy a striking interlocking between past and present, general and personal, universal and particular, mythical and real. Just as *Incendies* has veiled but identifiable references to historical occurrences (the Lebanese civil war, as discussed above) so does *Forêts*; in it are depicted the activities undertaken by French underground resistance movements during the Second World War, such as falsified identities and underground rescue missions of stranded Allied soldiers. Also portrayed are public executions by the Nazis of members of the Resistance, and the heroic refusal of the latter to disclose the names of their fellow associates even as they are being tortured and killed, sometimes in the presence of their parents or children who manage to maintain an indifferent demeanor.[124]

Moreover, the imbrication of individual histories with historical incidents typical of *Incendies* is apparent once more in *Forêts*, forming the starting point of the action. For instance, the very opening of that third play stages a party held on November 16th by Aimée and her husband in honor of Aimée's newly discovered pregnancy. Several times there is mention of the start of the fall of the Berlin Wall occurring a week before the said party, namely on November 9th, 1989. Additionally, that same date is repeatedly recalled in the opening scenes in connection to the Crystal Night or the *Kristallnacht* of November 9 and 10, 1938, when the Jewish quarters in Austria and Germany were destroyed, the victims having to sweep tons of shattered glass from the broken shop windows of Jewish-owned stores, and when 30,000 Jews were put in concentration camps and mistreated by the infamous Schutzstaffel (SS).[125]

To mark the connection between the real and the mythical mentioned above, one that endows the opening of the play with a poetic breath, one of the guests in the November 1989 party quotes a passage from Racine's *Iphigénie*,[126] in which Clytemnestra bitterly chastises her husband Agamemnon for listening to the oracle's advice to sacrifice their daughter Iphigenia. This reference foreshadows and endorses Aimée's own endeavor to convince her husband Baptiste to keep the baby despite medical opinion. In fact, when given the choice between undergoing chemotherapy and aborting her female fetus or continuing the pregnancy, Aimée, who has initially decided in favor of chemotherapy and abortion suddenly changes her mind hours after the historical December 6, 1989 horrendous bloodshed that occurred at the Ecole Polytechnique of the University of Montréal, when, on the last day of classes, a gunman stormed in a lecture room, ordered the men out, and shot to death the fourteen remaining female students before killing himself. The incident is decisive in preserving the life of the unborn child as Aimée spends the whole night of that fateful December 6th reciting the names of the victims (in a gesture reminiscent of Joséphine in *Littoral*) and declares the following day (when her first chemotherapy session is supposed to take place) that she refuses to proceed; refuses to add "a fifteenth victim" to the toll of the evening massacre:[127] "Trop de morts" [too many deaths],[128] she repeats to her puzzled husband. Thus, it seems that in *Forêts* the memory of the start of the Jewish holocaust, the fall of the Berlin Wall, and the Montréal massacre have played their part as catalysts between life and death, between individual and collective destinies, contributing to the creation of a new link, a harbinger of hope, in a long chain of more or less broken existences, in what makes for a play on chance occurrences and the arbitrary sets of synchronicities that shape human existence.

As seen from the analysis above, the three plays studied in this chapter have a common setting: Montréal at the outset, Lebanon and/or Europe thereafter. All three plays harbor the themes of kept and forsaken promises, of great friendships supplanting kinship, of war and the horrors of it (including forced displacement and loss), as well as the search for one's origin, and the intersection of the historical and the personal. The middle volume is one where the exile of the characters and their *dispersment*, as a result of dire circumstances, is vastly pronounced. All three plays are akin to tragedies, yet they also have in common an indelible sense of humor worth noting, albeit briefly so. This humor is situational, as in *Littoral* when the dead father's cadaver acts out, makes a pest of himself, and wants to lead the show, or when in *Forêts* the roles are reversed at the end of the play between the rebellious teenager Loup and the Paleontologist who suddenly adopts her awkward and immature linguistic mannerisms. The humor is also, on occasion, linguistic, as in *Incendies* when the notary Hermile Lebel, in his naivety, distorts idiomatic French expressions to fit the present situation, such as when he substitutes the expression "des chevaux dans la soupe"[129] [like a fly in the appointment],[130] to indicate a sudden disruption, for "un cheveu dans la soupe" [out of the blue] and "mettre la charue avant les oeufs"[131] [putting the house before the cart][132] for "mettre la charue devant le boeuf" [putting the horse before the cart], and "ce n'est pas la mer à voir"[133] [It wasn't the Taj Nepal][134] for "ce n'est pas la mer à boire" [it is not the end of the world] when speaking about the location of his new office. The overall effect of this humor infused to otherwise somber plots is one that adds tremendously to *le plaisir du texte*, or the pleasure of the text, to borrow a cherished expression of Roland Barthes.'

MOUAWAD ON HIS OWN EXILE AND HIS CRAFT

Are Mouawad's plays, often staging exiled individuals living in Montréal and traveling overseas in search of their origin, all about exile? "Exile and literature have always been linked," remarks Mouawad when asked.[135] In fact, in a heartfelt article entitled "Wajdi Mouawad ou l'irruption de l'Autre" [Wajdi Mouawad or the eruption of the Other] written by his admirer/colleague Stéphane Lépine, the critic qualifies the sort of exile found in Mouawad's oeuvre in the following terms: "non pas ... l'exil de la terre d'origine, mais l'exil de soi, ... l'exil des mots qui nous nomment" [not exile from the native land, but exile from the self, from the words that describe us].[136] In this sense, yes, Mouawad is quintessentially a writer of exile, both metaphorical and actual. Need I to recall that Edward Said used the notion of metaphorical exile as opposed to actual exile to characterize the role of the intellectual as outsider: "Exile for the intellectual in this metaphysical sense is restlessness, movement, constantly being unsettled, and unsettling others,"[137] a statement that rings true in light of

Wajdi Mouawad's dramaturgy and the unsettling emotional impact it has had on national and international audiences alike.

Mouawad's own exile is to be taken in the existential acceptance of the term, reminiscent of the Kafka he admires so much as to reply, somewhat impatiently, when questioned about his professed ethnic identity (Lebanese, French, or Québécois), that he thinks he is Jewish because he feels very close to Kafka.[138] A revealing comment indeed, since Kafka himself was a "minor" writer (Jewish and living in Prague) writing in a major language (German), much like Mouawad who writes in French instead of the Arabic he does not master. Mouawad's is the sort of exile great writers dwell in, a metaphorical one linked to the essence of the human condition, and one his theatre excels in delineating in sweeping strokes of genius.

It is nearly impossible to do justice to the figure of Wajdi Mouawad without taking into account his own personal trajectory, one imminently tied to the accidental and serendipitous discovery of his vocation as an actor and playwright at a turning point in his life when he felt aimless and his mother was dying. Hence *Architecture d'un marcheur* [Architecture of a Walker], subtitled "Entretiens avec Wajdi Mouawad" [Conversations with Majdi Mouawad], a book that sheds light on the playwright's intentions and methods. It consists of a series of interviews conducted in 2005 by the Québécois sociologist Jean-François Côté. The book is organized as a novel written by the latter, with chapter headings under the all-encompassing title, *trajectoire* [trajectory]. There are nine chapters whose titles read as a list of the influences at play on Mouawad's development as an artist: from "La Route d'Antigone" [Antigone's route], this classical figure of rebellion whose voice is heard through such protagonists as Wilfrid, Joséphine, and Nawal, to "Le détour de Gregor" [Gregor's Detour], alluding to the protagonist of Kafka's *Metamorphosis*, to "La Piste de Persée" [Perseus's trail], where Mouawad recounts vanquishing his fear of failure as well as his efforts to conquer the craft of a stage-director and playwright.

"Antigone's Route" (chapter 2) expatiates on the author's artistic commitment and the distinction he makes between "engagement and participation," the latter defined as the management of one's life in order to partake in the "functioning of the machine that will ensure our survival,"[139] and the former as "the courage to choose one's life as it stirs in one."[140] The inference at play here is that Antigone's personal struggle against her uncle and king Creon, verging on the political, is a witness to the sort of courage Mouawad emulates, the courage "to accept to be devoured" by art, this "famished tiger," and to become, "in the tiger's stomach, the tiger itself."[141] "Gregor's Detour" (chapter 5) is where Mouawad recognizes Kafka's influence on his art, an influence he also invokes in 2004, in the introduction to *Willy Protagoras Enfermé dans les toilettes*. "I am the bug of the metamorphosis,"[142] he asserts, recalling the day he read Kafka's story at the age of fourteen, and the shock that catapulted him to the certitude that some day he would be writing "stories to attempt, as Kafka did, to say the unnamable [he] sensed at the heart of [his] adolescence."[143] The protagonist-bug of Kafka's story with which Mouawad identifies stands perhaps for the breakage caused successively by the author's dual immigration (Lebanon-France-Québec), one which entailed the construction of a new persona each time.

At the insistence of Côté, who attempted to lead the line of discussion in the direction of the creative influence of immigration on Mouawad's art, Mouawad refuses to yield, holding a stance much reminiscent of Naïm Kattan's before him, as we have seen. In the playwright's words:

je vous dirai que, de cette expérience de l'immigration, artistiquement, je ne tire rien. Si j'en tirais quelque chose, je devrais reconnaitre la pertinence de l'exil, de la guerre. Je refuse. Je ne suis pas un auteur "sur" l'immigration.

[I will tell you that, from this experience of immigration, artistically speaking, I do not benefit at all. If I did, I would have to recognize the pertinence of exile, of war. I refuse to do so. I am not an author "on" immigration.][144]

The view expressed in the above quotation is vehemently endorsed by Lépine when he asserts:

il n'y a pas de nostalgie du pays perdu chez cet auteur; il y a plutôt une nostalgie de nous-mêmes qui ne sommes jamais suffisamment.

[there is no nostalgia of the lost country in this writer; there is, rather, a nostalgia of ourselves who never *are* sufficiently.][145]

Furthermore, taking aim at those who like to marginalize Mouawad and to dismiss his creative genius by reducing him to the figure of the "néo-Québécois"[146] writer in search of the "lost country," that fervent critic asserts, against all biographical evidence, that it is not Arabic but Yiddish that informs Mouawad's poetic oeuvre, reiterating, after Paul Celan, that "All poets are Jewish."[147] In the same vein, and taking aim at those who love to pigeonhole some authors under the handy rubric of "ethnic writers," Lépine is quick to respond to the question of whether Mouawad is a minority writer: Certainly so, he asserts, but not *because of his geographical* or linguistic origin, but *because of his literary legacy*, one that would make him an exile in his own country as well, in the same manner as the Austrian Jewish writers of Central Europe (those "hunger artists") and, in my view, much like Adorno who lived in actual exile in the United States after being, as Edward Said pointed out, in metaphysical exile in his native Germany.[148] To avoid the trap of national origin Lépine is warning against does not mean, however, to negate geographical affiliations. All the while admitting the presence of Lebanon and the Lebanese civil war in the background of Mouawad's plays, Lépine likes to point out that this background actually stands for the internal rifts and moral struggles characteristic of the human condition.[149] "A Hunger Artist," the title of Kafka's story, also speaks of Mouawad's relentless quest.

It is noteworthy that a number of the protagonists in Mouawad's works have a variation of the author's first name, beginning with W (Wilfrid in *Littoral*, Walter, in *Journée de noces chez les Cro-magnons*, Wahab in both *Incendies* and *Visage retrouvé*, Willy in *Willy Protagoras*, and Willem in *Rêves*), a fact noted by a critic[150] who sees in this phenomenon of condensation proof of an "autobiographical investment" related to Mouawad's concept of the stage as the space for a *prise de parole*, as mentioned above. Though I agree with Lépine that one should avoid the trap of "autobiographical inscription" when speaking of Mouawad, and that the *je* inscribed in his plays is a literary, Proustian, first-person pronoun,[151] it is still worthwhile detecting, without according overdue importance to it, a certain identification at work between the playwright and his characters, one that exists on more than one level, and one that sheds some light on author and text alike. As shown above, the recurring burning bus incident in *Incendies* was witnessed by Mouawad-the-child. Similarly, one of the biggest fears haunting Wahab, the adolescent protagonist of *Visage retrouvé*, the fear of an imaginary woman with wooden legs, is reportedly one Mouawad himself experienced as a child.[152]

Moreover, of note is the idea of the sensation of a virtual, interchangeable life, a disembodiment effect equivalent to deterritorialization inasmuch as it relates to the concept of self in the same way deterritorialization relates to the loss of space or territory. We encounter it in *Littoral* expressed by Wilfrid to the judge: the letters left by the father to Wilfrid, revealing to the latter his infancy and his past, reportedly gave Wilfrid a sense of *irreality*, as if they were addressed to someone else living in another country, someone who happened to be inhabiting his own skin.[153] Mouawad expresses the same sensation in *Architecture d'un marcheur*, in the context of his return to Lebanon as stage director, meeting with his aunts and cousins who remembered his likes and dislikes as a child, a memory Mouawad himself no longer held. "je voyais dans leurs yeux l'enfant que j'avais été" [I saw in their eyes the child I had been],[154] he adds, commenting that both lives consequently seemed unreal to him: his former life in Lebanon that he did not recall and that was being resurrected, on the one hand, and his life in Québec, which was geographically removed and which was being negated by the memory of another self.

Perhaps on a symbolic level, the title of the 2005 book is itself a pointer in the direction of a further identification between playwright and characters, witness the fact that Mouawad stages his own plays and sometimes acts in them, much in the same manner Molière did, becoming one of the characters he invents. Moreover, the title *Architecture d'un marcheur* is first encountered in the 2002 play, *Rêves*, a metatextual, self-reflexive text staging Willem, a young author who writes all night in a hotel room. The people he comes across—the hotel owner and a woman trapped behind the wallpaper—get enmeshed in the plot alongside the characters they evoke. When asked about the title he will give to his story, Willem declares that he wants to call it "Architecture of a Walker,"[155] a title that becomes, three years later, that of the above-mentioned collection of interviews.

The word *marcheur* (walker), at once literal and figurative, is highly evocative since it alludes to the way in which Mouawad constructs his work: *walking* throughout the city, relentlessly, sometimes by night, then coming back and putting his ideas on paper. The architecture of Mouawad's "walk in the dark," as he calls the making of *Incendies*,[156] is symbolically that of his craft as a stage director, one who creates his plays as he goes along, using a style intensely actor-oriented: the queries Mouawad puts to his cast about what they want to speak about on stage, which fantasies they want to enact, and the suggestions and desires expressed by the actors during those roundtable sessions, all provide the impetus for the night writing and the stage setup, witness the detail of the clown nose in *Incendies*, a detail that provides a solution to the narrative fabric, and one inspired by an actress who verbalized the fantasy of portraying a sad clown. In the introduction to *Incendies*, Mouawad writes about the rationale behind his approach in the following terms:

> *Il s'agissait de révéler l'acteur par le personnage et de révéler le personnage par l'acteur, pour qu'il n'y ait plus d'espace psychologique qui puisse les séparer.*
>
> [My aim was to reveal the actor through the character and to reveal the character through the actor, so that there would no longer be any psychological space that could separate them.][157]

Given the method harbored as well as the tight connection between actors and characters, it is of no surprise then that Wilfrid, the protagonist of *Littoral*, is the outcome of Mouawad's own "straying" (*égarement*), and Simone, that of the rebellion of Isabelle Leblanc (the actress who plays Simone, the violinist) who is further credited with the idea of the heavy name directories carried by Joséphine; that *Forêts* was rehearsed for 600 hours by opening night, five times longer than standard, according to actress Anne-Marie Olivier,[158] and that Mouawad's *carnets de création* [writer's diaries] abound in details regarding the agonizing intensity involved in the making of his plays.

In this regard, it is noteworthy to mention Pirandello's influence at work in Mouawad's creative endeavors, witness that the Italian playwright's *Six Characters in Search of an Author* was stage-produced by Mouawad between 2000 and 2004 at the time he was director of the *théâtre de Quat'Sous*. Reflecting on "the mystery of artistic creation" (an idea also present in Pirandello's "A Character's Tragedy") in the preface to *Six Characters* that establishes the *metatheatricality* of his art, namely the self-conscious exposure of the stage itself as a metaphor for human life, Pirandello writes about the six characters:

> I can only say that, without having made any effort to seek them out, I found them before me, alive—you could touch them and even hear them breathe—the six characters now seen on the stage. And they stayed there in my presence, each with his secret torment and all bound together by the one common origin and mutual entanglement of their affairs. . . .[159]

The similarity of the above statement with Mouawad's own pronouncements on the genesis of the two middle plays of his tetralogy-in-the-making will be apparent in the following passages taken from the introductions to the two plays:

> *Une histoire, ce n'est pas quelque chose que j'invente. Je la rencontre dans la rue. Et c'est en général une beauté à couper le souffle et je me demande comment ça se fait que les autres ne la regardent pas. . . . Alors on va prendre un café, on s'assoit l'un en face de l'autre et je lui demande comment elle s'appelle. Je m'appelle* Incendies.
>
> [A story is not something I invent. I meet it on the street. And in general it is a breathtaking beauty and I wonder how others do not notice it. . . . So we go for a coffee, we sit in front of each other and I ask it its name. My name is *Incendies*.][160]

> *de cet horizon, j'ai vu venir quelqu'un, une ombre magnifique et passionante à contempler dans cette marche qui l'a menée jusqu'à moi pour me dire: "C'est moi, je suis* Forêts."
>
> [from that horizon, I saw someone come, a magnificent shadow, fascinating to watch in that walk which led her to me and to tell me: "It's me. My name is *Forests*."][161]

The above statements and similar ones, perhaps meant to mystify Mouawad's readers and to ward off heavy-handed questions from interviewers, contain nevertheless an indication as to the genesis of his plays, for time and again Mouawad stresses the fact that he simply welcomes the stories that choose him, much in the same manner Pirandello before him asserted, notably in "A Character's Tragedy," that he often held audience with characters who selected him as their prospective author. Moreover, just as Pirandello declared his belonging to that category of philosophical writers who admit only affairs, landscapes, and figures that have been imbibed, as it were, "in a particular sense of life and acquire from it a universal value,"[162] so too Mouawad asserts that his art is steeped in a "unquenchable thirst of the infinite"[163] and that his actors, whom he never fails to thank profusely in the prefaces to his plays, typically allow his texts to change their lives.[164] Given those facts, Mouawad is undoubtedly a most "dedicated playwright" and one who refuses to be "a part-time tiger" with regard to the fierce exigencies of his craft.[165] In the words of a circular from the National Arts Centre announcing Mouawad's appointment as director of NAC French Theatre: "He has built an international reputation for his deeply humanist theatre that examines the human experience with keenness and compassion, and emphasizes the power of the actor as spokesperson in the fullest sense of the word."[166]

NOTES

1. Wajdi Mouawad, *Incendies* (Montréal: Actes-Sud Papiers, 2003): 29, 69; *Scorched*, translated from the French by Linda Gaboriau (Toronto: Playwrights Canada Press, 2005): 22. Henceforth, I will be giving the page numbers for the quotes in the French text and the page numbers for the English translation in two separate endnotes, unless the quote is very short.

2. Mouawad, *Incendies*, 14, 88.

3. Gaboriau, *Scorched*, 6, 81.

4. Mouawad's early works were first published in Montréal by Leméac. With the new millennium, they were published in Montréal and also in France, Belgium, and Switzerland by Actes Sud-Papiers.

5. Directed by French stage director Dominique Pitoiset.

6. Alphonse has the following long subtitle: *ou les aventures extraordinaires de Pierre-Paul-René, un enfant doux, monocorde et qui ne s'étonne jamais de rien*. In the English translation: *The Adventures of Pierre-Paul-René: A Gentle Boy with a One-note Voice Who Was Never Surprised by Anything*.

7. Stéphane Lépine, "Wajdi Mouawad ou l'irruption de l'autre," *Jeu* 73 (1994): 80–87, 83.

8. Fabienne Darge, "Wajdi Mouawad: Le Théâtre comme antidote de l'exil," *Le Monde*, October 28, 2006, abonnés.lemonde.fr/cgi-bin/ACAHTS/ARCHIVES/archives.cg (accessed January 9, 2007): 1–2, 1.

9. Fabienne Darge, "Wajdi Mouawad," 2.

10. Répertoire des membres du CEAD, Press Review of *Littoral*, www.cead.qc.ca/repw3/mouawadwajdi.html (accessed January 3, 2007), 1–9, 5. CEAD stands for Centre des auteurs dramatiques.

11. Michel Arsenault, "Solidarity of the Shaken: Wajdi Mouawad's Theatre of War," *Walrus Magazine* (December 31, 2006), www.walrusmagazine.com/print/art-solidarity-of-the-shaken/ (accessed December 31, 2006): 1–6, 5.

12. Darge, "Wajdi Mouawad," 1.
13. The first date refers to when the play was first performed on stage, and the second to the publication date.
14. Catherine Richon, "Wajdi Mouawad: Interviews sur Fluctuat.net," www.fluctuat.net/1317-Wajdi-Mouawad (accessed January 4, 2007): 1–3, 1. Mouawad produced his first film in 2004 based on the play *Littoral*.
15. "Wajdi Mouawad refuse un Molière," *Radio canada*, www.radio-canada.ca/culture/modele-document-printd.asp (accessed January 1, 2007): 1–2, 1.
16. Rainier Grutman and Héba Alah Ghadie, "Incendies de Wajdi Mouawad: les méandres de la mémoire," *Neohelicon* 30.1 (2006): 91–108, 91–92.
17. Arsenault, "Solidarity of the shaken," 4.
18. Jean-François Côté, *Architecture d'un marcheur; Entretiens avec Wajdi Mouawad* (Montréal: Leméac, 2005), 129. Henceforth, *Marcheur*.
19. Wajdi Mouawad, *Incendies* (Montréal Leméac, 2003), 6.
20. Wajdi Mouawad, *Littoral* (Montréal: Leméac, 1999), 6.
21. Michel Vais, "Les Nouveaux visages de l'engagement," *Jeu* 94 (2000): 120–134.
22. An English translation of *Forêts*, under the title *Forests*, is being prepared for publication by Playwrights Canada Press by the same translator who translated *Incendies*, Linda Gaboriau.

Alphonse (Montréal: Leméac, 1996) was translated by Shelley Tepperman (Toronto: Playwrights Canada Press, 2001). The forthcoming *Journée de noces chez les Cro-Magnons*, still an unpublished manuscript read in 1992 at the Centre des Auteurs dramatiques (CDEA) appeared in English under the title *Wedding Day at the Cro-Magnons'* (Toronto: Playwrights Canada Press, 2001), translated by Shelley Tepperman who also translated *Littoral* and *Alphonse*. It may seem strange that *Wedding Day at the Cro-Magnons* was published in English before the French original that preceded it. When I inquired as to the reason for such, I was told that Leméac had an agreement with Mouawad to publish his plays a year after they have been staged.

23. Mouawad, *Forêts*, 8.
24. Mouawad, *Forêts*, 9.
25. Pierre L'Hérault, "Impitoyable consolation. *Incendies* de Wajdi Mouawad," *Spirale* (September/October 2004): 54–55, 54.
26. Arsenault, "Solidarity . . . ," 2. Also see Jane Moss, "Immigrant Theatre: Traumatic Departures and Unsettling Arrivals," in *Textualizing the Immigrant Experience in Contemporary Quebec*, ed. Susan Ireland and Patrice J. Proulx (Westport, Connecticut: Praeger, 2004): 65–82, 70.
27. Mouawad, *Littoral*, 135.
28. Wajdi Mouawad, *Tideline*, translated by Shelley Tepperman (Toronto: Playwrights Canada Press, 2002): 166.
29. Jane Moss, "The Drama of Survival: Staging Posttraumatic Memory in Plays by Lebanese-Québécois Dramatists," *Theatre Research in Canada/Recherches Théâtrales au Canada* 22.3 (Fall 2001): 173–179, 179.
30. Mouawad, *Littoral*, 85 and 84, 92, 117.
31. Mouawad, *Littoral*, 71.
32. Mouawad, *Tideline*, 81.
33. Mouawad, *Littoral*, 8.

34. Pierre L'Hérault, "*Littoral* de Wajdi Mouawad: l'hospitalité comme instance dramatique," in *Le Dire de l'Hospitalité*, eds. Lise Gauvin, Pierre l'Hérault, and Alain Montandon (Clermont-Ferrand, France: Presses universitaires Blaise Pascal, 2004): 179–187, 182–183.

35. Mouawad, *Littoral*, 116.
36. Mouawad, *Littoral*, 8.
37. Mouawad, *Littoral*, 102.
38. Mouawad, *Tideline*, 124.
39. Mouawad, *Littoral*, 116.
40. Mouawad, *Tideline*, 144.
41. Mouawad, *Forêts*, 8.
42. Mouawad, CEAD repertoire, 7.
43. Mouawad, *Incendies*, 7.
44. Sylviest Jacques, "Ensemble, c'est tout," *La Presse Montréal*, lundi, 6 novembre 2006 (arts et spectacles), 4.
45. Mouawad, *Incendies*, 52.
46. Mouawad, *Scorched*, 46.
47. Mouawad, *Incendies*, 38.
48. On page 62, Nawal and Sawda recite the poem *Al-Atlal*, which is a known poem sung by Om Kalthoum, the famous Egyptian singer.
49. Mouawad, *Incendies*, 14.
50. Mouawad, *Scorched*, translated from the French by Linda Gaboriau (Toronto: Playwrights Canada Press, 2005): 6–7.
51. Mouawad, *Incendies*, 27, 33, 87 (six times).
52. Mouawad, *Scorched*, 27.
53. Mouawad, *Scorched*, 22.
54. Mouawad, *Incendies*, 29, 89.
55. Mouawad, *Incendies*, 29, 69.
56. Mouawad, *Scorched*, 22.
57. Mouawad, *Incendies*, 29, 89.
58. Mouawad, *Incendies*, 49.
59. Mouawad, *Scorched*, 44.
60. Mouawad, *Incendies*, 14–15.
61. Mouawad, *Incendies*, 62; also see 56, 68.
62. Mouawad, Scenes 36–39.
63. Instead of killing a great number of people (children included), Nawal chooses to kill the head of the militia responsible for masterminding the carnage.
64. Mouawad, *Incendies*, 60; also see 33 and 69, with variations.
65. Mouawad, *Scorched*, 54.
66. Mouawad, *Incendies*, 69.
67. Mouawad, *Scorched*, 64.
68. Emphasis mine.
69. Mouawad, *Incendies*, 90.
70. Mouawad, *Incendies*, 28.
71. Mouawad, *Incendies*, 26.
72. Mouawad, *Scorched*, 20.
73. Mouawad, *Incendies*, 14, 15, 26, 27 (five times), 88.

74. Mouawad, *Incendies*, 89.
75. Mouawad, *Scorched*, 81–82.
76. Mouawad, *Scorched*, 82–83.
77. Mouawad, *Incendies*, 67.
78. Mouawad, *Scorched*, 62.
79. Mouawad, *Scorched*, 63.
80. Mouawad, *Incendies*, 87. My translation.
81. Mouawad, *Incendies*, 18, 24, 26 (six times), 31, 42 (three times). My translation.
82. Mouawad, *Incendies*, 62, 92.
83. Mouawad, *Scorched*, 56.
84. Mouawad, *Incendies*, 88.
85. Mouawad, *Scorched*, 29; "La terre est blessée par un loup rouge qui la dévore," *Incendies*, 35.
86. Mouawad, *Incendies*, 71.
87. Mouawad, *Scorched*, 65.
88. Mouawad, *Incendies*, 48, 46.
89. Mouawad, *Incendies*, 48.
90. Mouawad, *Incendies*, 46.
91. Mouawad, *Visage retrouvé*, 22.
92. Mouawad, *Incendies*, 39, 79.
93. Mouawad, *Incendies*, 43.
94. See Rainier Grutman and Heba Alah Ghadie, "Incendies de Wajdi Mouawad: les méandres de la mémoire," *Neohelicon* 30.1 (2006): 91–108.
95. Mouawad, *Incendies*, 83. My translation.
96. Mouawad, *Incendies*, 57–58.
97. Mouawad, *Scorched*, 51–52.
98. Mouawad, *Scorched*, 52; "elle s'est mise à hurler que c'était elle qui avait tué ses fils. Avec son corps trop lourd, elle disait qu'elle était l'assassin de ses enfants," *Incendies*, 58.
99. Caroline Barrière, "Le Testament d'une mère brisée," *Le Droit*, 4 October 2005, 1. Mouawad is quoted speaking about that prison.
100. Le Devoir.com, Tuesday 21 Mars 2006, Théâtre, www.ledevoir.com/2006/03/21/104845.html (Press Release), no author (accessed June 6, 2008).
101. Mouawad, *Forêts*, 8.
102. Mouawad, *Forêts*, 8.
103. Mouawad, *Forêts*, 75. Unless otherwise indicated, all the translations of the quotes from the forthcoming *Forêts* are by Linda Gaboriau, published by Playwrights Canada Press.
104. Those titles are my translation.
105. Arsenault, "Solidarity of the Shaken," 5.
106. Darge, "Wajdi Mouawad . . . ," 1.
107. Mouawad, *Forêts*, 39. My translation.
108. Mouawad, *Forêts*, 40.
109. Mouawad, *Forêts*, 41.
110. Mouawad, *Forêts*, 91.
111. Mouawad, *Forêts*, 55.

112. No fewer than twelve times on pages 88–89. It also occurs throughout, see 73, 74, 75, 106, 108.
113. Mouawad, *Forêts*, 73.
114. Mouawad, *Forêts*, 93.
115. Mouawad, *Forêts* , 52.
116. Mouawad, *Forêts*, 91.
117. "Wajdi Mouawad Crée Forêts en France," Le Devoir.com, Tuesday 21 Mars 2006, Théâtre, www.ledevoir.com/2006/03/21/104845.html (Press Release), no author (accessed June 6, 2008).
118. Mouawad, *Forêts*, 104.
119. Translation mine.
120. She says: "J'ai peur de ne pas trouver ma place dans le monde"[I am scared not to find my place in the world], 71.
121. Mouawad, *Forêts*, 108.
122. Mouawad, *Forêts*, 108: "celle qui viendra après moi/pas encore née."
123. Mouawad, *Forêts*, 106.
124. See p. 94–95, with a detailed description of a public execution of Damien, a sixteen-year-old who was, along with his father, a member of the resistance. He was arrested and interrogated on the street, and when he refused to reveal his parents' names and the secret codes used, he was shot three times, and his father, a passerby on the street, witnessed the whole scene, and went his way.
125. Mouawad, *Forêts*, 12–13.
126. Mouawad, *Forêts*, 14.
127. Mouawad, *Forêts*, 27.
128. Mouawad, *Forêts*, 27.
129. Mouawad, *Incendies*, 45.
130. Mouawad, *Scorched*, 40.
131. Mouawad, *Incendies*, 80.
132. Mouawad, *Scorched*, 73.
133. Mouawad, *Incendies*, 11.
134. Mouawad, *Scorched*, 3.
135. Darge, "Wajdi Mouawad," 1.
136. Stéphane Lépine, "Wajdi Mouawad ou l'irruption de l'autre," *Jeu* 73 (1994): 80–87, 87.
137. Edward Said, "Intellectual Exile: Expatriates and Marginals," *Representations of the Intellectual: The Reith Lectures* (New York: Vintage Books): 47–64, 53.
138. Darge, "Wajdi Mouawad," 1.
139. Mouawad, *Marcheur*, 33.
140. Mouawad, *Marcheur*, 34.
141. Mouawad, *Marcheur*, 36.
142. Mouawad, *Marcheur*, 69.
143. Mouawad, *Marcheur*, 69.
144. Mouawad, *Marcheur*, 81.
145. Mouawad, *Marcheur*, 85.
146. Lépine, "Wajdi Mouawad," 84.
147. Lépine, "Wajdi Mouawad," 87.
148 Said, "Intellectual Exile," 58.

149. Lépine, "Wajdi Mouawad," 85.
150. Pierre L'Hérault, "De Wajdi . . . à Wahab," *Jeu* 111 (June 2004): 97–103, 103.
151. Lépine, "Wajdi Mouawad . . . ," 86.
152. Mouawad, *Marcheur*, 73.
153. Mouawad, *Littoral*, 56.
154. Mouawad, *Marcheur*, 78.
155. Mouawad, *Marcheur*, 61.
156. Mouawad, *Incendies* 7.
157. Mouawad, *Incendies* 8.
158. Arsenault, "Solidarity," 4.
159. Luigi Pirandello, *Six Characters in Search of an Author* (London: Penguin Books, 1998), xix.
160. Richon, "Wajdi Mouawad," 2.
161. Mouawad, *Forêts*, 8.
162. Pirandello, *Six Characters . . .* , xix.
163. Mouawad, *Littoral*, 7.
164. Mouawad, *Forêts*, 9.
165. Mouawad, *Marcheur*, 36.
166. National Art Centre, September 13, 2006, www.nac-cna.ca/en/nacnews/viewnews.cfm, 1–4, 1 (accessed October 3, 2007).

6

✢

"Fragments and Enigmas":[1] Hédi Bouraoui and *La Femme d'entre les lignes*

Je la ramènerai à moi par des mots silencieux qui brûlent

[I will bring her back to myself with silent words that burn].

Hédi Bouraoui (*La femme d'entre les lignes*, 19)

Mon écriture procède par fragments et énigmes: fragments qui ouvrent les portes de l'imaginaire, et énigmes qui ouvrent le seuil aux possibilities méditatives.

[My writing proceeds by fragments and enigmas: fragments that open the doors of the imaginary, and enigmas that open the threshold of meditative possibilities.]

Hédi Bouraoui (*Transpoétique: Eloge du nomadisme*, 35)

Le texte est (devrait être) cette personne désinvolte qui montre son derrière au Père politique

[The text is (should be) this carefree person who shows his behind to *Father Politics*].

Roland Barthes (*Le Plaisir du texte*, 84)

BOURAOUI (1932–) AND HIS OEUVRE

University Professor Emeritus of French Studies at York University, Hédi Bouraoui is a Toronto-based poet, novelist, short-story writer, literary critic, and academic whose vast production—over forty volumes to date—spans four decades, from the mid-sixties to the present. He is credited for having considerably promoted the growth of French studies and *francophonie* in Ontario, a merit for which he was recognized when awarded the *Prix du Nouvel Ontario* in 1999 for "his contribution in the field of poetry, fiction and interculturalism."[2] He was one of the cofounders of the African Literature Association (ALA) over which he presided, promoting studies on the Maghreb within it. The culmination of Bouraoui's efforts with regard to francophone literatures and cultures seems to be the 2002 *Centre Canada Maghreb* (York University) he was instrumental in implementing, with the aim of housing a large collection of literatures of French expression, mainly from the Maghreb, Québec, the Maritimes, and Ontario, but also from the Caribbean and sub-Saharan Africa. More than any of his counterparts in Arabic-Canadian literature, he has devoted himself to fostering awareness of Canada's *other* literatures, specifically through bringing the francophone Maghreb to the foreground of the literary map. Transculturalism, a term he is credited to have coined along with the parallel concept of *transpoétique* (the crossing of genres) pervades at once his life, his creative writing, and his academic interests. Moreover, he is said to have "made [Transculturalism] a dominant concept in the establishment of the Canadian identity,"[3] favoring the concept of the Canadian Mosaic over that of the American melting pot. To quote Elizabeth Sabiston, a scholar who has studied Bouraoui's oeuvre extensively:

> Bouraoui is a one-man example of Transculturalism in that he has lived and worked on three continents [Africa, Europe, and North America]. . . . His desire to make connections between and among his native and adopted cultures, and the cultures he has visited, has also driven him to break traditional boundaries of language and poetry.[4]

In fact, Africa is Bouraoui's native continent, France the country of his "heart and language," and Canada his adoptive country,[5] a view faithfully reflecting his own personal and professional trajectory, which incidentally is also reflected in his multilingual skills: French, English, Italian, Spanish, and Tunisian Arabic.

Hédi Bouraoui was born on July 16, 1932, in Sfax, Tunisia, where he grew up. He left for France as a teenager and studied in Toulouse where he received his Bachelor of Arts degree, which was shortly followed by a Fulbright to the United States, where he studied at the University of Indiana, then at Cornell, writing his dissertation under Paul de Man, and earning his Ph.D. in Comparative Literature. He moved to Canada in 1966, settling in Toronto where he held an academic and administrative career at York University, and traveling extensively.

In the image of his life, Hédi Bouraoui's oeuvre bears the mark of plurality, multiplicity, and diversity. The most prominent features of his creative and academic work are a constant exploration entailing the crossing of linguistic and spatial boundaries; the experimentation with form and content across genres; and the attempt to reinvent and invigorate the French language by coining new constructs, concepts, and notions. Those are features that ground Bouraoui's oeuvre in a postmodern framework, as we will see below. Moreover, the entirety of Bouraoui's literary production is informed by the love of peace and tolerance between all nations and between individuals, across religions, across cultures, and even across genders.[6] In this regard, it is an interesting happenstance that the author's first name, Hédi, is usually encountered in the Arab world as a girl's name.

As an academic, Bouraoui produced a number of critical works, with a total of ten published titles. The first twin volumes appeared in Montréal in 1971, bearing the evocative title of *Créaculture I* and *Créaculture II*, a neologism that combines the notions of creation and culture, suggesting that culture is the result of a dialectic between man and his environment. Bouraoui's latest critical essay, *Transpoétique: Eloge du nomadisme* [Transpoetic: A Praise of Nomadism] received the *Prix du meilleur livre d'érudit de l'année 2005* [Best erudite book of the year 2005] from the *l'Association des Professeurs de Français des Universités et des Collèges Canadiens* (APFUCC). It was published in Montréal as well, three decades after the first title, namely in 2005. Between 1971 and 2005, a number of critical works were produced: *Structure intentionnelle du Grand Meaulnes: vers le poème romancé* (Paris, 1976) [Intentional Structure of *Le Grand Meaulnes*: Towards the Novel-Poem] where Bouraoui fuses a structuralist and phenomenological approach to demonstrate that the morphology of a given work has its own intention and logic, one at odds with the writer's own; *The Critical Strategy*,[7] (Toronto, 1983) published at York University (where Bouraoui held a faculty position); and *La Francophonie à l'estomac* (Paris, 1995), an essay promoting the idea of a global, plural *francophonie*, equally integrating all French-speaking people inside and outside France. The balance of critical essays by Bouraoui appeared in Paris and Ontario and includes four edited collections of essays. Those are: *Robert Champigny: Poète et philosophe* (Paris, 1987), *Littérature Franco-Ontarienne* (Sudbury, 2000), *Pierre Léon: Poète de l'humour* (Ottawa, 2003), and *The Canadian Alternative* (Toronto, 1980). In the latter, transculturalism is presented as an alternative construct ranging somewhere between ethnicity and total assimilation; it entails the pursuit of an enlightened, tolerant policy away from the homogeneity and conformity characteristic of manipulated mass culture.

Predominantly a poet, Bouraoui has published twenty-two collections of poems over the last four decades, with titles such as *Vers et l'Envers* (1982) [Towards and Reverse], *Reflet Pluriel* (1986) [Plural Reflection], and most recently, *Livr'Errance* (2005) [Book'Errance] published in Paris, along with several other earlier collections. The vast majority of his poetic production, however, appeared in Toronto or Ottawa. The most memorable of these include *Emigressence* (1992) [Emigressence], a title combining the self-explanatory terms *essence* and *émigrer* to evoke the essence of emigration, and *Nomadaime* (1995) [Nomadeen], a neologism combining the noun *nomade* [nomad] with the verb *aime* [love]. Three volumes have appeared in Montréal. Those are: *Eclate-Module* (1972) [Module Burst], *Haîtuvois* (1980) [Haitusee], and *Struga suivi de Margelle d'un festival* (2003) [Struga Followed by the Border of a Festival].

The very first literary prize (*Prix International de Poésie* [International Poetry Prize]) Bouraoui was ever awarded was for an earlier collection of poems titled *Echosmos* (1986), a self-explanatory neologism combining the constructs of echo and cosmos. While as early as 1994, Bouraoui received the prestigious *Prix France-Canada* [France-Canada Prize], the new millennium saw a flurry of worthy prizes awarded to several of his poetry volumes, notably *Grand Prix de la ville de Bergerac* (France) [Grand Prize of the City of Bergerac] in 2005 for *Iluminations Autistes* (2004) [Autistic Illuminations], a poignant and telling illustrated collection of poems written from the viewpoint of an autistic youngster, and *Prix International de Poésie Emmanuel Roblès* [International Emmanuel Roblès Poetry Prize] in 2004, for the entirety of his poetic oeuvre.[8]

As for Bouraoui's production of creative prose, it started almost twenty years after his very first published volume of poetry (a 1966 collection creatively titled *Musocktail*),[9] a fact which makes of the writer a relatively latecomer to the world of novel publishing. *L'Icônaison* (1985),[10] the first in a sequence of nine novels and the only one to be published in Québec (incidentally by the Egyptian academic/publisher, Antoine Naaman) is labeled by its author a *romanpoème* [poemnovel], one "marking the transition from poetry to fiction";[11] in it all punctuation is absent (except for the occasional question mark) and replaced by additional spacing within the text. That first avant-garde work was followed by eight additional novels, two of which appeared in Tunis, namely, *Retour à Thyna* (1996) [Return to Thyna], recipient of *Grand prix littéraire de la ville de Sfax* [Grand Literary Prize of the City of Sfax], and *La Pharaone* (1998) [The Woman Pharaoh], recipient of the Tunisian award *Grand Prix Comar d'Or*. Three more novels appeared at once in Ontario and in Tunis, published respectively in 1999 and 2002. Those are *Ainsi parle la tour CN* [Thus Spoke the CN Tower]—it received the French award *Prix Afrique Méditerranée/Maghreb* in 2000 and *Prix du Salon du livre de Toronto* the same year—and *La Femme d'entre les lignes* [The Woman between the Lines], subtitled in the Tunisian edition[12] *Etrange amour* [Strange Love]. The remaining novels, namely *Bangkok Blues* (1994), *La Composée* (2001), and *Sept portes pour une brûlance* (2005), appeared in French in Ottawa, published by Editions L'Interligne and

Editions du Vermillon;[13] the latest novel to date, *Cap Nord* (2008) was just published in Toronto.

As one browses through the history of Bouraoui's books, one may wonder why the recognition of this most prolific writer's work has not reached the Québécois literary consciousness and publishing houses in a more pronounced manner. One may speculate as to the reasons behind this omission, one of which perhaps being that Québec is still busy building its own self-image and consequently does not always want to extend itself to the adjacent English Canada from which it is still seeking independence, even when the latter contributes to the body of Francophone literature in which Québec itself is immersed. Another reason could also be the fact that the *littérature Franco-Ontarienne* is alive and well, counting over fifty productive writers, and having its own outlets of production. All things considered, one fact remains clear: the positive and relatively prolific reception Bouraoui's work has enjoyed, especially in Ontario but also in France, has reached new heights in recent years, particularly over the last decade, witness the surge of conferences on and critical appraisal of his work since the midnineties, again in his adoptive Ontario. Of mention are titles such as *Hédi Bouraoui: Iconoclaste et chantre du transculturel* (1996) [Hédi Bouraoui: Iconoclaste and Pioneer of the Transcultural], a collection of seventeen essays written by international figures, and two monographs, *The Muse Strikes Back: Female Narratology in the Novels of Hédi Bouraoui* (2005) and *Le Texte d'Hédi Bouraoui: Approche par le ça* (2007) [Hédi Bouraoui's text: Approach from the Id]. Equally noteworthy is *Perspectives critiques; L'Oeuvre d'Hédi Bouraoui* (2006) [Critical Perspectives: Hédi Bouraoui's Oeuvre], an impressive collection of twenty-five essays by literary critics and writers alike. It is the outcome of an international conference held at York University in May 2005 on Bouraoui's oeuvre. Moreover, the May 2007 international colloquium held in Paris on *"Identité plurielle et émigressence dans l'oeuvre d'Hédi Bouraoui"* [plural identity and *emigressence* in the oeuvre of Hédi Bouraoui] at the *Institut supérieur des sciences techniques, économiques et commerciales* (ISTEC) [Institute of Higher Learning for Technical, Economic, and Commercial sciences], featuring nineteen speakers from France, Canada, and the United States, is another endeavor likely to result in a new collection of essays on Bouraoui and the body of his works.

Bouraoui's first four novels,[14] namely *Bangkok Blues* (1994), *La Pharaone* (1998), *Retour à Thyna* (1996), and *Ainsi parle la tour CN* (1999) have been dubbed by Bouraoui's eminent critic[15] "literature of cities"[16] in that in them are portrayed a manner of exotic-yet-familiar return "to other roots," respectively to Bangkok, Cairo, Thyna/Sfax (Tunisia), and lastly, to Bouraoui's beloved hometown, Toronto. *Ainsi Parle la tour CN*, with the somewhat Nietzschean title, finalist for the Ontario Trillium Award, a "timely and uncannily prophetic, as well as disturbing"[17] complex novel, features that super-tower itself as the narrator evoking its origins on which is grafted the history of the complex multicultural mosaic of people who have helped it reach the sky, as well as that of the individuals who still manage to keep it turning. The main narrative is set against the backdrop of the bold act of the aboriginal Peter Deloon who throws himself safely from atop the tower, and subsequently loses his job as a result. The CN Tower, reminiscent of Nietzsche's Zarathustra, intervenes, with her injunctions,[18] as a harbinger of reconciliation, hope, and understanding, in favor of the Canadian cultural mosaic. In the words of Sabiston:

> The tower . . . offers a vision of liberty and tolerance, a dream for all people who shelter in this Canada, from the original inhabitants, the Amerindians and Inuit, to the founding nations, French and British, to the recent immigrants.[19]

The language Bouraoui uses throughout the vast body of his works belongs to a multiplicity of registers: the familiar bordering on the vulgar, the slang, the eloquent, the scholarly, and the erudite.[20] Moreover, the high number of neologisms that permeate the writer's entire oeuvre (witness the titles of some of the books mentioned above), and more particularly his poetry and novels where colloquial language is the mark, seems quite striking, constituting, so to speak, the author's own hallmark. Bouraoui's neologisms, sometimes constructed with suffixes bearing negative connotations, are meant to retain the attention of the readers and to appeal to their sensitivity, surprising and unsettling them with a plethora of unexpected words, a fact that adds to the eroticism of the text, as we shall see below. In the words of Jacques Cotnam, who is otherwise quick to point out the "ill-defined" neologism *narratoème* (or narrative poem) coined by the author:

> *Iconoclaste passioné, Bouraoui s'applique non seulement à prendre le contre-pied d'idées reçues ou tout simplement à la mode, à mélanger les niveaux de langue, à subvertir le lexique et la grammaire, à fragmenter la syntaxe et à user de la ponctuation comme bon lui semble, mais aussi à transgresser, en les rejetant, les frontières qui séparent les genres.*
>
> [As a passionate iconoclast, Bouraoui strives, not only to take a stance against fashionable or generally accepted ideas, to mix the levels of language, to subvert grammar and vocabulary, to fragment syntax and to use punctuation as he fancies, but also to transgress, by rejecting them, the frontiers that separate the genres.][21]

Transgressing "by rejecting them, the frontiers that separate the genres" is indeed, as mentioned before, a feature highly characteristic of Bouraoui's writing. Interestingly, this transgression ties in with the author's refusal of the constraints of nationalism and his equal refusal to abide by "the linguistic and generic conventions generally accepted by each culture."²² His is a world of *émigressence,* where the migratory nature of words converges toward the migratory nature of a life without borders. Writes Bouraoui in the first poem that tellingly gives its title to the entire 1992 collection:

> *J'ai choisi de vivre dans les mots*
> *Au Coeur d'alphabets inconnus*
> *Là où les oiseaux chantent*
> *Leur silence immémorial*
> *Aux quatre coins des cinq continents*
> *Ainsi les langues me transportent*
> *Sur l'arcane même de mon corps éclaté.*
>
> [I have chosen to live within words
> In the heart of unknown alphabets
> There where birds sing
> Their immemorial silence
> In the four corners of the five continents
> Thus languages transport me
> On the very arcane of my exploded body.]²³

In the remainder of this chapter, I will undertake an in-depth study of Bouraoui's novel, *La Femme d'entre les lignes* (2002), a personal favorite of the author's himself, a fact that is partially responsible for my choice, notwithstanding that undoubtedly this novel happens to encapsulate par excellence some of the experimental devices characteristic of Bouraoui's innovative approach to his craft as a writer.²⁴

LA FEMME D'ENTRE LES LIGNES (2002)
[THE WOMAN BETWEEN THE LINES]

In a 2007 study entitled "Au pays du Migramour, la transfusion des mots sans visage" [In the Country of Migralove, the Transfusion of Words without Face], the critic, Claudette Broucq,²⁵ has very aptly qualified *La Femme d'entre les lignes* as "a rare book, written with a language other than the one we know," a remark highly evocative of Roland Barthes's judicious pronouncement²⁶ (inspired by an expression used by Arabic scholars to qualify the body of a text as the definite body or in the words of Barthes, *le corps certain*) in *Le Plaisir du texte*²⁷ (1973). This notion refers to the double nature or reality of the human body and the literary text alike: a reality belonging to the realm of the physical (the object of study of physiologists and philologists, respectively) on the one hand, and a second reality pertaining to the realm of intense enjoyment or *jouissance,* on the other hand. That *dédoublement,* or twinning,²⁸ one akin to symbolist esthetics, with particular emphasis here, in my view, on the *jouissance* aspect of the reading and writing experience that occurs throughout, is the mark of this singular novel of Bouraoui's. The novel reads like a partial application of Barthes's semiotic interpretation of amorous discourse and the interaction between reader and writer in literary texts. A love story is enmeshed in the meager, self-reflexive plot of Bouraoui's novel, and *dédoublement* is seen here as well with regard to the loving subject (the writer) and his female devoted reader, each of whom is supplanted by a mirror reflection or a double at the very end of that highly metafictional, self-reflexive work of fiction that revels in its own making, ultimately supplanting itself. To quote Elizabeth Sabiston at the conclusion of a chapter devoted to the novel, "*La Femme d'entre les lignes* is, in the final analysis, a book about art, and the love of art. Only in that sense is it a love story."[29]

The title itself, *La Femme d'entre les lignes*, occurs no fewer than six times throughout the novel. Does it speak of Lisa, a protagonist born between the lines, who will transfer into reality and back between the lines, or vanish altogether, throughout the narrative? "Entre les lignes" [between the lines] also comes to refer to the silent complicity at work between the two characters, the delight sensed by the male narrator and his female reader, Lisa, in seeking pleasure around the text itself or "in-between the lines that intoxicate [them], in the euphoria of blank spaces where lie stacks of delicious sheets of silent feelings."[30] The notion evoked here pertains to *jouissance*, qualitatively different from *plaisir*, which, unlike the latter, cannot be expressed. In the words of Barthes:

> *La jouissance est in-dicible, inter-dite. Je renvoie à Lacan ("ce à à quoi il faut se tenir, c'est que la jouisssance est interdite à qui parle comme tel, ou encore qu'elle ne puisse être dite qu'entre les lignes").*[31]
>
> [Jouissance is inexpressible, for-bidden. I recall Lacan ("it is important to remember that jouissance is forbidden to the one who speaks as such; it can only be said *in-between the lines*").][32]

"In-between the lines" is in essence the intent of the novel titled after this common expression. That silence, necessary for the survival of the love relationship, is best expressed by the narrator speaking of the correspondence he held with Lisa for a decade, in the following terms:

> *De toute façon, ce n'est pas dans le corps de ses lettres que j'ai flairé cette attirance pour la substantifique moelle de mon écriture, mais dans les non-dits éloquents, dans les écarts entre les signifiés de ces mots que nous parvenins à échanger entre nous.*
>
> [Anyway, it was not in the body of her letters that I sensed that attraction to the substantial marrow of my writing, but in the eloquent unsaid, in the discrepancies between the signified of the words we managed to exchange.][33]

In fact, though there is constant allusion, throughout this first-person narrative, to the intense textual enjoyment occurring in the discretional space *entre les lignes*, there is also reluctance of speaking or naming that joy, lest by so doing it gets tarnished: "Une fois nommée, toute chose perd sa force et son mystère" [Once named, everything loses its strength and its mystery],[34] a statement highly reminiscent of Barthes's aforementioned pronouncement on the impossibility of discoursing on the *jouissance* type of text (one that remains impervious to external appraisal) unless one speaks from within it: "en lui, à sa manière"[35] [in it, in its own way], a fact that explains, as pointed out by Sabiston, that critics have found but few "handholds" with which to tackle this novel.[36]

The book is divided into two parts, the first entitled "Le parchemin de la mémoire" [The Parchment of Memory] and the second and significantly longer part, "Migramour" [Migralove], a term encountered in an earlier novel of Bouraoui's *La Pharaone* (1998) and a neologism constructed so as to include love, death, and nomadism (migration) as will be shown below. Part one introduces Marguarita Felice, nicknamed Lisa, an avid reader of an unnamed narrator who sells *The Encyclopedia Britannica* to support himself. Lisa is a journalist stationed in Milan where she works for a newspaper (*La Republica*) as editor of the literary section where she includes sympathetic book reviews of the narrator's works. The nameless narrator is a francophone writer who belongs to three continents and whose origins are in North Africa. He is single; he has had at least one major love relationship with a woman reminiscent of Lisa, and he travels extensively. For ten years the pair has communicated in absentia about the narrator's work, and about art and poetry. Finally they meet in Lisa's native Italy where they enjoy other than textual pleasures (though this remains ambiguous and intimately intertwined with the textual *jouissance* that is the hallmark of their rapport) before he returns home by Québec Air, thus suggesting Canada is his home. The little we learn about Lisa's life is as follows: she lives with her invalid and tyrannical mother for whom she cares; she is single, childless and has a niece, Anna, whom she dotes over.[37]

Throughout this first-person narrative, there is an abundance of references to the avid pleasure Lisa derives from reading the work of the narrator who lives as much to be read by her as she herself lives to read him. Most significantly, the word *mots* (words) is the most frequently encountered term, occurring no fewer than forty times.[38] In fact, *mots* constitutes the very last word of the novel; we find it as well on the second page where the narrative convention on which the book-in-the-making rests is still being established, and where it stands for the only remaining expedient of the unhappy narrator separated from and madly in love with Lisa: "je n'ai aucun recours sauf celui de l'aimer avec mes mots" [my only recourse is to love her with my words].³⁹ This statement evokes the quip by Francis Ponge (taken up by Roland Barthes in *Fragments de discours amoureux* [A Lover's Discourse]): "Je parle et tu m'entends, donc nous sommes" [I speak and you listen to me, therefore we are].⁴⁰ This aphorism can easily be rephrased in the novel at hand to read, "I write and you read me, therefore we are," in what comes to suggest the "extreme solitude," ("l'extrême solitude") that, Barthes held, characterizes a lover's discourse.⁴¹ By extension, I would add, this extreme solitude is an attribute of the creative process as well, since in *La Femme d'entre les lignes*, both themes, love and the making of a novel, are woven into the very fabric of the narrative. But perhaps the closed circuit in which the narrator-poet and his reader-critic communicate partakes in a self-reflexive process of which the narrator-lover is increasingly aware; indeed, he tends to reiterate, perhaps in order to understand it, the phenomenon that links him to his admirer. In his own words:

Pendant dix ans, elle s'est penchée sur mon corps textuel glanant, comme une abeille laborieuse, le pollen de mes mots pour en faire son miel journalier, et ses ébats nocturnes.

[For ten years, she has bent over my text-body, collecting, like a laborious bee, the pollen of my words to make of it her daily honey and her nightly pleasures.]⁴²

Et c'est dans mon alphabet pasionnel, dans sa glorieuse disponiblité que Lisa, s'articulant poème, s'identifie à moi.

[And it is in my bodily alphabet, in its glorious availability, that Lisa, becoming a poem, identifies with me.]⁴³

Mes poèmes sont une rivière où Lisa s'abreuve.

[My poems are a river where Lisa quenches her thirst.]⁴⁴

Incapable de résister à la chimie particulière des mots.

[Incapable of resisting the special chemistry of my words.]⁴⁵

Elle se laisse éclabousser . . . par les mots qui la tiennent en éveil.

[She lets herself be splashed . . . by words that keep her awake.]⁴⁶

Les mots deviennent des baisers lancés à la sauvette.

[Words become kisses stealthily given.]⁴⁷

Lisa m'a déclaré qu'elle était fécondée, au tournant d'un quatrain irrégulier aux rimes internes.

[Lisa declared to me, at the turn of a quatrain with internal rimes, that she was impregnated.][48]

Nous ne sommes pas seulement tombés amoureux de l'amour, ce farceur de première classe, mais par les 'mots', nous en avons fait la passion de notre vie.

[We did not only fall in love with love, this first-rate prankster, but with "words" we made it the very passion of our life.][49]

Throughout the narrative *amour* and *mots* can almost be used as interchangeable terms, in what comes to constitute what I have called *amour-mots*, a self-explanatory construct pregnant with implications worth pointing out: in order to speak itself, the language of love in the narrative will have to be infused with metaphors pertaining to the human body. It will heavily draw on images evoking the latter, eventually displacing those images to become itself *body*. The novel is replete with such examples, the ones just cited belonging to them: "smeared by words," "chemistry of my words," "my bodily alphabet," and of course, "fertilized at the turn of a quatrain." The expression *corps-texte* or "text-body," belonging to the first one of the list of quotations above, and occurring a number of times in the novel,[50] is a prime instance of the attempt by Bouraoui, whether conscious or not, to bring an idea across, namely that of a heavy interlinking between love, words, and eroticism. From bodily flesh to the flesh of words, such is the key concept of the *corps-texte*—the narrator will distinguish *le corps-texte* from "le corps tout court"[51] in keeping with a dual notion, physical and immaterial, of reality—and the essence of that "rare love extracted from books"[52] displayed in *La Femme d'entre les lignes*. But how does this mechanism work in relation to the two main protagonists, the reader and the narrator of this novel?

To reply to this question, we need to recall that Barthes has advanced the notion that the pleasure of a text in the act of reading lies in an erotic rapport between two subjects, two personal pronouns, a *je* (I) narrator-writer who calls for a *tu* (you), the reader who is, so to speak, courted by the writer: "Sans ce mouvement amoureux, ce mouvement du désir, il n'y a pas de texte possible" [Without that amorous movement, that movement of desire, there is no possible text].[53] The reader undertakes a sensual operation whose foundation is the body itself (or, more precisely, the reader as a specific subject) to (re)structure a given text in order to attain what Barthes will call *signifiance*, defined as meaning produced sensually.[54] "Le corps, c'est la différence irréductible, et c'est en même temps le principe de toute structuration" [The body is the irreducible difference, and at the same time the principle of every structuration], contends Barthes.[55] In this sense, the act of reading and the organization that happens therein are akin to the act of courting. Both the lover and the reader embark on a trip of desire where they seek novelty through the Other.⁵⁶ This inner mechanism underlying the reader-writer relationship (as well as the role of the reader as creator of the text) is at work throughout *La Femme d'entre les lignes*, a novel that can be read as an illustration of the said mechanism.⁵⁷ Says the narrator about Lisa-the-reader:

> *Dans l'enchantement, son corps avance vers la vie qui circule dans le texte, vers les choses qui lui racontent leurs histoires.*
>
> [With delight, her body advances towards the life that circulates in the text, towards things that tell her their stories.]⁵⁸

The sensuality of the text (especially related to the sense of taste) in *La Femme d'entre les lignes* is visually established in a passage very early in the narrative, during the very first live encounter between the two main protagonists after their ten-year correspondence. The narrator offers Lisa, his *narrataire* (*narratee*) or privileged reader, four copies of an art book and in between the books he puts a package of dates stuffed with almond paste flavored with orange blossom (a gift that is hardly appreciated), with the aim of compensating the otherwise abstract nature of writing with an immediate touch of sensuality: "le goût, l'odorat de ce fruit-là sortiront, peut-être, de l'abstraction de l'écrit"⁵⁹ [the taste and smell of that fruit will perhaps emerge from the abstraction of the writing]. The "delectation" that Lisa is supposed to experience when eating the dates is corroborated, this time explicitly, in the second part of the novel. Speaking of a social occasion where Lisa was present, the narrator-lover delights in the silent complicity charged with love, at work between him and Lisa:

> *Ainsi, nous faisons l'amour en plein public sans que personne ne puisse en décoder le moindre signe, à la manière d'une dégustation de texte dans l'intimité de la lecture.*
>
> [So we make love in public without anybody being able to decode the slightest sign, in the manner of a *text tasting* in the intimacy of reading.]⁶⁰

The key expression here is *dégustation de texte*, equated with the intimacy of love-making. Here again, it is the notion of text-body, explained above, that comes through, a notion that will subsume every aspect of the novel, including the love of art, crystallized in the second part of the novel.

In Part two of *La Femme d'entre les lignes*, entitled *Migramour*, the narrative becomes highly allegorical, as Lisa is supplanted by her own palimpsest created by her lover-narrator, and as she in turn creates a fictional character, Virebaroud (incidentally an anagram containing two of the three syllables of Bouraoui's name)⁶¹ whom she takes as lover, displacing her writer-narrator. She then "kills the father who nourishes her fantasies,"[62] Virebaroud himself who seems to have mutated from created character to writer-creator, as Lisa in turn, not unlike the troubadour who appropriates the words of the poet, is transformed from reader/critic into writer-creator before she disappears altogether. Once more, the key issue here is *mots*, words that have entranced her and in which she found her *raison d'être*. In one of her letters to the narrator, she writes:

> *Séduite par le pouvoir des mots, je suis tentée de voguer à ma guise, recréant le héros que je nomme Virebaroud, et qui incarne la synthèse de tous tes personnages. Ce protagoniste principal erre en moi, comme s'il était en chair et en os.*

> [Seduced by the power of words, I am tempted to wander at my leisure, recreating the hero that I name Virebaroud, one who incarnates the synthesis of all your characters. This protagonist wanders in me, as if of flesh and bone.][63]

The narrator-lover in turn feels the necessity to set himself free from the father figure presiding over his creative process, in order to master his own destiny: "dans mon acte d'écriture, il est nécessaire que je me débarrasse du père" [In my act of writing, I must get rid of the father].[64] He kills that paternal presence just as Lisa-Palimpsest has killed him in Virebaroud, and toward the end of the narrative, he is carrying his father's cadaver, trying to find him a burial place as he wanders across the five continents, in a gesture much reminiscent of the protagonist of Mouawad's *Littoral*, Wilfrid. But whereas the latter managed to find at least a burial place in the bottom of the sea, our narrator-lover is condemned, in his own words, "to perpetual wandering" ("à l'errance perpétuelle").[65] Lisa-Palimpsest and Virebaroud, perhaps more real than the pair who created them, will end the narrative with a new set of epistolary exchanges, themselves a mirror reflection of the pretransformation epistolary exchanges between Lisa and the narrator in Part one. Perhaps the novel ends when the process of its making has reached maturation or when pleasure has become impossible with the death of the father. Says Barthes, "La mort du père enlèvera à la littérature beaucoup de ses plaisirs" [The death of the father will take away from literature a lot of its pleasures].[66] Perhaps Lisa had to leave her writer confronted to a blank page to set him free from the tyranny of love and words, or *amour-mots*, in order to become a creator in her own right: "elle se débarrasse ainsi de l'auteur, et s'y substituant, elle devient, elle-même, l'auteur" [she gets rid of the author, and, by taking his place, she thus becomes herself the author"], says the narrator.[67]

The narrator-lover "who is subtly undermined by his creator, and finally displaced,"[68] to quote Sabiston, will have to begin a new book or become a character himself, as he begins a new amorous relationship with Pia, the incarnation of Lisa-Palimpsest. Thus the reading/writing adventure continues through renewed/transferred love and pleasure. Significantly, Pia is involved, if not in writing, at least in all aspects of book production. Is this new love triangle (the narrator, Palimpsest, and the possibility of a new book) foreshadowed in Part one by the umbrella that awkwardly stands between Lisa and the narrator during their first encounter, as suggested by Sabiston?[69] Does the sliding back and forth from reader (Lisa) to character (Virebaroud and Lisa-Palimpsest) to writer-creator (the narrator and then Lisa), a constant shift occurring in the narrative between characters, functions, and roles, suggest that, ultimately, reading and writing, the reader and the writer, the narrator and the protagonist, are one and the same, interchangeable so to speak? Toward the end of the narrative, the narrator proclaims the twinning/*dédoublement* that is the essence of the novel, in the following terms:

> *Je viens donc de me détacher d'un moi pour narrer à la troisième personne, l'histoire de mon autre en moi qui est attelé au couple créé pour l'amour de percer l'énigme d'un migramour à l'aube d'un siècle nouveau. Narrateur et personnage sont, en effet, distanciés et confondus. . . .*
>
> [So, I have just walked out of myself in order to narrate in the third person, the story of my-other-in-myself attached to the couple created for the love of piercing the enigma of a *migramour* at the dawn of a new Century. Narrator and character are, in fact, distanced and fused together. . . .][70]

The novel is in fact an exteriorization or an outward manifestation of a phenomenon akin to semiosis, understood as a verbal space where the play of signs can occur, and as an illustration of the erotic literary effect on reader and writer alike. *La Femme d'entre les lignes* can easily be entitled "Adventures of a Reader," after the story by Italo Calvino, since it partakes in the postmodernist tradition of fragmentation, parody, pastiche, allegory, and *fouillis* (hodgepodge). A ludic dimension is also at play here, such as when Lisa kills the author and re-creates him in the image of Virebaroud.

La Femme d'entre les lignes can also be said to stand as a metaphor for the relationship at work between the two subjects that constitute the polarity of the writing/reading axis. As early as *Le Plaisir du texte*, Barthes advanced the thought that there is no such thing on the textual scene as a passive body behind the text (the reader) and an active body in front of it (the writer). Rather, there are two subjects who act upon each other in a relationship of creation and re-creation. The book creates its reader who thus exists as a result of having encountered it, restructuring and re-creating it in turn. The initial trio that forms the characters in *La Femme d'entre les lignes*, namely the narrator, Lisa and her Palimpsest, followed by the fourth and fifth Virebaroud and Pia (the latter herself the incarnation of Lisa-Palimpsest) are all attempts to model a process of perpetual duplication and *dédoublement,* whereby the book that is *lived* is also the one being *read* and the one being *written* and whereby one can be at once a reader, a character in a book, and a created, living character. Here, a second order character may claim to be the "original verbal conceptor"[71] [concepteur verbal origina] and to displace the author. Says the reconciled narrator-lover in a Pirandellian, metafictional moment very much reminiscent of *Six Characters in Search of an Author*:

> *Je ne suis plus l'auteur à la recherche de personnages ou d'histoires. Mes personnages, à leur tour, ne sont plus à la recherche de leur auteur.*
>
> [I am no longer the author in search of characters or stories. My characters are in turn no longer in search of their author.][72]

The metafictional nature of the book-in-the-making is emphasized at the end of the narrative by one of the characters who asserts that "the work contains a part of reflection on its own creative process."[73] In this regard, Sabiston has rightly asserted that "the novel ... denounces its own fictivity, but by the same token celebrates it."[74] Thus Lisa-the-reader tells the narrator-writer about the style of his books:

> *souvent en état de crise ... un post-modernisme ... y éclate de partout sur fond de conservatisme prônant la stabilité.*
>
> [often in a state of crisis ... a postmodernism is bursting everywhere from them against the background advocating stability.][75]

Wherein lies that *stability,* if at all? The constant *mise en abyme* and mirror reflections of book, reader, and character at work in this novel call to mind a *Matrioshka,* the Russian doll that self-contains a series of duplicate-selves in decreasing sizes, until the smallest unit, the quintessential *Matrioshka,* possibly itself a symbol of the ultimate book, or "Le livre absolu" evoked by the narrator.[76] It is perhaps because of the combination of factors outlined above that a novelist/critic has rightly dubbed *La femme d'entre les lignes* "a linguistic novel,"[77] an appellation worth mulling over, witness the constant play of signifiers present in the novel and the neologisms that permeate it.[78]

Transexuer, a neologism built upon the adjective *transexual,* referring this time to sex and gender exchange with someone else, is hinted at in the first part of the novel and constitutes a transitional point between the two sections of the narrative, foreshadowing the *migramour* of the second, with its state of flux, transfer, and interchangeability. Gender switch is already implicit and latent in the following statement by the narrator-lover: "Lisa se nourrit de mes mots comme jadis maman me nourrissait de son amour" [Lisa feeds on my words as Mother used to feed me with her love],[79] setting the terms of the comparison as follows: the narrator's mother/himself on the one hand (as nurturing figures) and Lisa/words on the other hand (as nurtured child and nourishment, respectively). What is equated here, at least by inference, are the following pairs, indicative of a twinning of roles and characters alike:

1. Lisa/the narrator-child (both recipients of love/words)
2. The dual act of nurturing/being nurtured
3. The narrator-lover/a loving mother
4. Love/words
5. Words/maternal love

From those equivalences, it seems that the narrator-lover, the purveyor of words, is also a mother figure besides being a male writer, in what constitutes another instance, amongst many, of *dédoublement*. It is during a walk on the beach with Lisa that he has the vivid impression of having exchanged bodies with her:

> *Nous avons échangé nos corps. Le mien transsexué en elle. Le sien transsexué en moi. Permutation de sexe et d'amour....*
>
> [We have exchanged our bodies. Mine transexed in her. Hers transexed in me. Permutation of sex and love.][80]

Furthermore, if traditionally the writer is a male figure, the fact that Lisa mutates from reader to writer toward the end of the narrative after getting rid of her own creation, Virebaroud, means that the gender crossing has carried over once more in a manner consistent with the above-mentioned foreshadowing, and that Lisa has also acquired *malehood* by *dédoublement*. The neologism *migramourir*, with its family of variants *(amourir, livramour, migramouriant, amourliser)* encountered throughout the novel, speaks precisely of the flux that is the essence of love, of creation; of the *migrating* nature of love; of the necessity to die *(mourir)* in order to be reborn to a new order of love (much as Lisa dies to the narrator-lover to be reborn in Lisa-Palimpsest), and of the creative process entailed in reading and writing alike, away from the stifling and petrifying effects of habituation, "the most banal routine of marital daily living."[81] This neologism also speaks of the necessity to distance oneself from erosion of emotions, and absence of pleasure, in view of reaching a love he calls "hors norme et hors catégorie" [exceptional and unclassifiable],[82] one that in essence defies death:

> *C'est pourquoi on peut parler d'amour "migrant" au lieu d'amour "mourant." Le néologisme "migramour" est parlant en ce sens. Il y a seulement permutation de*

sujet, non du sentiment. Et si l'on assiste à une migration horizontale sur le plan de l'action, on est en droit de se demander s'il n'existe pas quelque part une migration verticale, celle de la mémoire qui ferait remonter les traces du passé dans le temps présent.

[This is why one can speak of migrant love instead of dying love. The neologism "migramour" is telling in this regard. There is only permutation of subject, not of feeling. And if there is at work a horizontal migration at the level of the action itself, we are entitled to wonder if there exists somewhere a vertical migration, that of memory which resurfaces traces of the past onto present time.][83]

Furthermore, when speaking of Lisa, the narrator-lover says "j'amourlisais en elle" [I was love-reading in her].[84] The neologism *amourliser* based on the combination of the noun *amour* (love) and *lisais* [was reading], which is at once the simple past of the verb *lire* (to read) and a play on the name Lisa itself (as in *lisais*), fuses the twin actions of loving and reading on the *corps-texte* [body-text] of the beloved, incidentally another frequently encountered term in the narrative, as mentioned above. *La Femme d'entre les lignes* seems to be first and foremost a quest for happiness through the power of books, an assertion that one can happily live immersed in the pleasure of reading, acting upon the text and being re-created by *it entre les lignes*. The constant linking outlined above between the pleasure of reading, erotic love, and *amour-mots*, are all pointers in that direction. Moreover, the love of love expressed in the last quote of the series of the aforementioned short quotes where the protagonist-narrator speaks of having made of love the "passion of [their] lives" reminds the careful critic, once more, of Barthes's pronouncement, in *Fragments de discours amoureux*, with regard to what he calls "aimer l'amour" [to love love], whereby, by an amorous perversion, love itself (rather than the loved person) becomes the object of love.[85]

If Love and The Book constitute the very fabric of the book-in-the-making, it means that everything else, all the themes encountered in the narrative, whether latent or explicit, including the stylistic features, will all be subservient to and reflective of that backbone, be it only indirectly. Such is the case with the intertextuality (and the parody or pastiche) found in the narrative. Echoes from Ronsard, Nerval,[86] Baudelaire, Mallarmé, Flaubert, and Proust are sometimes heard scattered throughout the narrative, often with no reference to the original author, but clearly enough to point the educated reader in the intended direction. Such is the case, for instance, when talking of the role of the writer. The narrator-lover comments that the latter is constantly looking not only for "le mot juste" [the exact word], the famous Flaubertian phrase, but especially for the "finely chiseled poetic expression" [l'expression poétique finement ciselée].[87]

Such is also the case when the narrator distorts the first verse of Mallarmé's poem, "Brise marine," namely "La chair est triste hélas et j'ai lu tous les livres" [Flesh is sad, alas, and I have read all the books] and makes it into "la chair est bistre, hélas, et il est possible de lire tous les *livramours*" . . . [Flesh is dark, alas, and it is possible to read all the *livramours*][88] without reference to the symbolist poet. We have already mentioned some side references to figures such as Baudelaire or Pirandello, but it is worth mentioning some other instances of intertextuality present in the novel. For instance, the expression "forêts de symboles" [forests of symbols] is taken from Baudelaire's poem "Correspondances," famous for establishing the premises of symbolist esthetics. It occurs on page 23 and again on page 72 where the narrator-lover speaks of "correspondances baudelairiennes" [Baudelairian correspondences] in reference to his amorous experiences with Lisa, and the translation of his sensations into various echoes. The critic Claudette Broucq has aptly applied the Baudelairian Symbolist correspondences to the very notion of writing as it appears in *La Femme d'entre les lignes*. Trying to capture the essence of the self-reflexivity and *dédoublement* phenomena that constantly occur in the narrative, she writes:

> L'écriture ici n'a pas d'importance en soi, elle est en priorité génératrice d'un autre sens. Elle tente simplement de démontrer qu'au delà du tangible existe un monde parallèle à la fois unique et universel, certes sémantique, mais qui reste à découvrir.
>
> [Writing here has no importance in itself, it is primarily the generator of another meaning. It tends to demonstrate that beyond the tangible exists a parallel world, at once unique and universal, that has yet to be discovered.][89]

The dual nature of everything permeates the narrative and conveys an atmosphere of mystery and complexity. Furthermore, we get the impression, as we advance in the reading, that *La Femme d'entre les lignes* may be "a book about the pleasure of reading and writing,"[90] but it is also a book about the refusal to see the literary text as an entity distinct from life, hence the comment made by the narrator against the "erudite critic who stupidly applies a given methodological scale."[91]

The central allegory of the narrative places the book at the heart of existence. As such, it represents the pervasive dialectic, book/reading, and the imbrication between erotic love and the love of art rampant in the novel and which a recent critic qualified as "a hymn to reading" [un hymne à la lecture].[92] From the erotic rapport between reader and writer/narrator, to the sensuality of the *corps-texte*, to the *amour-mots*, to the love of art, such is the gradual evolution at work in the narrative, with the love of art encompassing and crystallizing all former steps. The allegory occurs at the beginning of Part two (*Migramour*) where the narrator describes the Bellini triptych he happened to see during a trip to Venice. He expatiates on why he fell in love with the Madonna on the face of whom he superposed the image of Lisa, in what makes for another duplication effect. The Virgin and Child are flanked on either side by a pair of monks, each one of whom is holding a closed and/or open book, in what constitutes, in the words of the narrator, "an invitation to reading" ["une invitation à la lecture"], as he, the Reader of this work of art, explains:

> *je ne suis pas tombé amoureux de cette femme exceptionnelle seulement pour sa beauté divine . . . mais aussi pour ces quatre lecteurs qui l'enlacent. Ce qui les unit encore davantage, ce n'est pas la ressemblance physique, mais cet air absorbé par la lecture, et cet appel à la méditation. Le Livre est au Coeur de leur vie.*
>
> [I did not fall in love with this exceptional woman only because of her divine beauty . . . but also because of those four readers surrounding her. What brings them together more acutely is not so much their physical resemblance but rather their being absorbed by reading and meditation. The Book is at the heart of their life.][93]

"Four readers," "absorbed by reading and meditation," "the Book is at the heart of their lives"; those are statements that all tend to emphasize and bring forth the sacred status of, perhaps, the Gospels, but certainly, by extension, the sacred status of all books where "l'amour du beau" [the love of beauty]—here we are reminded of Baudelaire—as well as "a vivid equation between art and love"[94] are part of their very fabric. From books, adds the narrator, depart and return all destinies "after their adventures and peregrinations":

> *C'est du Livre que partent et reviennent les destins après les périples et les pérégrinations, les aventures et les sédentarismes, tous vécus entre les lignes.*
>
> [It is from the Book that depart and come back destinies after all vicissitudes and peregrinations, adventures or sedentary times, all lived between the lines.][95]

Books are essential to one's trajectory and one could not emphasize enough the importance of creating them, perhaps as one's mission in life:

> *Semer, à tous les vents, des livres inutiles d'où l'on pourra, peut-être, cueillir une fleur, une rose, une marguerite, un jasmin.*
>
> [To sow in all winds useless books from which one could pick a flower, a rose, a daisy, a jasmin.][96]

This seems to be the ultimate message of the strange narrator-lover and perhaps of Bouraoui himself, in what seems to form a synesthetic experience where the Barthesean *Plaisir du texte* evoked at the beginning of this chapter entails a transfer, across the senses, of the *jouissance* involved in the dual/simultaneous act of reading and writing. In this regard, the following statement by a sympathetic critic is pertinent indeed as a concluding remark on this novel:

> La Femme d'entre les lignes *apparaît comme un roman initiatique si captivant que sa lecture ne souffre pas d'interruptions. Le lecteur, fasciné, passe ainsi sans transition du passé au présent, du rêve à la réalité, d'un personnage à l'autre, sans heurts ni difficultés.*
>
> [*La Femme d'entre les lignes* appears as a bildungsroman so captivating that the reading of it cannot allow for an interruption. The fascinated reader goes without transition from past to present, from dream to reality, from character to character, without difficulties or clashes.][97]

All things considered, *La Femme d'entre les lignes* may be, albeit unwittingly so, a statement on literature and a reflection on language, its functions and its limitations. Who is "the woman between the lines" who gives the book its title? In this context, one is reminded of *The Treason of Images*, Magritte's famous painting of a pipe with the caption "Ceci n'est pas une pipe" [This is not a pipe] accompanying it, and the irony thus upheld. In the case of Bouraoui's novel, likewise, the title seems to be a manifesto of sorts about language and the way meaning is either transmitted or blocked by symbols. Just as a painting may not be what it represents, a novel is not what it claims to portray. *La Femme d'entre les lignes* is perhaps not a novel about a woman, nor a love triangle, nor is it a novel at all, but merely a passageway in the world of illusions, where things may lose their signifiers (appellations) or, if they maintain them, their signified (meanings) and identities get shifted or switched. Furthermore, when trying to analyze this book, the critic is constantly reminded of what Barthes calls *texte de jouissance* (a category to which *La Femme d'entre les lignes* surely belongs, as noted above) as opposed to *texte de plaisir*, in that the former cannot be told. It escapes criticism because of its being untenable, impossible and perverse (in that it is located outside all imaginable finality, even that of pleasure), characteristics that make it unattainable and unreachable except by a fellow *texte de jouissance*. Discoursing on it can only be done from within,[98] (and even then, there is the risk of emulating it), hence the aforementioned difficulty encountered by literary critics who try to tackle this novel.[99] The third epigraph at the outset of this chapter, namely the Barthesean aphorism about the irreverence that should be an attribute of the literary text, is well served here by Bouraoui's writing.

The refraction/interchangeability of the characters demonstrated above in the analysis of *La Femme d'entre les lignes* is in line with Bouraoui's rewriting of "Je est un autre" [I is another], Rimbaud's well-known distortion of the Cartesian aphorism. Bouraoui's "Je est nôtre" [I is ours], advocated in his 2005 essay, *Transpoétique*, incidentally subtitled *Eloge du nomadisme* [Praise of Nomadism],[100] speaks of an exigency of tolerance stemming from the depth of oneself toward the unlike-oneself-Other, for, indeed, fraternity and a call for peace seem to be the quintessence of Bouraoui's postmodern legacy.

NOTES

1. Hédi Bouraoui, *Transpoétique: Eloge du nomadisme* (Montréal: Mémoire D'encrier, 2005): 35. A small version of this paper, under the title, "A semiotic Reading of Hédi Bouraoui's *La Femme d'entre les lignes*" was read at the Annual Conference of the Canadian Comparative Literature Association, University of British Columbia, May 31, 2008.
2. Elizabeth Sabiston, "Introduction," *The Muse Strikes Back: Female Narratology in the Novels of Hédi Bouraoui* (Sudbury, Ontario: Human Sciences Monograph Series, 2005): 9–15, 15.
3. Elizabeth Sabiston, "Introduction," *The Muse Strikes Back: Female Narratology in the Novels of Hédi Bouraoui* (Sudbury, Ontario: Human Sciences Monograph Series, 2005): 9–15, 11.
4. Elizabeth Sabiston, "Introduction," *The Muse Strikes Back: Female Narratology in the Novels of Hédi Bouraoui* (Sudbury, Ontario: Human Sciences Monograph Series, 2005): 9–15, 14.
5. www.hedibouraoui.com/lhomme.php (accessed June 5, 2008).
6. When I asked Bouraoui about his religious affiliation, he refused to abide (in an email dated December 22, 2006), perhaps in a spirit of tolerance toward all religions, which, he added, are equally represented in his books.
7. In this book Bouraoui creatively responds to such innovative artists as John Cage, William Burroughs, Michel Butor, and Samuel Beckett. By critical strategy is meant an approach involving the notion of *mediatrix* (that was the original title of the book), a neologism combining the words matrix and mediator, or the critic's function being "to mediate between art and life, creator and audience, text and reader" (7), with the enlightened critic providing this very matrix, or structure. Furthermore, Bouraoui advances the notion that creativity and criticism are parallel, sometimes congruent processes, and that there is a constant *frottement* (friction) between the two activities, one which bears happy results, much in keeping with Baudelaire's injunction that a true critic (as opposed to a parasitic tormenter) must contain a poet.
8. *Illuminations Autistes* appeared in an Italian translation by Nicola D'Ambrosio under the title *Illuminazioni Autistiche* (Bari, Italy: WIP Edizioni) in 2007.
9. A title which is itself a neologism combining the words *cocktail* and *muse* and signifying a mixed collection of poems.

10. Here again, we have a neologism combining the suffix *aison* with the noun *icône* suggesting that the book is a recitative of icons, or strong, concrete images.

11. Elizabeth Sabiston, "Introduction," *The Muse Strikes Back: Female Narratology in the Novels of Hédi Bouraoui* (Sudbury, Ontario: Human Sciences Monograph Series, 2005): 9–15, 15.

12. *L'Or du temps*.

13. *La Composée* appeared in an Italian translation by Nicola D'Ambrosio under the title *Frammenti di Donna* (Napoli, Italy: Ed. Specchio del Mediterraneo) in 2005.

14. *L'Icônaison* (1985) is actually the very first prose title of Bouraoui's; however, it belongs to a hybrid genre of poem-novel or novel-poem and as such deserves a classification on its own. *Retour à Thyna* appeared in an Italian translation (*Ritorno a Thyna*), translated by Maria Michela Scamardella in 1998 (Palermo: Ed. Dora Marcus). As for *La Pharaone*, it appeared in an Italian translation (with an interview) by Nicola D'Ambrosio in 2007 (Bari, Italia: WIP Edizioni).

15. Elizabeth Sabiston, *The Muse Strikes Back: Female Narratology in the Novels of Hédi Bouraoui* (Sudbury, Ontario: Human Sciences Monograph Series, 2005): 9–15, 15.

16. Elizabeth Sabiston, *The Muse Strikes Back: Female Narratology in the Novels of Hédi Bouraoui* (Sudbury, Ontario: Human Sciences Monograph Series, 2005): 89.

17. Elizabeth Sabiston, *The Muse Strikes Back*, 90.

18. In her study entitled "Ainsi parle la tour CN: of Moose and Women and Talking Towers," in *The Muse Strikes Back: Female Narratology in the Novels of Hédi Bouraoui* (Sudbury, Ontario: Human Sciences Monograph Series, 2005): 89–119, 89.

19. Elizabeth Sabiston, *The Muse Strikes Back*, 119.

20. On this issue, see Jacques Cotnam, ed., *Hédi Bouraoui: Iconoclaste et chantre du transculturel* (Ottawa: Le Nordir, 1996): 214–215.

21. Jacques Cotnam, ed., "Présentation" [introduction], *Hédi Bouraoui: Iconoclaste et chantre du transculturel* (Ottawa: Le Nordir, 1996): 7–11, 9.

22. Elizabeth Sabiston, "Bâtir des ponts: Transculturel et résistance négociée du lecteur," *Perspectives critiques: L'oeuvre d'Hédi Bouraoui* (Sudbury, Ontario: Human Sciences Monograph Series, 2006): 9–25, 13.

23. Hédi Bouraoui, *Emigressence* (Ottawa: Editions du Vermillon, 1992), 13. The page numbering throughout this collection of poems is written out in French rather than in Arabic numbers, such as *treize* [13] for the quotation in question here.

24. Emails by Bouraoui to myself in July 2007.

25. Claudette Broucq, in *Le Texte D'Hédi Bouraoui: Approche par le "ça"* (Toronto: CMC Editions, 2007): 73–87, 87.

26. The *rapprochement* between Barthes and Bouraoui found in this study is one also made by another critic in 1996, years before the publication of *La Femme d'entre les lignes*. See Robert Elbaz, "Sur la sémiotique matricielle de Bouraoui," in *Hédi Bouraoui: Iconoclaste et chantre du transculturel* (Ottawa: Le Nordir, 1996): 167–172.

27. Roland Barthes, *Le Plaisir du texte* (Paris: Editions du Seuil, 1973): 29.

28. That twinning is suggested at the outset by the book cover illustration representing Leda and Jupiter in the form of a swan. As pointed out by E. Sabiston (in "The Man Behind *La Femme d'entre les lignes*," in *The Muse Strikes Back: Female Narratology in the Novels of Hédi Bouraoui* (Sudbury, Ontario: Human Sciences

Monograph Series, 2005, 143–160, 144–145). What comes to mind is the image of the twins begotten by Leda as a result of the rape.

29. Elizabeth Sabiston, "The Man Behind *La Femme d'entre les lignes*," in *The Muse Strikes Back: Female Narratology in the Novels of Hédi Bouraoui* (Sudbury, Ontario: Human Sciences Monograph Series, 2005): 143–160, 146.

30. "L'entre-les-lignes qui nous enivre, dans l'euphorie des blancs où stagnent des millefeuilles de sentiments muets," Hédi Bouraoui, *La Femme d'entre les lignes* (Toronto: Editions du gref, 2002), 62. Also see pages 88, 99, 139, 140. Henceforth referred to as *La Femme*.

31. Emphasis mine.

32. Barthes, *Le Plaisir du texte*, 36.

33. Bouraoui, *La Femme*, 96.

34. Bouraoui, *La Femme*, 94.

35. Barthes, *Le Plaisir du texte*, 37–38.

36. "The Man Behind *La Femme d'entre les lignes*," 143. It is also worth noting the collection of essays edited by E. Sabiston and S. Crosta, entitled *Perspecties critiques: L'oeuvre d'Hédi Bouraoui* (Sudbury, Ontario: Série monographique en sciences humaines) and published in 2006 as an outcome of a 2005 conference at York University (Canada) on the work of Hédi Bouraoui. This collection contains no fewer than four critical articles dedicated to *La Femme d'entre les lignes*, out of a total of twenty-four articles, a significant percentage.

37. Anna is involved in a relationship where she is brutalized by her lover, a failed North African artist, and it seems that the *amour-larmes* of Anna and Ali parallels the *amour-mots* of Lisa and the narrator.

38. See *La Femme*, pages 10, 11, 15, 22, 23, 25, 26, 15, 40, 41, 28, 30, 36, 37, 49, 62, 63, 65, 66, 69, 70, 79, 83, 84, 88, 90, 96, 129.

39. *La Femme* . . . 10.

40. Roland Barthes, "Je suis odieux," in *Fragments de discours amoureux* (Paris: Editions du Seuil, 1977), 197–198, 198. The quote from Ponge is as follows: "Puisque tu nous lis (mon livre et moi), cher lecteur, donc nous sommes (toi, lui, et moi)" [Since you read us (my book and me), dear reader, we hence are (you, it, and myself)].

41. Roland Barthes, Notice, in *Fragments de discours amoureux* (Paris: Editions du Seuil, 1977): 5.

42. Bouraoui, *La Femme*, 11.

43. Bouraoui, *La Femme*, 91.

44. Bouraoui, *La Femme*, 71.

45. Bouraoui, *La Femme*, 63.

46. Bouraoui, *La Femme*, 83.

47. Bouraoui, *La Femme*, 83.

48. Bouraoui, *La Femme*, 125.

49. Bouraoui, *La Femme*, 70.

50. See for instance pages 11, 28, 85, 127, 131, 64.

51. Bouraoui, *La Femme*, 64.

52. "Un amour rare qu'on extrait des livres," *La Femme* . . . 13.

53. Vincent Jouve, *La Littérature selon Roland Barthes* (Paris: Editions de Minuit, 1986), 103.

54. "Qu'est-ce que la signifiance? *C'est le sens en ce qu'il est produit sensuellement*" [What is significance? It is meaning produced sensually], Roland Barthes, *Le Plaisir du texte*, 97.

55. Vincent Jouve, *La Littérature selon Roland Barthes* (Paris: Editions de Minuit, 1986), 101.

56. Writes Jouve in *La Littérature selon Roland Barthes*, "le rapport érotique de deux sujets à l'intérieur d'un texte: tel semble être le plaisir profond de la littérature" [the erotic rapport of two subjects inside a text, such is the profound pleasure of literature], 104.

57. The erotic rapport to a text can be more violent if it is replete with unexpected, baroque, eccentric words, will assert Jouve. Such is the case with the number of neologisms used by Bouraoui, neologisms that are almost always surprising and unexpected. "On pourrait Presque parler du viol du texte sur la personne du lecteur" [one can almost speak of rape on the person of the reader] (102) will say Jouve, in *La Littérature selon Roland Barthes* (Paris: Editions de Minuit, 1986): 102.

58. Bouraoui, *La Femme*, 96.

59. Bouraoui, *La Femme*, 14.

60. Bouraoui, *La Femme*, 116. Emphasis mine.

61. In her study entitled *"La Femme d'entre les lignes*: Au pays du Migramour, la transfusion des mots sans visage," in *Le Texte D'Hédi Bouraoui: Approche par le "ça"* (Toronto: CMC Editions, 2007, 73–88) Claudette Broucq sees in the name Virebaroud a reference to the adjective "baroudeur," signifying someone who likes struggles, 80.

62. Bouraoui, *La Femme*, 107.

63. Bouraoui, *La Femme*, 103.

64. Bouraoui, *La Femme*, 139.

65. Bouraoui, *La Femme*, 139.

66. Bouraoui, *Le Plaisir du texte*, 75.

67. Bouraoui, *La Femme*, 137.

68. Elizabeth Sabiston, "The Man Behind *La Femme d'entre les lignes*," in *The Muse Strikes Back: Female Narratology in the Novels of Hédi Bouraoui* (Sudbury, Ontario: Human Sciences Monograph Series, 2005): 143–160, 153.

69. Elizabeth Sabiston, "The Man Behind *La Femme d'entre les lignes*," in *The Muse Strikes Back: Female Narratology in the Novels of Hédi Bouraoui* (Sudbury, Ontario: Human Sciences Monograph Series, 2005): 143–160, 151.

70. Bouraoui, *La Femme*, 133.

71. Bouraoui, *La Femme*, 139.

72. Bouraoui, *La Femme*, 86. Also see page 88.

73. Bouraoui, *La Femme*, 137.

74. Elizabeth Sabiston, "The Man Behind *La Femme d'entre les lignes*," in *The Muse Strikes Back: Female Narratology in the Novels of Hédi Bouraoui* (Sudbury, Ontario: Human Sciences Monograph Series, 2005): 143–160, 159.

75. Bouraoui, *La Femme*, 100.

76. Bouraoui, *La Femme*, 123.

77. Jean-Max Tixier, "La Fonction de transfert dans *La Femme d'entre les lignes*," in *Perspectives Critiques: L'oeuvre d'Hédi Bouraoui*, ed. Elizabeth Sabiston and

Suzanne Crosta (Sudbury, Canada: Human Sciences Monograph Series, 2006): 365–371, 366.

78. For instance, on page 99, *expir* and *inspir* when speaking about the movement of waves. Both nouns are derived from *expirer* and *inspirer*, verbs that refer to breathing. Also see page 90, with the word *élastiqué*, meaning exercised, derived from the word *élastique*, or elastic. Speaking of Lisa, the narrator writes: "Dès ma naissance . . . je me suis élastiqué dans des mots dont la vraie langue lui est inconnue" [Ever since my birth I have stretched myself in words whose real meaning are unknown to her].

79. Bouraoui, *La Femme*, 56.
80. Bouraoui, *La Femme*, 38.
81. Bouraoui, *La Femme*, 88, "la routine d'une quotidienneté maritale des plus banales."
82. Bouraoui, *La Femme*, 94.
83. Editor, Du Gref, Toronto: "*La Femme d'entre les lignes*," www.hedibouraoui.com/details.php?id=29 (accessed July 5, 2008).
84. Bouraoui, *La Femme*, 85.
85. Roland Barthes, "Aimer l'amour," in *Fragments de discours amoureux* (Paris: Editions du Seuil, 1977): 39–40, 39.
86. On page 128 of *La Femme*, part of Nerval's famous line is quoted, "le ténébreux, le veuf, l'inconsolé."
87. Bouraoui, *La Femme*, 81.
88. Bouraoui, *La Femme*, 93.
89. Claudette Broucq, in *Le Texte D'Hédi Bouraoui: Approche par le "ça"* (Toronto: CMC Editions, 2007): 73–87, 82.
90. Email of Bouraoui's to myself, dated July 7, 2007.
91. "Un critique 'savant" qui applique stupidement une certaine grille méthodologique," *La Femme*, 50.
92. Giuseppina Igonetti, "L'écriture et l'errance dans *La femme d'entre les lignes*," in "*Perspectives Critiques: L'oeuvre d'Hédi Bouraoui*," eds. Elizabeth Sabiston and Suzanne Crosta (Sudbury, Canada: Human Sciences Monograph Series, 2006): 343–355, 344. Writes Igonetti: "Dans cet hymne à la lecture, Bouraoui démontre qu'il aime, au sens propre du terme, écrire, qu'il en éprouve du plaisir et compte bien qu'il se manifestera dans ses livres assez de ce plaisir pour que le lecteur (tout comme Lisa, son personnage-lectrice) le partage à son tour" [In this hymn to reading, Bouraoui shows that he loves, in the literal meaning of the word, writing; that he derives pleasure from it, and that he hopes that the reader (just as Lisa, the character-reader) will also partake in it], 344–345.
93. Bouraoui, *La Femme*, 110.
94. Bouraoui, *La Femme*, 122.
95. Bouraoui, *La Femme*, 110.
96. Bouraoui, *La Femme*, 126.
97. www.hedibouraoui.com/details.php?id=29.
98. Barthes, *Le Plaisir du texte*, 37–38.
99. Such critics as Jouve speak of "l'érotisme particulier du fouillis de l'écriture dans le texte moderne" [the special eroticism of the hodge-podge of the style in the modern text] whereby the reader is on the lookout for the sentence, the detail,

the word that will directly and deeply touch him or her. See Vincent Jouve, *La Littérature selon Roland Barthes* (Paris: Editions de Minuit, 1986), 104.

100. Hédi Bouraoui, *Transpoétique; Eloge du nomadisme* (Montréal: Mémoire d'encrier, 2005), 45. On that issue, also see Suzanne Crosta, "Transculturalisme et transpoétique chez Hédi Bouraoui," in *Perspectives Critiques: l'oeuvre d'Hédi Bouraoui* (Sudbury, Ontario: Human Sciences Monograph Series): 380-382.

Conclusion

Engaging a sociohistorical framework for the apprehension of minor literatures in Canada, the present study consists of a historiographic profile of the writing produced by Canadians of Arabic origins, coupled with a detailed portrayal of five of its distinguished (mostly francophone) figures; it delineates the specificity of this contemporary trilingual literature and sets the stage for the appreciation and enjoyment of the authors portrayed, in and of themselves and also as part and parcel of a distinct literary system they were instrumental in shaping.

When I first embarked on this project I did not suspect that the final outcome would have the table of contents it presently has. Initially I was inclined to write a monograph mostly devoted to some of the nine women writers whose works are sampled in my 2002 anthology, namely, Nadia Ghalem, Anne-Marie Alonzo, Rubba Nadda, Mona Latif Ghattas, Andrée Dahan, Nadine Ltaif, Yamina Mouhoub, Yolande Geadah, and Abla Farhoud.[1] Only the latter, however, made it in the present book in a chapter devoted entirely to her. Serendipity aiding, the definitive shape and content of this book took a slightly different turn than initially projected. To give but one example: I received one day in the mail an awaited package of books from Leméac, in which the librarian kindly slipped two volumes by Wajdi Mouawad, "in case of interest," said the accompanying note. Indeed I became interested and I rejoiced at the discovery, then at the succeeding new thought of devoting an entire chapter to him, as I read and examined more of his strikingly beautiful plays.

The first chapter is a general, inclusive one. Here I looked at the vast body of works produced by Canadian writers hailing from various Arabic countries, writers who produced a trilingual literature befitting the diversity of their cultural backgrounds. I accepted to begin with the presence of multiple relations within this body of works, without knowing beforehand exactly what the nature of those relations was. I looked for the modalities of the existence of this literature. I examined its emergence and development over the last three decades. I focused on production patterns and then dealt with the writing itself, observing thematic and structural tendencies, differences and similarities. I also studied the writers themselves, their bio-bibliographical profile, and instances of their reception by the Canadian literary institution. Moreover, I placed this corpus of writing in the context where it initially came into being, mostly in Québec and Ontario, and I further examined reasons that make the former a choice site for the study of exilic literatures in Canada. I gave some illustrations of the more salient characteristics found in this literature as a whole, characteristics partially shared by other literatures of exile. I showed examples of how it bears the mark of the political, the collective value of utterances, and the deterritorialization of language. Having done so, it was time to give a detailed study—including an overview of their oeuvre and an *explication de texte* of selected works—of the five chosen figures, namely, Saad Elkhadem, Naïm Kattan, Abla Farhoud, Wajdi Mouawad, and Hédi Bouraoui, in the order enumerated.

My choice of *precisely* those five authors was dictated by the same taste for breadth and balance that informs my entire endeavor: I have chosen one writer who is deceased, as a way of paying tribute to his memory (Elkhadem); two who are at a stage of their careers where they can reap the benefits of a lifelong commitment to their craft (Bouraoui and Kattan); one who is in the prime of her creative endeavors (Farhoud), and yet another whose successful career as playwright was launched at a relatively young age (Mouawad).[2] Those Canadian writers have created drama, poetry, fiction (long and short), film scripts, children's books, and essays. Among them, there are a combined total of approximately 120 volumes published across the said genres.

Of the five writers brought together in this monograph, four have in common the decision to write in French (namely, Kattan, Farhoud, Mouawad, and Bouaoui) and one, the late Saad Elkhadem, chose Arabic and English as his languages of literary expression. All five writers—they are Moslem, Christian, and Jewish—share Arabic as their primary language. They are highly educated, and three of them taught at the university level in some capacity. "Errant et polygraphe," to borrow an expression by a French Tunisian poet,[3] are attributes that could qualify the individual trajectory of some of them; yet, they mostly resist being pigeonholed as writers of immigration. All five authors left their native countries a long time ago, mainly because of sociopolitical conditions that made life there highly unwieldy. In two cases (Mouawad and Farhoud), the Lebanese civil war was a determining factor for their parents to seek departure. In one case (Kattan), the 1948 creation of the State of Israel precluded a return to his native Iraq as an Arab Jew, and in yet another case (Elkhadem), the motivation for leaving Egypt was escaping life under Nasser's tyrannical rule. As for Bouraoui, he left his native Tunisia when it was still a French protectorate. Except for Saad Elkhadem who transited through Austria prior to landing in Canada, these writers all lived in France for a few years before making Canada their final home.

Throughout this study, I have preferred using the term *exile/exilic* over *immigration/immigrant*, for while both constructs and their derivatives imply movement from the original country and the ensuing estrangement, exile connotes, to various degrees, terminal loss and forced displacement, which are associated with sociopolitical conditions that render living in the native land (or returning to it) anywhere from undesirable to hardly possible. Hence, the noun/adjective *exile*, with its wealth of metaphorical shades of meaning, seems directly or indirectly more appropriate in the present context than the bland, nonevocative, and generic terms *immigration/immigrant*. If I were to describe the state of being in exile in terms of its single, most relevant attribute, then I would concur that "its essential sadness can never be surmounted."[4] Perhaps this is why the texts marked by it tend to appear rather somber, albeit occasionally shot with luminous spots and horizons of hope.

Since there is no reliable theory that comes to the rescue to explain what it means *not to be* Québécois, French, or Canadian, and how much one is or is not so and to what degree one can be Egyptian and Lebanese but not Swedish and Senegalese, I attempted for the most part to gather my scholarly insights and pronouncements from examination of the texts at hand, and to listen primarily to *the voice therein*. When theorists and researchers working in the area of minor and exilic literatures have inspired me, I did not hesitate to be informed by their views and to be influenced by them, especially so when their methods of analyses were likewise based on a sympathetic inside view of the material examined.

Instead of being lumped together under one rubric or another, each of the five authors portrayed in this book deserved a separate narrative, with a careful examination of paratextual facets, including career, profile, and reception of their respective works. I had no a priori stance except the exigency to approach their writing objectively, conscientiously, empirically so to speak, with rigor and exactitude, and with receptivity. I was also aware of the necessity to seek the quality of *literariness*, dear to comparatists, inherent in their texts. When dealing with Kattan, I did not know that I would find the key to his worldview in some of his early essays; likewise, when I studied Elkhadem, I sensed that the key to his love-hate relationship with his native land resides in his Flying Egyptian trilogy; however, I had to look at three more of his novels in order to get a full picture of his methods, his anger, and his style. When examining Farhoud, I had initially intended to deal only with her plays, since she mostly defined herself as a playwright. However, I was compelled to look at and to present her three novels as well, as they curiously show strong structural and thematic crossovers with her dramaturgy, thus shedding light on her entire endeavor. Likewise, when dealing with Bouraoui, I realized halfway that an in-depth analysis of a single novel of his could prove more significant in his particular case than an in-breadth study of a collection of his novels. Furthermore, when examining Mouawad, I devoted the entire chapter on his trilogy of broken promises and salvaged lives, since it encapsulates, in my view, the gist of his preoccupations as an artist. Furthermore, I realized that to deal with Mouawad as a playwright and not to look at his style as stage director would be insufficient and misleading, and I wrapped up the chapter devoted to him on that note. When similarities, sometimes embedded in differences, surged up across or between the writers, I pointed them out. In the final analysis and as I close this book, I do not know all the answers to questions I may have elicited, and I hope others will seek to find out.

At the conclusion of this monograph, I find myself pondering about the future of that predominantly francophone writing dubbed Québécois/Canadian-Arabic or Arabic-Canadian/Québécois, one that has created a large body of works bearing the indelible signs of talent and exile; a writing marked with a creativity and originality bound to enrich the cultural context in which it was born, infusing that locus with memorial vestiges of the old countries left behind forever.

However, if Canadian-Arabic literature, produced in three languages, is to become fully institutionalized, something it truly deserves, it should be researched, studied, and disseminated among scholars and the wider public. Further work on the topic could be concerned with:

1. Studying the production of individual texts of Arabic-Canadian literature in a "situated" and "circumstantial" way, in the sense given to those terms by Edward Said, and in keeping with his well-documented hypothesis that for the literary critic "the genesis of a literary work is as relevantly interesting as its being."[5]
2. Producing studies of the characteristics, patterns, tendencies, peculiarities and diversity of Arabic-Canadian writing; the thematic fabric that permeates it and the language that transmits this thematic fabric.
3. Drawing a diachronic (historical) and synchronic (descriptive and analytic) profile of the emergence and the degree of institutional insertion in Canadian Literature of Arabic-Canadian writing. This will

entail a detailed study of the reception of this literature by the two major literary systems in Canada as reflected in academic articles, the press, universities, libraries, bookstores, publishers, information media, and literary prizes earned.
4. Writing monographs with in-depth studies of individual writers and their works.
5. Studying the relations between Arabic-Canadian writing and other literary systems in Canada.

It is my hope that the present monograph has contributed a fortunate step toward the canonization of the literature of Canadians of Arabic origins.

NOTES

1. *Voices in the Desert: An Anthology of Arabic-Canadian Women Writers.* Toronto: Guernica, 2002.
2. Since my 2002 anthology featured nine women writers, I think the present monograph featuring four men writers and one woman also establishes a semblance of balance.
3. Abdelwahab Meddeb, *L'Exil occidental* (Paris: Albin Michel, 2005): 9; the expression "errant et polygraphe" [wandering and polygraph] is the title of the first chapter, 9–18.
4. Edward Said, "Reflections on Exile," *Reflections on Exile and Other Essays* (Cambridge, Massachusetts: Harvard University Press, 2000): 173–186, 173.
5. Edward Said, *The World, the Text and the Critic* (Cambridge, Massachusetts: Harvard University Press, 1983): 152, 157.

Bibliography

Abitbol Oré, Bob. *Le Goût des confitures*. Montréal: Hurtubise HMH, 1986. Short stories.
———. *Les Faucons de Mogador*. Montréal: Balzac, 1994. Novel.
Abu-Laban, Baha. *An Olive Branch on the Family Tree: The Arabs in Canada*. Toronto: McLelland and Stewart Ltd., 1980.
———. "Arabs," in *Encyclopedia of Canada's Peoples*, ed. Paul Magosci. Toronto: University of Toronto Press, 1998: 203–212.
Achebe, Chinua. *Things Fall Apart*. New York: Fawcett Crest, 1959.
Allard, Jacques. "Entrevue avec Naïm Kattan." *Voix et Images* 11.1 (1985): 10–32.
———. *Le Roman du Québec: Histoire, Perspectives, Lectures*. Montréal: Québec-Amérique, 2000.
———. "L'Anniversaire ou l'hommage raconté," in *L'Ecrivain de passage. D'où je viens, où je vais. Saluts. hommages et lectures*. Montréal: Hurtubise HMH, 2002. 151–155.
Allen, Roger. "Saad Elkhadem: *Canadian Adventures of the Flying Egyptian*." *World Literature Today* 65.2 (Spring 1991): 356–357.
Alonzo, Anne-Marie and Denise Desautels. *Lettres à Cassandre*. Laval: Editions Trois, 1994. Fiction.
Alonzo, Anne-Marie. *Geste*. Paris: Editions des femmes, 1979. Poetic fragments.
———. *Veille*. Paris: Editions des Femmes, 1982. Poetic fragments.
———. *Droite et de profil*. Montréal: Lèvres urbaines 7, 1984. Poetic fragments.
———. *Bleus de mine*. Ville St-Laurent: Editions du Noroît, 1985. Poetry.
———. *Ecoute Sultane*. Montréal: Editions de l'Hexagone, 1987. "Fiction."
———. *Seul le désir*. Montréal: NBJ éditeur, 1987. Poetry.
———. *Le Livre des ruptures*. Montréal: Editions de l'Hexagone, 1988. Poetry.
———. *L'Immobile*. Montréal: Editions de L'Hexagone, 1990. Letters.
———. *Lead Blues*. Translated from the French (*Bleus de mine*) with a preface by W. Donoghue. Montréal: Guernica, 1990. Fiction.

———. *Galia qu'elle nommait Amour*. Montréal: Editions Trois, 1992. Tale.
———. *Margie Gillis: La danse des marches*. Montréal: Editions du Noroît, 1993. Poetic fragments.
———. *Lettres à Cassandre*. Montréal: Trois, 1994. "Fiction."
———. *Et la nuit*. Laval: Editions Trois, 2001. Poetry.
Angenot, Marc. "Préface." *Romanciers immigrés: Biographies et oeuvres publiées au Québec entre 1970 et 1990*, éds. D. Helly and A. Vassal. Montréal: IQRC/CIAD-EST, 1993. xi–xiii.
Annuaire de l'Afrique du Nord. Paris: Centre National de Recherche Scientifique, 1981: 1220–1221.
Anonymous. "Antoine Naaman, un écrivain au service de la littérature." *La Tribune*, Sherbrooke, May 26 (1983): B3.
———. "In Memoriam: Saad E. A. Elkhadem: 1932–2003." *The International Fiction Review* (January 2004), no page.
———. "Wajdi Mouawad refuse un Molière." *Radio canada*, www.radio-canada.ca/culture/modele-document-printd.asp (January 1, 2007): 1–2.
———. "Wajdi Mouawad Crée Forêts en France," Le Devoir.com, Tuesday, 21 Mars 2006, Théâtre, www.ledevoir.com/2006/03/21/104845.html (Press Release), no author (6 June 2008).
Anthologie critique de la littérature Canadienne française et québécoise., éd. G. Marcotte. Montréal: Librairie Beauchemin, 1994. Two volumes.
Antoun, Bernard. *Les Anémones*. Montréal: Humanitas, 1991. Poetic tale.
———. *Fragments arbitraries*. Québec: Editions Trois, 1989. Poetry.
Arsenault, Michel. "Solidarity of the Shaken: Wajdi Mouawad's Theatre of War." *Walrus Magazine* (December 31, 2006), www.walrusmagazine.com/print/art-solidarity-of-the-shaken/ (accessed December 31, 2006): 1–6.
Barrière, Caroline. "Le Testament d'une mère brisée." *Le Droit*, 4 October 2005, 1.
Barthes, Roland. *Le Degré zéro de l'écriture*. Paris: Editions duSeuil, 1953 and 1972.
———. *Le Plaisir du texte*. Paris: Editions du Seuil, 1973.
———. *Fragments de discours amoureux*. Paris: Editions du Seuil, 1977.
Basile, Jean. "Lori Saint-Martin et Nadia Ghalem." *Le Devoir*, April 13, 1991.
Baudot, Alain. "*La femme d'entre les lignes*," www.hedibouraoui.com/details.php?id=29 (accessed July 6, 2007).
de Beaugrande, Robert. "Toward the Empirical Study of Literature: A Synoptic Sketch of a New 'Society.'" *Poetics* 18 (1989): 7–27.
Bernatchez, Raymond. "Abla Farhoud: 'S'il n'y avait pas la mort, je n'écrirais pas,'" *La Presse Montréal*, Théâtre, Samedi, 13 Septembre 1997, D5.
Berrouët-Oriol, Robert and Robert Fournier. "L'effet d'exil." *Vice versa* 17 (Décembre 1986–Janvier 1987): 20–21.
———. "L'Emergence des écritures migrantes et métisses au Québec." *Litte Réalité: Une revue d'écrits originaux: A Journal of Creative and Original Writing* 3.2 (Fall 1991): 9–35.
Berry, J. W., and J. A. Laponce, eds. *Ethnicity and Culture in Canada: The Research Landscape*. Toronto: University of Toronto Press, 1994.

Biron, Michel. "L'Histoire littéraire est inadmissible: le cas du Québec," in *Les Etudes littéraires francophones: état des lieux*, ed. Lieven D'Hulst and Jean-Marc Moura. Lille: Conseil Scientifique de l'Université Charles-de-Gaulle, 2002: 209–219.

Bisztray, George. *Canadian Hungarian Literature: A Preliminary Survey*. Ottawa: Secretary of State, 1988.

———. "Language and Literary Institution: Hungarian-Canadian Examples." *Canadian Review of Comparative Literature/Revue Canadienne de Littérature Comparée* 16.3–4 (1989): 826–838.

Bouraoui, Hédi and Jacques Flamand, eds. *Ecriture Franco-Ontarienne*. Ottawa: editions du Vermilon, 1998.

———. *Ecriture franco-ontarienne*. Ottawa: Editions du Vermillon, 2003.

Bouraoui, Hèdi and Micheline Mongomery. *Musocktail*. Chicago: Tower Publications, 1966. Poetry.

———. *In-Side Faces: Visages du dedans*. Toronto: Centre Canada Maghreb, 2008. Illustrated poems.

Bouraoui, Hédi. *Créaculture I and II*. Philadelphia: Centre for Curriculum Development/Montréal: Marcel Didier, 1971. Essay.

———. *Eclate-Module*. Montréal: Cosmos, 1972. Poetry.

———. *Structure intentionnelle du grand Meaulnes: vers le poème romancé*. Paris: Nizet, 1976. Essay.

———. *The Canadian Alternative*. Toronto: ECW Press, 1980.

———. *Haituvois suivi de Antillades*. Québec: Nouvelle optique, 1980.

———. *Vers et l'Envers*. Toronto: ECW Press, 1982. Poetry.

———. *L'Icônaison*. Sherbrooke: Editions Naaman, 1985. Novel-Poem.

———. *Echosmos*. Toronto: Mosaic Press, 1986. Poetry.

———. *Reflet Pluriel*. Bordeaux: Presses Universitaires de Bordeaux, 1986. Poetry.

———. *Robert Champigny: Poète et philosophe*. Paris: Champion, 1987. Essay.

———. *Emigressence*. Ottawa: Editions du Vermillon, 1992. Poetry.

———. *Bangkok Blues*. Ottawa: Editions du Vermillon, 1994. Novel.

———. *Nomadaime*. Toronto: Editions du Gref, 1995. Poetry.

———. *Retour à Thyna*. Gazelle, Tunis: Or du Temps, 1996.

———. *La Pharaone*. Tunis: or du temps, 1998. Novel.

———. *La Composée*. Toronto: Editions l'Interligne, 2001. Novel.

———. *La Femme d'entre les lignes*. Toronto: Editions du Gref, collection "Le beau Mentir," 2002 Novel.

———. *Struga suivi de Margelle d'un festival*. Montréal: Mémoire d'encrier, 2003. Poetry.

———. *La Femme d'entre les lignes*. Gazelle, Tunis: L'or du temps, 2003.

———. *Illuminations Autistes*. Toronto: Editions du Gref. Collection Athéna, 2004. Children's book.

———. *La Francophonie à l'estomac*. Paris: Nouvelles du Sud, 2004. Essay.

———. *Sept portes pour une brûlance*. Ottawa: Editions du Vermillon, 2005. Novel.

———. *Transpoétique: Eloge du nomadisme*. Montréal: Mémoire D'encrier, 2005. Essay.

———. *Livr'Errance*. Mareuil: D'ici et d'ailleurs, 2005. Poetry.

———. *Cap Nord*. Ottawa: Editions du Vermillon, 2008. Novel.

Bourdieu, Pierre. *Leçon sur la leçon*. Paris: Les Editions de Minuit, 1982.

Brière, Eloïse. "Mère Solitude D'Emile Ollivier: Apport migratoire à la société québécoise." *International Journal of Canadian Studies/Revue Internationale d'études canadiennes* 13 (1996): 61–70.

Broucq, Claudette. *Le Texte D'Hédi Bouraoui: Approche par le "ça."* Toronto: CMC Editions, 2007.

Bumsted, J. M., ed. "Introduction." *A/Part*, Papers from the 1984 Ottawa Conference on Language, Culture, and Literary Identity in Canada, *Canadian Literature*, Supplement 1 (May 1987): 7–20.

Cassidy, Richard. "Anglo-Québec Literature and the Figures of National Literary Identity." Paper Presented on May 31st at the annual meeting of the Canadian Comparative Literature Association, University of British Columbia, Vancouver, May–June 2008.

Cassis, A. F. "*One Night in Cairo* by Said Elkhadem" *The International Fiction Review* 29 (January 2002): 97–98.

Chatton, Jean-françois and Joanna Mazuryk Bapst. *Le Défi francophone*. Bruxelles: Bruylant, 1991.

Chouinard, Marie-André. "La Voix de Dounia." *Le Devoir*, Montréal, Saturday and Sunday, March 28/29, 1998, D1–D2.

Cloutier, Mario. *La Presse, Montréal*, Monday, 24 avril 1995, A17.

Colombo, J. Robert. "Our Cosmopolitans: The Ethnic Canadian Writer in a Provincial Society." *A/Part*, Papers from the 1984 Ottawa Conference on Language, Culture, and Literary Identity in Canada, *Canadian Literature*, Supplement 1 (May 1987): 90–101.

Corneau, Guy. *Lost Sons: The Search for Masculine Identity*. New York: Random House, 1991.

Costas, Gilles. "Le Français tel qu'ils le jouent." *Le Quotidien de Paris*, Friday, 2 October 1992, "Festival des francophonies."

Côté, Jean-François. *Architecture d'un marcheur; Entretiens avec Wajdi Mouawad*. Montréal: Leméac, 2005, 129.

Cotnam, Jacques, ed., "Présentation" [introduction]. *Hédi Bouraoui: Iconoclaste et chantre du transculturel*. Ottawa: Le Nordir, 1996: 7–11.

Dahab, F. Elizabeth. "Visages de la francophonie: du politique, du littéraire, du sociologique." *Postcolonial Literatures: Theory and Practice*, eds. S. Tötösy de Zepetnek and S. Gunew. *Canadian Review of Comparative Literature/Revue Canadienne de Littérature Comparée* 22.3-4 (1995): 693–705.

———. "Des littératures migrantes d'expression française au Québec." *Collectif Interculturel: La Revue de l'Institut de Recherche et de Formation Interculturelles de Québec*, III-2 (1998): 5–19.

———. "L'Exil aux portes du paradis. Ecritures et écrivains canadiens du Moyen-Orient." *Comparative Literature Now: Theories and Practice, La Littérature comparée à l'heure actuelle Théories et réalisations*. eds. Steven Tötösy de Zepetnek, Milan V. Dimic, and Irene Sywenky. Paris: Honoré Champion, 1999: 319–331.

———. "Arabic-Canadian Literature: Overview and Preliminary Bibliography." *Canadian Ethnic Studies*, 2 (1999): 101–111.

———. "Francophonie en exil et littératures mineures: Le cas du Québec." *Colonizer and Colonized, Proceedings of the XVth Congress of the International Comparative Literature Association: "Literature as Cultural Memory"* (Leiden, Netherlands,

July 1997), eds. Theo D'Haen and Patricia Krüs. Amsterdam /Atlanta: Rodopi, 2000: 321–333.

———. "Voices of Exile: The Trilingual Odyssey of Canadian Writers of Arabic Origins." *The Canadian Review of Comparative Literature/Revue canadienne de littérature comparée* 28.1 (March 2001): 48–69.

———. *Voices In The Desert: An Anthology of Arabic-Canadian Women Writers.* Toronto: Guernica, 2002.

———. "Exilic Writer Saad Elkhadem and Two Transnational Novellas," in *Representing Minorities: Studies in Literature and Criticism,* eds. Larbi Touaf and Soumia Boutkhil. Newcastle: Cambridge Scholars Press, 2006: 183–194.

———. "Poetics of Exile and Dislocation in Saad Elkhadem's *Wings of Lead* (1971), *The Plague* (1989), and *Trilogy of the Flying Egyptian* (1990–1992)." *Canadian Ethnic Studies,* volume 30.2, 2006: 72–86.

———. "A Semiotic Reading of Hédi Bouraoui's *La Femme d'entre les lignes.*" Paper read at the Annual Conference of the Canadian Comparative Literature Association, University of British Columbia, Vancouver, May 31, 2008.

D'Alfonso, Antonio. *L'Autre rivage.* Montréal: VLB Editeur, 1987. Essay.

———. *In Italics: In Defense of Ethnicity.* Toronto: Guernica, 1996.

Dahan, Andrée. *Le Printemps peut attendre.* Montréal: Quinze, 1985. Novel.

———. *L'Exil aux portes du paradis.* Montréal: Québec-Amérique, 1993. Novel.

———. *La Jeune fille au luth.* Laval: Editions Trois, 2002. Novel.

———. *Chants de la terre morte.* Laval: Editions Trois, 2005. Poetry.

Darge, Fabienne. "Wajdi Mouawad: Le Théâtre comme antidote de l'exil." *Le Monde,* October 28, 2006, abonnés.lemonde.fr/cgi-bin/ACAHTS/ARCHIVES/archives.cg (9 January 2007): 1–2.

David, Gilbert. "Ecrire pour surmonter son impuissance." *Le Devoir,* Montréal, 27 February 1991, Théâtre, C3.

Déjeux, Jean. *Dictionnaire des auteurs maghrébiens de langue française.* Paris: Karthala, 1984.

Deleuze, Gilles and Félix Guattari. *Kafka: Pour une Littérature Mineure.* Paris: Les Editions de Minuit, 1975.

Déniau, Xavier. *La Francophonie.* Paris: Presses Universitaires de France, 1983.

D'Hulst and Jean-Marc Moura, eds. *Les Etudes littéraires francophones: Etat des Lieux.* Lille: Editions du conseil scientifique de l'université Charles-de-Gaulle, 2004.

Donoghue, William. "Preface," *Lead Blues* by Anne Marie-Alonzo. trans. W. Donoghue. Montréal: Guernica, 1990: 5–10.

Douek, Simone. "Naïm Kattan: *D'où je viens, où je vais,*" in *L'Ecrivain du passage. D'où je viens, où je vais. Saluts. hommages et lectures.* ed. Jacques Allard. Montréal: Hurtubise HMH, 2002: 11–76.

Doyon, Frédérique. "Littérature-Femmes dans le Paysage; Des écritures de l'exil inscrites dans le territoire américain," *Le Devoir* (Montréal), October 21–22, 2006. www.ledevoir.com/2006/10/21/120733.html (accessed December 28, 2008). Email exchange with Elizabeth Dahab.

Du'ûn, Najîb. Unpublished Memoirs, Montréal: 1960.

Dupré, Louise. "Ecrire comme vivre: dans l'hybridité. Entretien avec Anne-Marie Alonzo." *Voix et Images* 56.2 (1994): 238–249.

Élia, Maurice. *L'homme des plages*. Montréal: Humanitas/Nouvelle Optique, 1988. Novel.

———. *Sur l'écran noir de mes nuits blanches*. Montréal: Humanitas/Nouvelle Optique, 1990. Novel.

———. *Lunes bleues d'Alexandrie*. Montréal: Humanitas, 1997. Short Stories.

El-Gabalawy, Saad. "Introduction," *Modern Egyptian Short Stories* by Saad Elkhadem. Fredericton: York Press, 1977: 5–11.

———. "Introduction," *The Ulysses Trilogy* by Saad Elkhadem. Fredericton: York Press, 1988: 1–9.

———. "Introduction," *The Plague* by Saad Elkhadem. Fredericton: York Press, 1989: 3–6.

———. "Introduction," *Canadian Adventures of the Flying Egyptian* by Saad Elkhadem. trans. S. El-Gabalawy. Fredericton: York Press Ltd., 1990: 3–8.

———. "Introduction," *Chronicle of the Flying Egyptian in Canada* by Saad Elkhadem, Fredericton: York Press, 1991: 1–6.

———. "Introduction," *Crash Landing of the Flying Egyptian* by Saad Elkhadem. Fredericton: York Press, 1992: 1–4.

Elkhadem, Saad. *"Rijal wa Khanazir" (Men and Pigs)*, Cairo: Dar al-Ma'ârif, 1967. Collection of Short Stories.

———. *Ajnihah min Rasâs*. Cairo: Dâr al-Ma'ârif, 1971. In Arabic. Novella.

———. *From Travels of the Egyptian Odysseus: Three Contemporary Egyptian Novels*. Translated by Saad El Gabalawy. Bilingual edition (English–Arabic). Fredericton: York Press, 1979.

———. *History of the Egyptian Novel: Its Rise and Early Beginning*. Fredericton: York Press, 1985. Essay.

———. *The Ulysses Trilogy*. Translated by Saad El Gabalawy. Bilingual edition (English–Arabic). Fredericton: York Press, 1988. Novellas.

———. "Nobody Complained." *Arab-Canadian Writing: Stories, Memoirs and Reminiscences*. ed. K. Rostom. Fredericton: York Press Ltd., 1989: 30–32. Short story.

———. *The Plague*. Translated by Saad El-Gabalawy. Bilingual edition (English–Arabic). Fredericton: York Press, 1989. Novella.

———. *Trilogy of the Flying Egyptian: Canadian Adventures of the Flying Egyptian* 1990. *Chronicle of the Flying Egyptian in Canada* 1991. *Crash Landing of the Flying Egyptian* 1992. Translated by Saad El Gabalawy. Bilingual edition (English–Arabic). Fredericton: York Press, 1990–1992.

———. *Life is Like a Cucumber, Colloquial Egyptian Proverbs, Coarse Sayings, and Popular Expressions*, edited and translated from the Arabic by Saad Elkhadem, Bilingual edition (Arabic/English). Fredericton: York Press, 1993.

———. "Men and Pigs," in *Five Innovative Egyptian Stories*. Translated by the author. Bilingual edition (Arabic–English). Fredericton: York Press, 1994. Short story.

———. *Wings of Lead: A Modern Egyptian Novella*. Translated by the author. Bilingual edition (English–Arabic). Fredericton: York Press, 1994. Novella.

———. *Five Innovative Egyptian Short Stories*. Translated by Saad Elkhadem. Bilingual edition (Arabic–English). Fredericton: York Press, 1994.

———. *Wings of Lead (Ajnihah Min Rasâs): A Modern Egyptian Novella*. Translated by the author. Fredericton: York Press, 1994. Novella.

———. *An Egyptian Satire about a Condemned Building*. Translated by the author, Bilingual edition (Arabic–English). Fredericton: York Press Ltd., 1996. Novella.

———. *The Blessed Movement*. Bilingual edition (Arabic–English). Fredericton: York Press Ltd., 1997. Novella.
———. *Two Avant-Garde Egyptian Novels*. Translated by Saad El-Gabalawy. Bilingual edition (English–Arabic). Fredericton: York Press, 1998.
———. *One Night in Cairo: An Egyptian Micronovel with Footnotes*. Translated by the author, Bilingual edition (Arabic–English). Fredericton: York Press Ltd., 2001. Novella.
Ertler, Klaus-Dieter and Martin Löschnigg. *Canada in the Sign of Migration and Trans-Culturalism*. New York: Peter Lang, 2004.
Fahmy, Jean. *Amina et le Mamelouk blanc*. Ontario, Vanier: Editions l'interligne, 1998. Novel.
Fanon, Frantz. *Peau noire, masques blancs*. Paris: le Seuil, 1952.
Farhoud, Abla. *The Girls from the Five and Ten*. Translated by Jill Mac Dougall, in *Plays by Women: An International Anthology*. New York: Ubu Repertory Theatre Publications, 1988. Play.
———. *When I Was Grown-up*. Translated by Jill Mac Dougall, in *Women and Performance* 5.1 (1990–1992): 121–143. Play.
———. *Les Filles du 5-10-15cents*. Carnières, Belgique: Lansman, 1993. Play.
———. *La Possession du prince*. Unpublished play, 1993.
———. *Quand j'étais grande*. Solignac, France: le Bruit des autres, 1994. Play.
———. *Games of Patience*. Translated by Jill Mac Dougall, in *Plays by Women: an International Anthology*. New York: Ubu Repertory Theatre Publications, Book 2, 1995. Play.
———. *Quand le vautour danse*. Carnières, Belgique: Lansman, 1997. Play.
———. *Jeux de patience*. Montréal: VLB Èditeur, 1997. Play.
———. *Le Bonheur a la queue glissante*. Montréal: L'Hexagone, 1998. Novel.
———. *Maudite machine*. Québec: Editions Troix Pistoles, 1999. Play.
———. *Splendide solitude*. Montréal: L'Hexagone, 2001. Novel.
———. *La felicità scivola tra le dita*. Translated by Elletra Bordino Zorzi, Rome: Sinnos Editrice, 2002.
———. *Les Rues de l'alligator*. Montréal: VLB Èditeur, 2003. Play.
———. *Le Fou d'Omar*. Montréal: vlb éditeur, 2005. Novel.
Farhoud, Samira. "Déchirement ou délivrance: écriture autobioraphique dans *Les Saisons de passage* d'Andrée Chédid. *Le Bonheur a la queue glissante* d'Abla farhoud et *La Prisonnière* de Malika Oufkir et Michèle Fitoussi." *Présence Francophone* 58 (2002): 138–151.
Forsyth, Louise. "Resistance to Exile by Girls and Women: Two Plays by Abla Farhoud." *Modern Drama* 48.4 (Winter 2005): 800–818.
Gandhi, Leela. *Postcolonial Theory: A Critical Introduction*. New York: Columbia University Press, 1998.
Gauvin, Lise, Pierre l'Hérault, and Alain Montandon, eds. *Le Dire de l'Hospitalité*. Clermont-Ferrand, France: Presses universitaires Blaise Pascal, 2004.
Geadah, Yolande. *Femmes voiles: Intégrismes démasqués*. Montréal: VLB Èditeur, 1996. Essay.
———. *La Prostitution: un métier comme un autre?* Montréal: VLB Èditeur, 2003. Essay.
———. *Accommodements raisonnables*. Montréal: VLB Èditeur, 2007. Essay.
Ghalem, Nadia. *Les Jardins de cristal*. Québec: Hurtubise 1981. Novel.

———. *La Villa désir*. Montréal: Guérin littérature, 1988. Novel.
———. *La Nuit bleue*. Montréal: VLB Èditeur, 1991. Short stories.
———. *La Rose des sables*. Québec: Hurtubise, 1993. Children's story.
———. *Le Huard et le Héron*. Montréal: Les Editions du Trécarré, 1995. Youth story.
Ghattas, Mona Latif and Loise Desjardins. *Momo et Loulou*. Montréal: Editions du remue ménage, 2004. Stories. Also published in Arabic (Cairo).
Ghattas, Mona Latif. *Nicolas, le fils du Nil*. Cairo: Elias Publishing House, 1985. Poetic novel. Second edition: Laval: Editions Trois, 1999. Novel.
———. *Les Voix du jour et de la nuit*. Montréal: Boréal, 1988. Novel.
———. *Quarante voiles pour un exil*. Laval: Trois, 1988. Poetry.
———. *Le Double conte de l'exil*. Montréal: Boréal, 1990. Novel.
———. *Le Livre ailé*. Laval: Editions Trois, 2004. Poetry.
———. *Ambre et lumière*. Montréal: Editions du Noroît, 2006. Poetry and CD.
Godbout, Jacques. *Les Têtes à Papineau*. Paris: Le Seuil, 1981.
Gould, Karen. *Writing in the Feminine: Feminism and Experimental Writing in Quebec*. Carbondale: Southern Illinois University Press, 1990.
Green, Mary Jean et al., eds. *Postcolonial Subjects: Francophone Women Writers*. Minneapolis: University of Minnesota Press, 1996.
Greenstein, Michael. "The Desert, the River and the Island: Naïm Kattan's Short Stories." *Canadian Literature* 103 (1984): 42–48.
———. "Iraquébec: Naïm Kattan's Trans-Mimetic Diaspora," in *Textualizing the Immigrant Experience in Contemporary Québec*, eds. Susan Ireland and Patrice Proulx. Westport, Connecticut: Praeger, 2004: 117–126.
Grutman, Rainier and Héba Alah Ghadie. "Incendies de Wajdi Mouawad: les méandres de la mémoire." *Neohelicon* 30.1 (2006): 91–108.
Hamel, R., J. Hare, and P. Wyczynski, eds. *Dictionnaire des auteurs de langue française en Amérique du Nord*. Montréal: Fides, 1989.
———. *Dictionnaire pratique des auteurs québécois*. Montréal: Fides, 1976.
Harel, Simon. "La Parole orpheline de l'écrivain migrant," in *Montréal imaginaire: ville et littérature*. Montréal: Fides, 1992: 373–418.
———. "L'Exil dans la langue maternelle: L'Expérience du bannissement." *Québec Studies* 14 (1992): 23–30.
———. *Les Passages obligés de l'écriture migrante*. Montréal: XYZ, 2005.
———. *Braconnage identitaire, Un Québec palimpseste*. Montréal: VLB, 2006.
Hassan, Marwan. *The Confusion of Stones: Two novellas*. Dunvegan, Ontario: Cormorant Books, 1989. Novellas.
———. *The Memory Garden of Miguel Carranza*. Dunvegan, Ontario: Cormorant Books, 1991. Novel.
———. *Velocities of Zero: Conquest, Colonization and the Destruction of Cultures*. Toronto: Tsar Publications, 2002. Essay.
———. *The Lost Patent*. Ottawa: Common Redpoll Books, 2004. Mystery novel.
———. *As the Crow Dies*. Ottawa: Common Redpoll Books, 2005. Mystery.
Hassoun, Jacques. "Préface." *Les Voix du jour et de la nuit*. Mona Latif-Ghattas, Montréal: Boréal, 1988: 7–9.
Helly, Denise and Anne Vassal, eds. *Romanciers Immigrés: Biographies et Oeuvres Publiées au Québec entre 1970 et 1990*. Montréal: IQRC/CIADEST, 1993.
Hodgson, Richard and Ralph Sarkonak. "Lire le roman québécois." *Oeuvres et critiques* 14.1 (1989): 7–17, 9.

Hutcheon, Linda and Marion Richmond, eds. *Other Solitudes: Canadian Multicultural Fictions.* Toronto: Oxford University Press, 1990.

Igonetti, Giuseppina. "L'écriture et l'errance dans *La Femme d'entre les lignes*," in *"Perspectives Critiques; L'oeuvre d'Hédi Bouraoui,"* eds. Elizabeth Sabiston and Suzanne Crosta (Sudbury, Canada: Human Sciences Monograph Series, 2006): 343–355.

Ireland, Susan and Patrice J. Proulx, eds. *Immigrant Narratives in Contemporary France.* Westport, Connecticut: Greenwood Press, 2001.

———. *Textualizing the Immigrant Experience in Contemporary Québec.* Westport, Connecticut: Praeger, 2004.

Jack, Belinda. *Francophone Literature; an Introductory Survey.* New York: Oxford University Press, 1996.

Jacques, Sylviest. "Ensemble, c'est tout." *La Presse Montréal.* lundi, 6 novembre 2006 (arts et
spectacles), 4.

Jakobson, Walter. "Breathing Words: Exile in (Other): Towards a Poetics of Anne-Marie Alonzo."
Unpublished talk delivered at a conference on "L'écriture des femmes migrantes en France et
aux Etats-Unis," Concordia University (Montréal), June 30, 1994.

Jama, Sophie, ed. *Les Temps du nomade: Itinéarire d'un écrivain.* Montréal: Liber, 2005.

Jameson, Frederic. "Third World Literature in the Era of Multinational Capital." *Social Text* (Fall 1986): 65–88, 69.

JanMohamed, Abdul J. "Worldliness-without-World, Homelessness-as-Home: Toward a Definition of the Specular Border Intellectual." *Edward Said: A Critical Reader*, ed. Michael Sprinker. Cambridge, Massachusetts: Blackwell Publishers, 1992.

Jouve, Vincent. *La Littérature selon Roland Barthes.* Paris: Editions de minuit, 1986.

Kamboureli, Smaro, ed. *Making a Difference: Canadian Multiculture Literature.* Toronto: Oxford University Press, 1996, Saad Elkhadem, "Nobody Complained," 95–98; Marwan Hassan, extract from *"The Confusion of Stones":* 330–339.

Kaminsky, Amy K. *Reading the Body Politic: Feminist Criticism and Latin American Women Writers.* Minneapolis: University of Minnesota Press, 1993.

Karamé, Antoine. *Le Raspoutine egyptien.* Sherbrooke: Editions Naaman, 1985. Short stories.

Kattan, Naïm."Romanciers canadiens-anglais et canadiens-français." *Liberté* 42 (November–December 1965): 479–83.

———. *Le Réel et le théâtral.* Montréal: Editions HMH, 1970. Essay.

———. *Reality and Theatre.* Translated from the French by Alan Brown. Toronto: Anansi, 1972. Essay.

———. *Dans le désert.* Montréal: Editions Leméac, 1974. Short stories.

———. *Adieu, Babylone.* Montréal: Leméac, 1986. First edition: 1975. Novel.

———. *La Traversée.* Montréal: L'Arbre HMH, 1976.

———. *Les Fruits arrachés.* Montréal: Hurtubise HMH, 1977. Novel.

———. *La Mémoire et la promesse.* Montréal: HMH, 1978. Essay.

———. *Le Rivage.* Montréal: Hurtubise HMH, 1979.

———. *Paris Interlude* (Les Fruits arrachés). Trans. Sheila Fischman. Toronto: McLleland and Stewart, 1979. Novel.

———. *Le Sable de l'île*. Montréal: L'Arbre HMH, 1981.
———. *Le Désir et le pouvoir*. Montréal: Hurtubise HMH 1983. Essay.
———. *La Fiancée promise*. Montréal: Hurtubise HMH, 1983. Novel.
———. *La Reprise*. Montréal: L'Arbre HMH, 1985. Short stories.
———. *Le Père*. Québec: Hurtubise HMH, 1990. Essay.
———. *Farida*. Québec: Hurtubise HMH, 1991. Novel.
———. *La Réconciliation: À la rencontre de l'autre*. Québec: Hurtubise HMH, 1993. Essay.
———. *La Distraction*. Québec: Hurtubise HMH, 1994. Short stories.
———. *Portrait d'un Pays*. Montréal: L'Hexagone, 1994. Essay.
———. *La Célébration*. Montréal: L'Hexagone, 1997.
———. "Les Ecrivians immigrants et les autres." *International Journal of Canadian Studies/Revue internationale d'études canadiennes* 18 (Fall 1998): 185–191. Article.
———. *L'Anniversaire*. Montréal: Québec-Amérique, 2000. Novel.
———. *L'Ecrivain migrant: Essais sur des cités et des hommes*. Montréal: Hurtubise HMH, 2001. Essay.
———. *L'Ecrivain du passage: D'où je viens, où je vais. Saluts. hommages et lectures*. ed. Jacques Allard. Montréal: Hurtubise HMH, 2002. Interviews, testimonials.
———. *Le Gardien de mon frère*. Montréal: Hurtubise HMH, 2003. Novel.
———. *Farewell Babylon; Coming of Age in Jewish Baghdad*, trans. Sheila Fischman. Vancouver: Raincoast Books, 2005. Novel.
———. *Je regarde les femmes*. Montréal: Hurtubise HMH, 2005. Short stories.
———. *Châteaux en Espagne*. Montréal: Hurtubise, 2006. Short stories.
———. *Farewell, Babylon: Coming of Age in Jewish Baghdad*. Boston, Massachusetts: David Godine, 2007. Novel.
Kett, Andrew. "Farewell, Babylon: Coming of Age in Jewish Baghdad." *Quill and Quire* (May 2005): 33–34.
Khalo, Michel. *L'Académie du Désir*. Montréal: VLB, 1987. Novel.
———. *Le Désir de l'Académie*. Genève: Éditions des Reprises, 2007. Novel.
Khouri, Rajwa G. *Arabs in Canada-Post 9/11*. Toronto: G7 Books and Canadian Arab Federation, 2006.
Kourouma, Ahmadou. *Les Soleils des indépendances*. Montréal: Presses de l'université de Montréal, 1968.
———. *Les Soleils des indépendances*. Paris: Le Seuil, 1970.
Kreisler, Henry. "The Ethnic Writer in Canada," in *Identifications: Ethnicity and the Writer in Canada*, ed. J. Balan. Edmonton: Canadian Institute of Ukrainian Studies, University of Alberta, 1982: 1–13.
Lamar, Celita. "'Resetting the Margins:' Abla Farhoud's Dramatization of the Female Immigrant Experience in Quebec," in *Women by Women: The Treatment of Female Characters by Women Writers of Fiction in Quebec since 1980*. London: Associated University Presses, 1997: 136–146.
Lambert, José. "Plaidoyer pour un programme des études comparatistes. Littérature comparée et théorie du polysystème." *Actes du XVIème Congrès de la Société Française de Littérature Générale et Comparée, Montpellier: 1980*. Montpellier: Université Paul-Valéry 1 (1984): 59–67.
———. "Les relations littéraires internationales comme problème de réception." *Oeuvres et critiques* 11.2 (1986): 173–189.

Lamonde, Yvan. "De la difficulté d'assumer un héritage pluriel." Interview by Daniel Vernet, *Le Monde* (France), Wednesday, July 2, 2008: V.
Lamontagne, André, ed. *Le Roman Québécois contemporain: Les Voix sous les mots*. Montréal: Fides, 2004.
Le Devoir.com, Tuesday, 21 Mars 2006, Théâtre, www.ledevoir.com/2006/03/21/104845.html (Press Release), no author (accessed June 6, 2008).
Ledoyen, Alberte. *Montréal au pluriel. Huit communautés ethno-culturelles de la région montréalaise*. Collection "documents de recherche." Institut Québécois de recherché sur la culture, 32, 1992: 392 pages.
Legaré, Yves, ed. *Dictionnaire Des Ecrivains Québécois Contemporains*. Montréal: Québec-Amérique, 1983.
Lépine, Stéphane. "Wajdi Mouawad ou l'irruption de l'autre." *Jeu* 73 (1994): 80–87.
Lequin, Lucie and Maïr Verthuy, eds. *Multi-Culture, Multi-Ecriture: La Voix migrante au féminin en France et au Canada*. Montréal: L'Harmattan, 1996.
Lequin, Lucie. "Quand le monde arabe traverse l'Atlantique," in *Multi-Culture, multi-écriture: La voix migrante au féminin en France et au Canada*, eds. Lucie Lequin and Maïr verthuy. Paris/Montréal: L'Harmattan, 1996: 209–219.
———. Abla Farhoud et la fragilité du bonheur." *Rocky Mountain Modern Language Association (RMMLA)* 58.1 (Spring 2004), rmmla.wsu.edu/ereview/58.1/articles/lequin.asp (accessed July 5, 2006).
L'Hérault, Pierre. "Pour une cartographie de l'hétérogène: Dérives identitaires des années 1980," in *Fictions de l'identitaire au Québec*, eds. Sherry Simon et al. Montréal: XYZ, 1991: 53–114.
———. "Ferron l'incertain: du même au mixte," in *L'Etranger dans tous ses états: Enjeux culturels et littéraires*. ed. Simon Harel. Montréal: XYZ, 1992: 39–52.
———. Préface. "*Les Rues de l'alligator* par Abla Farhoud." Montréal: VLN Èditeur, 2003: 7–10.
———. "De Wajdi…à Wahab." Jeu 111 (June 2004): 97–103
———. "*Impitoyable consolation. Incendies* de Wajdi Mouawad." *Spirale* (September/October 2004): 54–55.
———. "*Littoral* de Wajdi Mouawad: l'hospitalité comme instance dramatique," in *Le Dire de l'Hospitalité*, ed. Lise Gauvin, Pierre l'Hérault, and Alain Montandon. Clermont-Ferrand, France: Presses Universitaires Blaise Pascal, 2004: 179–187.
Louder, Dean and Eric Waddell. "Le Défi de la francophonie nord-américaine." *Québec Studies* 7 (1988): 28–47.
Lotfi, Mohamed. "Racism, Made in Quebec." citoyen.onf.ca/extraits/media/racism_quebec.pdf
(accessed January 9, 2009).
Ltaif, Nadine. *Les Métamorphoses d'Ishtar*. Montréal: Guernica, 1987. Novel.
———. *Entre les fleuves*. Montréal: Guernica, 1991. Poetry.
———. *Elégies du Levant*. Montréal: Editions du Noroît, 1995. Poetry
———. *Le Livre des dunes*. Montréal: Editions du Noroît, 1999. Poetry.
———. *Le Rire de l'eau*. Montréal: Le Noroît, 2004. Poetry.
Malpede, Karen. "Theatre at 2000: A Witnessing Project." *The Year 2000: Essays on the End*, eds. Charles Strozier and Michael Flynn. New York and London: New York University Press, 1997: 299–308.

Marcotte, Gilles, ed. *Anthologie critique de la littérature Canadienne française et québécoise*. Montréal: Librairie Beauchemin, 1994. Two volumes.

———. "Neil Bissondath disait. . . ." *Québec Studies*, 26 (Fall/Winter 1998/1999): 6–11.

McClennen, Sophia A. *The Dialectics of Exile*. West Lafayette, Indiana: Purdue University Press, 2004.

Meddeb, Abdelwahab. *L'exil occidental*. Paris: Albin Michel, 2005.

Micone, Marc. "Speak What." *Jeu* 50 (mars 1989): 84–85.

Miller, Christopher. *Theories of Africans: Francophone Literature and Anthropology in Africa*. Chicago: University of Chicago Press, 1990.

Moss, Jane. "Multiculturalism and Postmodern Theater: Staging Québec's Otherness." *Mosaic* 29.3 (1996): 75–96.

———. "The Drama of Survival: Staging Post-Traumatic Memories in Plays by Lebanese-Québécois Dramatists." *Theatre Research in Canada* 22.2 (Fall 2001): 172–189.

———. "Immigrant Theatre: Traumatic Departures and Unsettling Arrivals," in *Textualizing the Immigrant Experience in Contemporary Québec*, eds. Susan Ireland and Patrice J. Proulx. Westport, Connecticut: Praeger, 2004: 65–82.

Mostow, Joshua S. "Complex Art of the Mosaic: Saad Elkhadem's *Canadian Adventures of the Flying Egyptian*." *Canadian Literature* 132 (1992): 174–176.

Mouawad, Wajdi. *Alphonse*. Montréal: Leméac, 1996. Play (youth).

———. *Littoral*. Montréal/Paris: Leméac, Actes Sud-Papiers, 1999. Play.

———. *Les Mains d'Edwidge au moment de la naissance*. Montréal: Leméac, 1999. Play.

———. *Pacamambo*. Montréal/Paris: Leméac/Actes Sud-Papiers, 2000. Children's play.

———. *Wedding Day at the Cro-Magnons'*. Translated by Shelley Tepperman (from the forthcoming *Journée de noces chez les Cro-Magnons*). Toronto: Playwrights Canada Press, 2001. Play.

———. *Alphonse*. Translated by Shelley Tepperman, Toronto: Playwrights Canada Press, 2001. Youth.

———. *Rêves*. Montréal/Paris: Leméac/Actes Sud-Papiers, 2002. Play.

———. *Tideline (Littoral)*. Translated from the French by Shelley Tepperman. Toronto: Playwrights Canada Press, 2002. Play.

———. *Visage retrouvé*. Montréal/Paris: Leméac/Actes Sud-Papiers, 2002. Novel.

———. *Incendies*. Montréal/Paris: Leméac/Actes Sud-Papiers, 2003.

———. *Je suis le méchant: Entretiens avec André Brassard*. Montréal: Leméac, 2004. Interview.

———. *Willy Protagoras Enfermé dans les toilettes*. Montréal/Paris: Leméac/Actes Sud-Papiers, 2004. Play (youth).

———. *Scorched (Incendies)*. Translated from the French by Linda Gaboriau. Toronto: Playwrights Canada Press, 2005. Play.

———. *Architecture d'un marcheur, Entretiens avec Wajdi Mouawad* (by Jean-François Côté), Montréal: Leméac, 2005. Interview.

———. *Forêts*, Montréal/Paris: Leméac/Actes Sud-Papiers, 2006. Play.

———. *Assoiffés*. Montréal/Paris: Leméac/Actes sud-papiers, 2007. Play.

———. *Un obus dans le Coeur*. Montréal: Leméac, 2007. Children's play.

———. *Le Soleil ni la mort ne peuvent se regarder en face*. Montréal: Leméac, 2008. Play.

———. *Forests (Forêts)*. Translated from the French by Linda Gaboriau, Toronto: Playwrights Canada Press, Forthcoming.
———. *Journée de noces chez les Cro-Magnons*. Montréal: Leméac, Forthcoming. Play.
Mouhoub, Yamina. *Qu'Importe le moment*. Laval: Teichtner, 1999. Poetry.
Moyes, Lianne, ed. "Ecrire en anglais au Québec: un devenir minoritaire?" *Quebec Studies* 26 (1998/1999): 3–37.
Mozejko, Edward. "Ethnic or National (?): Polish Literature in Canada." *Canadian Review of Comparative Literature/Revue Canadienne de Littérature Comparée* 16.3-4 (1989): 809–825.
Naaman, Antoine, trans. (from Arabic). *Légendes Pharaoniques*. Sherbrooke: Editions Naaman, 1985. Tales.
Nepveu, Pierre. *L'Ecologie du reel: Mort et naissance de la littérature québécoise contemporaine*. Montréal: Boréal, Collection Papiers collés, 1988.
Nora, Pierre, "Discours sur les prix littéraires." www.academie-francaise.fr/immortels/discours_SPA/nora_2007.html (accessed November 29, 2007).
Orlando, Valérie. *Of Suffocated Hearts and Tortured Souls: Seeking Subjecthood through Madness in Francophone Women Writing of Africa and the Carribbean*. Lanham: Maryland: Lexington Books, 2003.
Owen, I. M. "Bridge of Tongues: Why an Arabic-speaking, Baghdad-born Jew Is a Perfect Guide to the Modern Canadian Experience." *Books in Canada* 12.5 (1976): 5–6.
Padolsky, Enoch. "Canadian Ethnic Minority Writing in English," in *Ethnicity and Culture in Canada: The Research Landscape*. eds. J. W. Berry and J. A. Laponce. Toronto: University of Toronto Press, 1994: 361–386.
Paradela, Nieves. "Arabic Literature in Exile: *The Plague* by Saad Elkhadem." *International Fiction Review* 22 (1995): 47–53.
Paré, François. *Les Littératures de l'exiguïté*. Hearst, Ontario: Nordir, 1992.
Pelletier, Jacques. "Avant-propos," *Voix et Images*. Special Issue on Anne-Marie Alonzo 14.2 (Winter 1994): 228–229.
Pirandello, Luigi. *Six Characters in Search of an Author*. London: Penguin Books, 1998.
Pivato, J. and S. Tötösy de Zepetnek, eds. *Literatures of Lesser Diffusion: Canadian Review of Comparative Literature/Revue Canadienne de Littérature Comparée* 16.3-4 (1989).
Pivato, Joseph. *Contrasts: Comparative Essays on Italian-Canadian Writing*. Montréal: Guernica, 1991.
Projean, Karine. "Le Fou D'Omar," *Choq FM*, August 3, 2005, web.choq.fm/article.php?id=1546 (accessed August 3, 2006).
Proulx, Patrice J. "Migration and Memory in Marie-Céline Agnant's *La dot de Sara* and Abla Farhoud's *Le Bonheur a la queue glissante*," in *Textualizing the Immigrant Experience in Contemporary Québec*, eds. Susan Ireland and Patrice P. Proulx. Wesport, ConnecticutT: Praeger, 2004: 127–136.
Rahimieh, Nasrin. "Naïm Kattan, *le discours arabe* and Empty Words." *Litteratures of Lesser Diffusion*, ed. Joseph Pivato, *Canadian Review of Comparative Literature/Revue Canadienne de Littérature Comparée* 16.3-4 (1989): 733–744.

———. *Missing Persians: Discovering Voices in Iranian Cultural Heritage*, Syracuse: Syracuse University Press, 2001

Répertoire des membres du CEAD, Press Review of *Littoral*, www.cead.qc.ca/repw3/mouawadwajdi.html (accessed January 3, 2007), 1–9.

Richon, Catherine. "Wajdi Mouawad: Interviews sur Fluctuat.net," fluctuat.net/1317-Wajdi-Mouawad (accessed January 4, 2007): 1–3.

Robin, Régine. *La Québécoite*. Montréal: Québec/Amérique, 1983.

———. "A propos de la notion Kafkaïenne de 'littérature mineure': quelques questions posées à la littérature québécoise." *Paragraphes* 2 (1989): 5–14.

———. *Le Roman mémoriel: de l'Histoire à l'écriture du hors-lieu*. Montréal: Le Préambule, 1989.

———. "Sortir de l'ethnicité." *Métamorphose d'une utopie*, eds. Jean-Michel Lacroix and Fulvio Caccia. Paris/Montréal: Presses de la Sorbonne/Nouvelle-Tryptique, 1992: 25–43.

Roorda, Julie. "Novel/Notable, *Voices in the Desert: The Anthology of Arabic-Canadian Women Writers*." *Pagicita in Toronto* 2.1 (2002): 123–124.

Rostom, Kamal, ed. *Arab-Canadian Writing: Stories, Memoirs, and Reminiscences*. Fredericton: York Press Ltd., 1989. Anthology of short stories.

———. *Arabi Takannad (An Arab Canadianized: Arab-Canadian Short Stories)* (in Arabic). Ottawa: Rostom Publishing, 1991. Short stories.

———. *Al Iswa Al Hassana: Arabic Canadian Children's Stories* (in Arabic). Ottawa: Rostom Publishing, 1994. Short stories.

———. *The Mustache and Other Stories*. Ottawa: Rostom Publishing, 2005 (?).

Sabiston, Elizabeth. *The Muse Strikes Back: Female Narratology in the Novels of Hédi Bouraoui*. Sudbury, Ontario: Human Sciences Monograph Series, 2005.

———. "Bâtir des ponts: Transculturel et résistance négociée du lecteur," in *Perspectives critiques: L'oeuvre d'Hédi Bouraoui*. Sudbury, Ontario: Human Sciences Monograph Series, 2006: 9–25, 13.

Said, Edward. *The World, the Text and the Critic*. Cambridge, Massachusetts: Harvard University Press, 1983.

———. *Representations of the Intellectual: The 1993 Reith Lectures*. New York: Vintage Books, 1996.

———. "Intellectual Exile: Expatriates and Marginals." *Representations of the Intellectual: The Reith Lectures*. New York: Vintage Books, 1996: 47–64, 58.

———. "On Defiance and Taking Positions." *Reflections on Exile and Other Essays*. Cambridge, Massachusetts: Harvard University Press, 2000: 500–506, 503.

———. *Out of Place*. New York: Alfred A. Knopf, 2000.

———. "Between Worlds." *Reflections on Exile and Other Essays*. Cambridge, Massachusetts: Harvard University Press, 2000: 554–568, 555.

———. *Reflections on Exile and Other Essays*. Cambridge, Massachusetts: Harvard University Press, 2000.

Salvatore, Filippo. "The Italian Writers of Quebec: Language, Culture, and Politics." Translated by David Homel, in *Contrasts: Comparative Essays on Italian-Canadian Writing*, ed. Joseph Pivato. Montréal: Guernica, 1991: 191–206, 199.

Schmidt, Siegfried. *Foundations for the Empirical Study of Literature: The Components of a Basic Theory*, R. de Beaugrande, trans. Hamburg: Buske, 1982.

———. "Looking Back-Looking Ahead." Editorial. *Poetics* 21 (1992): 1–4.

Senghor, S. Léopold. "Le Français, langue de culture." *Esprit* (1962), www.esprit .presse.fr/review/article.php (accessed January 9, 2009).
Serrano, Richard. *Against the Postcolonial: "Francophone" Writers at the Ends of French Empire*. Lanham, Maryland: Lexington Books, 2005.
Sgard, Jean. "Conclusion," in *Exil et Littérature*, ed. Jacques Mounier. Grenoble: Ellug, 1986: 291–299.
Simard, Mathieu. "Abla Farhoud: Le Fou d'Omar ou être à l'origine de sa propre vie." *Le Libraire* 28 (May–June 2005): 1–16.
Simard, Sylvain. "Kattan romancier: La Promesse du temps retrouvé." *Voix et Images* 11.1 (1985): 33–54.
———. "Lettre à qui refuse le tragique," in *L'écrivain du passage, D'où je viens, où je vais, Saluts. hommages et lectures*, ed. Jacques Allard (Montréal: Hurtubise HMH, 2002): 84.
Simon, Sherry and D. Leahy. "La recherche au Québec portant sur la littérature ethnique," in *Ethnicity and Culture in Canada: The Research Landscape*. eds. J. W. Berry and J. A. Laponce. Toronto: University of Toronto Press, 1994. 387–409.
Simon, Sherry, et al. eds. *Fictions de l'identitaire au Québec*. Montréal: XYZ, 1991.
Simon, Sherry. "The Language of Difference: Minority Writers in Québec." *A/Part*, Papers from the 1984 Ottawa Conference on Language, Culture, and Literary Identity in Canada. *Canadian Literature, Supplement 1* (May 1987): 119–128.
Sky, Lee. "Complex Art of the Mosaic." *Canadian Literature* 132 (1992): 174–176.
Soderstrom, Mary. "Farewell, Babylon: Coming of Age in Jewish Baghdad." *Montréal Review of Books* 9.1 (2005). aelaq.org/mrb/article.php?issue=15452&cat=4 (accessed February 13, 2006).
Spettigue, D. O. "Farewell, Babylon." *Queen's Quarterly* 84.3 (1977): 510–511.
Suleiman, Michael W., ed. *Arabs in America: Building a New Future*. Philadelphia: Temple University Press, 1999.
Sylviest, Jacques. "Ensemble, c'est tout." *La Presse de Montréal*, Lundi, 6 novembre 2006, (arts et spectacles), 4.
Tarakdjian, Elie. *Entre l'Arbre et l'écorce*. Athabasca: Editions Pourquoi pas, 1982. Novel.
Tétu, Michel. *La Francophonie; histoire, problématique et perspectives*. Montréal: Guérin littérature 1987.
Tixier, Jean-Max. "La Fonction de transfert dans *La Femme d'entre les lignes*," in *Perspectives Critiques: L'oeuvre d'Hédi Bouraoui*, ed. Elizabeth Sabiston and Suzanne Crosta. Sudbury, Canada: Human Sciences Monograph Series, 2006: 365–371.
Tötösy de Zepetnek, Steven. "Systemic Approaches to Literature: An Introduction with Selected Bibliographies." *Canadian Review of Comparative Literature/Revue Canadienne de Littérature Comparée* 19.1-2 (1992): 21–93.
———. "Comparative Literature and Systemic/Institutional Approaches to Literature: New Developments." *Systems Research* 2.2 (1994): 43–57.
Vachon, G.-André. "La Francité." *Etudes Françaises* 4.2 (1968): 117.
Vaïs, Michel. "Les Nouveaux visages de l'engagement." *Jeu* 94 (2000): 120–134.
Vaïs, Michel and Philip Wickham. "Le Brassage des cultures: Table ronde." (Interviews), *Jeu* 72 (no issue number) (1994): 8–38.
Vallières, Pierre. *Nègres blancs d'Amérique*. Montréal: Parti-Pris, 1968.

Varoujean, Vasco. *Calligraphies pour le temps présent*. Unpublished manuscript. Poems.

———. *Des jours, comme ça, fortuitement*. Unpublished manuscript. Short stories.

———. *Espaces singuliers*. Unpublished manuscript. Poems.

———. *Le Moulin du diable*. Ottawa: Le Cercle du Livre de France, 1972. Short stories.

———. *Les Fous de la cité*. Unpublished manuscript. Novel.

———. *Les Raisins verts*. Ottawa: le Cercle du Livre de France, 1975. Narrative.

———. *Les Pâturages de la rancoeur*. Montréal: Pierre Tisseyre, 1977. Novel.

———. *Les Plaisirs des petits fauves de Késsab*. Unpublished manuscript. Novel.

Vasseur, Annie Molin. "Entretien avec Anne-Marie Alonzo." *Arcade* 34 (1995): 80–89.

Verduyn, Christl. "Ecriture et migration au féminin au Québec: de mère en fille," in *Multi-Culture, multi-écriture: La voix migrante au féminin en France et au Canada*, ed. Lucie Lequin and Maïr Verthuy. Paris, Montréal: L'Harmattan, 1996: 131–144.

———. "Relatively Political: Comparing (examples of) Québec/Canadian 'ethnic'/ immigrant 'writings,'" in *Cultural Identities in Canadian Literature*, ed. Bénédicte Maugière. New York: Peter Lang, 1998: 213–225.

Vigneault, Jean. "Splendide Solitude." *Le Courrier*, Montréal, 12 December 2001, www.lecourrier.qc.ca/archives/2001/2001_12_12/707L15X.html (accessed February 9, 2006).

Werner-King, Janeen. "Review of *The Plague*, by Saad Elkhadem." *The International Fiction Review* 16.2 (1989): 154–156.

Wyl, Jean-Michel. *Quebec Banana State*. Montréal: Beauchemein, 1978. Novel.

———. *Quand meurent les dauphins*. Montréal: Beauchemin, 1979. Novel.

Index

Absence, vii, 4, 5, 20, 30, 36, 51, 69, 73, 83, 87, 88, 116, 142, 150, 188
Abu Laban, Baha, xii, xiv
Alienation, 4, 5, 6, 24, 31, 36, 77, 87, 101, 125
Allard, Jacques, 9, 40, 67, 69, 71, 78, 83, 86, 88, 92, 93
Allen, Roger, 66n64
Alonzo, Anne-Marie, ix, 7, 9, 11, 17–20, 23, 27, 29–34, 199
Antoun, Bernard, 19, 20, 23
Arabic-Canadian writers, v, vii, viii-xiv; profile, 1–3, 5, 7, 9, 10, 11; patterns in writing, 17–23, 25–41, 43; 47, 51, 54, 59, 61, 64, 65; and Kattan, 68, 70, 71–73, 76, 82, 87, 90; and Farhoud, 99–103, 105, 109, 110, 118, 119, 122, 123, 125; and Mouawad, 139, 143, 145, 161, 162
Arsenault, Michel: on Mouawad, 166n11, 167n17, 169n105, 171n158

Barthes, Roland, 69, 92, 160, 173, 179, 180, 183, 185, 186, 189, 192, 194–198, 206
Baudelaire, Charles, 117, 189, 190, 191, 193

Berrouët-Oriol, Robert/Robert Fournier, 29, 35, 36, 42, 95
Bouraoui, Hédi, v, x, 17–20, 23, 28, 31–32, 34–35, 173–198
Bourdieu, Pierre, 1, 207
Bouyoucas, Pan, 11, 17
Brière, Eloise, 9, 38n51
Brossard, Nicole, 5, 26, 68
Broucq, Claudette: on Mouawad, 179, 190, 194n25, 196n61, 197n89

Caccia, Fulvio, 6, 8, 43n140
Cairo, 19, 20, 32, 39, 45, 47, 48, 50, 52, 55, 57; *One Night in Cairo*, 59, 66
Camus, Albert, 69, 117
Canada: viii-x, xii-xiv, 1, 2, 4, 10, 11, 17–19, 21–23, 25–29, 35, 39, 40, 42; in Elkhadem's works, 45, 47, 48, 49, 53, 55, 56, 63, 65, 66; in Kattan's works, 67, 70, 76, 78, 80, 81, 87–89, 91, 93; and Farhoud, 98, 109–111, 119; and Mouawad, 136, 139, 153; and Bouraoui, 174, 176–178, 181; and writers, 199, 200–201, 203
Cassis, A. F.: on Elkhadem, 64n4, 66n67

Chamberland, Paul, 5, 26
Chouinard, Marie-André: on Farhoud, 130n56
Christian, xi, 11, 20, 31, 51; and Kattan, 75, 77, 86, 93; and Mouawad, 136, 151, 152
Collective: value of utterances, ii, 29, 32, 54, 82, 99, 138, 200; personal and collective, 30, 82, 127, 151, 153, 154, 159
Côté, Jean-François: and Mouawad, 161, 167n18
Cotnam, Jacques, 178, 194n21
Crémazie, Octave, 4, 36n22

Dahan, Andrée, xiii, 17, 23, 31, 33, 38, 43, 199
D'Alfonso, Antonio, 8, 21, 30, 37–39
Darge, Fabienne: on Mouawad, 155, 166n8, 167n12, 169n106, 170n135
Death, 2, 7, 20, 27, 39, 46–48, 533, 61, 85, 88, 100, 102, 103, 109, 110, 116, 122, 124, 125, 140–145, 150, 155, 159, 181, 128, 188
Deleuze /Guattari, ix, x1, xii, 3, 22, 24, 32, 33, 35, 40, 41, 43, 51, 87, 88, 95, 99
Despair, v, 33, 45, 49, 51, 53, 55, 57, 59, 111
Déterritorialisation, 4, 87, 142, 163
Diaspora, 3, 35, 63, 69, 92, 94, 95, 96n129
Displacement, xiii, 54, 63, 127, 160, 201
Doyon, Frédérique, xiiin15, 38n49
Dupré, Louise, 40n87, 42n124, 43n135

El-Gabalawy, Saad: and Elkhadem, 47, 55, 63, 64n6, 65n26, 66n80
Elkhadem, Saad, v, ix, x, xiii, 1, 17–19, 23, 26, 29, 30, 32, 39–42, 45–66, 200, 201, 205, 208–209, 210, 213, 215, 219
Escape, 11, 32, 50, 54, 74, 76, 80, 84, 104, 106, 124, 147, 151, 156, 192
Exile, x-xii, xiv, 1–4, 5–9, 21–24, 27–29, 30, 32–35, 38, 41, 42, 52–54, 55, 59, 62–64; and Kattan, 70, 73, 80, 82, 88–92; and Farhoud, 99, 106, 116, 125, 128, 130; and Farhoud, 139, 140; and Mouawad, 160–162, 170, 200, 201, 208, 211, 211–212, 215, 217–218, 223; exilic, vii, x, x1, 2, 5, 31, 78, 138
Expatriation, 35n14, 48, 70

Fanon, Frantz, 5
Farhoud, Abla, v, x, xiii, 17, 19, 20, 23, 28, 74, 97–134, 138, 141, 146, 200, 202, 206, 210, 214–215, 222
Fear, 32, 51, 52, 55, 58, 61, 74, 88, 120, 125, 127, 151, 161, 163
Forsyth, Louise, 99, 128n6
Francophonie, xiii, 3, 10, 28, 35, 36, 37, 68, 69, 98, 128, 137, 174, 175, 207, 208; Francophone, ix, x, xii, xiiin16, xivn18, 1, 3, 4, 6, 7, 8, 9, 18, 23, 25, 26–27, 38n45, 58, 77, 87, 117, 136, 138, 155, 181, 199, 202

Gandhi, Leela, 35n10, 36n31
Geadah, Yolande, 28, 199
Ghalem, Nadia, xiii, 17, 19, 23, 25, 26, 28, 30, 34, 41, 199
Ghattas, Mona Latif, xiii, 17–20, 29, 30–32, 34, 38, 199
Godbout, Jacques, 3, 5, 26, 37n33, 68
Greenstein, Michael, 69, 81, 82, 83, 87, 90
Grutman, Rainier, 167n16, 169n94
Guernica, xiiin13, 18, 34n5

Harel, Simon, xi, 8, 36, 37, 38, 87
Hassan, Marwan, ix, xiii, 3, 17, 19, 23
Helly, Denise, 36, 38, 40, 41
Hutcheon, Linda, xii, xiii, 34
Hybridity, 3, 6, 7, 8, 31

Immigration, Arabic in Canada, x, xiv, 4, 10–11, 17; theme of, 29, 32, 53–55, 58; in Kattan's works, 58, 70, 82, 89; in Farhoud's works, 99, 109, 110–111, 126, 127; experience, 162, 200, 201; *also see* immigrants
Immigrants in Canada, xi, xiv; Arab, 10, 11; Egyptian, 29, 38, 39, 53, 54;

and Québec language law, 58, 101; and CN Tower, 178
Intertextuality, 56, 107, 117, 189, 190
Iraq, x, xi, 8, 10–12, 22, 23, 31, 69, 72–78, 87–90, 92, 95, 201
Ireland, Susan, xiiin12, 38n50, 92n8, 94n71, 95n104, 96n129, 131n104, 167n25
Islam, 22, 71, 83, 120; also see Moslem, x, 11, 71–75, 86, 93, 118, 200
Israeli, 29, 55, 74, 76, 87, 105, 126, 152, 153, 201

Jakobson, Walter, 27, 42n114, 43n134
Jama, Sophie: and Kattan, 69, 93n58
Jameson, Frederic, 3, 16
Janmohamed, Abdul, xivn24
Judaism, 72, 90; also see Jews, 22, 31, 57, 72, 73–76, 81, 82, 87, 90, 93

Kafka, Franz, xii, 3, 35, 36, 40, 41, 43, 54, 95; and Mouawad, 161, 163
Karamé, Antoine, 19
Kattan, Naim, v, x, xii, 8–9, 17–20, 22, 23, 25–27, 28, 31, 34, 38, 40–41, 43, 67–96, 108, 130, 162, 200–201, 205, 209, 211, 213, 214, 217–222
Khalo, Michel, 19
Kourouma, Ahmadou, 7, 37n35

Laframboise, Alain, 18
Lambert, José, 2, 35n6
Lamonde, Ivan, 5, 9, 36
Language choice for minority writers in Canada, 2, 20, 22, 40
Lebanon, x, 10, 17, 40, 97, 100, 101, 103, 110, 112, 128, 136, 137, 139, 143, 144, 146, 151, 153, 158, 159, 162, 163
Le Devoir (Montréal daily), x, xiii, 9, 17, 26, 38, 41, 68, 128, 130, 153
Le Monde, 75, 136, 166
L'Hérault, Pierre, 8, 37, 38, 42, 105, 129, 141, 167, 171
Lépine, Stéphane: on Mouawad, 160, 162, 163, 166n7, 170n136, 171n149

Lequin, Lucie, ix, xiii, xv, 42, 99, 100, 117, 128
Literary Prizes, ix, 2, 7, 19, 25, 26, 28, 33, 41, 68, 70, 91, 98, 99, 138, 137, 139, 176, 203
Literatures of exile, xi, xiii, 3–4, 6, 7, 9, 200
Lorey, Chris, 64n2
Ltaif, Nadine, xiii, 17, 19, 23, 28, 31, 34, 199

Magritte, René, 192
Mallarmé, Stéphane, 189
Marcotte, Gilles, 25, 41
Meddeb, Abdelwahab, 203n3
Memory, ii, 21, 24, 28, 29, 30, 60, 76, 88, 113, 127, 141, 154, 159, 163, 167, 181, 189, 200
Mental illness, 4, 112, 30, 109, 118, 119, 121, 124, 125, 126
Miller, Christopher, 37n36
Minor Literatures: in Québec, ix, xii, 1–4, 6–9; 21, 32, 33, 35, 51, 54, 88, 99, 199, 201
Moss, Jane, 129n36, 141, 167n26
Mouawad, Wajdi, v, x, xiii, 17, 18, 20, 34, 38, 135–172, 200, 202, 206, 209, 212, 214–217, 221, 222
Mouhoub, Yamina, 199
Multiculturalism, 35, 38, 66, 88, 38, 82, 178

Naaman, Antoine, 11, 17, 18, 25–27, 38, 39, 46
Nadda, Rubba, 17, 23, 199
Nelligan, Emile, ix, 4, 7, 19, 28
Nepveu, Pierre, xi, 4–7, 26, 36, 37n40, 37, 41, 68, 88, 95n116
Nomadism, 20, 35n14, 78, 104, 173, 175, 181, 193, 198n100

Ollivier, Emile, 8, 9, 30
Ontario, x, xiii, 2, 10, 11, 18, 34, 35, 58, 174, 177, 193–196, 200
Ottawa, 18, 21, 22, 26; and Kattan, 68, 70; and Mouawad, 137; and Bouraoui, 175, 176

Palestininian, 10, 11, 31, 33, 126, 151, 152
Paradela, Nieves, 47, 64n23, 65n31
Paratextual, 3, 201
Paré, François, xv, 1, 2, 34
Pelletier, Jacques, 27, 41
Pirandello, Luigi, 103, 137, 165, 166, 171n159, 190
Pivato, Joseph, 15, 34n5
Postmodernism: Language in, 6; and exile, 32, 47; and Bouraoui, 175, 186, 193
Proulx, Patrice, 13n12, 92n8, 94n71, 129n36, 167n26; *also see* Ireland, Susan
Proust, Marcel, 117, 163, 189

Québec: choice of, vii, xii, xiii, 1–11; exilic writers in, 17–22, 23–29, 31; 33–42; and language bills, 36, 37; Egyptians in, 54, 58; and Kattan, 67–69, 78–79, 82, 86, 91–95; and Farhoud, 101, 105, 109, 118, 127–129, 131; and Mouawad, 137–138, 144, 157, 162–163; and Bouraoui, 174, 177

Rahimieh, Nasrin, xii, xv, 25, 73, 87, 91n2, 93n29, 95n107, 95n108
Reception, x, xi, 3, 20, 24, 25, 28, 37, 48, 56, 177, 200, 201, 203
Refugee, 10, 126, 147, 151, 152
Resistance, 4, 7, 27, 105, 128, 146, 156, 158, 170
Robin, Régine, 8, 9, 30, 34, 36, 42, 43
Rostom, Kamal, xii, 18, 20, 23, 29

Sabiston, Elizabeth, 174, 178, 180, 185, 186, 193, 193–196, 197
Said, Edward, ix, xii, xiv, 1, 3, 7, 20, 28, 29, 35, 41, 42, 55, 65, 106, 130160, 170, 202, 203
Serrano, Richard, xivn18, 37n34
Sgard, Jean, xi, xivn23, 28, 42n117
Spettigue, D. O., 87, 92n6, 95n105

Structure, viii, 2, 3, 34, 35; and Elkhadem, 50, and Kattan, 70, 75, 78, 79, 82; and Mouawad, 144; and Bouraoui, 175, 183, 193
Style, ix, xi, 2, 29, 34; and Elkhadem, 49, 61, 62, 65; and Kattan, 69; and Farhoud, 108; and Mouawad, 158, 164; and Bouraoui, 187, 197, 202
Suicide, 60, 105, 118, 126, 156

Terrorism, 54, 126
Tötösy, Steven, xv, 208
Transcultural, 4, 6, 8, 69, 70, 87, 139; and Bouraoui, 174, 175, 179, 198
Translation, ix, 18, 19, 25, 27; and Elkhadem's works, 47, 54; and Kattan's works, 68, 70, 92; and Mouawad's works, 137, 144, 166, 167, 169; and Bouraoui's works, 190, 193, 194

Varoujean, Vasco, 11, 17, 19 23, 25, 30, 34, 43
Vassal, Anne. *See* Helly, Denise
Vasseur, Annie, 27, 42n113, 42n125
Verthuy, Mair: see Lequin
Voix et Images, 17, 27

Wanderer, 78, 82, 89
War, ii, v, vii, ix, xii, xiv, 1, 2, 5, 7, 8–11, 20–22, 24–30, 32, 33, 35, 38, 40–43; and Elkhadem, 46, 47, 50, 52–55, 61; in Kattan's works, 68, 72, 77; in Farhoud's works, 98, 99, 100, 101, 103–105, 106, 11–113, 114, 116, 119–121; in Mouawad's works, 135, 136, 140, 141, 145–146, 150, 153, 160–162; in Bouraoui's works 185, 186, 201, 202, 203

York Press, vii, 18, 40n90, 40n118, 45, 47, 65n26, 66n66

Credits

The author and publisher are grateful for permissions to quote from the following copyrighted materials:

Thanks to Editions du Gref (collection le beau mentir) for permissions to quote from:

-*La Femme d'entre les lignes* (2002) by Hédi Bouraoui, by permission of Alain Baudot, Editions du Gref (Toronto), Le beau Mentir series.

Thanks to Leméac editeur for granting permission to quote from:

-Wajdi Mouawad's *Littoral* © Leméac Editeur, 1999, by permission of Leméac Editeur
-Wajdi Mouawad's *Incendies* © Leméac Editeur, 2003, by permission of Leméac Editeur
-Wajdi Mouawad's *Forêts* © Leméac Editeur, 2006, by permission of Leméac Editeur

Thanks to Playwrights Canada Press for granting permission for use of the English translations from:

-Wajdi Mouawad's 2002 *Tideline* (*Littoral*) translated from the French by Shelley Tepperman, by permission of Playwrights Canada Press (Toronto)

-Wajdi Mouawad's 2005 *Scorched (Incendies)* translated from the French by Linda Gaboriau, by permission of Playwrights Canada Press (Toronto)
-Wajdi Mouawad's yet unpublished *Forests (Forêts)* translated from the French by Linda Gaboriau, by permission of Playwrights Canada Press (Toronto)

Thanks to Naïm Kattan for granting permission to quote from:

-*Adieu, Babylone* (Leméac Editeur, 1986), © Naïm Kattan, by permission of Naïm Kattan
-*Farewell, Babylon: Coming of Age in Jewish Baghdad* (Raincoast Books, 2005), © Naïm Kattan, by permission of Naïm Kattan

Thanks to Editions Hurtubise HMH LTEE for granting permission to quote from:

-Kattan, Naïm. *Le Réel et le Théâtral*. Montréal: Editions HMH, 1970
-Kattan, Naïm. *Les Fruits arrachés*. Montréal: Hurtubise HMH, 1977
-Kattan, Naïm. *La Mémoire et la promesse*. Montréal: Hurtubise HMH, 1978
-Kattan, Naïm. *La Fiancée promise*. Montréal: Hurtubise HMH, 1983
-Kattan, Naïm. *Le Désir et le pouvoir*. Montréal: Hurtubise HMH, 1983
-Kattan, Naïm. *L'Ecrivain du passage. D'où je viens, où je vais. Saluts, hommages et lectures*, Jacques Allard, ed., Montréal: Hurtubise HMH, 2002
-Kattan, Naïm. *Le Gardien de mon frère*. Montréal: Hurtubise HMH, 2003
-Kattan, Naïm. *Je regarde les femmes*. Montréal: Hurtubise HMH 2005

Thanks to Editions Québec Amérique for granting permission to quote from

-Naim Kattan's *L'Anniversaire* (2000), by permission of Editions Québec-Amérique (Montréal)

Thanks to VLB éditeur and Abla Farhoud for granting permission to quote from

-Abla Farhoud's *Jeux de patience*, VLB éditeur, 1997 © 1997 VLB éditeur and Abla Farhoud
-Abla Farhoud, *Splendide solitude*, VLB éditeur, 2001 © 2001 VLB éditeur and Abla Farhoud

-Abla Farhoud, *Les Rues de l'alligator*, VLB éditeur, 2003 © 2003 VLB éditeur and Abla Farhoud
-Abla Farhoud, *Le Bonheur a la queue glissante*, Editions de L'Hexagone, 1998; Editions Typo 2004 © 2004 Editions Typo and Abla Farhoud
-Abla Farhoud, *Le Fou d'Omar*, VLB éditeur, 2005 © 2005 VLB éditeur and Abla Farhoud

Thanks to Editions Lansman and Abla Farhoud for granting permission to quote from:

-Abla Farhoud's *Les Filles du 5-10-15 cents* (1993) by permission of Emile Lansman, éditeur and Abla Farhoud

Thanks to the editors of the *Canadian Review of Comparative Literature* for granting permission to quote from:

-A smaller version of my article, "Voices of Exile: The Trilingual Odyssey of Canadian Writers of Arabic Origin," *The Canadian Review of Comparative Literature* 28.1 (March 2001): 48-69.

About the Author

F. Elizabeth Dahab (edahab@csulb.edu) is Associate Professor of Comparative Literature in the Department of Comparative World Literature and Classics at California State University, Long Beach. Prior to this, she taught French language and literature in the United States and in Canada. She has given numerous talks and published a number of research articles in her fields of specialization (including exilic Canadian/Québécois literature of Arabic provenance), as well as a translation into English of a book on *Comparative Literature Today: Methods and Perspectives*. In addition, she also authored a children's book titled *Hurly and the Bone*. Her edited anthology, *Voices in the Desert; An Anthology of Arabic-Canadian Women Writers*, appeared in Toronto in 2002. F. Elizabeth Dahab earned her Bachelor of Arts from McGill University (Montréal) and her Master's from the University of Alberta (Canada). She received her *doctorat de littérature comparée* in Comparative Literature from the Université de Paris IV-Sorbonne. She is currently working on two collections of poems, a French and an English one, as well as a translation of modern Arabic texts.

Breinigsville, PA USA
04 February 2010
231939BV00001B/8/P